YORCK
AND THE ERA OF PRUSSIAN REFORM

Drawn by P.E.Stroehling Historical Painter to H.R.H.the Prince Regent. — Engraved by I.Vendramini.

YORCK

AND THE ERA

OF PRUSSIAN REFORM

1807-1815

BY PETER PARET

PRINCETON UNIVERSITY PRESS
PRINCETON, NEW JERSEY
1966

ACKNOWLEDGMENTS

Many individuals and institutions helped in writing this book. I am grateful to the Central Research Fund of the University of London, the Committee on Research of the University of California, and the Social Science Research Council for their financial support, and to the staffs of the Algemeen Rijksarchief in the Hague, the Bundesarchiv-Militärarchiv in Koblenz, the Militärgeschichtliche Forschungsamt in Freiburg im Breisgau, and the Manuscript Section of the Library of the University of Münster for making their holdings available to me. Colonel Dr. Günther Gieraths, Professor Werner Hahlweg, Major S. G. P. Ward, and Count Paul York von Wartenburg each gave me useful information, for which I am deeply appreciative. Mrs. Carol Ladd of the Department of History, University of California, Davis, made my work much easier by her intelligent and efficient typing of the manuscript. Miss Jean MacLachlan proved once again to be the best imaginable of editors. It is a pleasure at last to be able to thank publicly Professors Felix Gilbert, Harold J. Gordon, Jr., and John Shy for their interest and their thoughtful suggestions. To Professor Michael Howard, who first introduced me to the study of war in the framework of intellectual, social, and political history, I owe a special debt of gratitude.

CONTENTS

A NOTE ON ILLUSTRATIONS

The frontispiece is taken from a sketch by Peter Eduard Ströhling (1768–after 1826), drawn in 1814, presumably during Yorck's visit to England after the First Peace of Paris.

Four diagrams illustrating the evolution from linear to columnar infantry tactics follow page 104.

C. Dalrymple, *A Military Essay*, London, 1761, plate 6.

Règlement concernant l'exercise et les manoeuvres de l'infanterie du premier août 1791, Paris, 1816, plate 26.

Exerzir-Reglement für die Infanterie der Königlich Preussischen Armee, Berlin, 1812, plate 1.

Exerzir-Reglement für die Infanterie der Königlich Preussischen Armee, Berlin, 1812, plate 2.

The designs for the jacket and for the chapter headings are taken from the first folio of Karl Friedrich Schinkel's *Album architektonischer Entwürfe*, published in Berlin in 1819.

YORCK
AND THE ERA OF PRUSSIAN REFORM

Introduction

THE CHANGES in the military institutions of Europe that occurred between the French Revolution and the final defeat of Napoleon resemble in magnitude the political and social changes of those years, to which they were closely linked. Innovation in one area made change elsewhere possible or necessary, and led to a reciprocal increase of military and political energies. The resulting wars have been studied as thoroughly as any in history; but more is known about the course of the campaigns and their exploitation by governments and individual genius than about the institutions that did the fighting and the methods that they employed. The great achievements are easily identified; the specifics of doctrine, administration, and execution that led to them and form part of their substance prove more elusive. To paraphrase Ranke: it is the concrete business of war that turns into history—we fail to pursue it at the cost of settling for abstractions.

To our understanding of the military revolution of the period, the changes that infantry organization and infantry tactics underwent are of peculiar importance. Foot-soldiers still dominated the battlefield; their central role and the nature of the armies in which they served meant that any alteration in their mode of employment would not only affect every aspect of military life but impinge as well on a multitude of other interests in government and nation. The content of the changes that took place, the reasons for them, and the processes by which they came about are matters of general rather than narrowly military significance. The new forms of fighting did not evolve in the isolation of staff college and drill-field, nor did they follow as a matter of course from technological and political developments. They were the expression of numerous, often conflicting, elements in their societies, and to the later observer they demonstrate the interaction between civil and military concerns of the age with a special clarity.

The civil factors that were conducive to military innovation never lacked allies in uniform. Even those armies that could not free themselves from social and operational rigidity possessed individual rebels and reformers, and—perhaps more significantly —institutional agents that pressed for change. In France during the 1790's, what may be termed the traditional forces of modernization, such as the long-established units of light troops, first combined effectively with new concepts and new men. After Jena and Tilsit a superior synthesis was achieved in the defeated Prussian monarchy, whose army during the next few years carried the military revolution farther towards its ideal potential, and eventually was able to turn it against its political progenitor.

The complexities of the Era of Prussian Reform have long been reflected in the critical evaluation of its civilian leaders. With growing sensitivity to the limitations of ideas and of the acting individual, historians have reconstructed the achievements and shortcomings of Stein, Hardenberg, and their fellow administrators and theorists. The military innovators by and large have fared differently. Scharnhorst and Gneisenau, and in their wake such men as Boyen and Clausewitz, are usually depicted as representatives of the most admirable type of reformer: practical idealists, who understand why the old order has failed, and who possess the inner freedom to bring about necessary change. Another figure—Yorck—is seen in a more ambiguous light.[1] He is remembered as the Prussian signatory of the Convention of Tauroggen, as a self-willed and successful general in the campaigns of 1813 and 1814, and above all as the antagonist of Stein, whose departure from office in November 1808 caused him to declare: "One mad head is already smashed; the remaining nest of vipers will dissolve in its own poison."[2] Words of such precise violence ensure their own immortality, and few accounts of Yorck have

---

[1] The name Yorck has been spelled both with and without "c." Yorck employed both versions, as did documents and letters addressed to him. On the patent elevating him to the dignity of Count the name is written "Yorck," but the "c" is deleted on his monument in Klein-Öls, the family's former estate in Silesia. His descendants have employed both spellings. Count Peter Yorck von Wartenburg, who was executed for complicity in the plot of 20 July 1944, generally used the "c," while his brother Paul, the present head of the family, does not. I have adopted the spelling "Yorck," but use the alternate version whenever it appears in a quoted passage or in the title of a book or article.

[2] J. G. Droysen, *Das Leben des Feldmarschalls Grafen York von Wartenburg*, Berlin, 1851–1852, I, 216–217.

thought it necessary to go beyond them. A modern English author with a penchant to shock has described him as the "most reactionary of Prussian officers," and even scholars of greater circumspection write of the "representative of the aristocratic-monarchic tradition of the Prussian state," and of the "soldier of decided legitimist-dynastic beliefs . . . the most severe opponent of Stein and his reforms." [3] But it is difficult to reconcile the obedient royal servant with the soldier who quit the French in the winter of 1812, an act that for its disdain of rule and tradition Clausewitz called one of the most daring in history.[4] The difficulty increases when we look past the decision at Tauroggen to the long process of change in Prussia's military institutions, and find Yorck on the side of modernization not only in the years of reform but well before Jena.

The need to bring such disparate actions and statements into agreement has usually been ignored by historians, or has led to interpretations that soon reveal themselves as unsatisfactory. Even the great nineteenth-century biography that Johann Gustav Droysen devoted to Yorck managed a consistent explanation only by having recourse to the "Frederician tradition" that governed Yorck's personality, to his roots in the military nobility of the state, to his old-Prussian sense of duty, to patriotism. These views harmonized with the author's political motives for writing the biography, but did not wholly accord with the facts. They were nevertheless far more satisfactory than later versions, which either label Yorck a "reactionary" or concentrate on his career in the field and dismiss any differences between him and other Prussian civil and military leaders in a few innocuous lines.

The following pages do not attempt a complete revision of

[3] A. J. P. Taylor, *The Course of German History*, New York, 1962, p. 46; H. Herzfeld, *Die moderne Welt, 1789–1945*, Braunschweig, 1957, I, 62; W. Mommsen, *Geschichte des Abendlandes von der französischen Revolution bis zur Gegenwart, 1789–1945*, Munich, 1951, p. 117.

[4] C. v. Clausewitz, *Der Feldzug von 1812 in Russland*, vol. VII of *Hinterlassene Werke*, Berlin, 1837, p. 218. Whether Yorck followed secret instructions in neutralizing his corps or acted on his own has been debated since the event first became known in Berlin in early January 1813. The most comprehensive and balanced analysis of the documents and the conflicting interpretations is still W. Elze's *Der Streit um Tauroggen*, Breslau, 1926. Elze's conclusion, p. 73, that "the long and involved path of research leads back to the recognition of Yorck's independence and responsibility at Tauroggen" seems unassailable.

Droysen's biography, which for all its shortcomings remains one of the great achievements of the early period of German historicism, marked by a respect for the past, a unity of conception, and a sustained energy of execution that later historians have rarely been able to muster. Our concern lies less with the man than with his times, and less with his times than with the course taken by military innovation from the age of Frederick to the defeat of Napoleon. The discussion of Yorck is limited to those aspects of his life that may cast further light on the changes in the military thought and institutions of Europe. Throughout his career Yorck was concerned with problems of modernization— particularly with the central military issue of his day, the proper selection, training, and use of infantry. To explore this issue, with its many non-military implications, and Yorck's part in resolving it is the purpose of this study. Its findings may indicate the need for adjustments in our view of Prussia's decline and reemergence as a major power, and perhaps suggest some questions about reform and its historical analysis in general.

CHAPTER II

The Frederician Age

H ANS DAVID LUDWIG VON YORCK was born at the height of the Seven Years' War, on 26 September 1759, in Potsdam, the eldest son of David Jonathan von Yorck, captain in a Prussian grenadier battalion, and Marie Sophie Pflug.[1] In the register of the garrison church the birth was listed as illegitimate.[2] Two years later Captain Yorck legitimized his son and a second child that had been born in the meantime, and in January 1763 he married the mother. The lateness of the wedding may have been due to a refusal of the King to consent to the marriage—not an unusual situation if, as was the case with Marie Pflug, the woman lacked property or social standing.[3] Despite his rank and title, however, the elder Yorck's background was not greatly superior to that of his wife. He was a man of modest means whose father, vicar in a Pomeranian village, had married the daughter of a fellow parson. Among his closer relatives were farmers, and sailors; his paternal ancestors almost certainly were German or Slav peasants settled on the Baltic coast.

[1] Droysen's reluctance to give up his view of Yorck as a characteristic Prussian noble of the Frederician Era makes him unreliable on Yorck's background. Major sources for this paragraph are: *Kleinoels: 1816–1871*, ed. L. v. Katte, a privately printed volume of Yorck family papers, which Count Paul York von Wartenburg kindly made available to me; the *Militair-Wochenblatt* of 27 February 1836, p. 93; "Notizen über den richtigen Familien-namen und die Abstammung des verstorbenen Feldmarschalls Grafen York von Wartenburg," *Preussische Provinzialblatter*, xx (August 1838), 156–160, which prints a number of documents unavailable elsewhere; the correspondence between Droysen and Theodor von Schön, one of his major informants on Yorck's career, which is printed in J. G. Droysen, *Briefwechsel*, ed. R. Hübner, 2 vols., Berlin-Leipzig, 1929; H. Berghaus, *York: Seine Geburtsstätte und seine Heimath*, Anclam, 1863; and H. Banniza v. Bazan and R. Müller, *Deutsche Geschichte in Ahnentafeln*, xi, Berlin, 1942, 188–190.

[2] Droysen, ii, 263. For further details, see Berghaus, p. 6.

[3] Her father had been a private in Frederick William I's giant guards, and later set up a smithy in Potsdam. Berghaus, pp. 12–15.

At an unknown date he and a younger brother assumed the title of nobility, and on that basis gained entry into the Prussian army.[4] Presumably to make their noble origin more convincing, the Yorcks claimed a remote relationship with the Earls of Hardwicke, adopted their coat of arms, and intimated that their ancestors supported the Stuarts and had been forced to flee England during the preceding century—a story that gained some acceptance in military circles.[5] The younger brother was killed in battle. Captain Yorck, however, survived numerous wounds, was apparently decorated with the order *Pour le mérite*, and seemed headed towards a promising future. But after the Peace of Hubertusburg his career faltered; twenty years later he still had not risen beyond the rank of captain. Lack of family influence, the effect of his wounds, and a brusque, independent nature may have combined to hold him back.[6]

It is not certain how much the son knew of his father's deception; but undoubtedly he would have regarded the assumption of nobility not as a romantic indulgence, but as a necessary step in the advancement of his family. In Frederician Prussia, service to the state held out by far the best promise to ambitious men who lacked connections or wealth. For such a career, especially in the army, noble status was, if not actually required, at least of the greatest assistance. An acknowledged bourgeois could make his way in some specialist forces, with their more limited social and professional rewards—the artillery, for instance, the technical units, and the hussars, who had not yet achieved status compa-

---

[4] Their original name, Jarcken, "was beautified only by the Field Marshal's father. . . . At best the family belongs to the local free peasantry." Banniza v. Bazan and Müller, p. 188. See also *ibid.*, p. 143.

[5] It is not inconceivable that this invention was inspired by the marriage of a sister to a member of a genuine Jacobite family—the Leslies—who had settled in Prussia, assumed the *von*, and provided the army with several officers.

[6] Colonel Günther Gieraths has informed me that the conduct reports of the Prussian army, which disappeared or were destroyed in 1945, contained several characterizations describing the elder Yorck as a difficult subordinate. Yorck himself later wrote that his father had fallen out of favor with Frederick, but gave no details. M. Lehmann, "Yorcks Wiedereintritt in den preussischen Dienst," *Historische Zeitschrift*, LXIV (1890), 253.

rable to that of the dragoons and cuirassiers.[7] If he distinguished himself, he might even hope for eventual elevation to the nobility. But in the major branches of the army—the infantry and heavy cavalry—the particule of nobility was taken for granted from the outset; indeed, it was insisted upon after 1763, when Frederick dismissed or transferred to reserve formations the middle-class officers he had been compelled to accept during the war. With a title the key to a career, it was no wonder that men would manufacture backgrounds that enabled them or at least their sons to give full rein to their abilities.

In the course of the century a circular social pattern had developed: the monarchs turned the army largely into a noble preserve, which it had not been under the Electors; but military service made it easier to gain access to the nobility. For an outsider with a spurious title to be accepted by one of the provincial bodies of nobility was very nearly impossible; he found it far less difficult to enter the army, particularly if he was helped by recommendations of the right kind. If his noble status was not reinforced by the possession of land, the new officer might be considered to belong only to the *Nominaladel*—to be noble in name only —but a successful career or a wealthy wife could enable him to buy a *Rittergut*, ownership of which qualified him to join a provincial *Ritterschaft*, and thus to become a member of the country's aristocracy. His first step—ascent to the military nobility—was often facilitated if he possessed ancestors who had been pastors or university professors, since genuine nobles tended to relinquish their titles on choosing these professions and the absence of *von* in one's father's or grandfather's name could thus be plausibly explained. Many officers besides the Yorcks rose in this fashion, Steuben and Clausewitz among them. But although the newcomers quickly took on the tone and manner of their comrades, the underlying division of attitudes between them could not be bridged as easily. The country noble with his close bonds to the land, his central position in the affairs of his native region, his nearly total authority over the peasants on his estate, who obeyed

---

[7] According to the *Army List* of 1789, all 180 officers of general and field grade in the heavy cavalry bore titles, while 55 were nobles and three were commoners in the hussars, and the division was 11 to 11 in the artillery. See also Appendix 2 of this work.

him as instinctively in the army as they did on his acres, was a very different man from the military professional.[8] What his name was to the one, his officer's patent was to the other, and their different origins and circumstances affected the way in which each met the social and military problems of the day. An old-established family could give its members a unique sense of independence that did not readily adjust itself to the emerging replacement of patriarchal loyalties by bureaucratic values, while the man who had nothing but his sword might be more receptive to the arguments of effectiveness and efficiency, or at least be unable to put up as strong a defense against them. That these were not exclusive categories, whose inherent interests completely determined individual behavior, hardly needs pointing out; the noble proprietor and the professional with little or no stake in the country did, however, constitute the two major social poles around which the officer corps was structured, and the heterogeneity that resulted had a bearing on the conflicts between military reformers and traditionalists that broke out in the open after Frederick's death.

The career of the young Yorck at first followed the standard pattern. Shortly after his thirteenth birthday he entered the army as *Gefreiter-Corporal*, a grade reserved for young nobles who expected to become officers. For some months he served in the Infantry Regiment von Borck, and then was transferred to the Regiment von Luck, one of the new units raised after the first partition of Poland. There he remained for the next seven years, being promoted to ensign and then to lieutenant. The regiment, though one of the least distinguished in the army, had the reputation of being particularly rigid in observing the minutiae of the service; its commanding officer was a pious pedant, who shone only on the drill-field, and did little to further the education of the young subalterns in his care. Yorck consequently was thrown onto his own devices. As his later friend, the philosopher and naturalist Henrich Steffens, was to write: "If it could be said of any man that life had educated him, it was true of Count York."[9] Yorck never achieved the universal culture of a Gneisenau or Clausewitz, but in time he acquired a sound if conven-

---

[8] See the good analyses of the relations between military authority and rural life in O. Büsch, *Militärsystem und Sozialleben im Alten Preussen, 1713–1807*, Berlin, 1962, particularly pp. 27–41.

[9] H. Steffens, *Was ich erlebte*, IX, Breslau, 1844, 308.

tional education, with a strong emphasis on French literature of the seventeenth and eighteenth centuries. In later life he came to admire Schiller's tragedies: *Wallensteins Tod* and *Don Carlos*, especially, provided him with pertinent quotations during the stormy years of Prussia's regeneration. Of works on military theory that he read as a young man he was particularly attracted by the writings of Maurice de Saxe.[10]

Yorck first saw active duty in the War of the Bavarian Succession. Among the few notable incidents of this uneventful campaign was the Austrian raid on Halberschwerdt, in which Croats captured the greater part of Luck's regiment, Yorck himself having the good fortune of not being involved in the disaster. In the fall of 1779, soon after the Peace of Teschen had been signed, the disgraced regiment returned to its West Prussian garrison. There Yorck committed an act of insubordination that caused him to be court-martialed, sentenced to a year's confinement in Königsberg, and cashiered from the service.

Droysen gives two rather different accounts of the events leading up to Yorck's trial, both of which are based on statements of officers serving with the regiment at the time.[11] Their gist is that Yorck objected to the presence in the regiment of an officer whom he suspected of having stolen an altarcloth during the recent campaign. A fuller and evidently more accurate version of the incident did not become known until 1890, when Max Lehmann published extracts from the regimental commander's *Immediatsbericht* to the King, which reported that one evening Yorck and two other lieutenants encountered an apothecary's assistant in the street, and beat him with their swords so that he suffered light wounds on his face and left hand. They then went to the quarters of *Stabscapitain* von Naurath, and in obscene language demanded that he come down to the street. Naurath was already in bed, and refused. The following day on the parade-ground Yorck called Naurath a bad fellow and a church robber. Ordered by two colonels to be silent, Yorck refused and insisted he spoke the truth. During the campaign two fusiliers had in fact suspected Naurath of stealing an altarcloth; but Naurath declared that the cloth in question was his own hankerchief. On General von

[10] Droysen, I, 26; E. Weniger, *Goethe und die Generale der Freiheitskriege*, Stuttgart, 1959, pp. 173–174.

[11] Droysen, I, 23–25.

Luck's report the King noted: "That's a dirty business. I confirm the court's sentence." [12]

At twenty-one, Yorck's career in Prussia seemed finished. On his release from the citadel, and after pleas for readmission to the army had been turned down by Frederick, he decided to seek service elsewhere. The war that had just broken out between England and the United Provinces offered an opportunity. He was able to acquire several introductions to the Dutch government, the most valuable among them being the recommendations sent by Dirk van Hogendorp, a lieutenant in his father's battalion, to his prominent relatives in Holland. [13] In May 1781 Yorck left Prussia.

· 2 ·

The service from which Yorck had been expelled was at the height of its fame. If the War of the Bavarian Succession had revealed flaws in leadership and administration, some slackness was only to be expected after sixteen years of peace, and even reform-minded officers retained their faith in the continued supremacy of Prussian arms. Their belief was shared in other states. More than one German prince now patterned the uniforms and drill of his miniature corps on the Potsdam model, as once his grandfather had looked to Versailles for hints on court architecture and life. The armies of the major European powers experimented with Prussian methods in an effort to increase the precision and rapidity of their evolutions, and from the 1760's onward

[12] M. Lehmann, "Yorcks Entlassung aus dem preussischen Dienst," *Historische Zeitschrift*, LXV (1890), 469. Later writers have ignored Lehmann's findings and continue to describe the incident as one that did Yorck honor. See W. v. Voss, *Yorck*, Berlin, 1906, p. 2; W. v. Bremen, *Yorck von Wartenburg*, Bielefeld-Leipzig [1913], p. 5; K. v. Priesdorff, *Soldatisches Führertum*, Hamburg, 1936–1945, No. 1120. Entries in the ten volumes of Priesdorff's biographical dictionary are here referred to by their identifying numbers.

[13] Dirk van Hogendorp became Minister of War of the Batavian Republic, and subsequently a general in the French army and Governor of West Prussia during the Russian campaign. His interesting memoirs, which contain numerous references to Yorck, were published in 1887. It is also possible that Yorck's mother had connections in Holland. The Hogendorp Papers in the Rijksarchief in the Hague (Inv. No. 11) contain two letters in reasonably fluent Dutch signed M[arie] S[ophie] York, addressed to Dirk's mother, Mme. van Hogendorp, "our dear benefactress."

the infantry manuals of at least two former opponents—Austria and France—were heavily indebted to the concepts of Frederick and his collaborators.[14] This vogue was the consequence of the Seven Years' War. The military world did not deny that Frederick's survival owed much to his genius and to the circumstances of accident and politics; these, however, were intangibles, while the Prussian drill could be studied and made one's own. The result frequently was an unhappy and ineffectual burlesque. And yet, at bottom, the adulation of the Philosopher of Sans-Souci expressed an accurate insight: he had discerned the essential conditions imposed on war by contemporary society, economics, technology, and he had organized and trained his forces to make the most of them. Not that he had discovered a new system, but that he had perfected a system known and common to all, turned Frederick into the military preceptor of the age.

Frederick's battle tactics were built around the infantry attack. Cavalry and artillery supported the advancing formations and disrupted the enemy order of battle; indeed, to several victories the cavalry contributed the largest share. But essentially cuirassiers and dragoons acted as a counterforce, protecting their own infantry against the enemy horse and giving it room to maneuver, and the King usually sought to achieve the decision with his infantry's movement and fire.

Frederick's views on the most effective method of attack changed over the years.[15] During the first Silesian campaigns the Austrian volleys tended to be ragged and slow, so that in theory at least the all-important advantages of speed and cohesion seemed to lie with units that did not stop to fire, but marched forward steadily, bayonet lowered—though, to be sure, they relinquished the effect their volleys might have on the enemy as well as the concealment provided by the smoke. "Let infantry fire as little as possible," the King wrote shortly before the Seven

---

[14] The influence of Prussian tactics on French military thought before the Revolution is analyzed in the third chapter of J. Colin's excellent study, *L'Infanterie au XVIIIe siècle: la tactique*, Paris, 1907. Nothing of substance is added in the more recent publication of R. Quimby, *The Background of Napoleonic Warfare*, New York, 1957.

[15] The stages of his thought are traced in *Die taktische Schulung der Preussischen Armee . . . 1745 bis 1756; Kriegsgeschichtliche Einzelschriften*, XXVIII–XXX, Berlin, 1900, pp. 440–451.

Years' War, "but charge with the bayonet." [16] In practice, however, it grew evident that against a well-trained opponent this was asking too much even of veteran troops, and after the first engagements in 1756 the Prussian attack reverted to rapidly alternating volleys and advances, culminating, if necessary, in a bayonet charge. "Battles are won by fire superiority," Frederick concluded in his *Military Testament* of 1768. "Infantry firing more rapidly will undoubtedly defeat infantry firing more slowly." [17]

The killing-power of a volley was, however, inconsiderable unless it was fired at close range.[18] The Prussian musket was an inaccurate weapon—less accurate, indeed, than contemporary armorers could have made it—and tactical doctrine depreciated aiming. Reliance was instead placed on volume, rapidity, and continuity of fire. In battle a well-trained grenadier, standing still and firing by command in unison with his fellows, achieved a rate of two or three unaimed rounds every minute—an effort that could be maintained only over brief periods of crisis, but that was rarely matched by his opponents.[19] The success of Prussian musketry depended no less on the moral effect of these rapid and continuous volleys than on the casualties they produced, and for the sake of appearance execution was often slighted. In the tension of combat many soldiers could not punctually perform the complex loading drill, which required from 19 to 22 separate actions to load and fire a single round, and they therefore fired muskets that were primed but not charged, whose ramrods had not been withdrawn from the barrel, or that had misfired and

---

[16] "Pensées et règles générales pour la guerre," *Oeuvres de Frédéric le Grand*, ed. J. D. E. Preuss, Berlin, 1846–1857, xxviii, 111.

[17] *Military Testament* of 1768, printed in Frederick II, *Militärische Schriften*, ed. A. v. Taysen, Dresden, 1893, p. 205.

[18] In a practice shoot in 1755, a Guards section firing volleys at a target 10 feet high by 10 feet wide scored 46.6 per cent hits at 120 yards and 16.6 per cent hits at 160 yards. In actual combat the results were far less satisfactory. *Die taktische Schulung*, p. 432. See also Appendix 5, Table 1, of this work.

[19] *Die taktische Schulung*, pp. 434–438, which must be supplemented by the discussion in H. Delbrück, *Geschichte der Kriegskunst im Rahmen der politischen Geschichte*, iv, Berlin, 1962, 329–332. See also the sound technical study by W. Eckardt and O. Morawietz, *Die Handwaffen des brandenburgisch-preussisch-deutschen Heeres*, Hamburg, 1957, pp. 32–33.

were loaded again without first clearing the barrel, resulting in a second misfire.[20] In the interest of massive, regular volleys, executed by steadily advancing lines, the ineffectiveness of the individual weapon was ignored. Aiming was in any case forbidden since it would have slowed the rate of fire—at most, the men were told to point their weapons waist-high.[21] Under these circumstances it was only to be expected that in the course of Frederick's reign Prussian muskets progressively became simpler to load and less accurate—the last model, the *Infanteriegewehr 1782*, being almost impossible to hold on a target because of its weight, imbalance, and shallow angle of butt to stock.[22] Other forces were better equipped; in particular the French *fusil 1777*, a reliable, mass-produced weapon, was far more accurate than the Prussian.[23] Not technological backwardness, but a tactical concept made the Prussian musket one of the worst in Europe.[24]

To exploit the greatest possible number of muskets for the volley, the deep and narrow formations of the preceding century had been gradually reduced in depth, the men thus spared being used to prolong the front. By the 1740's a Prussian battalion habitually fought in three ranks, its 700 men extended over a front of 150 yards or more. But the very thinness of the formation created a new problem. The battalion was fully committed from the start, it lacked its own tactical reserve, and enemy pressure on intervals between units could quickly lead to local breakthroughs or worse.[25] Consequently the battalions had to be deployed in close echelons or in practically continuous lines, which in turn limited maneuverability. The extent, complexity, and brittleness of the tactical patterns, as well as the difficulty of maintaining an orderly and rapid fire, demanded intensive training of the sol-

---

[20] Eckardt and Morawietz, pp. 35–36.

[21] Since the rapidity of loading and firing led men to fire high, some officers ordered them to point their weapons at the enemy's feet. *Ibid.*, p. 32.

[22] *Ibid.*, pp. 38–41, 43–44.

[23] J. Margerand, *Armement et équipement de l'infanterie française du XVI° au XX° siècle*, Paris, 1945, pp. 41–43, 107–108. See also Appendix 5, Table 1, of this work.

[24] By 1806, unqualifiedly the worst, according to Clausewitz in his *Nachrichten über Preussen in seiner grossen Katastrophe; Kriegsgeschichtliche Einzelschriften*, x, Berlin, 1888, 426.

[25] Delbrück, IV, 317, n. 1.

diers, and their most stringent supervision, particularly in combat. For the man in the ranks, if not for all his officers, this meant renouncing his will to reason and his total submersion into the unit, the strength and safety of which resided largely in the degree to which its members could act as one. "Moving batteries" was Frederick's description of his ideal battalions.[26]

The need for close supervision was heightened further by the very large number of foreigners in the ranks.[27] Without foreign soldiers the mercantilist state would not have been able to maintain an army that even in peacetime amounted to more than 3 per cent of the population, but outsiders could not be expected to share the patriarchal and regional loyalties of the native peasantry. Minimizing the opportunities for desertion became an additional task for the march and combat formations, and it was entirely in keeping with this necessity that Frederick devoted the first section of his *General Principles of War* to the subject.[28] Close linear formations seemed to answer most adequately not only the requirements of tactical control and effect, but those of disciplinary control as well.

Prussian discipline, whose notorious severity reached its height in Frederick's reign, was the necessary adjunct of these organizational and tactical concepts. If deserters were whipped or exe-

[26] Frederick II, "Histoire de mon temps," *Oeuvres*, ii, 42. On the preceding page Leopold von Dessau is called "un mécanicien militaire." Already in his "Réfutation du Prince de Machiavel," *Oeuvres*, viii, 242, the Crown Prince speaks of the rank and file as "des animaux grossiers et mécaniques." To liken Prussian infantry—indeed, the troops of all nations —to machines and automata became a hardy cliché of eighteenth-century literature, and is to be met with even in official correspondence. Often the simile was employed in a critical or pejorative sense, but sometimes it was used approvingly. At the turn of the century the able, conservative, military publicist Friedrich v. d. Decken could still express profound agreement with the statement of Maurice de Saxe that most soldiers should be "transformed into machines, which can take on life only through the voices of their officers." See his *Betrachtungen über das Verhältniss des Kriegsstandes zu dem Zwecke der Staaten*, Hanover, 1800, p. 270.

[27] In the last decades of Frederick's reign, foreigners constituted about 50 per cent of the troops, a proportion that sank to 35 per cent by the beginning of the new century. C. Jany, *Geschichte der Königlich Preussischen Armee*, Berlin, 1928–1933, iii, 50, 436.

[28] Frederick II, "Les Principes généraux de la guerre, appliqués à la tactique et à la discipline des troupes prussiennes," *Oeuvres*, xxviii, 4–7.

cuted even in peacetime, it seemed a small matter to use the cane or the flat of the sword on soldiers who were awkward on the parade-ground. Fear alone could produce the conditioned reactions necessary for carrying out the Prussian drill; and fear and compulsion, linked perhaps with habit and *esprit de corps*, were the factors counted on to keep the men tractable and effective in combat. The absolutist age found it difficult to hold out other motives; particularly among the hundreds of states and principalities that fragmented Central Europe, love of country was hard put to grow into a dynamic force. By the middle of the century, nevertheless, German writers were beginning to speculate on the possible military implications of patriotism in the contemporary world. A distinction had to be drawn between officers and men. Unlike his subordinate, the officer was not isolated in society. Even as a foreigner he stood in a direct and mutually advantageous relationship to his monarch. Both were members of an elite governed by aristocratic ideals, they held in common certain views on honor and duty, and they were joined by bonds of reciprocal obligations. The officer's social and professional interests and loyalties might be deepened by an attachment to the region of his birth and by his partisan feeling for the state to which it belonged. With his military tasks, therefore, the officer gradually came to combine a function of more general significance to the monarchy. In Hintze's words, "It was primarily the nobility that became the carrier of that Prussian sentiment for the state which the King exemplified for his country." [29]

The common soldier still stood apart from this development. For him the reciprocity of his relationship with the monarch limited itself to the state's obligation to clothe, feed, and pay him during his period of service. Even if he were a native, his attachment to the Uckermark or to West Prussia was not reinforced by elements of class and professional loyalty, of professional advantage, least of all by an appreciation of *raison d'état*. During the Seven Years' War the Prussian Professor Thomas Abbt might call on the underprivileged, even the *Pöbel*, to love their

---

[29] O. Hintze, "Die Hohenzollern und der Adel," *Historische Zeitschrift*, CXLI (1914), 495. Cf. the same author's "Der preussische Militär- und Beamtenstaat im 18. Jahrhundert," reprinted in *Geist und Epochen der Preussischen Geschichte*, Leipzig, 1943, p. 461; and "Das politische Testament Friedrich des Grossen von 1752," *ibid.*, p. 476.

country, to foster a noble enthusiasm and a Roman spirit of self-sacrifice; but such appeals, while they did not fail to raise echoes in intellectual circles, scarcely touched the rank and file.[30] Neither in his own mind nor in the eyes of his commanders was the common soldier the man to be inspired by the ideals of the state or of a national community.[31] His monarch—except on a few complimentary occasions—even held that like most commoners he lacked a sense of honor, and it was the exceptional officer who disagreed with a view that fitted so perfectly the prevailing social and military structure.

Again the literature of the day contains signs of a coming change in attitude. Among its early expressions is an essay published shortly before the Seven Years' War in a Prussian military journal. The anonymous author does not consider beating as such to be dishonorable, but feels that nevertheless "it would be best if no one is punished at drill except the inattentive and the trouble-maker. . . . To educate the soldier only in a machine-like manner, to do nothing in accordance with his likes, to regard soldiers as automata that have no thought but only physical movements: these are notions that dishonor man." If officers were humane, "soldiers would obey without being slaves, they would bear all difficulties and be only half-aware of them from their love of honor, from the affection and respect in which they held their commander, and the trust they placed in his abilities." The section headed *On honor as the basis of discipline* presents such characteristic arguments as "Love of honor can rouse the inactive. . . . It can be rewarded at least expense. As it is innate in human beings, it needs only to be given a lawful direction." [32] These sentiments are harbingers of a milder spirit that was to

---

[30] T. Abbt, *Vom Thode für das Vaterland*, Frankfurt a. O., 1761.

[31] The attempts of National Socialist writers to discern a political awakening of the Prussian army and people under Frederick can only be termed anti-history. For a sophisticated example, see the essay by the SS historian R. Höhn, *Der Soldat und das Vaterland während und nach dem Siebenjährigen Krieg*, Weimar, 1940.

[32] "Versuch von der Kriegeszucht," *Krieges-Bibliothek*, I, Breslau, 1755, 100, 52, 54, 87. Its author very probably was the Prussian cavalry officer, later general, G. D. v. d. Groeben, who edited the publication, called by M. Jähns the earliest European military journal. See his *Geschichte der Kriegswissenschaften vornehmlich in Deutschland*, Munich-Leipzig, 1889–1891, III, 1813.

spread among the officer corps in the last decades of the century, with momentous implications for army and state. The soldier's dignity and his ability to reason became important, though he continued to be denuded of all political and most social and economic privileges. A relaxation of tactical rigidity was to accompany these autumnal rays of the enlightenment; until then discipline remained harsh and drill narrowly formalistic. The soldier fought in linear formations, elbow to elbow with his neighbors, forbidden to show initiative or independent judgment, even to the extent of aiming, trained to direct all his psychic and physical energies towards the prompt and precise execution of the command.

To win battles with these methods, the commander had to satisfy three fundamental requirements.[33] Tactical surprise could be achieved only if the army developed its battle formations with great rapidity. To enable the deep marching columns to shift smoothly into the thin, extended lines of attack or defense, the regiments must arrive on the battlefield in proper order, readiness, and with exact intervals between themselves and their neighbors. The approach march became a vital and complicated part of the battle—the most difficult part of the art of war it was often called, at least by staff officers. Secondly, direction and lateral extent of the attack must be accurately projected, since once set in motion the far-stretched lines could change only at the cost of time and order. To some degree this lack of flexibility could be counteracted by deploying the lines so that they would eventually outflank the enemy, and by concentrating from the outset the greatest strength on the wing that was to make the decisive effort: the two components of Frederick's oblique order. Finally, once the attack was launched it must move forward with little or no interruption; halting and engaging the enemy in a static, prolonged fire-fight—as Grawert's division was to do disastrously at Jena—went against the nature of the process.

The advantages of volleys, of linear cohesion, and of tactical control exerted by the commander-in-chief could be utilized to the fullest only on relatively level, unobstructed ground. This fact, together with the fear of losing disciplinary control over their men, caused Frederician generals to avoid woods and hills. On

[33] Here I follow the analysis of W. Rüstow in his *Geschichte der Infanterie*, Nordhausen, 1864, II, 258–261.

occasion sizable infantry masses did maneuver and fight over broken terrain—most notably in 1762 at Burkersdorf, where the Austrians refused to be lured from their entrenched positions. But Frederick preferred to keep to the plains. "As for the Prussian infantry," he wrote after the second Silesian War, "it is above all rules. However, open country suits it best."[34]

The implications of the linear system and of its related disciplinary principles did not stop at the boundaries of the battlefield. The same fear of laxness and desertion, of seeing the tight formations unravel into clusters of possibly willing but necessarily ineffective individuals, that turned the approach march into an operation calling for the most careful planning and execution, made it difficult to exploit a victory once it had been won. Darkness usually put an end to the fighting. Tactical pursuit of the enemy was rare and lacked conviction; strategic pursuit did not exist. At most some hussar squadrons irritated the rearguard, but a commander could reasonably count on having an opportunity to sort out and reorganize his defeated forces, undisturbed by serious interference. Even the costliest engagement rarely led to a break-up of the beaten army, with its attendant military and political consequences.[35]

Disciplinary and tactical demands not only stood in the way of achieving decisive results in battle, but acted as a retarding element throughout the campaign. They handicapped reconnaissance, precluded improvisation, favored systematic rather than rapid movement, and placed the heaviest of burdens on the supply

[34] *Die Instruktion Friedrichs des Grossen für seine Generale von 1747*, ed. R. Fester, Berlin, 1936, p. 44. Cf. also articles 51, 55, and 56 of the "Aphorismen des Königs" of 1757, *Oeuvres*, xxx, 238–240; and the "Principes généraux de la guerre," *ibid.*, xxviii, 5.

[35] In his classic history of the Seven Years' War, G. F. v. Tempelhoff writes that "not once, following a defeat, was the Prussian army seen to evacuate entire provinces on the run. . . . Victory was always made so costly that the effort of the enemy to achieve it exhausted him to such an extent that for a while he had to abstain from any further projects." *Geschichte des Siebenjährigen Krieges in Deutschland*, Berlin, 1783–1801, II, 26. The mechanical and psychological factors that inhibited pursuit in the eighteenth century are analyzed in an interesting study on the aftermath of Leuthen in *Rückzug und Verfolgung*, ed. H. Meier-Welcker, Stuttgart, 1960. See also the older but still valuable study by Captain Liebert, "Über Verfolgung," *Militär-Wochenblatt* (1883), Supplement 8.

and transportation system. The problem of feeding the army was compounded by the social and political principles of the age. While rounding up cattle and levying contributions were far from unheard of, their scope was nevertheless limited. Living off the country in Napoleonic fashion would have called for a radical adjustment of attitudes on the part of soldiers and governments alike. The proliferating network of magazines on which reliance was placed instead, guarded by a large part of the army, and linked by bad roads over which thousands of wagons and carts made their ponderous, uncertain way, became the leg-irons of eighteenth-century war. The sluggish operations were the counterpiece to the rapid and precise, but short-winded, evolutions that became dominant when battle was joined at last.

· 3 ·

Highly developed drill, comprehensive control of the men, professional expertise of generals and subordinate commanders— necessary as these were, they could not by themselves render the linear system effective on campaign. The precisely tooled parts of the machine required a lubricating substance before they could be set and kept in motion. This oil was provided by the light troops. In contrast to the armies' major operations, their area of activity was called the "little war." [36]

In the lectures on the little war that Clausewitz gave at the Berlin War Academy in 1810 and 1811, he formulated the meaning of the term in these words: "By *little war* we understand the employment of small units in the field; actions involving 20, 50, 100, or 300 or 400 men belong to the *little war*, unless they form part of a larger action." [37] Characteristically he approached his

[36] The term "little war" as a translation of "petite guerre" or "kleiner Krieg" has not gained acceptance in English. It is used here since no exact equivalent exists in the language. "Partisan war" and "guerrilla war," which may suggest that at least one side consists of irregulars, are not always suitable. The same objection applies to "small war," which has had some currency in the United Kingdom, though not in America. See C. Callwell, *Small Wars*, London, 1909, p. 21, for a definition of this term, which is meant to apply particularly to colonial operations. "War of detachments" is perhaps the most nearly correct of all alternatives, but it seems even more cumbersome than "little war."

[37] C. v. Clausewitz, *Meine Vorlesungen über den kleinen Krieg*, Introduction. Manuscript deposited at the University of Münster.

definition from the element of power: what mattered was the proportion of the force committed. Earlier writers attempted to define the concept by listing the specific tasks in which these forces were engaged. In 1752, the French officer de la Croix, in what appears to be the earliest work in military literature wholly devoted to the subject, wrote that the duties of soldiers engaged in the little war "consisted mainly in covering the marches of the army, in always moving against the enemy ahead of the army, and in bringing information to the generals." [38] Four years later, another French officer elaborated on this list: "Aside from detached service and constant patrolling carried out by a unit of light troops, there are frequent occasions when a commanding general employs it as an advance- or rear-guard of the army, to attack small positions along the line of march, to reconnoiter enemy movements, to guard wooded areas or defiles during battle, and finally to pursue a defeated and fleeing enemy." [39] At the end of the century a Prussian *Jäger* officer wrote: "By the so-called *little war* I understand all those undertakings in war that only assist the operations of an army or corps, without having an immediate bearing on *conquest or defense* of the territory [at stake], that secure and even mask the main force whether in battle-order or on the move: in other words, those actions that only intend to damage the enemy." [40] Another treatise, four decades later, amended the last phrase to read: ". . . those actions that only intend to damage the enemy without trying to force a decision by battle." [41] Finally a soldier and military historian, drawing the balance of a century's discussion, proposed the following, very much in the Clausewitzian tradition: "The little war is that manner of fighting which attempts to achieve the second-

[38] de la Croix, *Traité de la petite guerre*, Paris, 1752. I am citing the somewhat shortened German translation of the book, which appeared in the journal *Krieges-Bibliothek*, I, Breslau, 1755. The quotation is from p. 106.

[39] de Grandmaison, *La petite guerre*, [Paris], 1756, p. 397. Frederick used Grandmaison's work in his course for staff officers. See Jähns, III, 2465. The book was translated into German as late as 1809 by the military hack writer, J. v. Voss.

[40] G. W. v. Valentini, *Der kleine Krieg*, 6th ed., Berlin, 1833, p. 1. The first edition appeared in 1799.

[41] G. v. Decker, *Der kleine Krieg*, Berlin, 1844, p. 3. See also Jähns, III, 2711.

ary aims present in all wars, by means that are small in relation to the over-all military effort." [42]

These secondary aims were to be realized by patrols, outposts, raids, ambushes of convoys, of forage parties and troops, and by the capture of prisoners—all undertakings that in their flexibility and need for improvisation contrasted with the prevailing system of measured evolutions. The little war filled the intervals of preparation and build-up between the climactic confrontations of armies; its specialists carried out those duties that the line generally could not or was not permitted to perform. As their tactics differed, so necessarily did their discipline and organization. To incorporate and accept such forces the Prussian service would find particularly trying, for the same social and military reasons that caused it particularly to be in need of them.

The regularization of armies during the seventeenth century, the decline of the military entrepreneur, the increasing standardization of drill and equipment, had brought with them a diminution of mounted and dismounted light troops, though even in Central and Western Europe these never entirely disappeared. Courts maintained squadrons of *towarczkys* or *pandurs*, as much for their decorative value as for military reasons, and small groups of *Jäger* or *chasseurs* could be found in many armies. In Prussia Frederick William I had established two weak hussar regiments, uniformed after the Hungarian model, which on his accession his son increased to three.[43] The experiences of his first Silesian campaign led Frederick to augment and reorganize this force, and to seek means of raising other light formations, both to dispose of a force sufficiently large and well-trained to carry out the necessary patrols and raids, and to counter the Austrian light troops, which had proved a considerable nuisance to his line infantry.[44] Other armies, too, were compelled to meet the Austrian threat in kind. "It was this multitude of men, distinguished by bonnets and capes of every kind and color," wrote Grandmaison, "that forced us in 1744 and the following years to raise the

[42] W. Rüstow, *Die Lehre vom kleinen Kriege*, Zurich, 1864, p. 3.
[43] *Stammliste aller Regimenter und Corps der Königlich-Preussischen Armee*, Berlin, 1798, pp. 213–221.
[44] The threat of Austrian hussars is already mentioned in the "Instruction für die Regimenter Infanterie," 28 March 1741, *Oeuvres*, xxx, 29–30, 32.

regiments de Grassin, de la Morlière, des Cantabres, Breton Volunteers, de Guesreick, and several free [i.e., partisan] companies, aside from countless detachments that daily set out from the lines." [45]

The special conditions in the Balkans, with their long sequence of Turkish wars, had forced Vienna to maintain a strong establishment of light units. The greater part was drawn from the "military border"—the *Militärgrenze*—a broad strip of settlements and camps of soldier-farmers, which by 1765 ran from the Adriatic to Transylvania. The *Grenzer*, mainly Serbo-Croats with strong Vlach, Hungarian, Rumanian, and some German minorities, were organized into militia commands under obligation to serve beyond their home territory if required, and even in peacetime were under arms between four and five months of the year. [46] Over the centuries, writes their modern historian, "the *Grenzer* developed a strong corporate unity, a reputation for military qualities, and above all a strong loyalty to the Imperial family. . . ." [47] Their strength was considerable. In 1740 they mustered over 45,000 men, of whom 20,000 could participate in the first campaign, out of a total Austrian force of 153,000. [48] At the outbreak of the Seven Years' War they mustered 34,000 foot and 6,000 horse, slightly more than a quarter of the army. [49] As significant as their numbers was the flexibility they contributed. The belief that the *Grenzer* were suited only for guerrilla warfare is not borne out by the campaigns in which they fought. [50] Against the Prussians they were employed not only for the little war but also for the standard duties of regular troops, but generally in

[45] Grandmaison, pp. 7–8.

[46] L. Jedlicka, "Das Milizwesen in Österreich," *Wehrwissenschaftliche Rundschau*, IX (1959), 380; M. Bernath, "Die Errichtung der Siebenbürgischen Militärgrenze . . . ," *Südost-Forschungen*, XIX (1960).

[47] G. E. Rothenberg, *The Austrian Military Border in Croatia, 1522–1747*, Urbana, Ill., 1960, p. 127.

[48] *Der Österreichische Erbfolgekrieg, 1740–1748*, ed. by the Kriegsgeschichtliche Abteilung des k. und k. Kriegsarchives, I, Vienna, 1896, 502.

[49] F. Vanicek, *Specialgeschichte der Militärgrenze*, II, Vienna, 1875, 403.

[50] See, for instance, E. Dette's interpretation—one of few flaws in his generally reliable work, *Friedrich der Grosse und sein Heer*, Göttingen, 1914, p. 78.

situations where these might be handicapped: in woods, hills, villages, and in the pursuit. The defensive screens they threw around their main forces were often so effective that enemy patrols found it impossible to operate.[51] Had it not been for the *Grenzer*, the Austrian command would have experienced even greater difficulties in avoiding the major confrontations that Frederick so often sought. Their exotic appearance and unregimented manner of fighting has, however, sometimes been held against them. General J. F. C. Fuller, for one, describes them as "cut-throats" and "a wild, thieving, murdering, plundering lot of scoundrels."[52] In reality they seem to have been neither better nor worse than their comrades of the line; but their loyalty being surer, their discipline was less restrictive, and on detached duty they lived off the land. Freed from the bondage of linear tactics and of supply depots, they possessed considerable mobility and power to surprise—even in larger units, as was shown by Count Hadik's raid on Berlin in 1757.[53] It was hardly more than a slight exaggeration for a contemporary to hold that Austria owed the greatest part of her military reputation to her Croats and hussars.[54]

These troops, particularly the cavalry, served as models for other European armies, whose light units often assumed Eastern names and uniforms. To raise the quality of his squadrons after their poor showing in 1741, Frederick made a point of recruiting as many Hungarians as possible, and also drew numerous Saxons and Poles to his new hussar regiments. But his own instructions and his energetic supervision of training did more than foreign recruits to improve this branch of the service. Within a few years the Prussian hussars became an elite force, and in time a sizable

[51] *Die taktische Schulung*, p. 522.

[52] J. F. C. Fuller, *British Light Infantry in the Eighteenth Century*, London, 1925, p. 47. Delbrück, IV, 322–323, calls the *Grenzer* "Naturburschen" and "halbe Barbaren," but more in praise than otherwise.

[53] Over half of his 3,500 men were *Grenzer* and hussars, the rest special detachments from German regiments. "Zur Geschichte der Einnahme von Berlin . . . im Oktober 1757," *Urkundliche Beiträge und Forschungen zur Geschichte des Preussischen Heeres*, I, No. 4 (1902), 52, n. 2. The General Staff study remarks on the commendable moderation shown by the raiders. *Ibid.*, p. 62.

[54] [F. v. Blankenburg], *Schilderung des Preussischen Kriegsheeres . . . aus dem Mirabeau-Mauvillonschen Werke . . .*, Leipzig, 1795, p. 31.

one. At his accession he had found barely a thousand hussars in an army of 71,000 men; at his death forty-six years later these figures had risen to over 15,000 out of 161,500 first-line troops— 9 per cent of total strength.[55] This was an uncommonly high proportion; the French, who established their first regular hussars in 1720, still had only six regiments in 1792. The Prussian increase, however, does not in fact reflect a true expansion of light cavalry.

Two principles remained constant in the hussar instructions throughout Frederick's reign: hussars were mainly responsible for reconnaissance and raids, and they were to prevent desertion. Since the cavalry tended to attract more reliable men as a rule, and the hussars received favored treatment, they were considered fairly immune to this plague of the army, though some loss nevertheless occurred: out of 56 officers in one regiment, 11 deserted between 1742 and 1751.[56] But if the hussars' other duties did not change, their role in battle developed over the years. The earliest surviving *Husaren Instruction* is almost wholly taken up with directions for patrols and raids; only one paragraph discusses the hussars' action in pitched battle, and that in case they came up against their Austrian counterparts. The squadrons were ordered to stay in close formation; at most, only one section out of three might fan out. In general the regiment was to charge the enemy in close order, since "all hussar skirmishing and firing never leads to anything." [57] This limitation of the hussars' traditional way of fighting, perhaps a necessary attempt to discipline the young arm, was not always obeyed in action, yet it expressed Frederick's basic attitude. The instructions of 1743 and 1744— though defining the hussars' main characteristics as flexibility, individual pursuit, and action in difficult terrain—continued to

[55] Jany, *Preussische Armee*, III, 134. The figures, which varied from month to month, are approximate, and do not include troops already budgeted for, but not yet in uniform.

[56] From a regimental list printed by E. Count zu Lippe-Weissenfels, *Husarenbuch*, Berlin, 1863, p. 555. In his discussion of the army after Frederick's death, G. H. v. Berenhorst wrote, "The hussars are treated with great gentleness, and few desert." *Betrachtungen über die Kriegskunst*, II, Leipzig, 1798, 359.

[57] "Instruction für die Obersten . . . von den Regimentern Husaren," 21 March 1742, *Oeuvres*, xxx, 61–62.

emphasize close formations.[58] At the same time, the hussars' tactical role was expanded; they were to cover the army's front, flanks,
and rear, and to constitute a general cavalry reserve.[59] Accord-
ingly, during the Seven Years' War they were often used as battle
cavalry; and though the instructions of 1763 again stressed the
light service, it continued to be pushed into the background both
in garrison and on maneuvers.[60] The opening sentence of the
section on hussars in the comprehensive *Eléments de castramétrie
et de tactique* of 1770: "We demand of our hussars that in battle
they perform the same service as the cuirassiers and dragoons"—
only states as doctrine what had already become accepted in
practice.[61] During the campaign of 1778 Frederick himself recognized how far the hussars had turned from their original role, and
the following July he issued an instruction that tried to recall
them to the "wirklichen Husarendienst," to use his phrase.[62] The
document urged the need for greater initiative among officers and
men, and better training in surprise attacks, patrolling, and the
gathering of information.

It may be taken as an indication of the hussars' tendency to
acquire all the characteristics—social as well as tactical—of
Prussian heavy cavalry that Frederick felt obliged to comment in
the same order on the absolute necessity "that not so many young
windbags serve as officers in the regiments, but that now and then
capable, long-serving sergeants be recommended for promotion to
lieutenant. . . ."[63] In this respect the King continued to draw a
distinction between the hussars and his other cavalry, from which
untitled officers were almost wholly excluded. From the day of
their formation, the hussars, in common with all light and techni-

---

[58] Extracts from the *Reglement* of 1743 are printed in Lippe-Weissenfels, pp. 131–154. "Disposition wie sich die Offiziere . . . zu verhalten
haben," 25 July 1744, *Oeuvres*, xxx, 125–136. The word *Reglement*,
incidentally, lost its *accent grave* in military German.

[59] *Ibid.*, pp. 135–136.

[60] "Instruction für die Commandeurs der Cavallerie-Regimenter," 11
May 1763, *Oeuvres*, xxx, 271–287. Cf. Jany, *Preussische Armee*, iii,
92–95.

[61] *Oeuvres*, xxix, 39.

[62] "Instruction für die Inspecteurs der Cavallerie," 20 July 1779,
Oeuvres, xxx, 351–358.

[63] *Ibid.*, p. 357.

cal troops in the Prussian army, accepted non-noble officers, many of whom they retained even after the weeding-out at the end of the Seven Years' War. How deep the social distinction ran may be learned from the last army list of the old monarchy; among them, 25 cuirassier and dragoon regiments shared one untitled officer, while ten regiments and one battalion of light cavalry had 73.[64]

The wish to possess a force that would be useful both as battle cavalry and for reconnaissance could not be faulted. Nor was the hussars' tendency towards regularization exceptional: in the history of armies the outsiders of one generation repeatedly turned respectable and even became the elite formations of the next. Neither versatility nor regularization represented a loss so long as the new function did not compromise the original purpose. In the Prussian army, however, a decided lack of imagination came to affect the employment of the light cavalry after Frederick's death. In the campaigns in France and Poland during the 1790's—when the armies were in any case fragmented and widely dispersed— hussars were assigned the missions of the little war and carried them out with distinction. In 1806, however, when it was a question of maneuvering large masses for a decisive encounter, the hussars' tasks of scouting and harassment were forgotten, their squadrons were concentrated with the main bodies, and instead of the eyes of the army they became simply another, and useless, muscle.

· 4 ·

Frederick did not attempt to bring about a similar amalgamation of light and line duties among his regular infantry. The framework of a militia existed in Prussia, and in times of crisis such units were even mobilized—for instance, against Swedish and Russian incursions during the Seven Years' War. The military value of these home-defense groups was small, however, and could only have been raised at the cost of radical changes in the country's social and administrative institutions. Nor was Frederick willing, for the sake of a minority of light units, to disrupt the peculiar system of discipline and precision with which Leopold

[64] *Rangliste der Königlich Preussischen Armee*, Berlin, 1806. Cf. also Appendix 2, Table 2, of this work, indicating social differences between more senior officers in various branches of the army.

von Dessau and he had molded the Prussian infantry. The result was that in wartime the special tasks of light infantry were carried out, if at all, by units hired for the duration, and by a few hundred *Jäger*.

The *Jäger* corps in the Prussian army owed its inception to Frederick, who, shortly after his accession, organized a group of fifty or sixty foresters and hunters on the model of similar units in other German forces, to serve as guides and to carry out patrols.[65] This first detachment was soon disbanded, but the scheme was revived in 1744 with the formation of two volunteer companies of rangers, or *Feldjäger zu Fuss*. The royal order declared that as far as possible the companies should be made up of sons of native foresters and of other woodsmen. "I don't doubt," wrote the King, "that young hunters will engage themselves the more readily as they can count on certain employment after having served for a few years as *Feldjäger*." [66] The order contains the basic characteristics that were to mark the corps throughout its history: the men are drawn from a skilled and loyal group; on return to civilian life they are given favorable consideration for appointments to positions in the royal domains and on private estates. A very high proportion of their officers was untitled—31 out of 133 serving between 1740 and the corps' reorganization in 1808.[67]

The *Jäger* carried rifles, which were far more accurate and powerful than the standard infantry musket, but took more than twice as long to load and fire, and required more careful maintenance.[68] Since there was little fear that the men would desert and since they were not expected to perform complex linear evolu-

---

[65] *Stammliste*, 1798, p. 120; R. de l'Homme de Courbière, *Geschichte der Brandenburgisch-Preussischen Heeres-Verfassung*, Berlin, 1852, p. 99. Details on the early history of the *Jäger* can be found in the first volume of C. F. Gumtau's fundamental *Die Jäger und Schützen des Preussischen Heeres*, 3 vols., Berlin, 1834–1838.

[66] Printed in D. v. Rentzell, *Geschichte des Garde-Jäger-Bataillons*, 2nd ed., Berlin, 1894, pp. 4–5. On recruitment, see also the Cabinet Order of 5 December 1786, in E. v. Frauenholz, *Das Heerwesen in der Zeit des Absolutismus*, Munich, 1940, pp. 297–298; and A. v. Lyncker, *Die Altpreussische Armee, 1714–1806, und ihre Militärkirchenbücher*, Berlin, 1937, pp. 151–152.

[67] Gumtau, I, Appendix 10.

[68] For comparative results at different ranges, see Appendix 5, Table 2, of this work.

tions, discipline could be freer than that generally prevailing in the army. Beatings were rare; transfer to a line regiment, with the consequent loss of future security, was considered the harshest punishment. The special qualifications looked for helped to limit the size of the new arm. After sixty years the *Jäger*, now a regiment, still numbered less than 2,000 men; over the decades they had gained a reputation for being effective fighters, and by 1806 the regiment ranked among the two or three most-decorated in the army.[69]

Although their primary duty was the pursuit of the little war, there were times when the *Jäger* took their place in the line of battle. During the Seven Years' War they fought a number of successful defensive engagements in woods, villages, and—at Hochkirch—even on open ground.[70] Their reliability made them useful to combat desertion. Backed by small groups of hussars, *Jäger* in twos and threes regularly surrounded Prussian armies in camp and on the march.[71] Occasionally they were employed on confidential missions; in 1756 Frederick planned to communicate from Saxony with the detached corps covering Berlin by sending Polish-speaking *Jäger* in disguise through the Russian lines.[72] Their versatility had its limits, however; they were at a greater disadvantage than line infantry when they faced superior opponents in unfavorable terrain. In 1760 the corps was completely destroyed when Cossacks caught it crossing an open plain, where the slow rate of fire of their rifles left the *Jäger* nearly defenseless.[73] Bayonets would have helped, but they were not part of the

[69] Rentzell's detailed breakdown, p. 34, adds up to 1,935 officers and men. Jany, *Preussische Armee*, III, 391, gives an unitemized figure of 2,007 for 1805–1806. The *Army List* for 1806 shows that seven officers of the *Feldjäger* were decorated with the order *Pour le mérite*, compared with fourteen in the other four regiments of the same *Inspection*, i.e., the same administrative command.

[70] *Der Siebenjährige Krieg*, ed. by the *Kriegsgeschichtliche Abteilung II* of the German General Staff, Berlin, 1901–1913. See particularly volumes IV, 204, and VIII, 290–291.

[71] See, for instance, "Instruction für die General-Majors von der Infanterie," 14 August 1748, *Oeuvres*, xxx, 155.

[72] "Militairische Instruction für den General-Feldmarschall von Lehwaldt," 23 June 1756, *ibid.*, xxx, 207–208.

[73] Rentzell, p. 13; Gumtau, I, 39–40.

Jäger equipment; an indication, possibly, of how difficult it was for the King to accept the idea of an all-purpose infantry.[74]

The *Jäger*, whether in battalion or regimental strength, were in any event too weak by themselves to achieve the secondary aims in any campaign. Rather than train a number of line battalions for the light service—whose ranks might have been filled entirely by native volunteers to allow the somewhat easier discipline without which the tactical pattern could not be opened up—Frederick took recourse to units raised solely for the duration of the war. These formations were given the name *Freibataillone*, or *Freicorps*—"free" because they did not come under the regular establishment, but formed separate administrative and tactical commands. Usually they were recruited and organized by officers who had concluded a contract or agreement with the King, an arrangement reminiscent of earlier days before the monarch had replaced the military entrepreneur in the Prussian army, and similar to that under which ranger companies were raised in America at the same period. The first of these corps came into being in the winter of 1756–1757; six years later they numbered more than twenty.[75] Several mounted corps were also raised during the war, as well as some larger commands that incorporated both foot and horse, on the pattern of the French *légions* of the time. After a period of experimentation, the standard *Freibatail-*

---

[74] *Jäger* formations of other German armies had been issued bayonets since the middle of the century, though as late as the American Revolution foreign observers considered this to be a novelty worthy of comment. A British officer, describing Hessian troops embarking for America in the spring of 1781, wrote that one "Company out of the Five, of which the Corps consists wear Leather Caps and carry Rifle Barrel Guns, with Bayonets to them, the other four have Hats, and are arm'd with the common Firelock." Quoted in A. Haarmann and D. Holst, "The Hesse-Hanau Free Corps of Light Infantry, 1781–1783," *Military Collector and Historian*, xv, No. 2 (Summer 1963), 41.

[75] The basic study is still Major Schnackenburg's "Die Freikorps Friedrich des Grossen," *Militär-Wochenblatt* (1883), Supplement 6. The circumstances in which these units were organized, their frequent amalgamation, disbandment, and change of name, make it difficult to give more than an estimate of their number and strengths. See also Lyncker, pp. 227–247; and G. Gieraths, *Die Kampfhandlungen der Brandenburgisch-Preussischen Armee, 1626–1807*, Berlin, 1964, pp. 326–340.

lon came to have, on paper, the same number of officers—21—as the Prussian musketeer battalion, but was somewhat stronger in the ranks—790 NCO's and privates as against 681. The men were equipped with the infantry musket, and their uniforms resembled those of the line infantry, except that waistcoats and pants were blue to match their coats, rather than the standard white or yellow. Later in the war some units adopted more colorful garb to attract recruits. Colonel Arndt von Kleist's "Prussian Croat" infantry, which carried out successful and profitable campaigns in Saxony and Franconia, were issued the high, cone-shaped felt cap of the Prussian hussars, a green jacket copied from the genuine Croats and decorated with white loops, green waistcoat and pants, short black hussar boots, and a red sash. Another unit received fur busbies with red and yellow bags, dark blue jackets lined in red with light-blue facings and white loops, blue waistcoats also decorated with white loops, and light blue pants.[76]

The majority of officers serving with the *Freicorps* held temporary commissions. They came from Prussia and other German states, as well as from France, Switzerland, Holland, and Eastern Europe. Many among them were untitled. "To the free battalions," Frederick wrote, "I assign competent and determined officers . . . who are however scoundrels and not really suitable for good line regiments." [77] Most of the men in the ranks were foreigners. Pressing prisoners into service was not uncommon, and contributed to the incidence of desertion and even of mutiny. In the hastily organized and drilled *Freicorps*, discipline could not be of the Prussian stamp; army regulations did not fully cover the men, and at times the attitude of the King actually favored their stepping out of bounds. "It is not customary," he wrote in 1759, "to give free battalions a winter allowance. They find their allowance in enemy territory, where they loot and plunder, which other regiments are forbidden to do by regulations and, therefore, are given allowances." [78] It was not surprising if the officers, as Frederick said of one battalion, "stole like ravens" or that the line

[76] Schnackenburg, pp. 326, 328.

[77] *Politische Korrespondenz Friedrichs des Grossen*, Berlin, 1879–1939, xvii, 142.

[78] *Ibid.*, xviii, 57.

generally held the *Freibataillone* in contempt.[79] When in 1760 the colonel of an elite cavalry regiment was ordered by the King to sack a chateau, he disobeyed on the grounds that "such an act might perhaps be seemly to officers of a *Freibataillon*, but not to the commander of His Majesty's *Gens d'armes*."[80] Some *Freicorps* officers nevertheless made their way in the service. The former Dutch lieutenant Wilhelm René de l'Homme de Courbière, an early advocate of establishing a regular body of light infantry in Prussia, rose to the dignity of *Generalfeldmarschall*. Among others who achieved senior rank were Wunsch, Chaumontet, Hordt, and Konstantin Nathaniel von Salemon, the son of Jewish parents living in Danzig, who ended his career as a lieutenant general and commandant of the town and fortress of Wesel.[81] Despite the arm's bad repute, Lessing had numerous models when he turned the idealized Prussian officer-hero of his happiest play, *Minna von Barnhelm*, into the commander of a *Freibataillon*.[82]

At the end of the war most of these units were disbanded, contrary to the King's promise that able *Freicorps* officers could look forward to a career in the Prussian service. Those officers and men not dismissed were transferred to line units, so that the next war found Prussia once more without a sufficient contingent of light infantry. Fifteen detachments were hurriedly raised in

[79] For Frederick's statement, see Schnackenburg, p. 333; and Dette, p. 78.

[80] The officer was J. F. A. v. d. Marwitz, an ancestor and namesake of the great representative of the conservative ethos during the Reform Era. His tomb bore the legend: "He witnessed Frederick's heroic age and fought with him in all his wars, chose disgrace where obedience brought dishonor." Priesdorff, No. 640. Tradition tells a similar story of disobedience involving General F. C. v. Saldern, the noted tactician of Frederick's last decades.

[81] On Courbière, see Priesdorff, No. 664; on Salemon, *ibid.*, No. 552; on Hordt, *ibid.*, No. 538. Hordt's memoirs, published both in a French and a German edition in 1788, contain interesting passages on the conflict between duty and honor to which command of a *Freiregiment* exposed him.

[82] The play's references to the current scene, especially the allusions to the *Freibataillone*, led the Prussian Resident in Hamburg to delay its *première* in 1767. The following year in Berlin, *Minna von Barnhelm* was presented without cuts to great public acclaim.

1778, but the campaign drew to a close before the majority had been equipped and organized.[83] It was this wasteful and inefficient episode together with the ever more obvious need for trained light troops that finally led Frederick to place light infantry regiments on the permanent establishment. In 1783 he drafted instructions for their use; three years later the necessary money was allocated for the organization of three regiments, which were termed *Frei-regimenter* in allusion to their predecessors in the light service. Little more than cadres at Frederick's death, the regiments were broken up in the first months of the new reign, and together with additional line units reorganized into twenty fusilier or "light" battalions.[84] Within a year—by June 1787—the total strength of dismounted light troops in the army had been increased nearly threefold.

· 5 ·

Frederick's recognition, in his last years, of the advantages to be gained from a permanent body of light infantry was not accompanied by new ideas on the employment of such troops in the field. His instructions for the *Freiregimenter* mark no advance over his earliest writings on the subject, though even then the Prussian army was falling behind others in the organization and use of the light service.

The tactics of the Prussian free battalions during the Seven Years' War might be termed irregular in a negative sense. By any standard, the close order they sometimes attempted was negligible; but, as Frederick said, compactness was of little benefit to such units.[85] Their open order was more a matter of instinct than of instruction. Being less dependent on alignment and volleyed fire than the regular infantry, they proved more effective in woods

[83] Schnackenburg, p. 339; Jany, *Preussische Armee*, iii, 112, 127–128.

[84] During Frederick's reign, fusilier battalions received the shortest men; otherwise they differed from grenadiers and musketeers only in slight variations of uniform and organization. After the King's death "fusilier" came to signify light infantry. On the word's change of meaning, see B. v. Poten, *Handwörterbuch der gesamten Militärwissenschaften*, Bielefeld-Leipzig, 1877–1880, iv, 20; and W. Transfeldt and K.-H. v. Brand, *Wort und Brauchtum des Soldaten*, Hamburg, 1959, pp. 34–35.

[85] "Instruction für die Frei-Regimenter . . . ," 5 December 1783, *Oeuvres*, xxx, 399.

and hills; but they were not trained in the individual movement and aimed fire of true skirmishing.[86] Their operational assignments were to protect the army's front, flanks, and rear, to raid in enemy territory, and to lead the first attack in a set battle. At the siege of Olmütz, in 1758, they effectively covered the lines of communication to Silesia, and then served as rearguard in the long retreat from Moravia. At Leuthen, three free battalions with two companies of *Jäger* constituted the advance guard that observed the Austrian right wing while the army marched against the other flank. In 1759 at Asch, and later at Herrnstadt, light troops stationed in suitable terrain withstood repeated infantry and cavalry attacks. The following year, during the fourth struggle for Dresden, Courbière's regiment and some *Jäger* fought from windows and rooftops.[87] This was more grateful and constructive work than the task Frederick often assigned them—leading a full-scale infantry attack as a forlorn hope.

In 1757, Frederick had written that since "the first infantry attack must always be considered a loss . . . the leading troops should not exactly be the best. One can take *Freibataillone* for the task, or other poor battalions, on which if need be one can fire should they retreat or refuse to attack with spirit." [88] The *Military Testament* of 1768 elaborated on this thought: "I shall let the *Freibataillone* make the first attack, not in alignment but *à la debandade et tiraillant*. The more they can draw enemy fire, the better is the order in which the regular troops can attack." [89] Two years later Frederick added further details to the free battalions' role in starting an attack: they must rush forward "heads down," urged on by the bayonets of the heavy infantry behind them.[90] Finally, the instruction for the *Freiregimenter*, while not ignoring the usual duties of raids and patrols, gave this example of their use in battle: "The enemy stands on high ground from which he is to be driven. In such a case one can take light troops for the

---

[86] "The free battalions become really useful in obstructed terrain." "Eléments de castramétrie et de tactique," *ibid.*, XXIX, 41.

[87] Gieraths, pp. 326–340, prints a valuable list of battles and engagements in which these units participated. Tactical details can be found in *Der Siebenjährige Krieg.*

[88] "Aphorismen," *Oeuvres*, XXX, 237.

[89] *Military Testament* of 1768, printed in Taysen, p. 218.

[90] "Eléments de castramétrie et de tactique," *Oeuvres*, XXIX, 40–41.

first assault; but this should not be carried out in a regular manner, rather they must run blindly up to the enemy and in no case fire until they have closed in hand-to-hand combat." [91]

The same rules laid down that in almost every eventuality light troops should fire by half-company volleys, the standard rolling fire of the Prussian infantry. The single reference to advancing and firing in open formations presents a highly schematic picture: against enemy troops lodged in a forest the companies open up to two or three times their ordinary distance, resulting in intervals of perhaps one yard between men, and the first rank fires until ammunition is exhausted. Then the second rank moves forward, while the first withdraws in sections around the flanks, and continues firing, until it, in turn, makes way for the third rank. [92] These evolutions, which attempt to solve their tactical problem by a minute opening up of the linear formation, contrast strikingly with the demand for a blind rush and the abandonment of all order. Neither method effectively exploits the forces of mobility and fire.

Frederick would have been astonished to learn that organizing three light infantry regiments on a permanent footing signified a departure from his traditional tactical concepts. Historians, however, have not hesitated to present the change in this light, sometimes going so far as to claim that with it the King moved in advance of his time. [93] This mistakes the course of tactical develop-

[91] "Instruction für die Frei-Regimenter . . . ," *ibid.*, xxx, 401.

[92] *Ibid.*, xxx, 400.

[93] The interpretation of Frederick as a pioneer of modern infantry tactics is put forward with special insistence in R. Sautermeister's *Die taktische Reform der preussischen Armee nach 1806*, Tübingen, 1935, a work sometimes cited in the recent literature. Sautermeister's view is derived from a superficial and selective reading of Frederick's military writings, buttressed with the arguments (pp. 7–10) that light troops increased during Frederick's reign (which ignores the great fluctuations in their numbers), that the King was impressed by the new forms of war in America (for which no evidence is cited), and that Frederick strengthened the *Jäger* corps (which passes in silence over their change in armament, a development discussed at the end of this chapter). Furthermore, Sautermeister does not distinguish between mobs and trained skirmishers. He sees "highly significant beginnings of *tirailleur* and column tactics" (p. 97) in any formation that is not strictly linear, even if it be no more than the forward rush of some *enfants perdus*, on whom, in the King's phrase that he ignores, "man allenfalls selber feuern kann, wen sie

ment both in Prussia and elsewhere. The instruction that the King drafted for the *Freiregimente* evidently looked to a previous age rather than forward; in comparison with doctrine in other armies it is antiquated. Nor were Frederick's views influenced by events overseas, as has been suggested, and, indeed, the fighting in America and India did not, as is often supposed, constitute the beginnings of a new era in tactics. A survey of the major lines of tactical evolution will clarify the role played by colonial experience and lead to a truer evaluation of Prussia's position at the conclusion of Frederick's reign.[94]

The decisive innovation in infantry fighting that was to occur at the end of the eighteenth century consisted in the acceptance of open-order tactics by the line infantry. Close-order methods—the line, the attack column, fire by volley—were now combined with skirmish groups and individual aimed fire. Furthermore, these methods were employed not by separate specialist units that mutually supported each other, but by the same men, or at least by subunits of the same tactical command.

Models or even primitive ancestors of the new tactical integration are difficult to find in colonial campaigns. Combat reports of the time make it apparent that open order itself, particularly in the attack, was rarely used overseas. During the Madras campaigns of the 1770's and 1780's all usually went well so long as the British and their native auxiliaries maintained close cohesion. In the American War for Independence, too, both armies relied primarily on linear formations, deployed on the cleared lands of

---

zurückgehen oder nicht beherzt angreifen wollen." Equally unwarranted is the suggestion that Frederick's attacking infantry made even rudimentary use of the column. No record exists of Prussian infantry fighting in columns during Frederick's reign, nor do the instructions ever mention columns as tactical formations. Sautermeister's error seems to lie in his failure to distinguish between route or marching columns and columns employed in combat. The latter did not appear in the Prussian service until some years after Frederick's death. Sautermeister's conclusion (pp. 8–9) that with the regulations for the light troops of 5 December 1783 "Frederick was far in advance of his age" suggests that his knowledge of other armies is similarly limited.

[94] The following paragraphs are based on my article "Colonial Experience and European Military Reform at the End of the Eighteenth Century," *Bulletin of the Institute of Historical Research*, xxxvii (May 1964), especially pp. 51–55.

the eastern seaboard. As their correspondence shows, it was an unceasing concern of the American leaders to teach their men not to scatter under fire, but to stand or move forward in serried ranks, and if possible to fire volleys by command. General Steuben's contribution to the American cause lies in the measure to which this goal was achieved.

The British light infantry, first raised in America during the 1750's, constituted an attempt to adapt linear methods to operations in difficult terrain. It must be noted, however, that these units derived many of their characteristics not from colonial society but from the European tradition of the *chasseur* and *Jäger*, and that their adjustment did not go very far.[95] Possibly their tactics were somewhat more flexible than those of the line; they served as advance guards, led assaults and landings, and at times were employed to pursue French and Indian raiding parties. Their drill, discipline, and equipment, however, were essentially those of the rest of the army, and more often than not they were used like regular infantry.

To contribute to march security and add versatility to their tactics, the British line battalions serving in America between 1756 and 1763 formed their own light companies on an *ad hoc* basis. These units tried to attract young, intelligent, and agile men, and came to rival the grenadiers as elite formations. In 1770 a light company was officially authorized for each line battalion. During the War for Independence, the light infantry was often grouped with grenadiers into improvised battalions for special missions—a development which, necessary though it was, nullified the companies' original purpose of adding flexibility to the line. It reflects, however, a common practice of European armies in the last decades of the century.

The one notable difference between infantry fighting in Europe and in the colonies lay in the greater emphasis placed on small-

[95] The first regiment of this kind, the 60th Royal Americans, was "recruited from settlers, mainly of Swiss and German origin . . . to which were added volunteers from British regiments and others from Europe. Many of the senior officers and a considerable number of the company officers were also drawn from the armies of Europe." Sir Edward Hutton, *A Brief History of the King's Royal Rifle Corps*, Winchester, 1917, p. 2. See also Fuller, p. 98. An excellent survey of British developments during this period is contained in S. G. P. Ward's *Faithful: The Story of the Durham Light Infantry*, London, 1963.

unit operations and, at least in America, on marksmanship. At a time when Frederick demanded volume of fire from his men rather than accuracy, Amherst wrote to Gage: "Firing at marks is so essential for forming a soldier for this country, that I am certain I need not mention it to you." [96] In 1765 Gage himself ordered Colonel Campbell in Detroit to "make every soldier in your Regiment a good Marksman," and two years later he wrote to Captain Edmonstone at Fort Pitt, "You have done very right in practicing the Recruits of the 34th Regiment to fire at Marks." [97] Similar statements occur in British military correspondence up to the end of the War for Independence, linked sometimes with advice to exercise troops in such manner as should be best for all sorts of service in the woods. But when large numbers of American and British came to face each other, they resorted to linear tactics; the troops deployed from columns into lines or squares, and attempted to kill or frighten the enemy by volleys that were certainly slower and more ragged, but perhaps more accurate, than those of their Prussian contemporaries.

The fabled rangers, sharpshooters, and riflemen performed the same auxiliary function in this linear pattern as did the *Jäger*, *Grenzer*, *Freibataillone*, and other specialists of the little war in Europe. It may be noted, incidentally, that at a time when the *Jäger* could already look back on a rich military past, his favorite weapon, the rifle, was still somewhat of a novelty overseas. Christopher Ward quotes a letter John Adams wrote to his wife while attending the First Continental Congress, in which he tells her of "a peculiar kind of musket, called a rifle," used by "riflemen . . . from Pennsylvania, Maryland and Virginia . . . the most accurate marksmen in the world." [98] Indeed, only one rifle-maker is said to have worked north of Pennsylvania before 1783. [99]

[96] Letter of 16 April 1761. Gage MSS., Amherst Papers, vol. v. William L. Clements Library, Ann Arbor, Mich.

[97] Letters of 20 April 1765, and 23 November 1767. Gage MSS., American Series.

[98] C. L. Ward, *The War of the Revolution*, ed. J. R. Alden, New York, 1952, I, 31.

[99] *Ibid.*, p. 435. The misconception that American rifles and American methods of loading were superior to those of Europe continues to be held even by specialists in eighteenth-century American military affairs. For example, H. H. Peckham writes in *The War for Independence: A Military History*, Chicago, 1959, p. 27: "Rifled barrels were known in Europe, but

Far from being decisively shaped by colonial wars, the new integrated infantry tactics that came to dominate European battlefields after the middle of the 1790's were the outcome of European experience and experimentation. Three separate but simultaneous developments, extending over a century, gradually joined to create the infantry methods of the Napoleonic Age.

The first was the amalgamation of irregular light troops with the regulars of the line. In Prussia, for example, we have seen the temporary *Freibataillone* turn into units on the permanent list; in 1787 they evolve into fusilier battalions, which after another two decades are so completely merged with the rest of the infantry that only their name and some bits of distinctive braid remain to set them apart.

The second development, already mentioned in connection with the British in America, was the addition to each line battalion of some specialists in open order and aimed fire. In France this practice could be found in rudimentary form as early as the Regency.[100] By the end of the *ancien régime* each French infantry battalion included a few dozen men who were trained to skirmish and fire at will—the *tirailleurs de bataillon*.

The third strand leading to tactical change was made up of the elite regular units, such as the *Jäger*, that most armies had possessed in small numbers since the turn of the century. The men were generally armed with rifles, rifled carbines, or carbines, instead of the cheaper and less accurate standard musket. In the last years of the monarchy, the French army—preeminent here, too—already had on its permanent establishment twelve battalions of *chasseurs à pied*, which were also called by the prophetic name *tirailleurs en grande bande*.[101]

---

the problem of making the lead bullet fit snugly, so that it would be set in a whirling motion by the rifle grooves when fired, had been ingeniously solved by some nameless backwoodsman who covered the bullet with a patch of greased linen. Both were inserted in the muzzle and rammed home against a pinch of powder. . . ." In reality this technique had been well known in Central Europe since the seventeenth century; indeed, the use of a patch or plaster suggested the word *Pflasterbüchse* to denote the rifle carried by German hunters and soldiers. Cf. Eckardt and Morawietz, pp. 73–80; *Thoughts on the Kentucky Rifle in Its Golden Age*, ed. M. A. Cresswell, York, Pa., 1960, pp. 26–27.

[100] Colin, *L'Infanterie au XVIIIᵉ siècle*, p. 47.

[101] *Ibid.*, pp. 274–276; and *Etat militaire de France*, Paris, 1788, pp. 301–313.

In France more than elsewhere, theory had speculated on the application of light tactics to the standard infantry encounter. Well before the Seven Years' War, Maurice de Saxe envisaged that one-tenth of the standard infantry unit was to fight as skirmishers.[102] Both light and line infantry should employ aimed fire —when they fired at all—since he considered unaimed volleys to be nearly useless.[103] The model of an infantry attack he outlined in these words:

In an attack the light infantry are dispersed a hundred, one hundred and fifty, or if desired two hundred paces ahead of the line. They should open fire when they are within three hundred paces of the enemy, without order or command, and at will. The light infantry captain must not signal retreat nor withdraw with his ensign until he is fifty paces from the enemy, then he slowly falls back on the regiment, keeping up his fire from time to time, until he has reached the intervals between the line battalions, which are already moving forward.[104]

De Saxe's proposed combined units, the *légions*, were never generally adopted by the French army; but in practice his ideas on the use of skirmishers gained considerable acceptance.[105] The conviction that aimed fire—which necessarily meant individual fire—was often of value survived even the Frederician fashion of the period after the Seven Years' War. The *Ordonnances* of 1776 and 1778 specified the use of both linear and skirmish formations.[106] In the following decade the new *chasseur* battalions were trained to fight either independently or interspersed among line formations, the latter use being strongly recommended in Lloyd's *Military Memoirs*, which appeared at this time. If called for by the tactical situation, the *chasseurs* could deploy entirely as skirmishers.[107]

---

[102] *Les Rêveries, ou mémoires sur l'art de la guerre*, The Hague, 1756, pp. 34–37. Not one-half, as in the modern translation by T. R. Phillips, *Reveries on the Art of War*, Harrison, Pa., 1953, p. 36, an edition that contains a number of serious errors.

[103] *Les Rêveries*, p. 44.

[104] *Ibid.*, p. 47. See also plate 11 of the Hague edition, which illustrates this maneuver.

[105] Colin, *L'Infanterie au XVIIIe siècle*, p. 50.

[106] *Ibid.*, pp. 180–184.

[107] The first English edition of Lloyd's work was published in 1781; three years later a French translation appeared under the title *Philosophie de la guerre*. For Lloyd's discussion of light units, see particularly Part I

Gradually, throughout Europe, differences in organization and tactics diminished between line infantry on the one hand, and irregular auxiliaries, regular specialists in open order, and elite light units on the other. These separate bodies were to join, with the eventual result of a new all-purpose infantry, in which each soldier could fight in the line, in column, as skirmisher, and on detached missions. The process was particularly advanced in the French army. When the Revolution released new sources of energy, of enthusiasm and patriotism, in government and people, it found well-developed military techniques ready to hand.

Under these circumstances it is not surprising that professional soldiers of the day showed little awareness of a supposed tactical influence from overseas. When Lafayette in his memoirs talks of the skirmishers he employed 1792, he alludes in no way to his experiences in America, though in other contexts these are mentioned often enough.[108] One of the most widely used practical guides to the little war and other types of detached service during the early years of the Revolution, Scharnhorst's *Militairisches Taschenbuch*, cites four examples of raids, patrols, and ambushes from the American War for Independence as against over sixty drawn from the Seven Years' War.[109] Some years later, when the great Napoleonic authority on light infantry, Count Duhesme, discussed in his fundamental work on light troops what he himself termed "the tactical revolution of the early 1790's," he wrote not one word about the experiences gained by the French or anyone

---

chapter XIII, of the latter edition. On the tactics of the chasseurs, see P. G. Duhesme, *Essai historique sur l'infanterie légère*, 3rd ed., Paris, 1864, pp. 66–67. The first edition of General Duhesme's work, one of the most important sources on the history of light infantry in France, was published in 1814. A German translation by "two Prussian officers" appeared in 1829 under the title *Die leichte Infanterie*. It contains numerous interesting notes comparing French and Prussian methods.

[108] Colin, *L'Infanterie au XVIIIᵉ siècle*, p. 275.

[109] G. Scharnhorst, *Militairisches Taschenbuch' zum Gebrauch im Felde*, Hanover, 1794. The work achieved at least four editions. Scharnhorst took the American incidents from the book of the Hessian officer, J. v. Ewald, *Abhandlung vom Dienst der leichten Truppen*, Flensburg, 1790. In a review of the work he wrote: "[It] contains quite useful rules for the service of light troops. However, those who know Jenny and Grandmaison will not find anything exactly new in it." *Jenaer Allgemeine Literatur-Zeitung* (1790), No. 352.

else in India and America. His analysis skips directly from the Seven Years' War to the wars of the French Revolution.

Frederick would have been the last to seek new ideas on war in the American campaigns. The political incompetence of the British government impressed him more strongly than the military abilities of the colonists, and he took an ironic view of the fascination with which Europe followed the distant and incomprehensible conflict. "We are like those German comedians," he wrote his brother Henry, "who during their holidays watch French actors and model themselves on them. We observe the Washingtons, the Howes, the Burgoynes, and the Carletons to learn from them that great art of war, which can never be wholly understood, to laugh at their stupidities, and to approve those things they can do according to the rules. His Britannic Majesty and his government occupy the boxes, we sit in the highest gallery, and even our whistles are ignored. Lord Bute, who is the author of the piece, should be hanged in the last act to make the scene properly pathetic." [110] When the young Gneisenau, who had spent some months in Canada with a German *Jäger* battalion, applied for a commission in the Prussian army, Frederick noted that he could not have learned the correct principles of war in America. An aide's favorable report on Gneisenau's character led the King to admit him to the Prussian service, with the judgment that "this man is quite suitable for a *Freiregiment.* . . . The people who come back from America imagine they know all there is to know about war, and yet they have to start learning war all over again in Europe." [111] The essential point, he thought, was missed by those of his contemporaries who held that the little war was the best school of the soldier since it fostered individual initiative and physical agility. [112]

If Frederick changed his views on infantry tactics during the last years of his life, it was in the direction of still more rapid and precise linear evolutions. He especially approved the efforts of one

[110] Letter of 3 November 1777. *Oeuvres*, xxvi, 401–402.

[111] Frederick's two memoranda are printed in K. v. Priesdorff, *Gneisenau*, Hamburg, 1943, pp. 21–22. Cf. also W. v. Unger, *Gneisenau*, Berlin, 1914, p. 11.

[112] Such enthusiastic statements occur in many texts on the little war and on light troops. See, for instance, de la Croix, p. 111; and G. v. Wissel, *Der Jäger im Felde*, Göttingen, 1778, p. 12.

of his Inspectors-General, Friedrich Christoph von Saldern, who refined parade-ground drill to an optimum of speed and complexity. Taking the King's dispositions in actual battles as his model, Saldern worked out new and surprising methods of deploying from the approach march into battle formations, preferably oblique ones.[113] More than ever this system demanded the correct initial tactical decision and minute exactness of execution. A contemporary observed that when after his death Saldern came to expound his principles to the spirits of Gustavus Adolphus and Montecuculi, he would be asked "whether since their time the surface of the whole globe had been planed flat." [114] And, indeed, these geometric evolutions could succeed only on level, unobstructed terrain. After Frederick's death the campaigns of the 1790's and the disasters of Jena and Auerstedt were to show how difficult it was for Prussian forces, all better insight to the contrary, to shed their dependence on methods that at best were useful as training exercises. "Those maneuvers made us forget war," Scharnhorst could write after the collapse; "everyone, even the English and French tacticians (not those natural soldiers who led the armies in 1793–1794, and later) regarded them as the basis of operations. Several able men—Tempelhoff and others—continued to respect these tactics-turned-into-formalities when they commanded in the field. That the mechanics of evolutions alone decided victory was generally believed. Since people occupied themselves very largely with the mathematical principles of fundamental tactics, these in turn became the basis of operations." [115]

Tactical preference and organizational, disciplinary, and technological considerations led the King to discount the value of light infantry—at least in the Prussian scheme of things. Like a fleet, light troops might be desirable; the state, however, could afford only what was essential. His professional view was reinforced by social and political preconceptions. Throughout his

---

[113] Saldern anonymously published an account of his system: *Taktische Grundsätze und Anweisung zu militärischen Evolutionen*, Frankfurt, 1781. K. v. Priesdorff has written a brief and disappointing book on his life and work: *Saldern*, Hamburg, 1943.

[114] Berenhorst, *Betrachtungen*, II, 423.

[115] *On Infantry Tactics*, ¶ 9. The complete essay is printed below, pp. 255–259.

reign Frederick disliked the presence of bourgeois officers in the army. His feelings were not entirely derived from aristocratic bias, though he did believe that only noblemen inherently possessed the qualities of command and representation, that sense of personal and family honor, of duty and *contenance*, which was needed by leaders of Prussian troops.[116] But the non-military functions of the noble officers also weighed heavily with the King. The army both molded an elite without whose efforts and sacrifices the state could not have raised itself from a minor principality, formed this elite's main source of honor, and constituted an important means for its economic support. The unwillingness to admit other elements was thus related to political concerns. But at no time were there enough suitable Prussian—or, indeed, foreign—nobles to fill all posts, and from necessity Frederick continued to accept bourgeois candidates in the auxiliary and special branches of the service, which had always maintained a non-aristocratic tradition: the artillery and engineer corps, the garrison regiments, and the light troops. Officers in these units, however, were not on a par in prestige or economic position with their comrades in the heavy cavalry and line infantry. They received lower pay and allowances, and enjoyed fewer prospects of advancement.[117] Even the hussars, who over the years had greatly gained in social standing, did not yet rank with the cuirassiers and dragoons, but had a seniority list of their own. Organization and tactics of the army were influenced by social factors, and certainly the light infantry's plebeian aura—its origins among militia, huntsmen, and irregulars—could recommend it neither to the King nor to the army as a whole.

Periodically during the forty-six years of his reign Frederick recognized the need for light troops; but, once established, these units were soon diverted from their original role by the force of the King's basic tactical convictions. Just as the hussars grew into something that often resembled a third branch of heavy cavalry, so the dismounted light troops turned into poor and

[116] A particularly clear expression of this attitude is contained in the "Mémoires depuis la Paix de Hubertsbourg . . . ," *Oeuvres*, VI, 94–95.

[117] Detailed comparisons between the various arms are given in B. v. Poten, "Das Preussische Heer vor hundert Jahren," *Militär-Wochenblatt* (1900), Supplement 1, 37. See also E. v. Höpfner, *Der Krieg von 1806 und 1807*, Berlin, 1855, I, 79.

expendable substitutes of line infantry. It is typical of this everlasting duality of recognition and denial that even in his final years Frederick increased the strength of his *Jäger* corps while simultaneously relieving three-fourths of the men of their characteristic arm, the rifle, and equipping them with smoothbore muskets and bayonets instead.[118] Developments in other countries—the French *chasseurs* and *tirailleurs de bataillon*, the British light infantry regiments and light companies, the light units in the Central and South German states—these and other harbingers of a new age were insufficiently heeded in Potsdam. Among his officers there were some to whom experience or reflection had opened wider horizons, but the King's mind remained fixed on the system that he had perfected and that had served him well.

[118] A Cabinet Order of 1 January 1784 called for an augmentation of the corps from 800 to 1,200 men, a total reached after two years. Rentzell, pp. 16–18. According to a contemporary, turning the *Jäger* into something akin to the line hurt morale, and some men deserted. Blankenburg, p. 32. The rifles were returned to the *Jäger* after Frederick's death. Rentzell, pp. 15, 16–19; Gumtau, I, 52–53.

CHAPTER III

The Last Years of the Old Monarchy

THE international character of eighteenth-century society was nowhere more pronounced than in the conditions of military service. Administrators and scholars shared the soldier's ability to transcend frontiers, but he alone represented the power of the state in the physical extreme of battle and yet remained free to join the side he had recently damaged. National and regional loyalties could still accommodate themselves without undue strain to the high degree of professional mobility. A more exclusive, self-assertive nationalism was gradually encroaching on this freedom, most seriously in Great Britain, without even there erecting insuperable barriers to the movement from service to service. On the Continent, especially east of the Rhine, obstacles to a change of allegiance had little real force.[1] Promising junior officers as well as men with established reputations were recruited by foreign comrades. Ambitious subalterns in the lesser principalities sought the more favorable opportunities for advancement held out by the major powers, while dissatisfied Prussians and Austrians offered their prestige and experience to the smaller armies, or took service overseas. This mobility helped diffuse new concepts and methods, and kept down professional insularity. Every establishment contained men who had fought in the most diverse conditions against very different types of opponents, and the lessons learnt in one theater of war were studied and discussed—if not always adopted—in every service. "Pendant la paix," one of the most distinguished soldiers of the age wrote of his fellow-officers, "nous ne formons qu'une patrie."[2] The numerous transfers from army to army while fighting was

[1] One-third of the men reaching the rank of general in the Prussian army between 1763 and Frederick's death were foreign-born.

[2] Prince de Ligne, in his proposal for an international military academy, contained in his *Fantaisies militaires*, Paris, 1914, p. 131. De Ligne himself held the rank of field marshal in the Austrian and Russian armies, and saw service in both.

actually in progress show how much of the officers' supranationality persisted even in times of war.

For Yorck, dismissal from the Prussian army and service under the Dutch flag brought with it changes of unusual magnitude. Until his twenty-third year he had known little beyond East Prussia and Silesia; now his horizons expanded, he was introduced to Western Europe and to the world overseas. The importance of this experience was commented on by his contemporaries and subsequently stressed by historians; its exact nature is more uncertain. Even during his lifetime legends, which he himself did little to clarify, developed around this stage of his career. Droysen's account, derived largely from family tradition, is obviously fanciful.[3] The Dutch Archives contain documents that permit a more accurate reconstruction of Yorck's life between 1781 and 1785, though even now some of its aspects remain uncertain.

The letters of recommendation that Yorck carried, and the interest the Hogendorp family took in his fate, quickly lifted him out of the mass of unknown and unemployed strangers crowding the Dutch capital. In July, as guest of a naval commander who was an intimate of the Hogendorps, he accompanied the Dutch squadron that was to guard merchantships against British attack on their way to the Baltic. Early in the morning of 5 August, off the Dogger Bank, they encountered a British force under Admiral Hyde Parker. After heavy and prolonged firing the Dutch convoy returned to the Texel, but the day was considered by both sides as a moral victory for the Dutch, who had stood up to the British guns with something of the old spirit of Tromp and Ruyter. According to Droysen, Yorck was sent back to the Hague with the first, unofficial news of the engagement.[4] In gratitude, Droysen continues the story, the Prince of Orange appointed him to the command of a company of his Guards; but Yorck sold his commission to pay gambling debts, and took service with the Dutch East India Company, which was hiring mercenaries to

---

[3] Droysen, I, 31–62.

[4] For Yorck's presence at the battle of the Dogger Bank, see W. G. Byvanck, *Vaderlandsche Figuren op den Overgang der Achttiende Eeuw*, The Hague, 1927, pp. 121–135. Byvanck, whose work is a collection of *feuilletons* first published in the Dutch press, drew much of his material from the Hogendorp Papers in the Algemeen Rijksarchief, but cites few specific references.

defend its possessions against the English. Apart from Yorck's weakness for gambling and his connection with the Company, little of this is true. The muster-roll of the Guards for 1781, now in the Algemeen Rijksarchief, does not include Yorck's name. This is not surprising since his captain's commission in the Company's service was issued on 1 June 1781, only a few weeks after his arrival in the United Provinces and well before the engagement of the Dogger Bank.[5] In May of that year, Colonel Charles Daniel de Meuron, a Swiss soldier of fortune, had signed a contract with the Company's directors, pledging himself to form a regiment of 1,120 men, to be recruited in the Swiss cantons and in Germany.[6] Yorck was among the first to be commissioned. The first six months of his new service he spent along the lower Rhine and in Paris, recruiting and buying uniforms and equipment.[7] We have no reason to doubt family tradition that he retained the impressions of these months with particular vividness into old age. He had the opportunity, Droysen writes, of witnessing the last flashes of brilliance of the *ancien régime.* "The theater, above all, was and remained the object of his admiration, and when he talked of it it might happen that he would jump to his feet and recite entire scenes from *Cinna*, from *Mahomet*, in the declamatory style he had heard during those early years." [8]

The Company's files in the Algemeen Rijksarchief show that on 2 September 1782 de Meuron's regiment left Rochefort in a small convoy. The sea passage, interrupted only by a brief halt at Teneriffe, lasted for more than five months and was a difficult

[5] Droysen prints the correct date of the patent, without noting that it does not fit his account.

[6] Capitulation of 28 May 1781, printed in "The Swiss Regiment de Meuron," anonymous article in the *Ceylon Literary Register*, i (1931), 108. Additional information on the regiment, which transferred to the British service in 1795, can be found in the *Musée neuchâtelois*, 1880–1885, 1921, 1923. Some documents concerning the regiment are deposited in the Algemeen Rijksarchief and in the Archives of the Dutch Central Government of Coastal Ceylon, formerly in Colombo, now in the Government Archives Department, Nuwara, Eliya, Ceylon.

[7] Droysen's statement that Yorck went to Paris at the beginning of September is supported by a Resolution of the Company's Council of Seventeen, of 13 September 1781, mentioning a recruiting officer of the regiment in Paris holding the rank of captain. Algemeen Rijksarchief, Kol. Arch. 286.

[8] Droysen, i, 44.

one. The vessel holding the greater part of the regiment, an old man-of-war named *Le Fier*, had not been converted to accommodate hundreds of troops. Captain and crew were uncooperative, not enough food had been taken on board, there was insufficient space for the regiment's guns and ammunition, and some supplies had to be stored in places that were "rotten and stifling." [9] If it had not been for the help of the French escort vessel, whose captain sent over food and other necessities, the death-rate from illness among the troops might have been disastrous.[10] In the first days of February 1783, the convoy arrived at the Cape. A regimental strength-return of 2 April, which lists Yorck as captain of the 8th company, gives the total number of officers and men as 985.[11]

Possibly Droysen is correct in writing that during the spring some companies of the regiment were sent to reinforce the French Admiral Suffren, who was operating with considerable success against a British force under Sir Edward Hughes along the eastern coast of Ceylon. If the companies did see action, it could not have been exceptionally arduous; according to one account no more than 42 men died in battle during the regiment's fourteen years in Dutch pay.[12] Droysen states that Yorck was a member of the contingent sent to Ceylon, that he was wounded during the final engagement between Suffren and Hughes off Goudelour in June, that he then remained for some months with the units occupying the island, where he formed a friendship with his fellow-officer Sandoz le Roi, and in action against the natives learned to appreciate and practice the "mobility, self-assurance, and calm boldness which is the most essential part of the light service."[13] Droysen gives no evidence for these statements, and

---

[9] Minute of 8–9 April 1783, addressed to the Governor of the Cape, of Meuron's report on the conditions of the voyage. Rijksarchief, Kol. Arch. 4280, fols. 55r–56v. See also the Governor's report of 12 March 1783 on the condition of *Le Fier* and on Meuron's complaints. *Ibid.*, fols. 8r–9v.

[10] Letter of thanks, dated 27 February 1783, by the Governor to the captain of the French frigate *Hermione*. *Ibid.*, fols. 15r–16r.

[11] *Ibid.*, fol. 220r.

[12] *Ceylon Literary Register*, I, 108. The article's statement that the regiment was fighting in Ceylon as early as the summer of 1782, i.e., at the time it was embarking in France, does not contribute to one's faith in the author's accuracy.

[13] Droysen, I, 52–53.

they are, in fact, disproved by the surviving minutes of a meeting held by the officers of the Regiment de Meuron, at the Cape on 7 July, only one week after all fighting had ceased in Ceylon. The document is signed by the participants, who include Yorck.[14] His presence in South Africa later in July or in August is further suggested by an undated letter of his friend Dirk van Hogendorp, who arrived at the Cape in July and wrote to Holland that he had encountered "two old comrades; first of all Yorck, and then the Chevalier de Sandol, who had been three years with me in garrison at Königsberg." [15] Towards the end of the year Yorck took Hogendorp's part in a quarrel with another member of the garrison, after which his continued presence at the Cape until his return to Europe is generally confirmed.[16] Presumably Yorck never entered the Indian Ocean—or, if at all, only for a brief voyage. His exposure to colonial warfare was slight at best. As in the somewhat similar case of Gneisenau, the claim of later biographers that their hero drew inspiration for a new and freer type of fighting from his experiences overseas is without foundation.[17]

Yorck remained in garrison at the Cape until the fall of 1784, when he sold his company and returned to Europe. The United Provinces were now on the verge of civil war, and he thought it more advantageous to seek employment elsewhere. Droysen mentions an attempt to gain entry into the Austrian service, which was rebuffed.[18] Yorck then decided to try to rejoin the Prussian army. His father had died while he was in Africa, but he retained some useful connections, and the augmentation of the army by three light infantry regiments that was now under way presented a favorable opportunity for officers who could claim overseas

[14] Algemeen Rijksarchief, Kol. Arch. 4286, fols. 823r–824v.

[15] Algemeen Rijksarchief, Hogendorp Papers, Inv. No. 82. The letter was probably written in August, but the internal evidence is not conclusive. In his interesting memoirs, Hogendorp mentions the reunion, which took place before the end of the hurricane season, when Hogendorp's vessel shifted anchorage, i.e., the end of summer. *Mémoires du général Dirk van Hogendorp*, ed. D. C. A. van Hogendorp, The Hague, 1887, pp. 25, 28–29.

[16] *Op. cit.*, p. 30. Droysen, I, 53–55.

[17] I have discussed some of the motives behind these interpretations in my article "Colonial Experience and European Military Reform at the End of the Eighteenth Century."

[18] Droysen, I, 62.

experience. Assisted by a loan from his old benefactress, Mme. van Hogendorp, he left the Hague on 5 January 1786.[19] His departure was nearly prevented by a quarrel, which, insignificant in itself, is so characteristic of Yorck's personality and mode of life at the time that the report on the incident which he sent to Mme. van Hogendorp may be worth citing in full:

Allow me, Madame, to give you in a few words the story of the unfortunate affair that took place between me and M. de la Lande yesterday. Finding myself in a coffeehouse between 9 and 10, while two gentlemen were playing billiards, I offered to bet with a spectator on M. Seliman, one of the players. The other, a Frenchman named de la Lande, commented on this, saying he found it very odd that people always offered to bet against him, that they had better change their ways, etc. I answered that in a public place everyone was free to bet without anything being said about it; he replied to me in a very loud voice. Growing impatient, I told him that we were both foreign visitors, that I did not know him, and that I begged him not to use unmannerly words with me. Thereupon he answered with the greatest rudeness; I replied that I would prove to him the following morning that I was not what he had called me, and turned to go home. A moment later I came back to the coffeehouse to talk to someone; he stepped up to me and whispered: Leave! I said, no! not this evening; I shall talk to you tomorrow. He left again. Returning to my lodgings by way of the Houtstraat, I heard a man running behind me. I turned, and saw M. de la Lande, sword drawn, telling me: defend yourself! and at the same time attacking me and giving me a thrust that pierced my cape and my coat. I immediately came on guard, and indignant at the manner in which he had attacked me, fell on him, and having disarmed him, I dealt him several blows with the flat of the blade. The guard of his sword broke during his struggle to get away, and he then ran off, leaving behind sword and hat.

The following morning, which was yesterday, I was chatting in the same coffeehouse with M. de Berestein, the *Grand Prévôt*. M. de la Lande entered and asked me, is it true that you have said that you gave me blows with the flat of the blade? I answered, yes! Whereupon he cried out, Gentlemen! I declare that M. de Jorcke is not worthy of wearing the uniform. At these words I rose in fury, and seeing M. de la Lande with his sword drawn, I drew mine, and after several strokes we were separated. Some time later, the Fiscal sent

[19] Letter of Yorck to Mme. van Hogendorp, 19 May 1787. Algemeen Rijksarchief, Hogendorp Papers, Inv. No. 82.

word for me to come to him, I gave him the above account and said that I planned to leave today. He told me that I first had to appear before the Court of Holland. This morning at eleven I appeared there, and made the same deposition under oath, and then asked whether I could leave as I had planned. One of the gentlemen told me that my presence at the Hague was no longer necessary, that he wished me a good journey, and that he was sorry for what had happened to me.[20]

In Prussia Yorck was soon shown that his behavior that had led to dismissal six years earlier was still held against him. Between January 1786 and February 1787 he sent ten appeals for readmission to Potsdam; their claim that the author had served in three campaigns under Suffren in the Indies no doubt became the basis for many of the misconceptions held by Droysen and others about Yorck's foreign career.[21] As long as Frederick was alive the pleas were ignored or rejected with his characteristic heavy irony. "After your recent naval service," the King replied once, "I must reasonably have doubts about reemploying you in the infantry; it would be the same as if a cook wanted to become a dancing teacher."[22] Only in the changed atmosphere after Frederick's death did Yorck's petitions begin to meet with some encouragement, until at last on 5 May 1787 he was appointed captain in one of the newly established light infantry battalions—the Fusilier Battalion von Plüskow.[23]

· 2 ·

The old King's death, though greeted with foreboding by some, released a brief surge of optimism and energy in the state. It seemed "as if the seeds that Frederick the Great's government had scattered only really came to grow and flourish since the hand of the strict gardener was no longer felt everywhere."[24] By the vigor and harshness of his personal rule the King had largely succeeded in insulating the army against the trends of the age;

[20] Unsigned document, headed "Ecrit sous la dictée de Mr. de Jorcke, le 5 janvier 1786." Algemeen Rijksarchief, Hogendorp Papers, Inv. No. 82.

[21] Petitions and answers are printed in Lehmann's "Yorcks Wiedereintritt in den preussischen Dienst," pp. 251–256.

[22] Droysen, I, 63–64.

[23] Priesdorff, No. 1120.

[24] O. Hintze, *Die Hohenzollern und ihr Werk*, Berlin, 1915, p. 409.

now, with his nephew's accession to the throne, the more humane notions entertained by the last generation of the Enlightenment gained ground even here.[25] These were most apparent in the general amelioration of discipline within the regiments, the government's effort to suppress cruelty and dishonesty in recruitment, the greater interest shown in the education of the common soldier and of his children, and in the foundation of invalid companies, asylums, and pension funds, to provide some security for the old or maimed soldier.[26] It was unfortunate for the army that

[25] Reforming tendencies were of course always present in the army. One or two instances are mentioned in the preceding chapter. In the latter part of Frederick's reign opposition to his military policies increased. The following are typical examples: An article, "Bemerkungen über das kleine Schiessgewehr," in *Krieges-Bibliothek*, VIII (1770), 101–158, argues that even rapid fire can accommodate aiming, that enemy troops are not impressed by inaccurate volleys, that Prussian muskets are of unnecessarily poor manufacture, that Prussian infantry units ought to include sharpshooters, etc. The anonymous author probably was G. D. v. d. Groeben, who earlier had pleaded in the same journal for the education and humane treatment of the common soldier. In 1782 Colonel J. A. v. Scholten, the ennobled son of a Hamburg merchant, anonymously published a pamphlet that called for higher standards in the education of Prussian officers and for the treatment of soldiers as rational and perfectible human beings. During the same period Scholten submitted proposals for a more effective corps of *Jäger*. In the *Militärische Monatsschrift*, which C. v. Massenbach, a member of Frederick's General Staff, published in Potsdam, an article, "Über die Aufklärung des Militairs," I (June 1785), 590–601, defended the educational ideals of Scholten and others against attacks launched by the traditionalist L. v. Brenkenhoff in his book *Paradoxa, mehrentheils militairischen Inhalts*, no place, 1780. In the same journal a whole series of anonymous contributions criticized Prussian methods, equipment, and uniforms; see, for instance, "Von der Ausrüstung der Soldaten," I (January 1785), 33–42; "Noch etwas über die Ausrüstung der Soldaten," I (June 1785), 602–611; and "Über die Ausrüstung und den Anzug des Soldaten, besonders des Infanteristen," II (October 1786), 394–409. The last article asked such questions as "Do we always have enough light troops to cover the flanks of a marching column? Don't we need patrols and skirmishers? How often does it happen that a regiment or a smaller unit is detached and must fend for itself?" In August 1785, incidentally, the *Militärische Monatsschrift* published a portrait of Colonel Scholten, who had become something of a hero to the intellectuals in the officer corps.

[26] See the orders and regulations on recruitment, maintenance, and pensions reprinted in Frauenholz, IV, 298–340, especially the fundamental "Bestimmungen über die Werbung" of 1 February 1787, pp. 298–

the laxness of central authority which soon came to characterize the new reign prevented these beginnings from being carried farther.

The first year of Frederick William II's rule also witnessed two events of potential importance for increasing the flexibility of infantry tactics. From 3 March 1787 on, ten *Schützen*—sharp-shooters—were added to each line company, whose duty was to fight outside the company line, heading the advance and covering the retreat.[27] It was an innovation that carried out—and expanded on—an idea of Frederick's which had not been implemented in his lifetime. In 1773, the King had suggested that whenever a battalion retreated, a few soldiers might be left behind to keep the enemy at a distance by their aimed fire.[28] The new sharpshooters were also supposed to patrol when necessary, and in every way "to fight just like the *Fussjäger*."[29] They were picked men; after 1788 they wore the NCO's plume and swordknot, and were treated as lance-corporals; their arm was the *Schützengewehr M. 1787*—a weapon whose accuracy lay halfway between musket and rifle.[30] Finally, on 26 February 1789, special regulations were issued for their service, which emphasized marksmanship and fighting in open order.[31] But the sharpshooters hardly affected infantry tactics. In an average battalion of 700 other ranks, skirmishing by forty *Schützen* could not amount to more than firing a few dozen aimed shots before the battalion front; they were too few to maintain a fire-fight for any length of time. Even more damaging, the institution of company sharpshooters

---

308. In the same year, disabled officers were finally granted a legal claim to pensions, which until then had been acts of royal grace and favor. See *Offiziere im Bild von Dokumenten aus drei Jahrhunderten*, published by the *Militärgeschichtliche Forschungsamt*, Stuttgart, 1964, p. 58.

[27] Jany, *Preussische Armee*, III, 160.

[28] "Règles de ce qu'on exige d'un bon commandeur . . . ," *Oeuvres*, XXIX, 60, 65.

[29] *Reglement für die Königl. Preuss. leichte Infanterie*, Berlin, 1788, p. 128. Cf. *Reglement für die Kgl. Preuss. Infanterie*, Berlin, 1788, Part V, Section 2.

[30] Eckardt and Morawietz, pp. 82–83; C. Kling, *Geschichte der Bekleidung, Bewaffnung, und Ausrüstung des Königlich Preuss. Heeres*, Weimar, 1902–1912, I, 157.

[31] *Instruction für sämtliche Infanterie-Regimenter und Fusilier-Bataillone. Exercieren der Schützen betreffend*, Berlin, 1789.

soon degenerated into an NCO replacement pool. According to the *Infantry Regulations* of 1788, the sharpshooter "must be intelligent, and have all those qualities which enable him to become an NCO, as no one may be promoted to this rank who has not already served some time as *Schütze*." [32] Sharpshooters were to be regarded as *Vice-Unteroffiziers*, and on guard and garrison duty assisted the company NCO's.[33] Under those circumstances there were frequent changes in the ranks of the *Schützen* and their special light infantry training was of necessity neglected.[34]

Of far greater significance was the formation between February and June 1787 of the twenty fusilier battalions, to which reference has already been made. Their officers were drawn from line units, and from among men who had fought overseas or served in the free regiments; together with the *Jäger* they were kept on a special seniority list, separate from the line infantry. Officially, noble status was a prerequisite for the commission, but this rule was not quite as rigorously enforced for the fusiliers as it was with the line regiments. A cabinet order of Frederick William II stated: "The posting of officer-cadets other than those of undoubted noble birth to line regiments as well as to the fusilier battalions is forbidden, and if an exception should be made in case of the latter—the fusilier battalions—and an officer-cadet of bourgeois descent is accepted, this should not occur until the explicit permission of His Majesty has been granted in each particular instance." [35] The *Reglement* even authorized battalion commanders to propose exceptionally competent sergeants for commissions.[36] The result of this equivocal policy was a rush of bourgeois to the fusiliers. In 1796, for example, of 61 fusilier officers in one brigade one-fourth had no title, while among the 223 line infantry officers stationed in the same area there was not a single commoner.[37] The proportion of 1 to 4 was maintained almost without alteration until 1806; if, as Jany suggests, Freder-

[32] *Reglement für die Königl. Preuss. leichte Infanterie*, p. 126.

[33] *Ibid.*, pp. 6–7, 130–131.

[34] Criticism of this arrangement is found in a number of memoirs by contemporaries. See, for instance, *Denkwürdigkeiten des Generals August Frhrn. Hiller v. Gaertringen*, ed. W. v. Unger, Berlin, 1912, pp. 15–16.

[35] Printed in Jany, *Preussische Armee*, III, 419.

[36] *Reglement für die . . . leichte Infanterie*, pp. 457–458.

[37] For the ratio of titled to untitled fusilier officers between 1789 and 1817, and the situation in other branches of the army, see Appendix 2.

ick William III was somewhat less rigid than his father in this matter, it in no way affected the composition of the fusiliers' officer corps.[38]

The light battalions' need for mobility and the lower prestige of the service combined to simplify their uniform and equipment.[39] They were clothed in green, resembling the dress of the *Jäger*, from whom they also took over the hunting-horn for signaling. The men were armed with the *Füsiliergewehr*, a lighter and more carefully manufactured version of the standard infantry musket; as in the line infantry, ten men of each company carried rifles.[40] Discipline relied less on corporal chastisement, and it was soon noted by observers that in these units the concept of honor attached to the common soldier differed somewhat from that of the line. The battalions were intended for action in wooded and hilly terrain, which was no longer quite the bugbear it had been under the old regime, and for the duties of the little war; they were to the army what the sharpshooters were to the grenadier and musketeer battalions—a means of adding elasticity to the rigid line. On 24 February 1788, the fusiliers were issued a special *Reglement*, the first Prussian field manual for the light infantry. In most points this work was identical with the new regulations for the line, which appeared half a year later, but it differed from these in two important respects: the battalions were formed in two ranks instead of the standard three, and some provision was made for fighting in open order.

The number of ranks in which infantry were drawn up greatly influenced the manner in which they fought.[41] The volleys of three ranks were not so effective as those of two, because of the difficulties in firing experienced by the third rank. Three ranks, however, possessed greater impetus in the advance; and, in general, the third rank added solidity to the formation. Two ranks,

---

[38] Jany, *Preussische Armee*, III, 419.

[39] *Reglement für die . . . leichte Infanterie*, pp. 182–183. See also Kling, III, 1–12, 40–57, 115–116; and Höpfner, I, 85.

[40] *Reglement für die . . . leichte Infanterie*, p. 3. W. Shanahan, *Prussian Military Reforms: 1786–1813*, New York, 1945, p. 23, incorrectly states that all fusiliers were armed with rifles.

[41] In the second of his three essays included in Appendix 1, Scharnhorst analyzes in some detail the varying depths of infantry formations, and their bearing on the changes in warfare during the Napoleonic Era.

on the other hand, were easier to keep aligned in difficult terrain, offered a less vulnerable target, and could deploy into extended order more rapidly. The introduction of two ranks by the *Reglement* of 1788 may therefore be seen as a step towards the opening up of infantry tactics, provided the two ranks were not fought in the old manner and used simply as rigid lines with which one tried to outflank the enemy.

The rules for fighting in open order are presented so obscurely in the *Reglement* that they do not even have a place in the table of contents, but are attached to Part III, Section 3: "How to fight standing still, advancing, and retreating." Nevertheless they mark a departure from the Frederician tradition. For the first time an official directive describes how Prussian infantry should form, and fight in, what may be called a skirmish line. The relevant passages read:

If in the advance the battalion is to make a skirmish attack, the battalion bugler gives the proper signal, which is immediately repeated by the buglers of the first and eighth sections [i.e., half-companies].

As soon as this has been given, the first and eighth sections—unless ordered otherwise—run forward fifty paces and spread out. In this connection it must be noted that though the skirmishers are not expected to keep such exact alignment as men marching in the ranks, they should nevertheless maintain an approximate direction; therefore the skirmishers must never separate too far from each other, and no one more than at most four or five paces from his neighbor. This should be particularly observed in attacking a forest, when everyone must at all times see his neighbors and remain aligned with them.

As soon as the attacking sections have moved out, they continue their advance at a good pace, and the supporting sections follow in close order.

If firing is to begin, the signal is given and the skirmishers open fire at will, all the time continuing their advance, never losing sight of their neighbors, and always retaining their alignment. Individual firing goes on in this manner until the signal is given to stop, after which no one—on punishment of whipping—may fire another shot.[42]

NOTE: His Majesty commands that when the light infantry battalions, or single platoons or squads, march in close formation, they should always shoulder their muskets, as is usual. But when light

---

[42] *Reglement für . . . die leichte Infanterie*, pp. 44–45.

infantry advance singly or as skirmishers, which particularly occurs in woods and hilly ground, they carry the musket with the right hand before the trigger guard and the left hand near the muzzle.[43]

When retreating, the battalion was also covered by a skirmish line, again consisting of one-quarter of the total force. All men were to be particularly well trained in musketry, although the less precisely regulated drill of individual firing was still held to be something of a specialty of the company riflemen.[44]

Historians have disagreed about the value of the light infantry *Reglement* of 1788. Jähns called it "wretched and pedantic," and condemned it for being "marked by the same rigid formalism as the manual for the line infantry." [45] Jany, who is rarely critical of the army, concluded his brief discussion of the regulations with the perplexing sentence: "If the regulations for close order drill take up far more space in the fusilier *Reglement* than do those for open order, it lies in the nature of the subject." [46] Gneisenau's first biographer, writing in the 1850's, even goes so far as to claim that at least the section on *Schützen* already expressed "what today are considered the essentials of the rifleman's duty." [47] The actual text hardly bears out such an evaluation. The timidity of the instructions, which even deem it necessary to specify that skirmishers should carry their muskets at port arms, shows how closely the army continued to be bound to the Frederician system. The manual is not an expression of radical reform but the product of a period of reluctant transition, a quality demonstrated not only by its contents but also by its language, which alternates between baroque convolutions and an exactness of expression almost approaching the classic lucidity of the *Reglement* of 1812. Certainly its paragraphs on skirmishing would have needed to be less unobtrusive, should have been much more emphatic, to make an impression on the compact faith in close order held by most Prussian officers. And, indeed, contemporary and specialist witnesses leave little doubt that on the whole these sections of the regulations were ignored. General von Höpfner writes that be-

[43] *Ibid.*, pp. 46–47.
[44] *Ibid.*, p. 47.
[45] Jähns, III, 2541–42.
[46] Jany, *Preussische Armee*, III, 166.
[47] [E. F. v. Fransecky], "Gneisenau," *Militair-Wochenblatt*, XLI (1856), Supplement for January–April, p. 44.

fore 1806 "the fusiliers trained for duty in the field much like the heavy infantry; in one case as in the other, hilly terrain was avoided as far as possible." Elsewhere he writes that "the riflemen lacked any training in extended order." [48] General von Witzleben, the intimate friend of Frederick William III, and a member of the footguards since 1799, is quoted as saying that during his early years as a subaltern "the *tirailleur* system was little known in our army"—a statement repeated in nearly the same words in General von Roeder's memoirs.[49] General von Wachholtz, in the Prussian service from 1798 to 1807, recalled that "musketry training consisted in shooting off a considerable number of dummy bullets," and that there was no target practice in the line battalions except for the riflemen.[50] In his memoirs, the fusilier officer and later General Friedrich Karl von Schmidt describes how difficult it was to procure real bullets even for the fusiliers' training.[51] Gumtau, the historian of the *Jäger* and *Schützen*, who served with the light infantry for over thirty years, claims that before 1806 each *Jäger* annually received powder sufficient for only

[48] Höpfner, i, 53, 56. Höpfner, to be sure, did not enter the service until 1813, and in this instance reports only hearsay.

[49] *Unter den Hohenzollern*, ed. G. E. v. Natzmer, Gotha, 1887–1889, ii, 124; *Für Euch, meine Kinder! Erinnerungen aus dem Leben des Königlichen General-Lieutenants Carl von Roeder*, printed as manuscript, Berlin, 1861, p. 30. On p. 19 Roeder writes that when his battalion marched against the French in 1806 only the forty sharpshooters had ever fired real bullets. Herr H. G. Schultz, Hamburg, kindly made available to me a copy of this rare work, which contains important material on Yorck as well as on the Prussian army of the time. Excerpts from Roeder's memoirs are incorporated in a volume treating the military experiences of his family, *Standhaft und Treu*, ed. M. Schultze, Berlin, 1912.

[50] *Aus dem Tagebuche des Generals Fr. L. von Wachholtz*, ed. C. v. Vechelde, Braunschweig, 1843, p. 71. Similar reports can be found in numerous regimental histories. See for example E. v. Conrady, *Geschichte des Königlich Preussischen Sechsten Infanterie-Regiments*, Berlin, 1857, p. 52.

[51] *Erinnerungen aus dem Leben des Generalleutnants Friedrich Karl von Schmidt*, ii, *Urkundliche Beiträge und Forschungen*, xii–xiii, Berlin, 1909, 22. Schmidt's father, a farm boy, served in the ranks during the War of the Austrian Succession, distinguished himself sufficiently to become lieutenant in a free regiment, and ended his career as colonel in command of a depot battalion. The son joined the fusiliers as cadet, and after ten years' service was elevated to the nobility. Priesdorff, No. 1423.

nine shots at the target, and had to provide the lead himself.[52]

There were nevertheless exceptions to the parsimony and unimaginativeness that marked Prussian training. In 1763, as a means of extending central control into every corner of the increasingly complex military organization, Frederick had divided the army into inspectorates, headed by men who possessed his particular trust. It lay in the nature of things that these *Inspectionen* took on a life of their own. Already in the final years of Frederick's reign several Inspectors-General experimented freely with tactical formations; under his less masterful successors they came to grant the units under their surveillance a sometimes surprising latitude in drill and administration. Many commanders reacted by pressing for further refinements of parade-ground evolutions; others strove to prepare their men for conditions that might reasonably be expected in the next war. Thus it was possible for Gneisenau and for other light infantry officers, such as the future generals Hinrichs and Schuler von Senden, to instruct their companies in skirmish tactics, marksmanship, and techniques of patrolling.[53] Yorck, too, even in the first years after his return to Prussia, while still a company-grade officer, seems to have been able to train his men with some degree of realism.

The political tremors that were beginning to course through Europe lent some urgency to these efforts. In 1787 a small Prussian corps intervened against the Patriot movement in Holland. Partial mobilizations followed against Denmark and Russia. In 1790 the major part of the army took up positions along the Saxon and Bohemian borders, but the threatened war with Austria was avoided under the pressure of new crises arising in the east and west. Two years later, in August 1792, 47,000 men crossed the frontiers of France.

For the moment Yorck's battalion still remained in its Silesian garrison. There, in November of 1792, he was promoted to major, after only five years' service as captain. He was now thirty-

---

[52] Gumtau, I, 59.

[53] Fransecky, pp. 41–42; Priesdorff, Nos. 1013 and 1154. Enterprising soldiers could refer to several unofficial works for models of light infantry training exercises. See, for instance, W. v. Reiche, *Der kleine Partheigänger und Krieger*, Leipzig, 1804, which contained numerous tactical examples for the "light infantry officer and non-commissioned officer."

three, one of the youngest men of his rank in the army; the time lost through his court-martial and dismissal he had more than made up. In this period, too, he married.[54] Like his father before him, Yorck chose a commoner; his bride was the daughter of a small Silesian merchant. Tradition has it that once, on being asked what family his young wife came from, he answered, "No family at all." [55] In 1794 his battalion was assigned to the force mobilized to combat the insurrection that had erupted in the territories Prussia had gained from the Second Partition of Poland. During the subsequent campaign against Kosciuszko Yorck distinguished himself both in major engagements and as commander of detachments and patrols. He received the personal commendation of the King, and for the next years the conduct reports, which annually analyzed the performance of every active officer, referred to him in increasingly complimentary terms. "An exceptionally efficient field-grade officer," reads one, "who possesses a high sense of honor, and is motivated by the best intentions." However, he was not promoted. With the frankness that characterized many officers in the matter of advancement, Yorck complained to the King's Adjutant-General, who could only reply that the decision was the monarch's alone. Not until 1797, when additional light units were raised, was Yorck given command of one of the new fusilier battalions. Two years later, after the accession of Frederick William III, he was appointed to the command of the *Jäger* regiment. The *Fussjäger*, the royal order read in part, formed "a very significant corps of the army, and it therefore must be particularly important for me to be assured that the regiment is in the proper state to fulfill its purpose. Your thorough familiarity with the service, which is known to me, combined with your laudable record, I regard as guarantee that you will always keep the *Jäger* regiment, now entrusted to your command, in the best condition. . . ." [56]

With this appointment Yorck was placed in charge of the unit

[54] On 6 July 1792, according to Droysen, I, 78; but this disagrees with the date, 7 June 1793, which Priesdorff gives for the royal marriage consent.

[55] Droysen, I, 78.

[56] The exact date of the royal order is uncertain: Droysen, I, 100, gives 6 November 1799; Priesdorff, 16 November 1799; Rentzell, p. 30, simply 1800. Droysen and Priesdorff publish the order with slight variants.

that had long been considered the elite of the Prussian light infantry, though indifferent leadership and uncertainty over the true function of the *Jäger* had recently brought about a lowering of standards. The uniqueness of the regiment, which in effect represented an officially sanctioned exception to the prevailing linear methods, afforded great opportunities for the independence and sense of realism of its new commander, at a time when the army's traditional principles of military organization, training, and tactics were being called seriously into question.

· 3 ·

The Polish campaign brought little distinction to the Prussian army. Against an enemy force made up as much of armed civilians as of regular troops, poorly equipped, but intensely patriotic and aided by the population, the Prussians and Russians waged a war that bears some resemblance to colonial expeditions of the following century. Eventually they gained their objectives—defeat of the insurgents and pacification of the newly acquired territories—but at far greater cost in time and casualties than had been expected and was necessary. Serious defects had shown up in the Prussian ranks: too many among the higher leadership proved inefficient and slow, two generals were court-martialed for incompetence, and the tactical concepts of others represented the most unrealistic extreme ever to be reached by parade-ground geometry—the *croix foudroyante*, for instance, a star-shaped grouping of mutually supporting infantry squares, with which its inventor, General Favrat, actually tried to maneuver against bands of peasants armed with scythes.[57] Only the light troop commanders—in particular Yorck's commanding officer, General von Günther—seem to have been untouched by the prevailing "anxiety that was entertained about the little war, and by the lack of resolution," and returned home with increased reputations.[58]

---

[57] Cf. H. v. Boyen, *Erinnerungen aus dem Leben des General-Feldmarschalls Hermann von Boyen*, ed. F. Nippold, Leipzig, 1889–1890, I, 47.

[58] *Ibid.*, I, 51, 61–62, 67f. Günther began his career as a volunteer in a *Freibataillon* during the Seven Years' War, was later ennobled, and became one of the best leaders of light troops of his day. Cf. Priesdorff, No. 791; and his biography by Boyen, who for a time served as his adjutant, *Erinnerungen aus dem Leben des Königl. Preuss. Generallieutenants Freiherrn v. Günther*, Berlin, 1834.

Compared with the fighting in Western Europe, however, the suppression of the Poles was a minor affair. In several respects the campaigns were not dissimilar: in Poland as in France the Allies faced an enemy who drew some of his strength from popular enthusiasm, and in both theaters of war the importance of light units quickly became apparent. But the differences were greater. Quite apart from her energetic, central leadership, France was neither hopelessly surrounded, nor numerically inferior; soon the offensive impetus of the legitimist powers faltered, and their punitive expeditions became transformed into a *cordon sanitaire*, made up of numerous dispersed corps and detachments, that attempted to shield Central Europe against the whole spectrum of new threats—military, political, and social—radiating from Paris. The nature of the ground over which the wars of the French Revolution were fought assisted this reversal. The Prussian and Polish plains were all but ideal for the movement of large regular forces, which might be handicapped only in certain areas, such as the Narew Swamps, and by the scarcity of roads and towns. The Rhine and Saar valleys, on the other hand, the forests of the Palatinate, and the Belgian network of canals and fortifications tended to cramp linear tactics, and lent themselves to a less regular, more flexible order of fighting.

To some extent, too, the French were pushed in this direction by the departure of thousands of royalist officers and the simultaneous incorporation of masses of untrained volunteers. The break with traditional leadership and the increasing size of the army facilitated experimentation in the field. But none of the methods that came to be adopted were new in themselves. The basic French infantry manual of the period was the *Règlement* of 1 August 1791, issued during the final weeks of the Constituent Assembly. It was far from being a revolutionary document. On the contrary, despite the many years during which it continued in force—a major revision was not prepared until 1831—the manual was in some points a regression from earlier tactical development. For instance, it revoked the formation by two ranks, which the *Instruction Provisoire* of 1788 had finally authorized after years of debate and trial.[59] The great value of the *Règlement* lay in

[59] The best analysis of the *Règlement concernant l'exercice et les manoeuvres de l'infanterie du premier août 1791* and of its predecessors is contained in Colin's *L'Infanterie au XVIIIᵉ siècle;* see also his earlier

the minimum of constraint it placed on tactical arrangement. The old controversy over column or line as the standard attack formation for the foot-soldier it resolved by authorizing the use of both. Provided with the needed doctrinal flexibility, the Republican infantry learned to deploy according to circumstances in battle lines, skirmishers, columns, and to change formation under fire. The methods were well known; new—and for the time being unique—was the ready cooperation achieved between different tactical forms, and their opportunistic adaptation to every kind of terrain.

The infantry line and the development of skirmishers during the eighteenth century have already been discussed. We must now look briefly at the third component of the new tactics. The column as an attack formation for infantry emerged from experiments with linear formations that were carried on throughout the eighteenth century, primarily in France. The disputes between adherents of the *ordre mince* and the *ordre profond* began as soon as the heavy rectangles, in which infantry still fought during the War of the Spanish Succession, had thinned into the elongated, fragile lines of the 1730's—or, rather, the disputes were a continuation of this process, stimulated by certain obvious weaknesses in the linear pattern. The disagreement of the two schools cannot be seen simply as a conflict between traditionalists and modernists. Each side had important disciplinary and technological arguments in its favor, and each shut its eyes to significant current developments. Many proponents of the *ordre profond*, for instance, distrusted the effectiveness of firearms, discounted the improvements that were being made in the design and construction of muskets, and advocated instead a return to pikes. The debate had not been settled at the onset of the Revolution; but it had created a tradition of tactical sophistication and versatility in the French army, which enabled commanders to give effective military form to the new social and psychological forces that were released in the nation.

Writers on the wars of the French Revolution and the Napoleonic Era do not always sufficiently distinguish the attack column from the marching column, a confusion compounded by the

---

work *La Tactique et la discipline dans les armées de la Révolution*, Paris, 1902.

common usage of the word "column" then and now for any large body of troops.[60] Occasionally, units on the march encountered the enemy, to the surprise of one or the other party, and men fought in the formation in which they happened to find themselves. In terrain that did not permit deployment on a broad front —in mountain and siege operations, in street fighting—marching and attack columns were essentially identical. But these were exceptions, and generally the two formations were quite different.

The narrow front and considerable depth which the word "column" suggests were the features of the marching column. The attack column, however, as developed in the French armies, was a rectangle, its front far more extensive than its depth. The description of the attack column as a battering ram, a favorite cliché of the military historian, is largely inaccurate.

The French infantry battalion generally formed an attack column with the front of one company and the depth of four—that is, a mass of about 40 men across and 12 men deep. Columns by sections or half-companies, which halved the front and doubled the depth, also occurred, but were rare. The ranks might close up or be separated by an interval. In major engagements fought over relatively open ground the columns might be considerably enlarged. At Wagram, Macdonald's attack column had a front of 1,100 meters and a depth of 700. At Waterloo, d'Erlon's attack in the early afternoon was carried out by four columns of 6, 7, 8, and 9 battalions respectively, each column occupying a front of 150 to 200 meters—the width of a battalion drawn up in three ranks—and a depth of 25 to 35 meters, not counting the space occupied by the skirmishers who proceeded the closed formations.[61] The attack column of the Napoleonic period continued to be more of a linear than a columnar formation.

---

[60] For example, in an order of the day of 5 October 1793, Kléber speaks of "attack columns," though the context makes it clear that he means attacking forces, whatever their formation. See the valuable documentary publication, *Kléber en Vendée (1793–1794)*, ed. H. Baguenier Desormeaux, Paris, 1907, pp. 355–356, and also 478–479.

[61] This unwieldy body, supported neither by artillery nor by cavalry, advancing uphill against a firm defensive line, had little chance of success. Some contemporaries as well as later writers have suggested that it was not the intended attack formation, but that British fire prevented the French from forming smaller columns or deploying into lines as they had planned.

The great tactical value of the column lay in its flexibility and versatility. It permitted the commander to move large numbers of men over the battlefield with better control and far more rapidly than had been possible before. The column could operate in hilly terrain. It could easily change into different formations. The deployment from marching column to attack column, in particular, took far less time than had the development of linear formations from the marching column. Skirmishers could be detached without necessitating major readjustments in the formation. Two- or three-rank firing lines could be formed rapidly, as could squares—the latter simply by the column's flanking files facing left and right, the rear ranks facing about, officers and musicians moving into the center. A battalion in attack column was thus able to some extent to act on its own; the need to maintain tight flank connections fell away: the tactical situation opened up and became more dynamic.

The attack column had two main functions. It could be used to bring men in close order rapidly to the enemy. The success of such an action was largely dependent on adequate preparation by gunners and skirmishers, and it was they who inflicted most of the casualties rather than the column itself, which possessed little or no firepower once it started to move. Throughout the period bayonet charges actually driven home against a steady enemy were rare.

The far more common employment of the attack column, certainly from the second half of the 1790's on, was that of a sustaining force. To use Napoleonic terminology, the *masse de rupture* often acted as a *masse d'usure*. The column sent out skirmishers to begin the fire-fight, served as a replacement pool for the skirmishers, and as their immediate tactical reserve. If it encountered firm resistance, the column might deploy into lines to carry on the fight with volleys. Once the enemy wavered these lines could resume the advance, or they might again reduce their front and move forward in column.

The attack column as well as the line were thoroughly discussed in the *Règlement* of 1791.[62] This was not the case with the third partner in the new system, the skirmisher, who was practi-

---

[62] *Titres* 4 and 5 of the *Règlement*. Some copies included supplements of plates illustrating in detail the employment of both formations in combat. See especially the edition of 1816.

cally ignored.[63] If we consider the great role open order played in the battles of the 1790's, this absence is surprising, and it has not gone unnoticed in the literature. It has confirmed some writers in their view of skirmishing as the military expression of the newly patriotic, or fanaticized, masses. Those who know the century-long experimentation with open order must seek other explanations. Colin suggests that the absence comes from the common conception in those days of the purpose and function of a military manual:

One wanted to find only formal *rules* in a *rulebook*, and anything susceptible to evaluation, to interpretation, was banished from it; indications for combat were no more found in the *règlement de manoeuvres*, than theories on the distribution of outposts in the field manual, or advice on the disposition of guards and sentry-boxes in the *service de places*. All this could be learned only from lessons taught in the military schools, by actual experience in war, and by tradition. The field manual imposed very strict duties on the commanders of outposts and on sentinels, the regulations for maneuvering carefully defined the formations and movements of closed ranks, all things where absolute rules were needed—but neither expanded on security in general nor on the course of battle.[64]

But for once Colin's analysis is in error. He not only ignores those contemporary manuals of other armies that regulate the actions of skirmishers, but for the moment forgets that some French manuals, too, contain instructions for the use of light troops in battle. The *Règlement provisoire* of 1792, for example, has the following paragraph on *tirailleurs*:

While battle lines are being formed and batteries placed, the commanding officers order the light infantry to advance ahead of the line infantry, so as to discover the positions of the enemy's guns and to diminish their effect. The light troops are placed in small thickets, behind hedges, ditches, or small rises, according to the nature of the ground. They are commanded to fire at the enemy batteries, and to try to kill the gunners. These men do not form in troops, so as not to

[63] Contrary to general assumption, the *Règlement* does contain at least one reference to *tirailleurs*. They are to be sent out to protect marching columns against cavalry. See *Titre V, cinquième partie, article 14*, and also Plate XL, figure 1, of the 1816 edition.

[64] Colin, *La Tactique et la discipline*, p. 109 of the Introduction.

draw artillery fire, but separate, profiting from any feature that may afford them cover, and remain attentive so that they can quickly reassemble at the first signal of their officers.

Once again the organic development rather than revolutionary emergence of the new tactics is demonstrated: the editors of the *Règlement provisoire* took these lines word for word from the *Règlement* of 1778, the only difference being the substitution of the term *infanterie légère* for *compagnies de chasseurs*.[65]

For a second, and more convincing, explanation for the absence of detailed skirmish rules, Colin called on a veteran of the Imperial light infantry, General Le Couturier, who declared that not much instruction was needed "for a type of warfare that was the most natural of all." Couturier's point was that since the movement of *tirailleurs* was not orderly, as was that of the columns and lines, but rather resembled a hunt, trying to impose order on skirmishers would spoil their effectiveness: "That which by its nature is irregular submits badly to rules." Colin concluded that "if the *Règlement* . . . does not mention *tirailleurs*, then [this was] simply because it was not considered useful to regulate the deployment of swarms of skirmishers."[66] And it is true that the French infantryman of the 1790's received little training in this function; he was told what to do, but not how to do it.[67] The release of his energy and intelligence, untrammeled in combat by detailed regulations, gradually proved effective. Yet improvisation had its drawbacks, not the least in open order fighting, always among the most demanding of tasks. Consequently, dur-

---

[65] *Règlement provisoire sur le service de l'infanterie en campagne du 5 avril 1792*, p. 124. In *L'Infanterie aux XVIII° siècle*, pp. 180–181, Colin prints the extract from the *Règlement* of 1778, stating that it "laid down rules for the employment of [the new] chasseur companies in battle." Possibly he was not aware of this document when he suggested in his earlier work that such rules had no place in an eighteenth-century manual.

[66] Colin, *La Tactique et la discipline*, pp. 99–102 of the Introduction. Compare the description of a Prussian observer: "They fought like hunters . . . akin to a pack of hounds." Valentini, pp. 1–2.

[67] Not all superior officers approved of this approach. Even General Le Couturier, despite his advocacy of laissez-faire, called for better musketry instruction and proposed the establishment of highly trained special units of light troops. See his article, "Essai sur les manoeuvres des voltigeurs," *Spectateur Militaire*, IV (1828), 266–267, 269.

ing the first campaigns of the Revolutionary War the *tirailleurs* either acted as snipers—at times digging in on the battlefield for that purpose—or formed dense swarms that attacked with dash but knew little of the refinements of mutual support and fire-control, panicked more easily than men fighting in line, and proved particularly vulnerable to counterattacks. Typical of French tactics at this stage is the battle of Kaiserslautern in November 1793, in which thousands attacked in open formations —*en debandade*—through woods, along creek-beds, over meadow and marshland, but were repeatedly driven back by the volleys and sharp counterattacks of the Prussian line.[68] Aimed fire and lack of alignment by themselves were not guarantors of success.

The divergence of views between the two opposing armies— the French, which gave its skirmishers a minimum of instruction, and the Prussian, which regulated their movements schematically —hardly confirms that difference in national character to which writers of the period so frequently allude. More likely it points to the very real contrasts in the troops' social characteristics, and in their discipline and attitudes. Even on the battlefield, individual initiative was made difficult for the Prussian *Schütze* and fusilier, while the French *tirailleur* could improvise, and was expected to do so. But until the French had gained greater tactical experience the military world was not convinced of the *tirailleur*'s superiority over his German counterparts. If Moreau, the companion and rival of Napoleon, declared the Prussian fusiliers to be the best light troops on earth he, no doubt, spoke with the voice of chivalry; that the allied *Jäger* and sharpshooters were outstanding no one could deny. Between 1792 and 1794 the Prussian *Jäger* regiment took part in 140 actions and emerged as one of the most decorated units in the army.[69] Possibly even more effective were the riflemen of the Central and South German contingents. In April 1793 a Prussian general observed the successful attack of a Hessian *Jäger* company, and afterwards congratulated the men: "Each had without orders taken the utmost advantage of even the smallest terrain feature, something he had never seen before,

[68] A. Chuquet, *Hoche*, Paris, n.d., pp. 81–89; *Pirmasens und Kaiserslautern, Kriegsgeschichtliche Einzelschriften*, xvi (1893), 347–368.

[69] *Rangliste für das Jahr 1796;* Gieraths, pp. 170–172.

indeed never had believed possible."[70] During the same campaign the Hessians mounted an assault on an entrenchment that exemplified the new tactics: two *Jäger* companies advanced in groups of skirmishers, an infantry battalion followed in close order, with two additional companies in column as reserve. The Republican troops defended their position in the traditional manner, firing unaimed volleys and deploying their front with care, and could not maintain themselves. Two tactical systems were in conflict, but the split did not run wholly along national lines. Even the percentages of light troops available on both sides were not dissimilar; on the day of battle it was not uncommon for the Allies to muster a higher proportion of light infantry than did their opponents.[71] And yet, regardless of training and numerical

[70] M. v. Ditfurth, *Die Hessen in den Feldzügen in der Champagne, am Maine und Rheine* . . . , Marburg, 1881, p. 318. See *ibid.*, pp. 326–330, for the following engagement.

[71] Exact figures are available on Allied strengths, but for the greater part of the 1790's the French did not know precisely how many men they had under arms. As late as 1798 the Ministry of War could complain that it was unable to rely on its records. At the outbreak of the Revolution the French army contained 12 battalions of light infantry. Their number rose to 25 by May 1793, more than doubled in the next twelve months; by the autumn of 1795 the rolls showed 119,000 light infantry of various appellations—*chasseurs, infanterie légère, tirailleurs,* and others. Belhomme, *Histoire de l'infanterie en France,* Paris, 1902, IV, 27, 66, 107. The decrees of 11 and 31 October 1795 fixed the line infantry at 323,000 officers and men, and the light infantry at 96,960 officers and men. P. Mahon, *Etudes sur les armées du directoire,* Paris, 1905, I, 31–32. But these figures represent nominal rather than actual strengths, which might differ by one-third or even more, and include very large garrison contingents. Useful comparative figures can be found in R. Phipps, *The Armies of the First French Republic,* London, 1926–1939—for instance, in vol. IV, 117, 148. See also the table published by M. Reinhard in his biography *Le Grand Carnot,* Paris, 1950–1952, II, 98. Between 190,000 and 230,000 appears to be a reasonable estimate of infantry strength available in the field in 1794 and 1795. Somewhat over one-ninth of this number habitually performed the duties of skirmishers and of the light service. *Jäger* and fusiliers made up between 11 and 12 per cent of Prussian first-line infantry in the years from 1792 to 1795 (however, 12 out of the 20 fusilier battalions were committed in Poland). The Austrian infantry during this period consisted of 60 line regiments and 17 *Grenz* or light regiments, to which must be added 26 *Jäger* companies and some temporary *Freicorps*. See the Austrian General Staff history, *Krieg gegen die*

strength, the Allied light troops played a far less significant role in the war than did the *tirailleurs*.

Their failure was due mainly to the inadequate psychological and material resources that the Allies mobilized against the Republic, and to the steady view that Carnot and his collaborators were able gradually to impose on French strategy and tactics. A Prussian *Jäger* officer wrote of those days: "In detached operations: surprise attacks, ambushes, and all actions where the various arms—particularly the cavalry—could participate, in outposts, and in everything that can be counted among the task of raiders, the superiority of the Allies was apparent. . . . But our frequently successful little war did not lead to decisions, exactly because it lacked [the French] system, which subordinated individual actions to a higher general purpose." [72] The Allies' employment of combined operations rarely broke the bounds of the little war, while tactical cooperation on the largest scale between heavy and light units came to be standard procedure in the French armies.[73] Even on conventional missions, the Allied heavy infantry too often lacked the protective screen of light troops, which their official doctrine now called for, since these specially trained men were constantly detached for reconnaissance or raids.[74] But few French close formations moved without their scouts and skirmishers. If the battalion *tirailleurs* went on patrol, an equivalent number of other soldiers took their places in the skirmish line. Eventually, most of the French line regiments could fight in some kind of open order—awkward and confused though it might be. It was this fundamental change that Duhesme, the Napoleonic specialist of the light service, tried to express when he wrote, "One can truthfully say that by the end of 1793 the French armies had only light infantry." [75] During the campaigns along

Französische Revolution: 1792–1797, Vienna, 1905, i, 228, 239–240. Austrian commands often reflected this proportion of 1 to 3 between light and line infantry. See, for example, C. de la Jonquière, *La Bataille de Jemappes*, Paris, 1902, p. 143.

[72] Valentini, p. 2.

[73] Rüstow, ii, 304–307, discusses this development with unsurpassed clarity.

[74] In addition the *Jäger* were often used as snipers. Goethe describes such a mission in the entry for 31 August 1792 in his *Campagne in Frankreich*.

[75] Duhesme, p. 71.

the Rhine and in the Low Countries, and later against increasingly inept opposition in Italy, the French system of improvisation did not unduly hinder their light troops. For a time, revolutionary armies tend to be lawless: an absence of rules best expresses their spirit and in the period of their *Sturm und Drang* enables them to function most effectively. But even as they accumulated experience and success, the French light infantry could not be expected to improve beyond a certain point unless their doctrine and training were perfected and became standardized. With the diminution of revolutionary *élan*, and the emergence of a supreme commander who on the whole possessed little interest in the refinements of infantry tactics, their effectiveness might even decline.

· 4 ·

Prussian tactical formations were not modified during the war against France. Change, for the time being, was a topic for discussion, to be advocated or condemned rather than carried out. Austrian commanders on the other hand, with their strong and well-integrated complements of light troops, were sometimes tempted to adapt to the new conditions. Their field expedients remained unsanctioned, however, and eventually were considerably restricted. The Austrian directions for general officers of 1796 declared:

The war in Flanders, on terrain usually so irregular that it was not possible to attack in closed lines, had the unfortunate consequence for the army of upsetting the ideas on the true method of attacking the enemy, held not only by the private soldier but by the officer as well. Even by the line infantry, attack *en tirailleurs* is almost the only method used on the most important occasions, or at least the attack degenerates into this as soon as the heat of battle reduces the original order of the advance. This misuse must be opposed because it weakens the impetus of the attack, and against unexpected resistance of the enemy may lose us our original advantage. . . .

Regular, trained, and solid infantry, if it advances in closed ranks, with rapid steps [*gestreckten Schritten*], courageously, supported by its artillery, cannot be held up by scattered skirmishers. It should therefore refuse to lose time either by skirmishing or by the fire of small groups [*Abteilungsfeuer*]. . . . It should close with the enemy as rapidly and orderly as possible, so as to drive him back and decide the action quickly.

This is the method that saves lives; firing and skirmishing costs casualties and decides nothing.

Therefore everything must be done to maintain cohesion and close order in rank and file among the troops, and not to permit skirmishing and scattering, either during attacks or pursuits, and still less in retreats. If when attacking a village or wood it be considered useful to employ a few companies or scattered *tirailleurs*, which would be supported by companies or battalions in close order, it should be impressed on the men that as soon as the company commander has the drummer beat alarm, they must gather by him without the least waste of time, and reform in rank and file.[76]

Old and new mingle in these directions. Some passages still sound the authentic note of the *ancien régime:* "Often as much can be gained by maneuvering as by a battle." On the other hand, the *Observationspunkte* permit the commander of a line battalion to deploy several of his companies into skirmish swarms at a time when even a Prussian fusilier battalion could use only two half-companies in this manner. Nor was the author of the directions mistaken in showing concern over the loss of impetus that resulted from opening up the serried ranks. The problem of innovation was partly one of timing. At first, any change, regardless how necessary, could lead only to confusion and reduced effectiveness.

Such practical considerations proved to be persuasive arguments with which to counter the reform proposals that were being brought forward insistently in the decade before Austerlitz and Jena. During these years a great debate between adherents and opponents of change was carried on in every German army, spilling from the committee rooms and staff meetings onto the pages of the proliferating professional literature. Books, pamphlets, and such journals as Hoyer's *Neues Militairisches Magazin*, Scharnhorst's and Decken's *Neues Militärisches Journal* and *Militärische Denkwürdigkeiten*, and Porbeck's *Neue Bellona*, to mention only the most important, gave expression to every con-

[76] [General K. v. Mack or Archduke Charles], "Observationspunkte für die Generale bei der Armee in Deutschland im Jahre 1796." *Beiträge zur Geschichte des österreichischen Heerwesens*, I, *Der Zeitraum von 1757–1814*, Vienna, 1872, 139. Excerpts are printed in Frauenholz, IV, 82–83, and Jähns, III, 2118–2120.

ceivable point of view.[77] The controversy dealt with the entire range of military life, from specifics of organization and equipment to the fundamental question of the army's position in the state. But the opposites had not yet crystallized, and, indeed, they were never to do so completely. The need for improvement was so extensive that is could be recognized in one or the other area, while elsewhere one kept faith with tradition. Even those men who were to revolutionize the Prussian army came to understand only slowly and reluctantly that comprehensive change was needed. It was altogether exceptional for Berenhorst, a man who had once served on Frederick's staff and remained one of the best-informed critics of the Prussian service, to point to the connections between political and military institutions, and plainly spell out the consequences. Echoing Guibert, Berenhorst declared that the absolutist principles of the state and the army corresponded to, and supported, one another. If a new kind of army were wanted, it could only be created by a new kind of state that would grant the individual a more active role in public affairs. He looked forward to a time, Berenhorst wrote, when monarchies were constitutional, when the rulers respected the rights of their subjects, and every citizen would also be a defender of the state.[78] The revolutionary *élan* of the French—even though it had faltered often enough—convinced Berenhorst that such a change was needed, since in the long run the enthusiastic and patriotic fighter would always defeat that "soulless automaton," that "lifeless work of art," the mercenary.[79] It was the experience of the early revolutionary campaigns that gave impetus to the controversy, and provided its frame of reference. It also set its limits. The course of the debate was largely guided by the fact that Prussia

[77] The role these and similar publications played in molding public opinion deserves study. Some efforts in this direction have been made by Otto Tschirch in his *Geschichte der öffentlichen Meinung in Preussen*, 2 vols., Weimar, 1933–1934, but his analysis suffers from his lack of knowledge of military affairs and from his methodology, which largely consists of measuring authors with the yardstick of an extreme, parochial chauvinism. Writers who do not pass are marked *freche Schwätzer*, *unbelehrbare Schwärmer*, their works are characterized as *undeutsche Feigheit und Verräterei*, etc.

[78] Berenhorst, II, 444.

[79] *Ibid.*, II, 431.

had withdrawn from the war against the French Republic in 1795; since the Peace of Basel Prussian soldiers followed events along the Rhine, in southern Germany, and in Italy only as distant observers. They spoke of the need to emulate and outdo the "new Franks"; but it was the early revolutionary forces they had in mind, and they perceived only dimly the steps by which the *levée en masse* was being transformed into the Imperial army.

In the debate between proponents and opponents of change, *tirailleur* tactics from the first assumed a central role.[80] To a remarkable, possibly unique, degree all problems concentrated in this issue. If skirmishing was to be more generally employed, the soldier's education, discipline, and drill—all of which bore directly on his ability to fight in open order—would need to be changed. Nor could the old methods of recruitment, exemption, and reliance on mercenaries be retained; a more representative cross-section of the population in the ranks would turn the army into a more national body; the relationship between officer and man, soldier and citizen, and between soldier and sovereign would be modified. Tactics and consequently strategy would become less limited; war as a whole, the "tamed Bellona" of the Age of Enlightenment, would burst through its carefully woven net of rules, limitations, and custom, to grow more universal. The importance of light troops lay in these connections and their interdependence with every aspect of a new kind of war that was gradually evolving, and conservatives who sensed this bond were provided with a further powerful reason for opposition.

The first issue to be determined was the true importance of the *tirailleur* in the campaigns between 1792 and 1795. His significance could be disparaged by interpreting his manner of fighting as a measure of despair brought about by the break-up of the royal army—and thus as a tactical system that no stable military institution need adopt. In any event, some traditionalists said, skirmishing was nothing new. In his work on the *Basic Reasons for the French Success*, Scharnhorst, at that time still a relatively obscure Hanoverian staff officer, wrote that people tried to deny

[80] For the following, compare especially Delbrück, IV, 522–526; M. Lehmann, *Scharnhorst*, Leipzig, 1886–1887, I, 203–280; and R. Höhn, *Revolution—Heer—Kriegsbild*, Darmstadt, 1944. Some problems of Höhn's methodology and interpretation are discussed in "A Note on Sources" at the conclusion of this work.

how valuable to the French and how different the *tirailleur* was by pretending that the *Jäger* and fusiliers had always done his work. Scharnhorst, on the contrary, termed it an undeniable truth that the *tirailleur*—a type of soldier until then always thought of as an auxiliary—had decided the greater part of the engagements in the war: [81]

The physical agility and high intelligence of the common man enables the French *tirailleurs* to profit from all advantages offered by the terrain and the general situation, while the phlegmatic Germans, Bohemians, and Dutch form on open ground and do nothing but what their officer orders them to do. . . . The "Commission de l'organisation et du mouvement des armées de terre" took account of these circumstances and based on them the system of always waging war in broken and covered terrain, where everything depends on the defense and attacks of positions, of avoiding large battles if possible, and instead wear out the Allied armies by skirmishes, outpost affairs, and isolated attacks in woods and ravines.[82]

Scharnhorst was far from giving all the credit for French successes to the light troops. Besides listing such other French military advantages as superior leadership and numbers operating from an exceedingly strong base, he believed that the fundamental political and moral conditions of the conflict favored the Republic—"The struggle was indeed too unequal: one side had everything to lose, the other little." [83] But the skirmisher remained for him the main tactical cause of victory. Years later, in 1811, when he had become the leader of military modernization in Prussia, and was removed from the immediate impact of these early struggles, he saw no reason to change his analysis, with the interesting exception that now he no longer thought of the French development as consciously planned. In a discussion of infantry tactics he wrote:

. . . the French armies, compelled by the situation in which they found themselves and aided by their national genius, had developed a

[81] "Entwicklung der allgemeinen Ursachen des Glücks der Franzosen in dem Revolutionskriege," *Militärische Schriften von Scharnhorst*, ed. C. v. d. Goltz, Dresden, 1891, pp. 224, 226 n.

[82] *Ibid.*, pp. 224–225.

[83] *Ibid.*, pp. 195 n., 203. Compare the discussion of Scharnhorst's and Clausewitz's analyses of the Revolutionary wars in my article, "Clausewitz and the Nineteenth Century," in *The Theory and Practice of War*, ed. M. Howard, London, 1965, pp. 25–28.

practical system of tactics that permitted them to fight over open or broken ground, in open or close order, but this *without their being aware of their system* [Scharnhorst's italics]. In the battle of Hondschoote, the actions of Dunkirk, Wervick, Tourcoing, the battles of Mouscron and Wassigny, the attacks on the Weissenburg Line—everywhere in the autumn of 1793 they won through their open order and their *tirailleurs*. In the spring of 1794 the battles of Courtrai, of Mouveaux and Fleurus, were won in the same manner. Decisive actions fought in close order were rare, though not excluded—they occurred only when it was impossible to gain the objective through skirmishers. The French *tirailleurs* attacked guns, and not infrequently silenced them. The fortress Crèvecoeur, covering the control locks of the inundation system around s'Hertogenbosch, was invested by *tirailleurs* who dug themselves in. No gun of the fortress could be loaded and aimed without some of the gunners being killed or wounded. Recently Peschiera was besieged in almost the same way.

Before the assault on Menin in April 1794, 4,000 *tirailleurs* approached the fortress and, firing from the ground, wounded or killed nearly all gunners who attempted to serve their pieces.

A lively regard for honor, for competition and distinctions, the ability to learn quickly and to adapt easily to different conditions and circumstances, make the French soldiers better skirmishers than those of any other nation. Because of this superiority the French were victorious whenever they fought in open order and avoided action in close formations. Often victory would not come until three or more days of fighting had passed, but then the more surely, since *they never involved themselves in pitched battles* [Scharnhorst's italics] where chance has such wide scope.[84]

One of Scharnhorst's most insidious opponents during the years of reform, the future Field Marshal von dem Knesebeck, who successfully combined an instinct for novelty with a profound faith in the established order of things, wrote as early as 1794 that the main reason for the reverses on the upper Rhine could be found in the enemy's ability to exhaust the Austrians by methods of the little war. The French, Knesebeck declared, used their entire infantry as light troops, "and do so with decided superiority. It is here that the education [*Aufklärung*] of the individual is of such great benefit to the Republicans, because situations too often occur during the combat of light forces in which the officer's control ceases completely . . . in which each

[84] See Scharnhorst's essay of 1811 in Appendix 1 of this volume, pp. 258–259.

man acts on his own." After suggesting that the firmness of line infantry depends entirely on the officer's example, while in light units "everything depends on the spirit, the ability, and skill of each individual," Knesebeck concluded with the explanation that he devoted so much time to the superiority of French light troops "because in this is to be found the key to so many unexpected events, and perhaps even the key to the outcome of the war." [85]

Such interpretations hardly met with general acceptance; they even earned their author a short-lived reputation for dangerous radicalism.[86] It was, nevertheless, acknowledged that some means had to be devised to deal with the *tirailleur*, whether he were a decisive force or only a nuisance. Those who did not wish to oppose the French open order with similar tactics or increase the number of sharpshooters in their units at least admitted that the traditional solutions would no longer serve. "There is no point in firing volleys at *tirailleurs*," a typical conservative statement went; "the best thing is to insert between one's infantry small groups of horses, which would attack as soon as the skirmishers showed themselves, and thus force them to stay together." [87] Nor would anyone dispute the need to raise the effectiveness of small-arms fire, both through better training of the men and improved construction of their muskets.[88]

But if agreement could be achieved on such relatively marginal points, it proved unattainable in the decisive matter of the standard tactical formations. Four generations had triumphed with the line and the mechanically responsive grenadier and musketeer.

[85] [K. F. v. d. Knesebeck], *Betrachtungen über den jetzigen Krieg*, Berlin, 1794, pp. 60–65.

[86] In his *Erinnerungen*, I, 360, Boyen commented that "in the Rhine campaigns of 1793 and 1794 . . . [Knesebeck] was generally thought to be a Jacobin," adding, "but later he became the total opposite."

[87] v. M., "Über die Beschaffenheit der französischen Armee," *Neues Militairisches Magazin*, I, No. 4 (1799), 62.

[88] See, for instance, the anonymous articles in the *Neues Militairisches Magazin*, I, No. 4 (1799); I, Nos. 5 and 8 (1800); II, No. 1 (1801). Other suggestions to assist infantry against skirmishers ranged from body armor and up-to-date Greek fire to anti-personnel grenades launched from specially adapted muskets. For the latter scheme, see J. J. Boreux's proposal, "Wie lässt sich wohl die Wirkung des Feuergewehres beträchtlich erhöhen, so dass nur wenig Truppen ihr zu widerstehen im Stande sein werden?" *ibid.*, I, No. 3 (1799).

Some slight adjustments were now permissible—the sending out of a few skirmishers, the introduction of more humane treatment, which accorded with the spirit of the age and by appealing to a man's intelligence and good intentions might incidentally be as useful a disciplinary device as the stick; but the great majority of officers, and the military and governmental institutions they represented, would not and could not move farther. Most troublesome to their position were the reasoned suggestions of those professional soldiers who like Scharnhorst were cautiously feeling their way from accepted doctrine towards the new. Far easier to dispose of, and at the same time maddening in their radicalism, were the enthusiasts who demanded nothing less than total abolition of every accepted method.

No one put the case for the *tirailleur* with greater enthusiasm than the retired Prussian lieutenant, world traveler, and bankrupt, Heinrich Dietrich von Bülow.[89] In a dozen ill-organized, repetitive, brilliantly written books, appearing in rapid succession between 1799 and his imprisonment by an outraged Prussian government two months before Jena, Bülow attacked every ideal of the Frederician army, including the great king himself. Prussian military institutions, he cried, should be turned into a true people's army, which not only defended the state but also, instead of being "a school for ***, a school for ***, and a school for ***, as at present, be changed into a purgatory in which young men were cleansed of the impurities of a poor upbringing."[90] Linear drill was "something complete within itself, in the sense of Goethe's and Schiller's aesthetic principles. It has its own purpose. Its purpose is to shine on the parade-ground."[91] For decades it seemed as if there was no stopping the drill-sergeant: " 'Will you dogs keep in step!' would have been the command

[89] Good analyses of Bülow's life and of his military theories are given in the two introductory essays in *Militärische und vermischte Schriften von Heinrich Dietrich von Bülow*, ed. E. Bülow and W. Rüstow, Leipzig, 1853. The excerpts of Bülow's writings reprinted in this volume are intelligently chosen, but the texts are unreliable. A fine shorter account of Bülow is contained in R. R. Palmer's chapter, "Frederick the Great, Guibert, Bülow: From Dynastic to National War," in *Makers of Modern Strategy*, ed. E. M. Earle, Princeton, 1961.

[90] [Bülow], *Neue Taktik der Neuern wie sie seyn sollte*, Leipzig, 1805, II, 7.

[91] *Ibid.*, II, 3.

even during surprise attacks at night, if the wars of the French Revolution hadn't disrupted the further development of Saldern's and Lacy's tactics. . . . It really would have come to that if the Revolutionary War hadn't threatened tactics with a revolution as well. Since then the adherents of dead-straight tactics have diminished, and there is less concern to achieve *this kind* of ideal. But it also deserves mention that since that time it is no longer quite so common to address human beings as dogs." [92] Sooner or later, Bülow prophesied, "skirmishing would certainly become the main feature of modern war." [93] Therefore all infantry should be turned into light infantry—that is, soldiers who can move easily, naturally, and rapidly—and their equipment and tactics should become those of the hunt: "The savior of France, I mean Carnot, declared . . . that modern war should really be a hunt for men, and that clockwork tactics would prove inadequate against his human tactics." [94] On the battlefield, infantry evolutions should be executed on the run and not in cadence; quick movement and accurate fire were the characteristics of the new soldier, who shattered the enemy line "not by shock but with bullets." [95] "A hollow square, surrounded by light, skirmishing infantry is among the most pitiable of objects." [96] All of Bülow's works sound the note of personal freedom, which he saw as the true source of military strength. The "servile tactics" of the line he opposed to skirmishing, which "restores to the individual his courage, his effectiveness, his intelligence, in one word his human dignity." His hatred of any kind of personal restraint went so far that he advocated making the troops slightly drunk before they attacked. [97] But he was never able to take the step from physical to abstract freedom, and his natural fighting man was inserted into an artificial strategic system made up of "points of domination," "angles of approach," and other rococo *jeux d'esprit*.

---

[92] *Ibid.*, I, 46–47.

[93] *Ibid.*, II, 24.

[94] *Ibid.*, II, 32, 85–89.

[95] *Ibid.*, II, 107, 113–115, 164. Compare the very similar arguments in [Bülow's] *Lehrsätze des neuern Krieges*, Berlin, 1805, pp. 491, 509–510, 625–626, 646–649.

[96] Quoted from Bülow's *Geist des neuern Kriegssystems*, Hamburg, 1799, in *Militärische und vermischte Schriften*, p. 238.

[97] *Neue Taktik der Neuern*, I, 146–147.

Bülow was very widely read at the time. Later, Varnhagen von Ense characterized his books as "phenomena of genius, meteors in the literary sky, before whose lightning whole masses of ancient prejudices collapsed, and whose effect still continues in many things that deny their origin or are not aware of it." [98] This took the intent for the act. A better estimate is Professor Palmer's. Bülow, he writes, "had the merit of sensing, though slowly and confusedly, the nature of the military revolution of his time." [99] His insights shocked; but they were random, inconsistent, handicapped by a fantastic and virulent presentation: on the coming generation of military leaders they had little lasting influence. Many officers who, like Scharnhorst and Clausewitz, disassociated themselves from his peculiar combination of geometric analysis and paeans on skirmishing, agreed with Bülow on the advantages of mass armies and open formations. But these did not imply the abolition of elite professional forces fighting in close order—on the contrary, the two systems somehow had to be combined.

The greatest advance in elaborating the new tactical experiences theoretically and fitting them into official doctrine took place not in Prussia but in the armies of the smaller Central and South German states. The leading figure here was Heinrich Philip von Porbeck, whose journal *Neue Bellona* published numerous historical and theoretical articles that urged changes in organization, strategy, and tactics, and incidentally printed the first article of the young Clausewitz—a critique of Bülow's scientific laws of strategy. Like Scharnhorst, Hoyer, and Decken, Porbeck was simultaneously an editor and a serving officer. His accounts

[98] In his biography of Bülow's more successful brother, *Leben des Generals Grafen Bülow von Dennewitz*, Berlin, 1853, p. 17. Compare this with Archduke Charles' judgment: "Bülow greatly resembles a thunderstorm from which we accept much darkness and superfluous noise for the sake of one brilliant bolt of lightning. Novices in the military profession are seduced by him." "Aphorismen," in *Erzherzog Karl: Ausgewählte militärische Schriften*, ed. v. Waldstätten, Berlin, 1882, p. 229. An interesting and rare attempt to adapt Bülow's visions to the realities of war can be found in the article by an anonymous Prussian officer, "Taktische Bemerkungen (vorzüglich in Rücksicht des Werkes: *Geist des neuen Kriegssystems*)," 2nd installment, *Neues Militairisches Magazin*, II, No. 4 (1802); see especially pp. 32–42.

[99] *Makers of Modern Strategy*, p. 73.

of the Revolutionary wars that appeared in those years are still occasionally quoted, but his work in bringing about actual tactical change has escaped notice.[100] He started his career in Hesse, and as a junior member of the general staff assisted Adam Ludwig von Ochs in the revision of the Hesse *Reglement* of 1796.[101] This work, although still suffused with the spirit of the parade-ground, is the first German manual to give detailed tactical instructions to light units, to lay down rules for their cooperation with the line, and to designate the entire third rank of the line infantry as skirmishers.[102] In 1803 Porbeck published a long study on riflemen, in which he argued that increasing their number was preferable to raising more badly trained light infantry battalions.[103] Soon afterwards he transferred to the army of Baden, for which he drafted new light infantry regulations. These he printed in his journal in 1806, despite, as he wrote, "the proneness of many military states to surround publication of their tactical instructions with three walls of horrible prohibitions." [104] The manual was modern in concept as well as in detail, and— excepting the new methods that Yorck was introducing to the *Jäger* regiment—far in advance of any official Prussian text. Tactical situations are analyzed in which entire companies maneuver as skirmishers. The men act in files of two or three, firing alternately; the basic interval between men in the skirmish line is five paces, but this may be doubled or even trebled; the skirmish line will usually attempt to outflank the enemy.[105] In a long introductory essay, which does not form part of the official manual,

[100] Höhn discusses Porbeck's literary activities, but ignores his practical work: *Revolution—Heer—Kriegsbild*, pp. 148, 171–172, 334, 341–342. See also B. v. Poten's article in the *Allgemeine Deutsche Biographie*, and C. v. d. Goltz, *Von Rossbach bis Jena*, Berlin, 1906, p. 383.

[101] Ochs came from a middle-class family, served as *Jäger* in America and against France, was commissioned and eventually ennobled. He is the author of several works on light infantry, among them "Ein kleiner Beitrag zur Berichtigung der Taktik für leichte Truppen," *Mars*, III, No. 2 (1805).

[102] *Hessen-Casselisches Militär-Reglement für die Infanterie, Artillerie, und leichten Truppen*, Cassel, 1802.

[103] *Neue Bellona*, v (1803), 252–292.

[104] *Ibid.*, x (1806), 78. The Baden *Reglement* formed the second part of Porbeck's series, "Versuch einer Instruction zur Abrichtung der Scharfschützen," in the *Neue Bellona*, x, 1–86, 125–177, and plates.

[105] *Ibid.*, x, 147–150.

Porbeck recalls the ineffectiveness against French *tirailleurs* of the Allied line infantry, "soldiers, whom the art of our lungs and sticks had partly transformed into stiff machines," and concludes that "the more enlightened the common people are, the more they reason, and the more they are suited and ready for skirmishing." [106]

Porbeck's work attracted sufficient attention to bring him an offer of a Prussian commission, which, however, he rejected. It is not known who arranged the invitation, but Porbeck would have proved a useful ally to the officers promoting innovation in the Prussian army. During the last pre-reform years these men found themselves in the frustrating situation of being accorded the widest possible hearing, unhampered by censorship or superiors, and yet incapable of making more than a dent in that "rare conceit" which in Clausewitz's words marked Prussian military society.[107] Their slowly evolving doctrines and the theoretical and practical resistance they engendered can be traced most clearly perhaps in the history of the *Militärische Gesellschaft* in Berlin. This society, of which Yorck was an early member, had been founded in 1802 by Scharnhorst together with several fellow-officers and two civilian teachers of military history.[108] The purpose of the society, according to Article 1 of its by-laws, was "to instruct its members through the exchange of ideas in all areas of the art of war, in a manner that would encourage them to seek out truth, that would avoid the difficulties of private studies with its tendency to onesidedness, and that would seem best suited to place theory and practice in proper relationship"—a typical Scharnhorstian turn of phrase.[109]

Soon after his transfer from the Hanoverian army in 1801,

---

[106] *Ibid.*, x, 23–24, 65.

[107] Clausewitz, *Nachrichten*, p. 428.

[108] After formal meetings during the summer and fall of 1801, the society was officially launched on 24 January 1802, the anniversary of Frederick the Great's birthday. The main source for the history of the society are its extremely rare *Proceedings*. See also G. H. Klippel, *Das Leben des Generals von Scharnhorst*, Leipzig, 1869–1871, III, 30–78, 255–262; Lehmann, *Scharnhorst*, I, 320–328; R. Stadelmann, *Scharnhorst: Schicksal und Geistige Welt*, Wiesbaden, 1952, pp. 60–64; and F. Meinecke, *Das Leben des Generalfeldmarschalls Hermann von Boyen*, Stuttgart, 1896–1899, I, 112–124.

[109] Klippel, III, 255.

Scharnhorst had been able to acquire a dominant influence over the very imperfect system of officer education in Prussia. He reorganized the existing officer schools in Berlin, assembled competent instructors—some from foreign services; in the Academy for Officers, with its three-year program in strategy, tactics, history, mathematics, and engineering, he created an institution for advanced military study. His aim was to introduce a measure of professional and technical competence into the so-called fighting branches, and to raise the educational standards of the officer corps in general—a goal that was far from enjoying universal approbation. The *Militärische Gesellschaft* formed another part in his campaign. A club outside the institutional structure, it was both more sophisticated and more prestigious than the service schools. Its membership, never quite reaching two hundred, included officers of all ranks, two princes of the royal house, as well as civilians interested in military affairs, among whom the Freiherr vom Stein was the most notable.[110] If no single direction could be developed in the lectures, discussions, and essay competitions, the exchange of ideas under Scharnhorst's guidance and inspiration at least gave him an excellent sounding board in the army that he had only recently joined. The society broke up with the general mobilization of 1805, but in the few years of its existence it had come to inform and unify the best intellectual efforts of the Prussian officer corps.[111]

A large number of articles dealing with light troops and the combination of light and linear tactics appeared in the five volumes of the privately circulated *Proceedings*—the *Denkwürdigkeiten der Militärischen Gesellschaft.*[112] Among the most valuable was an essay by Hermann von Boyen, the future Minister of War and champion of the militia, which in 1804 gained first place in the competition on the question: "Should line infantry be

[110] Shanahan, p. 64, mistakenly writes that an average of 188 members attended the meetings. This was the figure of the total membership in 1805. Klippel, III, 31; Lehmann, *Scharnhorst*, I, 322.

[111] Stadelmann, p. 61.

[112] Shanahan, p. 64, writes that "for the general public a lively popular journal was issued," and discusses the kinds of articles that appeared in it. This publication never existed. Scharnhorst proposed that the society publish a journal for general circulation, but the mobilization of 1805 put an end to the scheme. Lehmann, *Scharnhorst*, I, 326–328.

taught the light service and how to fight *à la debandade?*" [113]
Boyen recognized that in the course of a campaign any line
battalion might become engaged under conditions in which skirmishing was the only effective tactic. For this reason he suggested that the third rank of the line battalions be trained to fight
in open order. His proposal was scarcely revolutionary. Not only
had this method already been officially adopted in Hesse, but
Scharnhorst in his lectures on tactics at the Academy for Officers
had explored the same means of making the standard line battalion more versatile, and had recommended the retraining of the
third rank to Frederick William. [114] Several Prussian units had
experimented with the system. But it needed the demonstration at
Jena of helpless grenadier lines being slowly destroyed by irregular fire to make this innovation acceptable to the Prussian army as
a whole.

Rather than training heavy infantry to skirmish, objected another member of the society, the desired tactical flexibility should
be achieved by increasing the number of fusilier units, since "a
line battalion is not suited for dispersed action." [115] Other members criticized Boyen's scheme on the grounds that "such a system would require twice as much drill . . . and prove detrimental to the accustomed routine of the line. . . . Skirmishing was
politically suspect and militarily unnecessary: in the French army
it had come about only through the nation's *levée en masse;* with
increasing regularization it was disappearing again." [116]

Boyen's essay did not ignore the political and moral implications of turning part of the line into light infantry. He recognized
that the skirmisher could not be a human machine; since his
effectiveness depended to some extent on his ingenuity and
good will, he required more humane and sympathetic treatment.
Indeed it was Boyen's concern over the excesses of Prussian
discipline that helped lead him to new tactical forms. Already

[113] See Scharnhorst's report on the society's activities in 1804 in vol. v
of the *Denkwürdigkeiten*, 1–10, and the discussion on the essay, *ibid.*,
154–158. Cf. Meinecke, *Boyen*, i, 120–124.

[114] In a memorandum submitted in 1800 or 1801. Lehmann, *Scharnhorst*, i, 257, 299–300.

[115] Lieutenant v. Beulwitz. His commander, Prince Hohenlohe, had
introduced skirmish training to his regiment, an experience Beulwitz may
have found discouraging.

[116] Lehmann, *Scharnhorst*, i, 323.

as a subaltern he had determined not to cane his men on the drill-field, and his first published article, written when he was twenty-nine, was a proposal to reform military punishment.[117] Humane treatment, the appeal to good will and intelligence, were the first steps in educating soldiers to better themselves and to become better servants of the state. By fostering the common man's ability and guiding him towards selfless service to the community the conflict that some saw coming between the individual and the state might be resolved. It was not surprising that the young Boyen also administered the garrison school for children of the rank and file, and himself taught men of his battalion to read and write.[118] On the small stage of his East Prussian garrison he was already putting into practice what came to be the main purpose of many Prussian reformers after 1806— to make the army the school of the nation.

To the opponents of the *tirailleur*, the moral issues attached to tactical change appeared in a different light. An anonymous officer wrote:

Of all means of fighting, skirmishing is the most natural, i.e. it best responds to our instinct of self-preservation; but this certainly does not imply, as some have attempted to prove, that it is the most suitable means of fighting. After all, war itself goes against human nature; to make the two correspond more closely would mean making war *unwarlike*, and that at least can never be an object of *military art*. Someone once said very justly: "Skirmishing fosters the instinctive cur [*natürlichen Hundsfott*], which, if we wish to be honest, exists in all of us, and which we must seek to suppress. . . ."

By becoming accustomed to his manner of fighting, the *tirailleur* loses the courage that is required for fighting in close formations. From this follows that line infantry must *never* skirmish if it would not lose its usefulness as line infantry.

---

[117] Boyen, *Erinnerungen*, I, 131–132; the essay is reprinted in *ibid.*, pp. 411–421.

[118] Meinecke, *Boyen*, I, 76, 89, 93–94. Boyen's years as a subaltern coincided with the first serious efforts of the state to educate the common soldier and his children. Meinecke, *ibid.*, pp. 94–101, discusses this important development and the connections between patriotism and the education of the soldier and worker. By the end of the century the garrison schools had become sufficiently institutionalized to require a reader, which J. F. Michaelis issued under the title *Lesebuch für preussische Soldatenschulen*, Berlin, 1798.

Besides, the writer continued, no tactical situation could be imagined that would ever oblige line infantry to skirmish, even in broken terrain, though an advance line of battalion *tirailleurs* might be useful to prevent the battalion from opening fire too early. In other words, the skirmisher was of use solely as a further means to maintain line discipline. The article concluded by expressing the hope that courageous men would not allow the flood of French *tirailleurs* now pouring over Europe to carry off the old principles.[119]

The new tactics, in this view, were not only unnecessary, but undermined moral values. Following the course usually adopted by critiques of the French system, the attack column, which restricted individual initiative as much as did the line, was ignored: the skirmisher became the sole object of disparagement. He was interpreted as the military expression of instinct and free will, which were deemed weak sources for effectiveness in war even when they were intensified by the dangerous element of enthusiasm. Here the critics linked the new system with the politics that employed it—the Revolution and French expansion. To many soldiers the defense against the threats emanating from Paris demanded the retention of old tactical forms, even the glorification of the line as a formation that stood for the aristocratic principle and German independence.

That French armies were not solely the military tools of the Revolution but sometimes its political agents as well rendered the objective analysis of their tactics more difficult. Everywhere, Porbeck wrote in his study of the Rhine campaigns, "the war of opinion meddled with the fighting men of the Allies, aroused indignation at this war, which the masses considered unjust . . . and thus was not infrequently created a boundless hatred and openly expressed repugnance, hidden and open insubordination, which was both detrimental to military discipline and to the offensive and defensive operations, and proved most obstructive to victory." [120] This contest the Allies lost almost by default. The

---

[119] Fransecky, pp. 63–67, prints what appears to be the entire article, with the exception of some technical passages, but gives neither the name of the author nor the place and date of publication.

[120] "Über die Ursachen der vielen Siege und des Kriegsglücks der Franzosen," *Neue Bellona*, II (1802), 225. Cf. P. Chalmin, "La Guerre 'révolutionnaire' sous la Legislative et la Convention," *Revue Historique*

traditional exhortations to their troops, the bombast and hatred of Brunswick's proclamation, could not match the Marseillaise and the policies and propaganda that aroused not only the enthusiasm of an army in times of crisis but more permanently affected the spirits of individual soldiers and of an entire society. Its association with these conditions handicapped the new tactics in German eyes. Far from increasing effectiveness, the new methods might in fact lead to military and social anarchy. For much the same reason, the attempt of some reformers to justify skirmishing as the logical development of the mode of fighting of Frederician light troops met with resistance: in the conflict of ideologies, these units with their bourgeois officers and undisciplined ways might themselves come to represent a danger to the status quo.

Light troops could be connected to new and undesirable forms of fighting in yet another area. As the literature pointed out, their organization and tactics made them particularly well-suited for collaboration with the armed populace. Even before the Revolution writers had discussed such combined operations, which had actually occurred a few times during the Seven Years' War, in Corsica, and in America.[121] It suggests the seriousness of the crisis in which the monarchical system found itself that in the Revolutionary wars the collaboration of armed civilians with regular forces first took place not on the French but on the German side, where an Imperial edict of 21 January 1794 called on the principalities on the east bank of the Rhine to arm their subjects as a last means of repelling the invader. The resultant efforts did little to affect the course of the war, but they aroused much interest among the military intelligentsia. The actions of armed peasant bands and light troops—generally Austrian—in the Palatinate and on the upper Rhine, which violated traditional concepts of war, were justified even by some conservatives on the grounds of extreme patriotic need, not however without accompanying warnings as to how difficult it might be to bank the fire

---

de l'Armée, IV (Summer 1958), a useful study of propaganda methods employed by the Revolutionary armies, though the author is overly influenced by French politico–military doctrine of the late 1950's.

[121] See, for instance, the anonymous work *Traité sur la constitution des troupes légères et sur l'emploi à la guerre*, Paris, 1782, particularly chapter IV, "Des opérations communes aux troupes légères et aux pesants."

once it had been permitted to break out.[122] Indeed, the emergency mobilization of the populace suggested the establishment of a permanent militia. Few would doubt that a militia, organized and trained in time of peace, was more useful than roving peasant bands; equally undeniable were the deep social and political changes that would result from a more general implementation of the principle of conscription, and the equipping of men with muskets outside the framework of the standing army. In Prussia, during the 1790's, concern over the growing numerical superiority of the French, Austrian, and Russian armies led a few soldiers and administrators to think seriously about the possibility of raising such a force.[123] In Pomerania and East Prussia, especially, the tradition of civilians fighting against foreign invaders had remained alive; but the step from an emergency measure to a regular organization proved too great for the state. When at last in 1803 a plan for a militia was officially considered, opponents, fearing that a force drawn from all sections of the population would lead to "a complete upheaval of the military and of its relations to the state," limited the scheme to the formation of closely controlled home defense groups.[124] None was raised before Jena. As late as spring 1806, Scharnhorst vainly called for the establishment of a truly national militia, its members motivated by patriotic enthusiasm, which was to be employed in conjunction with trained soldiers, by preference "wherever skilled exploitation of circumstances, the fighting in open order, is more essential than regular combat." [125]

It was the most searching critic of the militia concept, the later Hanoverian general Friedrich von der Decken, who also most

[122] A typical analysis is contained in the work of the Prussian officer and military writer, C. v. Massenbach, *Übersicht des merkwürdigen Feldzuges am Rhein im Jahr 1796*, n.p., 1797, pp. 71–82. Massenbach, whose career was to end disastrously in 1806 as Hohenlohe's chief of staff, also supported the establishment of a militia in Prussia. Like Bülow, he could recognize the importance of numbers and the value of enthusiasm and patriotism in the common soldier while holding fast to the most artificial principles of maneuver strategy.

[123] Courbière, pp. 139–150; Jany, *Preussische Armee*, III, 450–465.

[124] The judgment is that of Field Marshal v. Möllendorf and General v. Rüchel, contained in a report to the King of 15 August 1803; Courbière, pp. 141–145; the quoted passage is on p. 141.

[125] In his memorial of April 1806, printed in v. d. Goltz, pp. 543–549.

effectively formulated the *ancien régime*'s answer to enthusiasm.[126] In his classic summing up of absolutist military theory, *Reflections on the Relation Between the Military Profession and the Purpose of States*, Decken devoted several chapters to the superiority standing armies enjoyed over militias, and suggested reasons why the latter were better suited to democracies than to monarchies.[127] He acknowledged that one of the characteristics of the citizen-soldier, enthusiasm—"that inseparable companion of civil war"—had proved of great value to the Revolutionary armies. If the French had not been defeated in the early 1790's it was because their disorganization and indiscipline had been compensated for by terror and enthusiasm.[128] Lately, he continued, they had reintroduced the principle of subordination; but patriotic fervor and the individual soldier's enthusiasm and good will remained factors that their opponents could ignore only at their own peril. What could the monarchies oppose to these emotions?

Love of country, or the wish from a belief in its excellence to maintain the condition of the country in which one lives, cannot be found to the same degree in standing armies as they exist in a volunteer militia. . . . What motive to fight for a fatherland, which to him does not exist, could possess the soldier who lives on his pay alone? He recognizes no other home than the company to which he belongs!

Greater effect on the military spirit can be expected from the *love the warrior bears for his own profession*.[129]

[126] Decken, member of a noble family that had been established in Lower Saxony for centuries, was Scharnhorst's co-editor on the *Neue Militärische Journal*. His career as soldier, government official, and historian still awaits detailed treatment. For the following, compare Lehmann, *Scharnhorst*, I, 264–280, and Höhn, *Revolution—Heer—Kriegsbild*, pp. 275–321. As in similar cases, Höhn's interpretation of this military writer, though interesting, is too abstract and fails to take account of the tactical realities. His extensive quotations from Decken's texts are marred by inaccuracies, which sometimes distort the original argument. See, for instance, p. 287, n. 1; p. 294, n. 3.

[127] The book, which has already been referred to in Chapter II, note 25, was dedicated to Scharnhorst, whose views on military institutions it almost wholly contradicted.

[128] Decken, pp. 281–282, 220.

[129] *Ibid.*, pp. 282–283. To be sure, Decken felt that too often the soldier's loyalty was insufficiently rewarded, a common complaint of the

The soldier's pride in his calling and in his unit was to counter the political and ideological strengths of his enemy. This was the traditional, timeless attitude of the military professional, echoing the belief of Frederick the Great, among others, that "all that can be done with a soldier is to give him *esprit de corps*, i.e., a deeper faith in his regiment than in all other troops on earth . . . and he must fear his officers more than the dangers to which he is exposed." [130] Decken added that professional pride could certainly be combined with enthusiasm for a great commander: "Love for their old Fritz, who led them like the God of War, enabled the Prussians to bear the indescribable burdens of the Seven Years' War." [131] He did not point out that this love was an emotion Frederick had attempted to arouse only in a few instances of supreme danger, that it played no part in the training and everyday life of the soldier, that it did not radiate steadily from a social or ethical principle. Unlike some other conservative minds —Mallet du Pan or Frederick Gentz, for instance—and unlike such military critics as Berenhorst, Decken denied that an involvement of a more fundamental nature than pride in one's commander and unit was required by the soldiers of France's neighbors to master the Revolutionary and Napoleonic challenge.

Yet, while Decken would not consider proposals that were incompatible with the principles of absolutism, he did recognize the need for change in less critical areas. Indeed, he concludes his book with a discussion on how reforms, once they have become inevitable, might be introduced with the greatest safety for state and army.[132] It is worthwhile to cite a few of his intelligent and balanced comments, whose only serious weakness is that their author could not recognize the full enormity of the dangers facing the old monarchies. "Any change in military institutions is subject to grave doubts," he begins.

---

times. See, for instance, the anonymous articles, "Gedanken eines Deutschen Offiziers über die jetzige Verfassung des Soldatenstandes . . . ," *Neues Militairisches Magazin*, ii, No. 6 (1802), and No. 7 (1803). Accompanying the usual pleas for higher pay and better service conditions for the professional soldier is an interesting protest against the increasing bureaucratization of modern armies.

[130] *Military Testament* of 1768, printed in Taysen, p. 205.

[131] Decken, p. 112.

[132] *Ibid.*, pp. 352–362.

. . . Nevertheless, conditions may develop that render a reform absolutely essential; conditions that cannot be avoided since the situation of peoples, like their physical and political circumstance, is subject to constant change. For this reason it is necessary to become acquainted with the difficulties that stand in the way of any improvement.

The first obstacle lies in recognizing the true nature of the defect. To deduce flaws in separate components from the irregular movement of the whole is easy enough; but it is very difficult to discover the seat of the illness, because generally this is not where the symptoms appear. Such a close relationship exists among the separate components of the military estate, which in turn is bound up so intimately with the state as a whole, that in order to achieve anything many wheels must be set in motion that often seem far removed from one another. It deserves notice in this connection that bias and partiality usually distort the accurate views of the person charged with such an investigation.

Furthermore, many defects are of the kind that cannot be cured. A state whose resources do not permit the maintenance of a powerful army will never, despite all efforts, be able to maintain one. . . . Other imperfections can be alleviated only little by little.

Another major impediment consists in the dislike of change felt by most men, and their resulting hatred of the individual who suggests change or is charged with bringing it about.

Much undoubtedly depends on the timing of the proposed reforms. Change encounters fewer obstacles shortly before the outbreak of a war that threatens the state with great danger. A danger sensed by all muffles the voice of intrigue, and the innovation appears as a smaller evil that must be accepted to avoid a greater. . . . Conditions are different when a reform is to be instituted in time of peace. Then the government tends to view the defect as insufficiently grave to subject itself willingly to a very painful operation. People are prepared to make some sacrifice to alleviate this or that abuse, but they cannot bring themselves to overturn and change everything.

Decken's speculations went so far as to touch on the problems of reforming an army that was in revolt against its ruler; but oddly enough his analysis did not penetrate to the condition that future events in Germany were to prove particularly favorable to decisive change: a society and its government recovering from a major military disaster.

So far as the infantry tactics of German armies were concerned, Decken conceded that they might in future come to approach more closely those of the French, if only from the Germans' desire to follow a new fashion; he permitted himself to add, "It cannot be predicted with certainty that this change will be a genuine improvement." [133] But the note of resignation evident in this passage, as elsewhere in his work, is rarely to be met with in the writings of those of his contemporaries who, broadly speaking, can be classed with him as defenders of the old order. At the end of the great debate, after the myriad of military and literary encounters of the 1790's and the first years of the new century, there was still no dearth of confident voices proclaiming the soundness of accustomed ways. Typical of these unreconstructed views is an attack on Bülow, which was printed during the months of Ulm and Austerlitz. The anonymous author stated bluntly that "open order tactics were created by the early events of the war with France; the latest developments should really make them vanish again." Only preconception and prejudice kept this fact from being universally acknowledged; nevertheless, the day of the skirmisher, who in the 1790's had "made so much noise and decided nothing," was past.[134]

Events of the following autumn were to prove that the prophecy of Bülow's unknown critic was as faulty as his analysis. Nevertheless certain German historians, writing in the Wilhelmine Era and later, tended to support their interpretations of the campaigns between 1792 and 1806 with such testimony, even at the risk of going against the views of men like Scharnhorst. At this point it may be useful to digress briefly and evaluate their writings, which have left a deep imprint on the literature. Most prominent among this group were the Prussian generals Freytag-Loringhoven and von der Goltz, and the future general Jany, whose historical studies published in the decade before Sarajevo were incorporated in his subsequent history of the Prussian army, which still remains the standard work on the subject. On the whole, these writers ignored or denied openly or by implication the reformers' analysis of the reasons for the French successes,

---

[133] *Ibid.*, p. 304.

[134] The untitled article from which these sentences are taken is the first of two printed as an appendix under the general heading "Anti-Bülow" in the second volume of Bülow's *Neue Taktik der Neuern*. The quotations are from pp. 181–183.

which had also found acceptance in the great civilian biographies —Pertz-Delbrück's *Gneisenau*, Lehmann's *Scharnhorst*, and Meinecke's *Boyen*, though, to be sure, sometimes with a misleading shift from the concrete to the idealistic. Freytag-Loringhoven wrote characteristically: "It was not the heroism of her armies that brought success to the French Republic, nor the so-called *levée en masse*. . . . Nor was the grouping of the French armies into divisions decisive . . . and of even less decisive importance were their *tirailleur* tactics. . . ." [135] In the view of these historians the real causes of the collapse of the old monarchies, and particularly of Prussia, were to be found not so much on the French as on the Allied side: their diplomatic errors and faulty strategy, and underlying these the frivolous, pacifist, and materialistic attitude which the Enlightenment had fostered among a smug populace. [136] Tactical deficiencies, if they existed at all, played only a very minor role. [137]

In some measure this was an understandable reaction to the puffed-up legend of the all-conquering, skirmishing volunteer, which contemporary Socialist writers perpetuated without regard to the very different conclusions reached by the detailed studies just then being published by the Historical Section of the French General Staff. Franz Mehring, for example, wrote of the "workers, peasants, mechanics, who fought for their own interests, who did not have to be driven into battle with the stick like mercenary armies. . . . They could move quickly, fight in open order, and give battle in any terrain. . . . The cancer of all mercenary armies, mass desertions, was entirely foreign to them." [138] This was pathetically doctrinaire, to be sure; but von der Goltz and Freytag-Loringhoven erred on the other side. With all their specialized knowledge they lacked objectivity; both put history to the service of the political and military disputes of their age. They

---

[135] *Krieg und Politik in der Neuzeit*, Berlin, 1911, p. 101. For a detailed criticism of Freytag-Loringhoven's interpretation of the Republican armies in his earlier work *Die Heerführung Napoleons*, see the article by G. L. [Fabry], "Soldats de la Révolution et de l'Empire," in *Revue d'Histoire*, XXXVII (1910), 237–258, 386–417.

[136] Freytag-Loringhoven, pp. 110–111; v. d. Goltz, pp. 495, 498–501, 507–509; Jany, *Preussische Armee*, III, 531–533.

[137] v. d. Goltz, p. 501.

[138] *Historische Aufsätze zur Preussisch-Deutschen Geschichte*, Berlin, 1946, p. 133.

were *Militärpolitiker*, who explicitly wrote their works as tracts for the times; political and social conservatism coupled with aggressive patriotism and a fervent belief in large, professional, standing armies could not but color their judgment of the revolutionary past.[139] Their arguments against the significance and importance of the French *tirailleur* were taken over and developed by Jany. They recur throughout his writings, but are most explicitly stated on pages 369–370 of the third volume of the *Geschichte der Preussischen Armee*, from which they may be summarized as follows:

(1) The tactics of the Prussian fusiliers were equal to the tactics of the French light infantry. (2) It was not true that fear of desertion made a more general use of *tirailleur* tactics impossible in the Prussian line infantry, since the French army suffered more from desertion than did the Prussian; besides, the Prussian light battalions contained as many supposedly unreliable foreigners as did the line battalions. (3) In any case, as long as smoothbore flintlocks were used, skirmish fire could never achieve decisive effects.

Jany's first argument is correct in a narrow sense: when the fusiliers were not heavily outnumbered, they could successfully oppose their superior steadiness to the greater dash and tactical flexibility of the French. But usually the *infanterie légère* and the *chasseurs* did outnumber them, and the French could employ most of their line units as skirmishers of sorts. Besides, the French generals used the *tirailleurs* aggressively and with imagination, while the fusiliers were kept on short leash by the formalism that continued to govern the Allied operations.

The second argument mixes up conditions before and after 1806. During Frederick the Great's reign, fear of desertion indeed helped restrict infantry tactics and operations in general. After Frederick's death, some easing of discipline and a limited opening up of tactics developed concurrently; but the new fusilier battalions were not true light troops. They still resembled line infantry. In combat they maneuvered either in close order or sent out at most one-fourth of their men as skirmishers, a proportion

---

[139] For Freytag-Loringhoven's and v. d. Goltz's motives in writing their historical studies, see respectively pp. iv–v and p. v of their cited works. Cf. also the favorable discussion of the contemporary import of v. d. Goltz's work by R. K. v. Caemmerer in a review in the *Forschungen zur Brandenburgischen und Preussischen Geschichte*, XVII (1904), 641.

that made disciplinary control a far easier matter than it would be in a French light infantry battalion, which might fight entirely *en débandade*. Certainly French desertion was heavy at times; but this is precisely one of the basic differences between the Revolutionary and the Allied forces which Jany ignores: tactical, administrative, and disciplinary irregularities, which would have crippled such an army as the Prussian or the Hanoverian, could be borne by the French.

Jany's third and most important point is equally misleading. True, skirmish fire alone was generally not decisive, but then it was rarely used by itself. In battle the primary task of the skirmishers was to enable the massed infantry to maneuver and attack. They did this by fixing and outflanking the opponent, by softening him for the assault, for which purpose artillery preparation alone was usually not sufficient, and by causing the enemy line to waste its musket fire, which artillery could never make them do. The *tirailleurs* opened the battle, masked the movement of the close formations, and supplied a measure of firepower to the column, which in the nature of things had little of its own. Indeed, without the *tirailleur*, columns in battle would have required far heavier artillery support than tended to be available. Since skirmish lines were intended to be backed up by close formations, Jany's argument that the Napoleonic skirmisher with his inaccurate musket could not be decisive in battle loses its significance.

It may be added parenthetically that the inferior Prussian musket did not prevent the Prussians from developing their open order tactics after Jena. Between 1812 and 1815 the Prussian line infantry frequently fought with one-third or more of its men deployed as skirmishers—evidently their weapons were not deemed so poor as to render this manner of fighting ineffective. The men however were not equipped with rifles, but with muskets either identical with or similar to those used during the 1790's and in the Jena campaign. At the time of mobilization in 1813 only 55,000 muskets of the new Prussian model were available, and most of the infantry had to be equipped with a conglomeration of foreign and obsolete weapons, which included sizable contingents of the old Frederician musket. In other words, the new tactics were carried out with the old weapons.[140]

[140] According to a table compiled by the Ministry of War, 22 July 1810, 14 infantry formations were equipped with the old Prussian mus-

A later generation of German military historians reasserted the importance of the French *tirailleur*, though without openly refuting Jany's authority. Two prominent National Socialist specialists in military history, Paul Schmitthenner and Reinhold Höhn, took the lead in rediscovering the skirmisher as a decisive force in the successes of the Republic—now however in combination with the factor of organized enthusiasm.[141] Professor Höhn even termed enthusiasm "the propelling motor of *tirailleur* fighting."[142] Intellectuals supporting the Third Reich knew better than members of the Imperial General Staff how powerfully a revolutionary regime could stir the masses. But these historians found it unnecessary to analyze the content of the emotion they valued so highly. In their hands enthusiasm became simply an absolute component of the Republican armies, and one shared equally by all its members—"the soldiers of the *ancien régime*, the enthusiastic volunteers of 1791, the mediocre drafts of 1792, and the rabble of 1793."[143] Their evaluation—at once mechanistic and exaggerated—spared them the trouble of inquiring into the ideas and feelings that moved the troops and the tactics that were actually employed. As a result, their interpretations proved as false as Mehring's. What insights they presented were unhistorical and schematic, formulated, as one courageous critic wrote at the time, "under the influence of the authoritarian Führer-state that our age has created."[144]

• 5 •

Since the death of Frederick the Great the administrative structure of the Prussian army had been somewhat elaborated, without

---

ket, eight with the new, one each with French, English, and Swedish muskets respectively, and three with both English and old Prussian muskets. The table is printed in Kling, III, 150. See also the analysis in Eckardt and Morawietz, pp. 48–54. Table 1 of Appendix 5 of the present work compares the effectiveness of these various muskets. It should be noted that the standard musket of 1782, when provided with an angled butt that made aiming possible, proved very nearly as accurate as the "New Prussian" musket of 1809.

[141] See Schmitthenner's *Politik und Kriegführung in der neueren Geschichte*, Hamburg, 1937, p. 191; and his *Das deutsche Soldatentum*, Cologne, 1938, p. 42.

[142] Höhn, *Revolution—Heer—Kriegsbild*, p. 131.

[143] The description is Reinhard's in his biography of Carnot, II, 91.

[144] F. Hartung in a review of Schmitthenner's *Politik und Kriegführung* in the *Historische Zeitschrift*, CLVIII (1938), 587.

in any sense approaching the complex divisions of responsibility that dominated the services in England, Austria, or indeed in the United States. On the contrary, the most serious flaw of the Prussian system lay in its simplicity. The principle that the monarch himself supervised every aspect of military organization was retained; subordinate authorities were seen as extensions of the King's will, not as organs possessing the power to initiate and implement on their own. In reality, the creation by Frederick of such intermediaries as the Inspectors-General showed that the concept of direct royal control could no longer be fully applied. This was again recognized by the establishment, in 1787, of the *Oberkriegskollegium*, a committee formed of the heads of various agencies and boards dealing with such matters as supply, personnel, mobilization, veteran affairs, as well as with the administration of the infantry, cavalry, artillery, and engineers. Not all service bodies were represented. Such agencies as the General War Fund continued in charge of the civil bureaucracy; other organizations retained a more or less independent position—notably, the General Staff, at that time still in its infancy. Nevertheless, the *Oberkriegskollegium* brought together most of the important strands of the service, and some officers expressed the hope that it would come to assume the functions of a central ministry of war. From its inception, however, the council's usefulness was compromised by inserting between it and the monarch a group of royal adjutants, the *Generaladjutantur*, headed by the Expediting Adjutant General, who reported to the King on all military matters, including the deliberations of the *Oberkriegskollegium*. This latter body consequently declined to the status of a secretariat, while the Expediting Adjutant General, through his direct access to the King and his opportunity to advocate and censor, gained vast influence, without himself possessing executive power and responsibility. Strengthened by the assistance of personal agents the King seemed again able to cope with the multitude of service problems, and the creation of true departmental authority was once more averted.[145]

In such a system everything depended on the ability of the man

---

[145] Clausewitz, *Nachrichten*, pp. 426–429, devotes some biting paragraphs to the higher military administration. The most complete modern analysis is Jany's, *Preussische Armee*, iii, 150–158, 338–341, 398–413. See also the excellent brief discussion in G. A. Craig, *The Politics of the Prussian Army, 1640–1945*, Oxford, 1955, pp. 29–30.

at the apex of the hierarchy and of his closest collaborators. Until the Treaty of Tilsit in 1807 the position of Expediting Adjutant General was filled by a succession of competent soldiers, who, if they were not themselves revolutionary innovators, could recognize inefficiency and often enough transmitted proposals for important reforms to their royal masters. Nor was Frederick William II without anxieties for the future; but after the early years of his reign he no longer applied the necessary sustained energy to the army's affairs. Frederick William III was perhaps more intensely interested in the army than his father had been—certainly so with the minutiae of uniforms and equipment—but here, as everywhere in life, his pessimistic character, too full, in Clausewitz's phrase "of that Nordic, cold sense of doubt," abhorred great innovations.[146] Had his senior commanders urged him in that direction, he might well have acquiesced; but such initiative could not be expected of Frederician veterans, and he was not the man to provide the lead for which some were secretly hoping.

The inadequacies of the state's military institutions in a rapidly changing Europe were, however, too obvious to ignore. Another method of meeting the new problems while still reserving the utmost degree of control to the monarch was the establishment of special committees, outside the regular military hierarchy, which reported directly to the King. The most important of these bodies, the *Immediat-Militär-Organisationskommission*, was formed in 1795, initially to direct the expansion of the army made possible by the newly acquired Polish territories, but subsequently "to investigate and ameliorate the defects that had appeared in military affairs."[147] The commission, made up of Field Marshal von Möllendorff, two junior generals, and a staff officer from the *Oberkriegskollegium*, became in effect the administrative head of the army, subject only to the King. During the ten years of its

---

[146] Clausewitz, *Nachrichten*, p. 422.

[147] Hintze, *Die Hohenzollern und ihr Werk*, p. 425. Shanahan is guilty of a mistranslation in rendering the commission's name as "Emergency Commission for Military Organization," *op. cit.*, pp. 73, 74, 76, 77, etc. The term "Immediat" in the commission's name signified its right of direct communication with the King, unscreened by other officials or boards. During the Reform Era, a government body might possibly have applied the term "emergency" to itself; its use before 1806 is unthinkable.

existence it was responsible for numerous changes: the conscription districts were reapportioned, the number of foreigners in the ranks was reduced, the supply system was modernized, the entire administration of the army was simplified by reducing the number of units while increasing their individual strength. In improving equipment and tactics the commission also effected useful developments without ever instituting a basic change. An early accomplishment in this area was the issue of the first Prussian manual dealing exclusively with small-arms fire, which was distributed to the army on 12 December 1795. The manual was not intended for the entire infantry, but solely for the battalion *Schützen*, who were to be taught to fire not only standing up, as did grenadiers and musketeers, but prone and kneeling as well, in which latter position they rested the rifle on a forked stick supplied for this purpose.[148] Here again, as so often during this period, an advance towards more modern methods of fighting was immediately compromised by some antiquated appendage. In 1796 the *Jäger* received their first standard rifle, the *alte Corps-Büchse*—a good though heavy weapon on which a straight cutlass could be fixed—while the *Schützen* were reequipped with an improved issue of their *Schützengewehr*.[149]

These cautious advances were not accelerated in the new reign. Although Frederick William III objected to certain extreme follies of the parade-ground, such as loosening the screws of the musket-butts so that the manual of arms could be executed with more martial noise, he found little to criticize in his troops' complex linear evolutions and rapid, unaimed volleys.[150] His concept

[148] Eckardt and Morawietz, p. 83.

[149] *Ibid.*, p. 80; Jany, *Preussische Armee*, III, 343.

[150] The nature of Frederick William's tactical ideas has been in some dispute. His most enthusiastic biographer, General A. v. Janson, claims for him a sensible and critical attitude, handicapped only by lack of experience and poor advisors. *König Friedrich Wilhelm III. in der Schlacht*, Berlin, 1907, pp. 39–41. Similar views are expressed in F. Thimme's panegyrical studies in the *Forschungen zur Brandenburgischen und Preussischen Geschichte*. Among the King's very numerous critics, Clausewitz deserves special mention, as does the military historian O. v. d. Osten-Sacken, who writes, "That such a complete negative attitude towards innovations in infantry tactics was maintained in Prussia was very largely due to the King." *Preussens Heer von seinen Anfängen bis zur Gegenwart*, Berlin, 1911, I, 357. The King's cabinet orders and correspondence seem to me to bear out fully the latter interpretation.

of infantry fighting at that time is illustrated by the provisional infantry instructions of 1798, which almost certainly were his own work.[151] They contain two provisions to speed up evolutions. Section V orders that deployment in action and the bayonet attack should no longer be executed at the ordinary slow cadence of 75 steps a minute, but in quicktime of 108 steps a minute, while Section X alters the fusiliers' method of deploying into the skirmish line. According to the *Reglement* of 1788 this had been formed by the two wing sections of the battalion, which was a slow procedure and tended to weaken the battalion's flanks. Henceforth, two squads of each company in the battalion line were to provide the skirmishers. The number of skirmishers remained unchanged, but there was some gain in mobility. Section X concludes with words that reflect the experience gained in France: "The application of evolutions for true maneuvering according to the terrain belongs to the realm of ideas, and in its great variety is left solely to the understanding and genius of each particular commander." [152]

Otherwise the manual remains entirely in the bondage of linear tactics, though some of its glosses would never have appeared in Frederick the Great's self-reliant, masterful texts. A note of decadence is clearly apparent in the famous statement in the introduction: "Uniformity is the first beauty of the soldier"—and perhaps even more so in the later sentence, "I don't understand why the most beautiful troops should not also be the best."

The *Reglement* was never generally adopted, and in the last years of the old monarchy the army was flooded with drill manuals, as well as "private" regulations, written by a regimental commander or a member of his staff, and designed for one particular unit, or *Inspection*.[153] Only a few of these local developments gained wider acceptance. In the Lower Silesian *Inspection* between 1803 and 1804 the number of sharpshooters in each light infantry battalion was raised from 40 to 88, or to somewhat over

---

[151] Jähns, III, 2551; v. d. Osten-Sacken, I, 357.

[152] Jähns, III, 2553.

[153] C. Jany, *Die Gefechtsausbildung der Preussischen Infanterie von 1806, Urkundliche Beiträge und Forschungen*, v, Berlin, 1903, 18. An example of the private manuals: as a fusilier lieutenant, the later General v. Schmidt wrote an instruction for the riflemen of his battalion which was copied by other officers, and still used in 1807. Schmidt, II, 21–22.

10 per cent of total strength. The following year the Guards adopted this change, which was extended to all fusilier battalions in the army by a Cabinet Order of 21 July 1806—too near the outbreak of war to be implemented in more than two or three units. Of greater significance could have been the new instructions issued by Prince Hohenlohe on 30 March 1803 to all infantry regiments of the Lower Silesian *Inspection*, in which, influenced by the theories of his protégé Bülow and by Scharnhorst's more concrete suggestions, he ordered that the third rank of all infantry formations be trained to fight in open as well as in close order.[154]

The section "On the Use of the Third Rank as Tirailleurs" begins with the general statement:

Often in war there are situations when it becomes necessary or advantageous to attack the enemy with skirmishers, or, if one is attacked in this manner . . . to defend oneself in the same way. Though this type of infantry fighting properly concerns only the light infantry and the *Schützen* of the line, experience teaches that light infantry is not always present where needed, and that the number of *Schützen* isn't sufficient to use this method in attack or defense. It might therefore be beneficial for the third rank of the line infantry to be employed for this purpose. . . .[155]

The manner of forming the skirmish group is spelled out in detail. After the men of the third rank have run around the flanks of the two closed ranks, the first skirmisher "runs 27 steps, or as far as he is told to, and stops. No. 2 runs three steps past him on the left, and also stops. No. 3 stops level with No. 1 about 1½ steps away . . . ," and so on, until the thirty-six or more men are positioned alternately in two parallel lines. A one-sentence paragraph prescribes the method of firing—each man alternating with his neighbor, a technique that had been adopted by the

---

[154] One of the very rare printed copies of this manual is contained in the personal collection of Dr. Hans Bleckwenn, Münster, who kindly made it available to me. Jany's excerpts of the passages on skirmishing, *Gefechtsausbildung*, pp. 89–90, agree in the main with the printed text, which is however rather more prescriptive in such matters as distance and interval between men.

[155] [Hohenlohe], *Reglement für die Niederschlesische Inspection*, Breslau, 1803, p. 214. The following references are to pp. 215–218 of the manual.

Jäger some years previously. Then follow complicated rules for advancing and withdrawing the skirmishers, and for their rapid reassembly into a closed third rank.

Hohenlohe's experiment had no practical results. Other commanding generals refused to follow his recommendation that a third of the line become at least acquainted with open order tactics; three years later at Jena even his own regiments failed to send out skirmish screens, which might have served them better against French musketry than their immobile, serried ranks.[156] The episode was characteristic of nearly all Prussian attempts at reform before 1806: they were belated, partial, and ineffective. Only in a few cases were the new demands of war understood and met. The reorganization of the General Staff in 1803 moved this body some way from map-making and the working out of march- and supply-routes towards strategic and operational planning, and gave it the structure with which it successfully functioned during the final campaigns against Napoleon. Another exception proved to be the reform of the *Feldjäger* regiment by Yorck.

After its return from the French campaigns, the regiment had fallen on evil days. Attempts were made—whether by their commanding officer or by higher authority cannot now be established —to have the *Jäger* conform more nearly to the prevailing standards of line drill and discipline. As a result, the *Jäger* had lost some of their knack for individual fighting without gaining much proficiency in close order tactics. An absurdly ragged march-past of the regiment during the great autumn review in 1799 may have been the incident that finally brought about the transfer of its commander.[157] When Yorck took over the regiment he found a body of dissatisfied, undisciplined men, led by officers whose concepts of their duties hovered doubtfully between the demands of the line and of the light service. These uncertainties were

[156] Shanahan, p. 69, states that the use of the third rank for open tactics "was eventually sanctioned by a royal order of October 5, 1805." This order specifies that the third rank be used as a reserve or extension of the linear formations; it does not mention open order or skirmishing. See the discussion of the order in Jany, *Gefechtsausbildung*, p. 91; and *Preussische Armee*, III, 495.

[157] Droysen, I, 103. For the condition of the regiment before Yorck assumed command, see also Priesdorff, No. 1120.

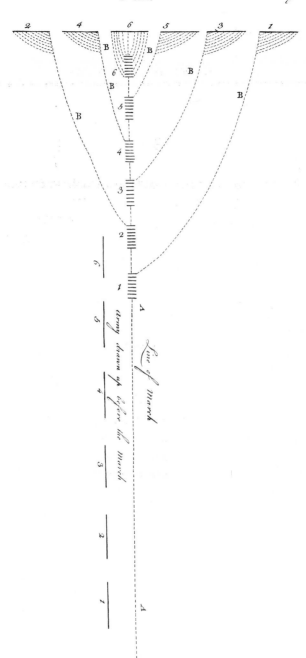

Infantry deploying from a marching column into the line of battle.
From C. Dalrymple, *A Military Essay*, London, 1761, plate 6

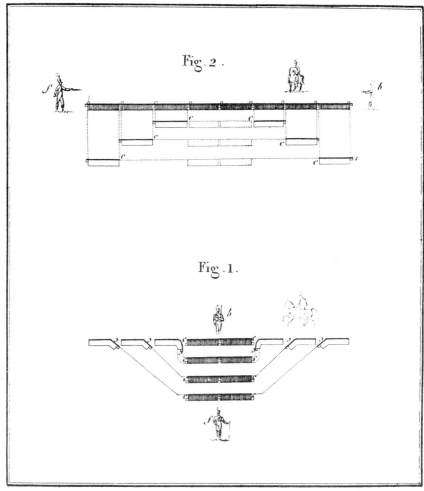

Figure 1. A battalion drawn up in three ranks deploys into an attack column

Figure 2. The attack column returns to the linear formation

From *Règlement concernant l'exercise et les manoeuvres de l'infanterie du premier aout 1791*, Paris, 1816, plate 26

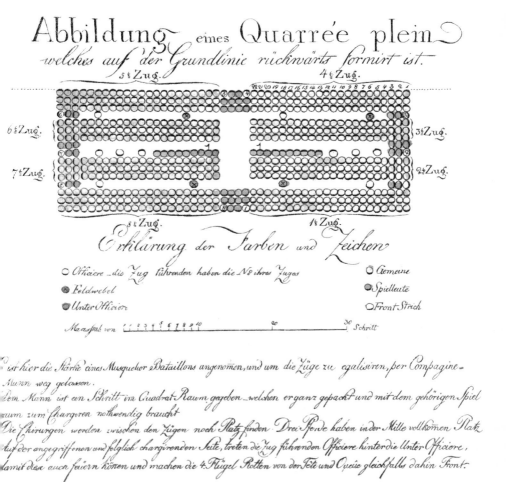

A battalion square. With some minor changes, the formation corresponds to the attack column. From *Exerzir-Reglement für die Infanterie der Königlich Preussischen Armee*, Berlin, 1812, plate 1

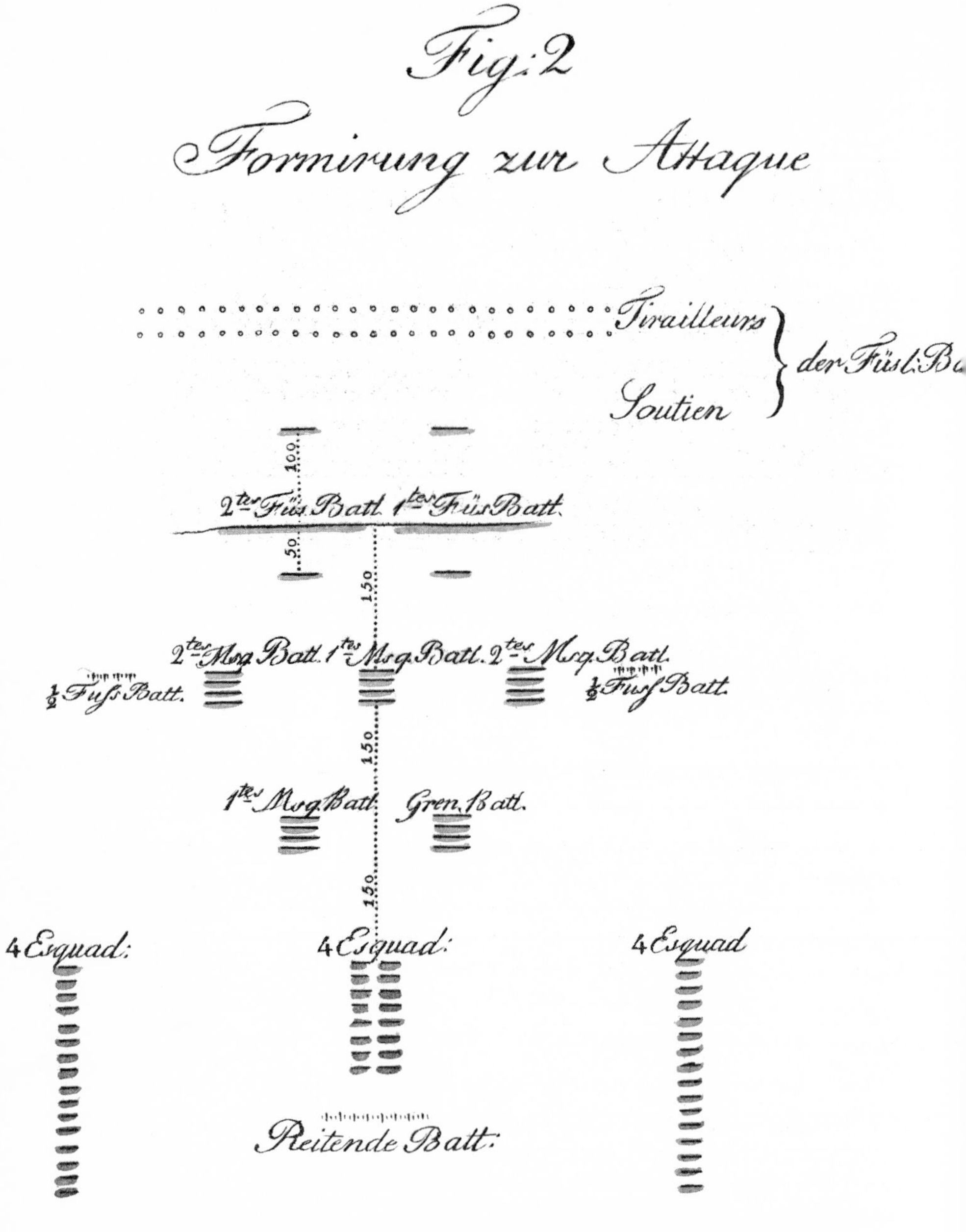

Fig. 2

Formirung zur Attaque

Tirailleurs ⎱
               ⎰ der Füsl. B..
Soutien ⎱
         ⎰

100.

2ᵗᵉˢ Füs Batl. 1ᵗᵉˢ Füs Batl.

50.

150.

½ Fufs Batl.   2ᵗᵉˢ Msg Batl. 1ᵗᵉˢ Msg Batl. 2ᵗᵉˢ Msg Batl.   ½ Fufs Batl.

150.

1ᵗᵉˢ Msg Batl.   Gren. Batl.

150.

4 Esquad: 4 Esquad: 4 Esquad

Reitende Batt:

Attack formation of a Prussian brigade. The *tirailleurs* of the fusilier battalions are at the head, supported by two sections of fusiliers in close order, which are followed by the main body of the fusiliers. Behind them comes the heavy infantry in five columns, with two sections of field artillery on the flanks. Cavalry and a battery of horse artillery bring up the rear. From *Exerzir-Reglement für die Infanterie der Königlich Preussischen Armee*, Berlin, 1812, plate 2

resolved early in 1800, when the new commander issued the first field instructions written especially for the Prussian *Jäger*. In their exploitation of open order and its integration with close formations, the brief directives went far beyond anything that had yet been seen in the army.[158]

Two methods of developing skirmish lines were authorized. As in the fusilier drill, the *Jäger* could deploy from the closed linear formation, though the number of skirmishers was not limited to one-fourth or one-third of the unit. If the commander saw fit, he could open up the whole regiment. However, the instructions preferred a second method of deployment. It should be the "basic rule" of open order, Yorck wrote, to deploy from columns of either company or battalion size. This evolution, by now basic practice in the French army, was new to Prussia. Its advantage lay not only in the column's far greater maneuverability, but in the fact that columns could coordinate their movement and fire with the actions of their skirmishers much more effectively than could the line. In training his men to use the column as a fighting formation, a mobile base for their individual efforts, Yorck introduced the Prussian infantry to a tactical combination that in the Wars of Liberation was to become its standard method of attack.

That the *Jäger* actually practiced fighting in attack columns is attested to by an eyewitness. A French *émigré* in the Prussian service, Count de la Roche-Aymon, writes that he observed "in 1805 at the Potsdam maneuvers numerous military men go into raptures over the marching cadence of the Jäger, and admire the precision with which these *chasseurs* formed their attack columns and their defensive squares. . . ." [159] This contemporary reference to attack columns in the old army is corroborated by Scharnhorst, who in his unpublished essay *On Infantry Tactics* reports that such formations were already seen on maneuvers in 1804, although he does not mention the unit or units involved.[160] It is

---

[158] The instructions, which were never printed, were distributed in manuscript to officers of the regiment. Extracts are printed in Gumtau, ɪ, 147–149.

[159] C. de la Roche-Aymon, *Des Troupes légères*, Paris, 1817, p. 72. Jähns, ɪɪɪ, 2719–2720, confuses Roche-Aymon with his father, who had published an *Essai sur la petite guerre* in 1770.

[160] Paragraph 4 of the essay in Appendix 1.

certain that the General Staff history of the Prussian army is mistaken in declaring that attack columns were not known in the service until after the defeats of Jena and Auerstedt.[161] The earliest appearance of attack columns in Prussian drill occurred not in the winter of 1806, but dates at least from Yorck's field instructions for the *Jäger* of 1800, and not defeat by Napoleon but the experience of the 1790's led to its introduction. Although Yorck's innovation bore no immediate fruit beyond his regiment, it was the most significant tactical advance in the Prussian army between the Seven Years' War and 1806.

The *Jäger* instructions called speed of execution "the first necessity," far more important than precision in drill: "It is a principal characteristic of the light service, and most particularly of the *Jäger* corps, to deploy with the greatest possible speed, to occupy ground at a moment's notice, so to speak." The men were always to act in pairs, and their fire had to be accurate.

The rifle [Yorck wrote] was not made for drill, and drilling is not the *Jäger*'s purpose. . . . In any eventuality it is an irrevocable basic rule that the *Jäger* never hurries his fire, but always shoots with effect. It is an equally irrevocable rule that two *Jäger* always defend one another, that is, always act in groups of two—front and rear man. These two *Jäger* must at all times consider themselves as one body; one defends the other, so that when one man has fired and therefore is defenseless, the other has loaded and is capable of defensive action. This rule must be an unbreakable law to every *Jäger*, since his honor and life depend on it.

These ideas were turned into reality by a painstaking training program that included practical field-exercises, something almost unknown to the army. Gumtau, whose account is based on regimental tradition as well as on the recollections of an officer who commanded a *Jäger* company at the time, writes that at first rigorous concepts of the service caused Yorck to be unpopular with most of the men.[162] The regiment possessed an unusual

---

[161] "Die in der Instruktion vom 23 November 1806 bereits empfohlene, bis dahin in der preussischen Armee unbekannte Kolonnenformation für den Angriff wurde in der Instruktion vom 17 Juli 1809 zum erstenmal amtlich vorgeschrieben. . . ." *Das Preussische Heer der Befreiungskriege*, I, *Das Preussische Heer im Jahre 1812*, p. 247.

[162] Gumtau, I, 142, 167.

tradition of independence: many of the *Jäger* still felt themselves to be members of a universal brotherhood of foresters, with their own skills, laws, and privileges. Not without encountering much passive resistance, Yorck broke down these remnants of guild mentality, and gradually succeeded in making the regiment an efficient military force while leaving intact the men's self-esteem. His willingness to foster an acceptable kind of individuality is illustrated by an incident in the early months of his appointment. His predecessor had ordered the *Jäger* to carry their rifles vertically, in the usual infantry manner, which the men resented not only because the angled rifle-butt made the vertical position awkward and tiring, but because the innovation seemed to reduce their status to that of the common musketeer. On 15 May 1800, the King approved Yorck's suggestion that the *Jäger* shoulder their rifles—a method that was both more practical and heretofore had been a special mark of distinction for the lance-corporals of the line.[163]

Yorck had never favored the stick, use of which in any case ran against *Jäger* traditions, and he had little or no recourse to it during his years of command. The history of the Guards *Jäger* battalion prints one of his orders, which declares that a soldier who had stolen a small sum of money, an offense ordinarily punished by running the gauntlet from six to twenty times, was simply to be deprived of his right to serve with the regiment.[164] If the *Jäger* was a native, and thus eligible for a post in the forestry service, the state was protected from a dishonest servant; but whether native or foreign, expulsion rather than corporal punishment safeguarded the regiment's pride and *esprit de corps*.

In his treatment of the private soldier Yorck shared with such men as Boyen and Gneisenau the most advanced attitude towards discipline then to be met with in the army. During the last years of the old monarchy the persuasion that all men were rational beings, deserving education and dignified treatment, was begin-

---

[163] Priesdorff, No. 1120.

[164] Rentzell, p. 31. See also Gumtau, I, 152–153. Very occasionally a *Jäger* received blows with the flat of the blade, but this seems to have called for a report to the King. For one such case, see the letter of J. R. v. Bischoffwerder to Frederick William II of 19 November 1793, in *J. A. Stargardt—Auktionskatalog*, No. 567 (May 1964), p. 171.

ning to mitigate the former total disregard of the private soldier. Once Frederick had written: "The troops' value lies exclusively in that of the officers: a good colonel, a good battalion." [165] Now this principle no longer held undisputed sway; little by little the individual was emerging from the purely mechanical role into which he had been forced half a century before. If he was still to fight as an unthinking member of a unified geometric formation, it was at least no longer universally accepted that only the stick could make him do so. In the afterglow of the Enlightenment the soldier's relation to his task and the officer's relation to his men seemed social questions, and for these the answer was not blind force but education. Officially—as in the Articles of War of 1797—the old concept of discipline was retained in all its harshness; but beatings on the drill-field were growing rarer, and somewhat greater attention was being paid to the soldier as a human being, to his life after duty-hours, and to his family. It was even beginning to be possible to think of him as a person of honor.

The mystical, knightly attributes of this quality never combined easily with the tenets of the Age of Reason, and its defenders had sometimes felt obliged to go to very great lengths to explain their aristocratic preconceptions in rationally acceptable terms. Frederick, for example, had declared that a commoner lacked honor because, unlike the nobleman's, his behavior was not shaped by the permanent threat of family ostracism.[166] And what the son of middle-class parents lacked was even more foreign to a day laborer or mercenary. To be sure, if the Articles of War and the oath of allegiance now appealed to the ethical standards of the common soldier, this did not attribute to him honor in the elevated, quasi-feudal sense. The terms were used more broadly to imply reliability, courage, and self-respect. To believe with Boyen that soldiers were dishonored by serving in the ranks with criminals, or to address them directly as men of honor, as Yorck did in his instructions, remained exceptional. Tactics and discipline, however, affected each other, and for an officer who experimented with flexibility to consider his subordinates as whipping boys was inadvisable, if not entirely impossible.

[165] "Règles de ce qu'on exige d'un bon commandeur," *Oeuvres*, XXIX, 58.

[166] "Mémoires depuis la paix de Hubertsbourg," *Oeuvres*, VI, 95.

Later Yorck said that he didn't train his *Jäger* "like wild animals to music," but as thinking men and independent soldiers.[167]

This attitude gradually won him confidence and loyalty. His regiment remained one of the few in the army that did not suffer from desertion, and it was to belong to the small group of units which survived the disintegration after Jena in reasonable order.[168] Its performance on maneuvers early impressed a few unprejudiced observers who, as one of them wrote, were struck by its "rationality and quality . . . which contrasted to a remarkable extent with the universal rigidity of the other infantry units." [169] Nor was official recognition withheld. In 1803, at the relatively early age of forty-nine, Yorck was promoted colonel; he became a member of the commission on rifle and musket design; as a reward for the regiment's improved showing on maneuvers the King presented him with the revenues of two small domains. In 1805, Yorck was appointed colonel-in-chief of the regiment, a dignity that brought him further financial benefits. A career that twenty years before had seemed ruined was now clearly destined to penetrate the upper reaches of rank and influence.

Yorck's rise had been much helped by his appointment to a unique regiment, which offered him both superior human material and an unusually free hand in their training. More than any others in the Prussian army, the *Jäger* were the men to pioneer flexible and individualistic modes of fighting; and since they were expected to differ from regular infantry, their innovations were not felt as threats to the parade-ground tacticians. An able officer in command of this elite could institute great changes in his area of responsibility, though the very factors that created the opportunity also precluded the results from achieving wider acceptance. The army leadership appears to have wished for no more than having the regiment brought back to an acceptable standard of discipline and performance. Yorck might have been content with perfecting the skill of the *Jäger* in the little war. Instead, during

---

[167] Priesdorff, No. 1120. Compare the admiring comment on Yorck's humaneness in Boyen's *Erinnerungen*, I, 480.

[168] *Mittheilungen aus dem Archiv des Königlichen Kriegsministeriums*, Berlin, 1895, III, 142.

[169] *Lebenserinnerungen des Generalleutnants Karl von Wedel*, ed. C. Troeger, Berlin, 1911, I, 14.

the six years in which he trained the regiment and developed his own concepts, he turned them from scouts and snipers into a force that could fulfill many of the tasks of line infantry as well. On individual fighters he imposed the discipline, cohesion, and maneuverability of the most advanced close order, just as after 1806 he was to open up the rigidity of the line by imposing on it some of the flexibility and initiative inherent in open formations. Both were shifts towards a common center of greater versatility, and both came from the recognition that the specialities of the little war of the *ancien régime* had become indispensable features on the nineteenth-century battlefield.

CHAPTER IV

Defeat and Reorganization

THE Prussian army went to war in 1806 with an invincible ponderousness of spirit and body. Despite the better knowledge of many of its leaders, the army was divided in the field rather than concentrated, its administration and logistics remained inefficient; a purely intellectual recognition of the need for speed and decision could not be translated into action. Even Yorck, the commander of Prussia's most mobile regiment, began the campaign encumbered with three trunks, two crates, two baskets, two bedrolls, a bedstead with mattress and bedding, and dozens of other items. A few weeks later these paraphernalia had vanished in the disintegration following Jena and Auerstedt.[1]

The campaign was more than half lost before the opening shot. In 1805 Prussia had remained aloof from the Third Coalition until the chance for concerted action was past, and by her indecision had helped make Austerlitz possible. The rearrangement of Germany's political map that now ensued worked increasingly to her disadvantage. Except for Russia's covert support and her alliance with Saxony, Prussia was politically isolated by the summer of 1806, and French pressure on her sovereignty had become

[1] See the list published in *Mittheilungen aus dem Archiv des Königlichen Kriegsministeriums*, III, 139–141. The two following paragraphs are based on my chapter "Jena" in *Great Military Battles*, ed. C. Falls, London–New York, 1964. Among the very extensive literature on the war of 1806–1807, the most important military studies are the already cited works by Clausewitz and E. v. Höpfner; O. v. Lettow-Vorbeck, *Der Krieg von 1806 und 1807*, 4 vols., Berlin, 1891–1896; A. v. Schlieffen, "1806," and "Jena," in *Gesammelte Schriften*, II, Berlin, 1913; P. J. Foucart, *Campagne de Prusse (1806), Jéna*, Paris, 1887, and *Campagne de Prusse (1806), Prenzlow-Lübeck*, Paris, 1890; P. Bressonnet, *Etudes tactiques sur la campagne de 1806*, Paris, 1909; H. Beseler, "Blüchers Zug nach Lübeck, 1806," *Militär-Wochenblatt* (1892), Supplement 2; and ch. 2 in *Rückzug und Verfolgung, Beriträge zur Militär- und Kriegsgeschichte*, I, published by the Militärgeschichtliche Forschungsamt, Stuttgart, 1960.

intense. It would have been wise to postpone an open break until Russian troops could again operate beyond the Vistula, but fear of the consequences of further passivity induced Frederick William to mobilize. French grand strategy now entered its military phase. Utilizing the bases in southern Germany that were among the prizes of last year's victory, Napoleon moved on Prussia from the south, threatening to separate his opponent's main forces from Berlin and from possible Russian assistance; by the time the exposed Prussians in central Germany sensed the danger and began a slow withdrawal north, their strategic defeat had become inevitable. Effective performance on the battlefield might still have minimized the loss and enabled the beaten armies to fight again; but lack of unified control, poor coordination between the different arms of the service, and the troops' inflexible methods of movement and fire led to disaster.

The Prussian order of battle had divided Yorck's 2,000 *Jäger* among four armies. One company was attached to the observation corps in Westphalia. Another, together with two fusilier battalions, constituted the light infantry of the Prussian advance guard commanded by Prince Louis Ferdinand, which was attacked on the morning of 10 October by a division of Lannes' 5th corps. Under cover of an extensive skirmish engagement the Prussian positions were enveloped. The *Jäger* retreated with the beaten advance guard to join the other five *Jäger* companies of Prince Hohenlohe's and General Rüchel's forces north of Jena. There on 14 October Hohenlohe's 43,000 men were totally defeated by Napoleon, who gradually concentrated 80,000 men against them. The sharp but limited advances and rapid volleys of the Prussians caused casualties but never posed a serious threat. In the first hours of battle, *tirailleur* tactics contributed to the French success by confusing and depleting the Prussian lines. "The impossibility of countering the devastating fire of the enemy *tirailleurs*, robbed the men of their composure." [2] In the early

---

[2] Report of the Grenadier Battalion Lecoq, in A. v. Montbé, *Die Chursächsischen Truppen im Feldzuge 1806–1807*, Dresden, 1860, ii, 16. Among the numerous eyewitness accounts that mention the effectiveness of the French *tirailleurs* during the campaign, the following are of particular interest: the memorandum of the *Jäger* lieutenant A. v. Seydlitz, in "Aus den Akten der Militär-Reorganisationskommission von 1808," ed. F. Meinecke, *Forschungen zur Brandenburgischen und Preussischen Ge-*

afternoon a general advance of thick skirmish swarms and battalions in line, followed by columns and supported at close range by artillery, decided the issue. On the same day, near Auerstedt 15 miles to the north, the main Prussian army was turned back in its attempt to regain its lines of communication. The Prussians, who proved unable to exploit their superior strength, withdrew in fair order; but having extricated himself, Frederick William panicked and instead of heading north he turned southwest to rejoin Hohenlohe. He was still unaware of the disaster at Jena, but under the best of circumstances this move would have been fatal since it took the army away from Berlin, deep into the French embrace. When word arrived of Hohenlohe's defeat during the night, the direction of the retreat was changed twice, and by morning the exhausted and scattered army had ceased to exist as a fighting force.

Yorck had not been involved in the battles. On 5 October he and four companies of his regiment left the main army with a corps commanded by the Duke of Saxe-Weimar, with the mission of raiding the French lines of communication. In circumstances that above all demanded the concentration of force their expedition was ill-advised; but the corps was not recalled until the 11th, and was still two days' march from the main army when it learned of the double defeat. The news caused the Duke to withdraw to the northeast, in a wide curve around the beaten armies and their pursuers, and he succeeded in gaining the Elbe without loss of men or order. The corps crossed the river on the 26th, covered against French attacks by Yorck, who in the skirmish of Altenzaun won the first Prussian victory of the campaign.[3] Three days later, on Napoleon's ultimatum that he would otherwise lose his throne, the Duke left the army and returned to Weimar, which

---

schichte, v (1892), 487–495, especially p. 491; the report of Major F. A. L. v. d. Marwitz in [Jany], *1806: Das Preussische Offizierkorps*, Berlin, 1906, pp. 151–181, especially p. 169; and the reports printed in Jany, *Gefechtsausbildung*, pp. 123–132.

[3] For decades Altenzaun, which was decided by open order and aimed fire, was referred to in the Prussian army as a model of modern infantry combat. Eyewitness reports of the fighting during the retreat are printed in Gumtau, I, 162–170; and Rentzell, pp. 39–44. Additional information can be found in the reports of Blücher, the Duke of Saxe-Weimar, and Yorck, printed in G. Lehmann, *Die Ritter des Ordens pour le mérite*, Berlin, 1913, I, entry for Yorck.

had been occupied by the French since the 14th. On 30 October the command was assumed by Blücher, who had extricated another small corps from the disaster. The combined Prussians now numbered some 22,000 men; Yorck commanded a rear guard of three fusilier battalions and the *Jäger*, of whom there were again six companies.

Blücher and his temporary chief of staff, Scharnhorst, set themselves two tasks: to draw away as many units as possible from the French advance on Mecklenburg and East Prussia, and to save their own force, if necessary by entering neutral territory. On 1 November the rear guard fought a second successful delaying action, in which Yorck was slightly wounded, and the main body was able to detach itself once more from the energetic pursuit of Bernadotte's men. After some hesitation, Blücher decided to head for Lübeck, where he hoped to rest and reorganize, protected by the walls of the town and its encircling river," and then entrust his fate to a decisive battle." [4] The town was reached late on the 5th; but the next morning French light cavalry attacked the forward positions beyond the river Trave, and at noon the infantry columns, deploying from their pursuit directly into the assault, marched against the walls on all sides, and broke into the town. In the street fighting that ensued, Yorck was wounded twice and taken prisoner. Blücher escaped with about 9,000 men, but was obliged to capitulate with this remnant the following day. In his report to Frederick William he singled out two officers: Scharnhorst, "to whose ceaseless activity, firm determination, and intelligent counsel are due a great part of the successful progress of my retreat," and Yorck, who fought "always at the head of the rear guard with the greatest determination and bravery." [5] A few days after the surrender Scharnhorst wrote, "On the whole no one mattered in the corps but Blücher, myself, and colonel Yorck." [6] When on Scharnhorst's urging Yorck was exchanged for a

[4] Blücher's report of 31 March 1808, in W. v. Unger, *Blücher*, Berlin, 1907–1908, I, 301.

[5] *Ibid.*, p. 318; and Blücher's report of 14 November 1806, in Droysen, I, 182.

[6] *Scharnhorsts Briefe*, ed. K. Linnebach, Munich-Leipzig, 1914, I, 296. The outbreak of war in 1914 interrupted work on the second volume of Scharnhorst's correspondence. The project was taken up again in the 1930's, only to be stopped once more by the Second World War.

French staff officer and in June 1807 reached royal headquarters in Königsberg, he was immediately decorated and promoted to major general; of the *Jäger* so many made their way to the Prussian lines that after a good deal of further fighting the regiment still numbered about 900 men at the end of the war.[7]

Yorck arrived in Königsberg during the days of Prussia's deepest degradation. On 14 June the French had beaten the Russians at Friedland, and Frederick William was engaged in armistice negotiations, which on 9 July ended in complete surrender. Napoleon did not content himself with the terms of capitulation that turned Prussia into a feeble tributary of his system, but immediately began his accustomed and not always well-informed interference in the personnel policies of subjugated governments. The King was compelled to dismiss his Minister of Foreign Affairs, Hardenberg, and General von Rüchel, who had efficiently administered the ragtag Prussian army during the last months of the war. They were replaced by Stein and by Yorck, who succeeded Rüchel as commandant of Memel, which until the beginning of 1808 became the seat of the Prussian government. The most important duty of Yorck's new position was the protection of Prussian interests vis-à-vis the French occupying authorities. His diplomatic scope was enlarged in September when he was appointed Prussian plenipotentiary in talks with Marshal Soult on drawing the frontier between the monarchy and the new Duchy of Warsaw, and on the time-table for the French evacuation of territory east of the Vistula. This settled, he was engaged in administrative business and with the demobilization of infantry units in West Prussia. These months, too, saw indications of a growing antagonism between Scharnhorst and Yorck, for which no specific reason can be identified, other than a sense of personal rivalry and envy on Yorck's part. His feelings were to be assuaged only gradually over the next two years. In April 1808 Yorck took charge of the coastal defenses of the Frische Nehrung on the Baltic, one of the last chinks in the French encirclement of the state. At the same time he organized the collection and reconditioning of muskets and rifles throughout the monarchy. Whenever the stock of a weapon needed to be replaced, it was provided with an angled

---

[7] Twenty officers and about 700 men of the regiment were killed or wounded during the war. Rentzell, pp. 47–49.

butt to make aiming possible—a tactical necessity that was at last officially recognized. In June Yorck became head of a new committee charged with the preparation of new training manuals for the services. In October he was ordered to supervise the army's musketry training, and the following month he assumed command of one of the six brigades in which the fighting branches of the reduced army were now organized. The range of his duties was lifting him out of the exclusively military sphere towards responsibility for major concerns of the state and society.[8]

At the outset of this new phase of Yorck's career, the King had intended him for a very different occupation. In August 1807, Frederick William's primitive and scheming crony, *Generaladjutant* von Köckritz, sounded out Yorck on his willingness to take charge of the education of the twelve-year old Crown Prince.[9] Yorck had rarely been at court; possibly during these weeks when the very existence of the monarchy was in doubt the dynasty wished to bind to itself any senior officer who had risen above the general level of resignation or incompetence. In his answering letter to Köckritz, a draft of which is printed in Droysen's biography, Yorck declined the "honorable and advantageous" offer, pleading insufficient prestige, knowledge, and experience to prepare a prince for his future role in life.[10] Oddly enough, he then proceeded to list some characteristics that he thought necessary in a ruler—a catalogue with overtones both of Helvetius and of Frederick the Great: the prince must consider only the purpose of the whole, his morality therefore differs from that of a private individual. Even in ordinary walks of life we must encounter people with care; a prince must encounter them with suspicion.

[8] For Yorck's appointments in 1807 and 1808, see Priesdorff, No. 1120, and the Cabinet Orders and memoranda printed or mentioned in *Die Reorganisation des Preussischen Staates unter Stein und Hardenberg*, Part II, *Das Preussische Heer vom Tilsiter Frieden bis zur Befreiung: 1807–1814*, ed. R. Vaupel, Leipzig, 1938, I, 43–44, 72, 127, 284, 367, 451, and 454. This work is henceforth cited as *Preussisches Archiv*.

[9] Cf. Hardenberg's report to the King of 15 September 1807 on the importance of acquiring an outstanding educator for the Crown Prince. *Die Reorganisation des Preussischen Staates unter Stein und Hardenberg*, Part I, *Allgemeine Verwaltungs- und Behördenreform*, ed. G. Winter, Leipzig, 1931, I, 298–299.

[10] Droysen, I, 193–197.

There are only two levers that move men to act for the common good—hope and fear. "If it be the case," Yorck concluded, "that his Royal Majesty should again think of me for a position in attendance to the Crown Prince, I beg you to be so kind as to assure the King that I am not suitable for this post, and under no circumstances can accept it without becoming guilty of betraying his confidence. . . . Whatever may be the consequence of my principles, they will remain, as they always have been, the guides of all my actions."

It may have been the current of assertive independence beneath the sheen of respectfulness and obedience that led a Victorian observer to discover a larger significance in these lines. The letter, Seeley wrote in his biography of Stein, "reveals a soldier-philosopher, who can put into words, as it were, the theory of the Prussian military monarchy." [11] Droysen, who did not share the English historian's austere detachment from the drama of Frederick William's relationship with his generals, limited himself to the discreet comment that Yorck's letter "is the first document of his hand in which we encounter the whole man." [12]

· 2 ·

To many civil servants and officers in the summer of 1807 the defeat seemed to offer opportunities for change in Prussia. Some went further: reform was not merely a desirable possibility, but necessary for survival. Behind their willingness to work for a system that they saw on the edge of dissolution lay different motives: attachment to the dynasty and its institutions, native patriotism, loyalty to the idea of the state, even the hope that a modern, strong Prussia might revitalize all of Germany. The elasticity of national loyalties, which throughout its history had permitted the kingdom to benefit from the talents of foreigners, would now enable some men to act in Prussian affairs from a sense of more general responsibility. Others in administration and army had been persuaded by the disaster that certain conditions at least could no longer continue; without any strong desire for change they became more receptive to it. The fourteen months of shock and impotence between the surrender of Tilsit and the

---

[11] J. R. Seeley, *Life and Times of Stein*, Cambridge, 1878, iii, 23.
[12] Droysen, i, 193.

Paris Convention of September 1808, which set the rules by which Prussia might continue to exist, were more favorable to reform than any period would ever be again in the course of the monarchy. At the same time actual conditions could scarcely have been less conducive to any exertion beyond the acceptance of the inevitable, and the gradual achievement of some security and well-being in the titan's shadow. The state was bankrupt, the loss of half of its territory and population had wiped out the work of generations. Its remaining possessions were controlled and exploited by the French. Every step leading back to more settled conditions was handicapped by uncertainty over French intentions. And while many men favored or accepted reform, as many resisted any but the most insignificant change. It was mainly due to Stein, with his masterful independence, his willingness to hate and destroy, and to the more withdrawn and diplomatic Scharnhorst that the psychological readiness of these months was used and the concrete difficulties were overcome sufficiently to raise the strength of the state to a point where it could function effectively in the continuing clash of the great powers.

Among the men whom Stein and Scharnhorst encouraged rather than led there was no unanimity on what might properly be termed a program of reforms in civil and military institutions. Their association was loose, pragmatic, changing; its lowest common denominator a conviction that in the new age Prussia could no longer afford a rigidly hierarchical society and the dynastically imposed isolation of the army. Their willingness to abolish a particular privilege might vary; but each believed—though with varying intensity—that important reserves of energy rested in the people, and that for the sake of the individual as well as of the state this psychic and physical force should no longer be wasted. At bottom they were educators. Men should be taught to deal more effectively with reality, and institutions had to be devised to accommodate and direct the freer action of intelligence. "We must train the nation to manage its own affairs," Stein wrote towards the end of 1807, "and to grow out of this condition of childhood in which an ever-restless and officious government wishes to keep the people." [13] During the same weeks and in

[13] Letter of 8 December 1807 to Hardenberg, quoted in G. Ritter, *Stein: Eine politische Biographie*, Stuttgart, 1958, p. 275.

similar terms Scharnhorst wrote to his student and friend Clausewitz that their purpose must be to "kindle a sense of independence in the nation; we must enable the nation to understand itself
and to take up its own affairs; only then will the nation acquire
self-respect and compel the respect of others. To work towards
that goal is all we can do. To destroy the old forms, remove the
ties of prejudice, guide and nurture our revival without inhibiting
its free growth—our work cannot go further than that." [14] The
interests of ruler, state, and people must be brought into closer
accord; such a rapprochement, the reformers knew, could proceed
only by a sequence of implied bargains. Possibly they saw the
connections between military and civil institutions more clearly
than did their opponents and the great mass that only wished to
do its duty and win a corner of security and repute, whatever the
circumstances. The French Revolution and Napoleon had taught
them something of the mechanics of power. Possibly, too, the
soldiers among them suffered less from doctrinaire conceptions
than did their civilian counterparts: the old system had permitted
them to gain a degree of experience that the others could not
obtain, and their immediate task—the regeneration of the army,
not of the state and of society—was more circumscribed. Scharnhorst, in particular, possessed a sympathetic understanding of
human and technical realities, and it was this which rendered his
idealism so politically effective. He still believed that anything—
whether a musket or the more complex mechanism of an army—
was subject to thoroughgoing improvement, if only an initial idea
could gradually be supported by reforms and innovations that
more nearly matched the organism's potential than did accepted
design or practice. In his widely used *Handbook of Gunnery* he
had recently outlined his concept of the process of change:
"Theory instigates suggestions for improvements, experiments
assist in the first investigation, and additional experience or large-
scale application serves to confirm their usefulness. In this way
improvements in artillery take place, which thus comes ever
nearer to perfection." [15] His views on the best constitution of an
army had long been formed; they had been tested in fifteen years

[14] Letter of 27 November 1807, *Scharnhorsts Briefe*, I, 333–336; the
quoted passage is from p. 334.

[15] G. D. v. Scharnhorst, *Handbuch der Artillerie*, Hanover, 1804–1814,
I, 7.

of European warfare, and after seven years in the Prussian service he had a pretty sound idea how much of the theory could be turned into practice in the prevailing circumstances.

The first steps in the army's modernization benefited from the character of the fighting that took place between the defeats in October and the end of the war in 1807. In East Prussia and Poland the remnants of the army often operated in mixed detachments, and coordination of the different arms under one commander lost some of its strangeness. Occasionally new tactical forms were improvised; at the battle of Preussisch Eylau, Prussian troops attempted attack columns. The defense of isolated towns and fortresses, a major element in the campaign, afforded scope for individual initiative, as did the *Freicorps*, partisan groups, and *Jäger* companies that harried the enemy's rear. Arming the rural population was considered, but had to be rejected since there was an insufficiency of weapons and no organization existed for the purpose—the long-debated home defense groups having never gone beyond the planning stage. In Silesia in the meantime a young officer, Count Friedrich Wilhelm von Goetzen, waged a patriotic partisan war in the hills and around the fortresses of the province. Goetzen possessed neither the manpower nor the inclination to maneuver in traditional patterns; instead his infantry was taught skirmishing and the use of squares and columns. Hundreds of civilians, among them members of the local nobility and bourgeoisie, responded to his appeals for support by serving in the ranks of *Freicorps*, companies of sharpshooters, the *Nationaljägerkorps*, and other predecessors of the volunteer *Jäger* of the Wars of Liberation.[16]

---

[16] Goetzen, one of the most talented Prussian officers of the period, had been a friend of Frederick William in the years before the King's accession to the throne. The war turned him into one of the warmest adherents of Stein and Scharnhorst. In the summer of 1808 he returned to Silesia to strengthen the defenses of the province, which was threatened by the impending war between Austria and France. Several of his letters and reports from this period are printed in *Preussisches Archiv*. He is the subject of a biography, which is good on the military aspects of his career but does not cover his political activities: H. v. Wiese und Kaiserswaldau, *Friedrich Wilhelm Graf v. Goetzen: Schlesiens Held in der Franzosenzeit, 1806 bis 1807*, Berlin, 1902. For Goetzen's support of the various Austrian and German insurgent movements during the war of 1809, see A. Ernstberger, *Die deutschen Freikorps 1809 in Böhmen*, Amsterdam-Berlin-Vienna, 1942.

On his flight to the northeastern corner of his realm, the King had reacted to the defeats and the subsequent loss of morale and discipline with a proclamation and a set of operational instructions. The so-called *Ortelsburger Publicandum* of 1 December 1806 threatened punishment of every officer and soldier remiss in his duties, authorized requisitioning without which Prussian troops could not have remained in the field, and declared that for the duration of the war NCO's and privates who particularly distinguished themselves could become officers.[17] The "Instruction for the Generals with the Army in East Prussia," issued the preceding week at Osterode, advised greater operational and tactical flexibility, and suggested a new attack formation for large commands of foot and horse, such as divisions or brigades, which resembled the scheme that Scharnhorst had recently presented in his lectures at the Academy for Officers, except that the King now included attack columns. The instruction also called for the training of ten reserve sharpshooters in each infantry company.[18] This minute increase in light infantry strength would not have sufficed to render the proposed formations practicable—Frederick William was speculating on concepts that he did not yet fully comprehend.

More to the point were the proposals sent to the King on 27 February 1807 by Gneisenau, who had proved himself an efficient light-infantry officer at Saalfeld and Jena.[19] Gneisenau wrote the King that it was essential for the Prussian army to adopt the French emphasis on light troops, and suggested the immediate formation of a large force of true light infantry, to be trained in skirmishing and sharpshooting. He even hinted that it might be advisable to give the line battalions some drill in open order, so

[17] The *Publicandum* is printed in a number of works; for instance, in [Jany], *1806: Das Preussische Offizierkorps*, pp. 7–10.

[18] The *Osteroder Instruktion* is printed in Höpfner, III, 717–722. Two preliminary memoranda by the King are printed in *Die Reorganisation der Preussischen Armee nach dem Tilsiter Frieden*, ed. R. K. v. Scherbening and K. W.[?] v. Willisen, Berlin, 1862–1866, I, 11–15. This work is henceforth cited as *Reorganisation*. Scharnhorst's lectures on "Battles," "Attack," and "Defense," given in the years 1802 to 1805, are printed in Goltz, *Militärische Schriften von Scharnhorst*, pp. 295–334.

[19] The memorandum is printed in G. H. Pertz and H. Delbrück, *Das Leben des Feldmarschalls Grafen Neithardt von Gneisenau*, Berlin, 1864–1880, I, 667–671. Frederick William's reply is printed in *ibid.*, p. 157.

that, he wrote, they would be able to help themselves when they were knocked about in battle. Frederick William answered that in the course of the planned reorganization of the army after the war he would certainly consider an increase in light infantry. During the same weeks Gneisenau discussed with an officer of the *Jäger* regiment the possibility of organizing detachments of civilian foresters and *Jäger* to fill some of the army's need for light troops, but this scheme also came to nothing, though similar groups were raised in Silesia.[20]

The disastrous war had improved the prestige of few senior officers; the most surprising advance in reputation was Scharnhorst's. His bravery at Auerstedt and his leadership during the retreat finally laid to rest the image of the bookworm in uniform, which he had never quite been able to shed. He was among the first prisoners to be exchanged after Blücher's capitulation, and at once made his way to East Prussia, where he added a note of moral and strategic vision to the tenacity of the Prussian effort. It was one of the real achievements in Frederick William's uninspired life that during the last months of the war he permitted himself to be impressed with the exceptional ability and selflessness of this foreigner to such an extent that he decided to entrust to him a large share in the work of reestablishing the army. On 15 July 1807, immediately after the conclusion of peace, he ordered Scharnhorst and one of the royal adjutants, Count Friedrich Karl von Lottum, to draw up plans for demobilization and for the distribution of garrisons over the territory remaining to the state.[21] Ten days later this working-team was expanded to a five-man group, the Military Reorganization Commission, which under Scharnhorst's chairmanship was to investigate and pass judgment on the army's performance during the war, and to propose changes for its improvement.[22] As had been the case with the *Immediat-Militair-Organisationskommission*, the new body stood outside the regular administrative and command structure, and enjoyed direct access to the King. To assist in its work, additional committees were formed to deal with specific problems, such as the development of tactical doctrine or the design of equipment, which frequently included a representative of the

[20] *Ibid.*, pp. 158–159.
[21] Cabinet Order of 15 July 1807, printed in *Preussisches Archiv*, pp. 1–2.
[22] Cabinet Order of 25 July 1808, printed in *ibid.*, p. 7.

commission. After its proposals were approved by the King, they were transmitted to the *Oberkriegskollegium* for execution.

The commission's preliminary frame of reference was outlined by Frederick William in a program of nineteen paragraphs.[23] The first five points of the King's *Guidelines* concerned the officer corps: investigation of its conduct during the war, punishment of those men "who evidently have not done their duty," improved methods of promotion, and the admission of greater numbers of bourgeois officers. Points 8 to 11, 18, and 19 discussed the reorganization of the infantry and cavalry, and the formation of permanent divisions and corps containing all branches of the service. Paragraphs 13, 14, and 17 dealt with the introduction of more practical uniforms, and with economic matters, in particular the abolition of the *Kompaniewirtschaft*, a system which by entrusting the company commander with the purchase of much of his men's necessities cast him in the profitable role of small entrepreneur. Point 6 demanded better proportions between the line infantry, light troops, and other branches of the service, and continued:

That we have too little genuine light infantry can hardly be doubted. But how could such a force be created? One might—and this appears to me most feasible and suitable—add a light battalion to each infantry regiment. . . . Or one could do away completely with the so-called light infantry, and the entire infantry would be trained to perform this duty as well, as is the case in the French army.

The following paragraph concerned recruiting, the end of hiring foreigners, and asked whether a free corps, "i.e., of light troops," might be raised on a semi-permanent basis. The twelfth paragraph stated that a change in recruiting procedures would necessitate a revision of the Articles of War: in the future punishment should be "equally strict, but less dishonoring" than in the past. Point 15 called for a reduction in the train, and point 16 for more realistic training. An appendix on the future organization of companies, battalions, and higher units included the statement that the third rank of the infantry would be trained for the light service, while the company *Schützen* would be abolished.[24]

[23] The King's *Richtlinien für die Reorganisation der Armee* are printed in *ibid.*, pp. 8–15.

[24] Shanahan, p. 103, writes that the *Richtlinien* called for "new regulations for each branch of the service," but there is no mention of this in the document.

Although some sections of the King's *Richtlinien* were couched in tones of command, their purpose was not to prescribe a given solution but rather to direct the commission's attention. On most issues Frederick William was undecided, and he changed his views frequently through the following years. He knew that his interests and those of the great nobility did not coincide everywhere; even less, it appeared to him, did they agree with the vast ambitions of some of the innovators. By temperament he might lean surprisingly often towards the bourgeoisie, but his background and environment pulled him elsewhere. In the end, each of the points in his July program became the subject of debate; some touched off intense disputes between traditionalists and the reform-minded within and outside the commission. Nor was the list complete. On 21 December 1807 the King sent the commission additional topics to work through; and other matters were entrusted to different groups, though here again a member of the commission might participate in the work—planning a Ministry of War was one such task. Nevertheless, the *Richtlinien* broached vital areas in the army and society, and the attitudes of the men appointed to investigate and make recommendations became of the greatest importance.

Much could have been done to improve the service without departing far from tradition; and carefully balanced adjustment was the goal of the three conservative officers who at first formed the majority on the commission. The ablest among them was Lieutenant Colonel Count Lottum, who was totally opposed to Stein's municipal reforms, and saw no military value but a good deal of political danger in Scharnhorst's militia proposals. In August 1807 he was appointed to the key position of Expediting General Adjutant, in which he was to gain the special confidence of the King. Until the defeat of Napoleon he served in administrative capacities; later he retired from active service and ended his career as Prussian Minister of the Interior and of Finance. Somewhat more sympathetic to the idea of a militia was a second administrative specialist, Lieutenant Colonel Karl Ludwig von Bronikowski, who had served as one of Frederick William's personal adjutants since 1800. The third, Lieutenant Colonel Karl Christoph von Massenbach (not the staff officer and military writer of the same name), was near retirement after an undistinguished career in the cavalry. These men could not comprehend, as Bronikowski once made clear, the reformers' belief that the state was in a crisis in which it might easily perish; they saw no necessity for subjecting the army to a revolution. Scharnhorst and the fifth member of the commission, Gneisenau, once again found themselves in the familiar position of distrusted outsiders, until Scharnhorst with the help of Stein was able to convince the King that the commission's make-up must be changed. Bronikowski and Massenbach were eased out of much of the work.[25] The appointment in October of another royal adjutant, Karl Leopold von Borstell, was terminated after less than two months by Scharnhorst's threat of resigning unless Borstell were removed. Their places were taken by Goetzen, Boyen—once a member of the *Militärische Gesellschaft*, and the future champion of the militia principle—and Major Karl Wilhelm von Grolman, who had fought with distinction in the winter campaign and was soon to reveal himself as the most extremist of Scharnhorst's supporters.

The commission thus reconstituted was representative of the Prussian officer corps neither in family descent nor in professional background. Of its six regularly participating members, only Boyen, Goetzen, and Lottum came from the established nobility. Scharnhorst, the son of a sergeant, had received the patent of nobility as an inducement to transfer to the Prussian service; Grolman's father, a judge, had been recently ennobled, and the genuineness of Gneisenau's title could not be proved. A fourth officer of middle-class descent might be named—Carl von Clausewitz, who, while not a member of the commission, was closely involved in its work after the summer of 1808 as Scharnhorst's aide and *chef de cabinet*.[26] Gneisenau, Goetzen, and

[25] Contrary to Lehmann, *Scharnhorst*, II, 20, and Shanahan, p. 102, Bronikowski and Massenbach did not quit the Commission altogether. Bronikowski, for example, participated in certain of its meetings as late as October 1808. He remained in opposition to Scharnhorst, who in July 1809 was driven to denounce him to Frederick William as a liar. Pertz-Delbrück, *Gneisenau*, I, 534. For service data on Bronikowski (Oppeln-Bronikowski), Lottum (Wylich und Lottum), and Massenbach, see Priesdorff, No. 1209, No. 1160, and No. 1164.

[26] In a letter of 4 September 1808 to his bride, he described himself as the general's *literarischer Faktor*, which might be translated as "ghost writer cum publicity agent." Printed in *Karl und Marie von Clausewitz: Ein Lebensbild in Briefen und Tagebuchblättern*, ed. K. Linnebach,

Clausewitz were specialists in the light service, officially or by personal preference, and Scharnhorst was a gunner. The composition of the other boards and commissions set up to assist the *Militär-Reorganisationskommission* was similar. The actual work of modernizing military institutions was thus to a considerable extent entrusted to men who until 1806 had been far removed from the social and professional center of the army.

From its inauguration the commission was the recipient of reform proposals submitted by officers, civil servants, and members of the public. Among the earliest was a memorandum written by Prince August of Prussia while still a prisoner of war in France.[27] The Prince was a competent officer; his suggestions, which very probably influenced the King's *Guidelines*, were the more important since they reflected the thinking of many enlightened conservatives in the army. The lost war had impressed on him the undue slowness of Prussian movements, and the imperfect coordination of infantry, cavalry, and artillery on the battlefield: he therefore suggested that Scharnhorst's scheme of grouping the branches of the service into permanent divisions should be adopted in the new army organization, that the troops should be relieved of cumbersome equipment, and the supply system made more flexible. Tactics also needed improving, in particular the cooperation between light troops and the line. Theorists of the preceding century, the Prince wrote, had already "recognized the advantages offered by an intelligent combination of line with light infantry. . . . The French were the first to carry out this excellent idea on a large scale . . . from which arrangement they derive . . . important advantages."[28] The Prince continued that the Prussian army had been one of the first to develop a corps of sharpshooters, but had not been clever in their employment. Since the *Schützen* of the line battalions rendered the closed formations more effective, they should never be separated

Berlin, 1917, pp. 170–171. On Clausewitz's training of skirmishers before 1806 and his battalion's employment of open tactics at Auerstedt, see W. Hahlweg, *Clausewitz*, Göttingen, 1957, p. 24; and Jany, *Preussische Armee*, III, 495.

[27] "Vorschläge zur Verbesserung der preussischen Militair-Verfassung," of 13 June 1807, printed in *Reorganisation*, I, 147–181. Clausewitz, the Prince's adjutant, contributed to the memorandum, but Professor Hahlweg informs me that the passages from his pen cannot be identified.

[28] *Ibid.*, p. 174. The discussion of tactics continues through p. 177.

from their units nor should they serve as replacement pools for NCO's. Perhaps the third rank might be used not only for backing up or lengthening the linear formation, but also for skirmishing.

From these very tentative tactical recommendations the memorandum proceeded to an evaluation of the abstract forces of patriotism and honor: "In modern times one generally cannot expect great results from patriotism. . . . In nearly all contemporary wars love of honor and ambition have been a greater influence, and have often replaced enthusiasm or patriotism." [29] The memory of demoralization and passivity after Jena may have played a part in this depreciation, and like many men of his time Prince August was less impressed by any sense of national loyalty the French soldier might possess than by his undoubted dash, pride, and rapaciousness. The Prince's belief that self-esteem and ambition were significant motives nevertheless led him to argue that military justice should agree with the principles of honor: "Nothing runs counter to this so much as corporal punishment and the unfortunately still widespread custom of forcing men to serve in the army. Both must necessarily be abolished if military justice is to agree with the principles according to which the soldier should act." Again the argument stopped halfway. The Prince would not advocate the complete abolition of corporal punishment. The stick should be done away with, but the rod might be retained; NCO's should not be beaten at all.

Scharnhorst and his friends, on the contrary, knew that the reform of state and army demanded the complete suppression of corporal punishment. A modern historian writes that in their deep appreciation of the "moral dignity of the individual, they realized that it was impossible to appeal to the sense of honor and national feeling in a man as long as his back was not yet safe from the corporal's rod." [30] The Reorganization Commission's report on

[29] *Ibid.*, pp. 178–179. The next quotation is from p. 179.

[30] H. Rosinski, *The German Army*, London, 1939, p. 70. It was not only NCO's who administered beatings. According to a memorial of the time addressed to the King by an anonymous Prussian officer, which was later printed as a pamphlet, some of the author's comrades possessed swords on one side of which was engraved the legend *Pro Deo, Gloria et Patria*, and on the other *Fuchtelklinge. Grundlinien zur Reorganisation der Armee*, Berlin, 1807, pp. 14–15.

military justice of 6 April 1808 stated that "public opinion now universally demands less dishonoring punishment for the soldier . . . and the system of conscription which now is also extended to the higher classes motivates this modern claim even more strongly."[31] But did a beating dishonor the soldier in the ranks as it surely would the officer? Was it realistic to equate the sensibilities and ethical standards of men in very different walks of life? In a memorandum on the power of the courts in cases involving both soldiers and civilians, Bronikowski wrote:

If officer and artisan are to be treated and judged . . . according to the same principle, then entirely different rules of honor will first have to be established, and in general a change of this nation's customs and a different view on all matters pertaining to honor must be introduced. However, this would not be as simple as those who love innovations might believe.

To judge an officer like a shoemaker, etc., in cases of insult or physical altercation can only lead to injustice. If, for instance, a shoemaker is the object of violence, he will not lose a penny of his earnings nor is he robbed of his reputation as a shoemaker. On the other hand, an officer who is beaten not only loses his position without fail, but is expelled forever from the community of his equals, and will therefore be unhappy for life.[32]

This echoed Frederick the Great's argument that honor is a function of the lack of economic alternatives, a claim that could no longer be officially upheld in a society that opened its professions and occupations to all. And yet, even the leaders of reform found it hard to draw the full practical conclusion from their stand. Even Stein—possibly "from a strange, romantic preference for

---

[31] *Preussisches Archiv*, p. 361.

[32] "Sondervotum" of 6 October 1808, printed in *ibid.*, pp. 590–591. The previous month Bronikowski had defended another privilege dear to conservatives: retention of the horse for infantry subalterns. His arguments presented to the King in a memorandum of 2 September 1808, *ibid.*, p. 574, included the point that members of the higher classes did not possess the physical strength of the common soldier, and therefore required special consideration. The majority opinion of the Reorganization Commission held, on the contrary, that dismounted junior officers set a good example to the men and eased the supply problem. *Ibid.*, p. 576. The new regulations concerning equipment in the field, of 26 September 1808, abolished the horse for all infantry lieutenants except those who served as adjutants or performed other staff duties.

medieval forms of legality"—would not at first admit that corporal punishment was out of place in the new state.[33] Caning was not wrong in itself, he wrote—only the emotional, arbitrary manner in which it had been administered in the past. To which Gneisenau commented, "I won't deny that during a regeneration of the state or in dangerous crises the stick might do wonders, only it would also have to be introduced to the other classes." As Scharnhorst more soberly wrote to Stein, corporal punishment simply could not be combined with universal conscription, and with the possibility of private soldiers' rising to the highest ranks in the service.[34] With the promulgation of the new articles of war on 3 August 1808, corporal punishment was forbidden, except for soldiers who had been found guilty of three serious offenses and had been transferred to a special category—the "second class."[35] Characteristically, some conservatives thought that if such a distinction were drawn at all, the first class should be exceptional, not the second. The brilliant and bitter spokesman for the *Junker* of the Mark Brandenburg, Friedrich August von der Marwitz, wrote: "It would have been better to turn the thing around, and to have a commission promote the honor-loving and useful soldiers into the first class."[36] Freedom from beating, like any other freedom, was to be a privilege, not a fundamental right. The defeat of this attitude in disciplinary matters was a signal and essential victory for the military reformers—the only complete victory, it has been pointed out, that they were able to gain.[37]

---

[33] Ritter, pp. 302–303. Stein's memorandum on this matter, and Gneisenau's marginal notes are printed in *Preussisches Archiv*, pp. 473–474.

[34] *Preussisches Archiv*, p. 500. See also Gneisenau's newspaper article "Freiheit der Rücken" of 9 July 1808, reprinted in Pertz-Delbrück, I, 385–387.

[35] The Articles of War and the supplementary decrees are printed in E. v. Frauenholz, *Das Heerwesen des XIX. Jahrhunderts*, Munich, 1941, pp. 101–120. The new code did not remove all cruel punishments: in 1810 a uhlan who had murdered his sergeant-major was sentenced to be broken on the wheel. See the issue of 7 November 1810 of the *Berliner Abendblätter*, republished in the facsimile edition, *Heinrich von Kleist's Berliner Abendblätter*, ed. G. Minde-Pouet, Leipzig, 1925.

[36] *Friedrich August Ludwig von der Marwitz: Ein märkischer Edelmann im Zeitalter der Befreiungskriege*, ed. F. Meusel, Berlin, 1908, I, 514.

[37] Rosinski, p. 70.

In the same year a second major reform was achieved with the abolition of the special claim of the nobility to officer positions. The bourgeoisie had always been represented in the officer corps; the purpose of the reform was not to increase their number immediately but to establish the principle that all subjects, regardless of social background, could aspire to every position in the army. In 1806, the *Ortelsburger Publicandum* had declared that for the duration of the war every NCO and private soldier had the same right to a commission as a prince. The Reorganization Commission recommended that this emergency regulation be made permanent. "A claim to officer rank," read the draft report of 25 September 1807, "shall in peacetime be warranted only by knowledge and education, in time of war by exceptional bravery, activity, and quickness of perception." [38] In place of privilege, by which regimental commanders could, if they wished, accept the sons of noblemen in early adolescence as officer cadets in their regiments, the reformers proposed to put education and competitive examinations. Successful candidates, who had to be at least seventeen years old and to have served for three months in the ranks, still needed to be approved by the officers of the units they wished to join—a condition that preserved the exclusive and unified character of the corps, though its ethical base would slowly change from the personal relationship between king and nobility to that of a patriotic, national-minded, and professionally competent order of knighthood. This reform, which theoretically could affect the entire balance of power in the state, was closely linked with events in the civilian realm, particularly the edict of 9 October 1807 that terminated the special legal and economic position of the nobility. Officially, writes Meinecke, "the estates of society changed into classes, which the individual could enter according to his free decision and the measure of his economic strength." [39] In fact this intermingling was to occur only very gradually over the decades, as did the increase of bourgeois officers in the army; nevertheless, the threatened loss of an important economic and social advantage was sharply resisted.

Yorck for one considered the commission's proposal doctrinaire

[38] *Preussisches Archiv*, p. 101.

[39] F. Meinecke, *Das Zeitalter der Deutschen Erhebung*, Göttingen, 1957, p. 90.

and unwise. He criticized the Prussian nobility often enough, and neither shared in the disdain with which some *Junker* affected to regard middle-class aspirations nor found it distasteful to associate with bourgeois comrades and to advance their careers. When his regiment had gone to war in 1806, it contained the greatest proportion of officers without titles—one fifth—of any first-line unit in the army, a condition partly dependent on the commanding officer's attitude. But now he doubted whether bourgeois would be willing to enter the army in sufficient numbers for the state to rely on them as a major source of officers, and he resented the annulment by fiat of the Frederician custom that enabled the sons of the country's nobility to count on a military career, if such was their inclination. He is credited during this period with words that contain the notes of violence, independence, and even rebelliousness which were coming to be associated with him. To Prince William, the King's youngest brother, who defended the abolition of the nobility's first claim to officer patents, he is quoted as having said: "If your Royal Highness deprives me and my children of our right, what is the basis of yours?" [40]

Others objected to the promotion of any bourgeois to officer rank. Lottum, in a memorandum presented to the King in the summer of 1807, wrote that "on the whole, judging from the experience of other German states, . . . no advantage could be expected to accrue to the army" if "non-nobles are to be accepted as cadets in the regiments on the same basis as nobles, and thus are granted a definite claim for advancement to officer." [41] If nevertheless it was thought advisable to admit non-noble cadets to help the state gain the attachment of the middle classes, their admission should be accompanied with the most stringent safeguards; in particular the regiments should submit their candidates to review by higher authority to avoid any possibility that graft or personal connections came to influence their choice. Lottum's position was rejected by Scharnhorst, who was opposed to giving military authority to adolescents, whether noble or not. Greater maturity and better preparation of the individual, the removal of legal advantages for one social group—only on these

[40] Droysen, I, 209.

[41] "Promemoria," undated, but written before 20 August 1807. *Preussisches Archiv*, p. 48.

bases could the officer corps begin to be improved. That the army was able to accommodate itself to this approach had been shown in the recent war. Early in 1807 two future members of the commission, Gneisenau and Goetzen, had taken advantage of the sanction granted by the *Ortelsburger Publicandum* to promote untitled men in their units. Goetzen had commissioned as many as 62 NCO's in 10 battalions of his Silesian command. After the war these officers became the special object of conservative ire, and nearly all were retired in the course of demobilization and army reduction. In June 1808 an officer in a letter to Gneisenau protested the vilification suffered by light infantry officers who had risen from the ranks, and begged him to protect these "good people, without whom, I believe, our light infantry can't at first improve." [42] Gneisenau chose this occasion to write two short articles in the Königsberg newspaper, the *Volksfreund*, "It has not escaped the enlightened monarch," stated the first, "that all forces must be awakened, and that every force must be given its proper area of action. High birth does not possess a monopoly of ability. . . . The new age demands more than old titles and parchment, it needs fresh deeds and strength." [43] The other piece satirized the opposition to reform, and concluded by asking who was more to blame in the Silesian campaign—Count Goetzen, who promoted deserving NCO's to officers while leaving inexperienced noblemen in the ranks, or the noblemen, "who so far demeaned themselves as to bear arms as privates without looking askance when old soldiers were raised over them? Is this not the world upside down?" [44]

The conflict over the method of appointing officers had gone on for a year, and a decision could no longer be avoided. On 6 August 1808 Frederick William signed the regulations on the selection of officers, which deprived the nobility of its special privileges while assuring its continued control of the actual ap-

[42] Major v. Putlitz to Gneisenau, 7 June 1808, *ibid.*, p. 457. See also the Cabinet Order of 5 July 1808 to the Governor of Silesia, concerning the retirement of men who had been commissioned during the war. *Ibid.*, pp. 503–504.

[43] The untitled article is reprinted in *ibid.*, p. 490, and with slight variants in Pertz-Delbrück, I, 688–689.

[44] "Verkehrte Welt," reprinted in *ibid.*, 380–381.

pointments.[45] The first words of the new law were almost identical with the key sentence in the Commission's proposal of 25 September 1807:

From now on a claim to officer rank shall in peacetime be warranted only by knowledge and education, in time of war by exceptional bravery and quickness of perception. From the whole nation, therefore, all individuals who posses these qualities can lay title to the highest positions of honor in the army. All social preference which has hitherto existed ceases completely in the army, and everyone, without regard for his background, has equal duties and equal rights.

Establishing the principle of equal rights had been difficult; far more difficult proved to be the imposition of equal duties. The nobility could learn to live with a gradually increasing proportion of bourgeois officers—the newcomers, it was pointed out, might even help strengthen and vitalize the aristocracy in the new age. Extending the obligation for military service to all classes, however, not only meant a total change in the basis of Prussia's military institutions, but would profoundly interfere with the economic, social, and political customs of the country. Not one privileged group, but all beneficiaries of the Frederician caste-state would be affected. Resistance to change in the method of manpower procurement therefore came from all sides: the wealthy peasants, the artisans, the bourgeoisie, the nobility, and the King.

During the eighteenth century the Prussian army had drawn its soldiers from two sources: foreign recruitment and the cantons, or draft-districts, within the country. As a rule each regiment possessed its particular canton, which supplied it with the needed recruits, who, since the state granted numerous exemptions, came almost entirely from the poor rural population. After 1807 foreign recruiting ceased as a matter of course, while French political pressures and the ruined economy demanded a reduction of

---

[45] The draft *Reglement über die Besetzung der Stellen der Portepee-Fähnriche* . . . of 30 July with the changes of the final version is printed in *Preussisches Archiv*, pp. 533–536, and with some variants in Frauenholz, *Das Heerwesen des XIX. Jahrhunderts*, pp. 121–123. The King reserved to himself the power to appoint "from time to time" officers who had not gone through the examination and election process.

army strength far below even the numbers that the cantons in the remaining Prussian territories could provide. It seemed feasible to continue with the canton system. But the political philosophies of many of the reformers, as well as the immediate political aims of those who worked towards a second war with France, required the destruction, or at least reduction, of every barrier that limited participation of the people in military affairs. Only an army made up of all classes could introduce to society a greater national awareness, help join dynasty and nation, exploit popular energies. In one of its first acts, the Reorganization Commission announced that "all inhabitants of the state are its born defenders," and proposed that the army be reconstituted into a standing force and a militia, both recruited from the entire native population.[46] The ranks of the standing army were to be filled by conscripts from the poorer classes, and presumably by volunteers; the militia was to consist of those who could afford to clothe and arm themselves and who could pay for their own training. Though favoring it in principle, Scharnhorst could not yet fully accept the reality of an army made up of all classes of the population, without exemptions or special privileges. In his thought, and in the debates during the following years, a politically reliable militia on the British model came to serve as a kind of halfway house on the road to true universal conscription. After further discussions, detailed plans for the new organizations were submitted to Frederick William on 15 March 1808, buttressed with the hint that the state might not survive without the efforts of all its able-bodied men and the assurance that a militia of property-owners would not prove a threat to the dynasty.[47] On this score the King's anxieties were not allayed, and though declaring in general terms that all Prussian subjects would in future be liable to bear arms,

[46] "Vorläufiger Entwurf der Verfassung der Reserve-Armee," 31 August 1807, printed in *Preussisches Archiv*, pp. 82–85. Any discussion of the broadening of military obligations in the era of Prussian reform is indebted to the research and interpretations of Max Lehmann. A brilliant modern synthesis of opposing ideas and personalities is contained in Craig's *Politics of the Prussian Army*, pp. 46–49. Also to be noted is W. Simon's analysis in his important book, *The Failure of the Prussian Reform Movement, 1807–1819*, Ithaca, N.Y., 1955, pp. 154–162.

[47] "Vorläufiger Entwurf zur Verfassung der Provinzialtruppen," *Preussisches Archiv*, pp. 320–332.

he postponed his decision.[48] The reformers' plans received a further check by the terms of the Paris Convention of September
1808, which limited the army to 42,000 men for a period of ten
years, and prohibited raising a militia. The question how the
regular army should be recruited was left open, and on this point
some of Scharnhorst's civilian sympathizers turned against him.
The idealistic Niebuhr denounced universal conscription as an
enemy of culture. Vincke, once head of the government in Westphalia and now Stein's advisor on constitutional questions, wrote
his minister that conscription was unnecessary since the state
would not again need a strong army, that it would most heavily
burden the propertied classes, that it was "the grave of all culture, of science and industry, of political freedom and all human
happiness." Vincke ended his letter with a threat to resign if
conscription were adopted, since such a step meant the end of his
hopes that "the Prussian state would continue to pursue elevated
concepts in its administration, that it would remain an asylum for
humanity, where men were still respected as valuable in themselves and not degraded to simple means to an end and blind
automata of obedience."[49] His was not a universal view; but
together with evidence of readiness and even eagerness to serve
there was much concern among the middle class over the brutali-
zation, financial loss, and disruption of careers that conscription
would entail. Several communities, among them the city of
Königsberg, enquired whether their former exemptions from recruiting might be retained under new conditions. No group in
Silesia, Goetzen wrote at the time, "opposed conscription as much
as did the wealthy merchants."[50]

Objections from the nobility came largely on the grounds that
conscription was egalitarian and that it would ruin the economy
and discipline of their estates. In November 1808 a characteristic

[48] The first article of the Articles of War for NCO's and private soldiers
of 3 August 1808 includes the statement: "In future every subject of the
state is to be obliged to perform military service . . . under yet to be
determined conditions." Frauenholz, *Das Heerwesen des XIX. Jahrhunderts*, p. 101.

[49] Letter of 30 September 1808, in *Preussisches Archiv*, pp. 598–601.
Cf., Lehmann, *Scharnhorst*, ii, 98.

[50] Letter to Gneisenau of 1 December 1808, *Preussisches Archiv*, p.
749.

135

petition of the nobles of the East Prussian district of Mohrungen stated: "Universal conscription extended to the nobility, which first saw the light of day as the child of a revolution that had smashed all existing arrangements and conditions in France, conscription which by its nature can be based only on the concept of universal equality, would, we dare assert, lead to the complete destruction of the nobility." [51] Frederick William responded that events had made conscription necessary; but when in the following month the Reorganization Commission submitted regulations for its implementation, he again refused to sign them into law.[52] Stein's departure from office removed the most powerful civilian supporter of the scheme, and not until the outbreak of war between France and Austria the next summer were radical mobilization policies again seriously considered. Scharnhorst proposed forming a reserve army from demobilized soldiers and volunteers, Gneisenau and his friends elaborated plans for a popular insurrection which they had first taken up the previous year, and a new civil-military commission was set up to study conscription, whose meetings continued even after Napoleon's defeat of Austria rendered fundamental innovation less likely than ever. Early in 1810 the commission recommended the adoption of universal conscription, without possibility of exemption. Stein's successors, the ministers Dohna and Altenstein, objected that such a measure of totality was proper only in war, that at the very least the French practice should be copied, permitting men who were selected for service to pay for substitutes—an attitude opposed to that of the reformers who held that universal military service must be permanent and, as far as possible, equitably imposed. By means of historical and contemporary examples Scharnhorst tried in vain to quiet Frederick William's suspicions of the militia and conscription being something dangerously alien.[53] Along the same lines, but in his brusque manner, Yorck wrote the King:

[51] Petition of 17 November 1808, *ibid.*, pp. 748–749, which also prints an excerpt of the King's reply of 30 November. Cf. the discussion in Lehmann, *Scharnhorst*, II, 295–296, of the petition against conscription of 2 March 1809 submitted by the Pomeranian nobility.

[52] "Regulativ über die allgemeine Konskription," of 20 December 1808, *Preussisches Archiv*, pp. 817–822.

[53] Overlooked, so far as I know, among Scharnhorst's studies on this subject is an incomplete and undated report on the Russian militia, which stresses the simplicity and cheapness of the organization and the fact that it cuts across class lines. *Nachlass Vaupel*, Nr. 51, Heft 20, 4–8, 9a.

The Canton *Reglement* protects everyone who is not a complete vagabond or beggar. The organization of the army makes it more than ever necessary not to exclude the wealthy from the military profession. The poor laborer, who is made to defend the property of his wealthy, healthy, strong, well-fed farmer, is a bad defender of his fatherland. In 1740 the army consisted almost wholly of sons of farmers and the middle class, and stood firm at Mollwitz. The hard campaign of 1744 did not lead to immediate desertion. The soldier had something worth defending; he stuck it out, fought well even in misfortune, and performed marvels in better circumstances.[54]

This was inspired if hardly accurate history, but Yorck claimed his criticism of the canton system was proved right by the many desertions that still took place. "Transgressions against discipline continue to be very frequent despite all efforts of the commanding officers, and this too is the result of the bad composition of the troops. Conscription alone can create a better spirit among the troops." In a letter to Scharnhorst the following year, Yorck praised the patriotism of the Poles in the Duchy of Warsaw, and continued, "How different it is here, where we have to fight over every recruit with his lord, and where miserable egotism is the only dominant passion." [55] Two days later he wrote that if war were to come again, the French soldiers would fight well, "since each one fights out of a feeling of personal honor and because he has national pride. Unfortunately this is not the case with us. Our system of recruiting is wrong; I have often said so, and shall continue to say it." [56] Not until 1813, and then only for the length of the war, were the reformers' ideas adopted. Universal conscription, volunteer *Jäger* companies for the wealthy and educated, militia formations—the *Landwehr*—for the poorer classes, backed in crises by the entire male population, the *Landsturm*,

---

[54] Quoted by Scharnhorst from General von Yorck's "most recent report on the subject to His Majesty" in a report on conscription written between April and June 1810; *Nachlass Vaupel*, Nr. 48, Heft 17, 28–29. Lehmann, *Scharnhorst*, ii, 332, excerpts several sentences of Yorck's report without citing the source.

[55] Letter of 22 August 1811, printed in Droysen, i, 285. In a letter to the East Prussian government of 19 February 1812, Yorck wrote that he did what he could to lighten the military burden on the province, but the local authorities were duty-bound "not to deprive the Royal service of any able-bodied draftee [*Cantonist*] for any reason whatever." *J. A. Stargardt —Auktionskatalog*, No. 576 (May 1966), p. 212.

[56] Droysen, i, p. 287.

seemed to fulfill, at least in theory, the aim of mobilizing "the physical and moral energies of the whole nation." [57]

Improving the treatment of the soldier, abolishing legal restrictions on access to officer rank, extending military obligations throughout society were the prerequisites for turning the wreck of the dynastic army into a force that could exploit the opportunities of the future. But to be effective these had to be complemented by other reforms. The behavior of the officers during the last war was investigated, and a few were tried and sentenced for a laxness that was no longer acceptable in the sterner present. The education of the soldier needed to be improved. Little continued to be done for the rank and file; but the new methods of officer selection demanded the immediate expansion of higher military education. Building on Scharnhorst's earlier work, the system of army education was restructured into cadet-schools, which prepared young men for the ensign examination, examination commissions, three schools where ensigns learned the essentials of the subaltern's duties, and a war school for officers—the later *Kriegsakademie*—in which young officers received advanced training and prepared for duty with the General Staff. Finally, the old principle of promotion by strict seniority was adjusted to permit more rapid acceleration, and able officers could now look forward to reaching positions of authority in their prime. The higher administration of the army was rescued from its petrified dependence on one man. Frederick William's programmatic memoranda had, understandably, not alluded to this problem, which Stein and Scharnhorst broached themselves. It was obvious to them that the *Generaladjutantur* like its civilian counterpart, the cabinet councillors, made responsible administration impossible. The reluctant King was compelled to remove the Expediting General Adjutant and his aides from their controlling positions, and to replace them and the *Oberkriegskollegium* with an effective Ministry of War, on a par with the other ministries of state, charged with the administration of the entire army and possessing the power to initiate and execute policy. The new arrangement removed the burden of routine from the King; but it was with these matters that Frederick William felt most at ease. He resented the loss of detailed and direct control over his subor-

[57] Scharnhorst and Gneisenau in their joint proposal for the organization of the *Landsturm*. Lehmann, *Scharnhorst*, II, 547.

dinates, and after some years the General Adjutants—the agents of his personal rule—regained much of their freedom to circumvent the regular channels of authority.

The formation of the troops was simplified, and their peacetime organization brought more in accord with likely employment in the field. The proposed grouping of the army into six divisions had to be scaled down to the equivalent number of brigades when the Convention of Paris reduced the permitted establishment to a figure lower than had been anticipated.[58] The essential feature of permanently combining infantry, cavalry, and auxiliary services under a single administrative and operational control was retained, nevertheless, and differences between the various branches of the service were reduced. Already in September 1807 the Reorganization Commission advocated that in future no distinction should be drawn between units other than that they were mounted or dismounted: "The internal formation of the army is therefore on the whole identical." [59] This remained an unattainable ideal; but gradually many of the inequalities in status, allowances, and professional opportunity that had proliferated in the old army were done away with. A Cabinet Order of 20 November 1807 introduced the new concepts to infantry organization. From now on each infantry regiment was to consist uniformly of two grenadier companies, two musketeer battalions, one light battalion, and one depot or garrison company.[60] The company *Schützen* disappeared; in their place the entire third rank of the line was to

[58] During the next few years a military force considerably in excess of the 42,000 men permitted by the French was maintained by keeping records of thousands of demobilized officers and men, and by giving leave to experienced men and replacing them with recruits. In August 1811, for instance, trained forces immediately available amounted to 74,413 men exclusive of officers. Jany, *Preussische Armee*, IV, 56.

[59] "Immediatbericht" of 25 September 1807, printed in *Preussisches Archiv*, p. 105.

[60] The order is printed in *ibid.*, pp. 160–162. Shanahan, p. 112, errs in thinking that after 1 December 1807 the light battalions were called "garrison companies." The latter, which until 1 December 1807 bore the name "depot companies," consisted of half-invalid veterans, still fit for garrison and guard duty. They had no connection with the fusilier battalions, whose name was changed to "light battalions" on 20 November of the same year. On 1 December 1809 the term "light battalion" was discarded and the light infantry battalions were again known as "fusiliers."

be trained as skirmishers, with an additional twenty to thirty musketeers in each company being given rudimentary instruction in open order to provide replacements for the third rank. On paper, about one-third of the infantry were now light troops—an enormous change from the proportion of only two years earlier. Musketeers and light infantry were to be considered as a single corps, their officers ranking together and liable for duty with both light and line units. One light infantry battalion was eventually incorporated into the Guards, another indication of the changing view taken of the descendants of Frederick's despised *Freicorps*. In each brigade the grenadiers were combined into a separate corps, and such elite and specialist formations as the Guards and the *Jäger* were also retained; but with these exceptions infantry organization had been standardized by the summer of 1808, and a general modernization of tactics now became possible. It still required the development of a tactical doctrine that paid regard to the lessons of the past twenty years, and the thorough training of the men according to its concepts, to turn the new force into reality.

· 3 ·

On 4 June 1808 a committee to draft training instructions was formed under Yorcks' chairmanship.[61] That the most urgent need lay in acquainting the army with the requirements of open order tactics was reflected in the committee's membership, which was drawn entirely from the light service. The two infantry representatives had served with the fusiliers—Gneisenau, and Colonel Friedrich Wilhelm von Bülow, a brother of the military critic and in years to come the successful defender of Berlin against Marshal Oudinot. The other two members of the committee were hussars—Lieutenant Colonel Wieprecht Hans von Zieten, who was to attain the rank of General Field Marshal, and Major Karl

---

[61] The Cabinet Order is printed in *Preussisches Archiv*, pp. 454–455, and extracted in Priesdorff's introduction to the period 1807–1812 in his biographical dictionary, III, 207. Important documents on the work of the committee, including letters by Frederick William III, Scharnhorst, Gneisenau, and Yorck, are contained in Roche-Aymon's work, *Des Troupes légères*, to which I have already referred in Chapter III, note 159.

Anton Count de la Roche-Aymon.[62] Roche-Aymon was a French *émigré*, who as a young man joined the Prussian hussars and was assigned to the household of Prince Henry, the brother of Frederick the Great. During his years at Rheinsberg he wrote a four-volume *Introduction à l'etude de l'art de la guerre*, which contained an informed discussion of columnar and skirmish tactics.[63] In the war of 1806–1807 he distinguished himself at the head of a hussar battalion, and from then on rose rapidly in the service. By 1810 he commanded a light brigade and was helping to draft the new cavalry regulations when Napoleon forced him to resign from the Prussian army and return to France, where he ended his career under the Restoration as *Pair* and Inspector-General of the cavalry. He proved to be a particularly useful member of Yorck's committee.

On 3 June 1808, the day before the committee was appointed, a "Provisional Instruction for the Training of Troops" had been issued over the King's signature.[64] It stressed the importance of teaching the essentials of field duty to subalterns and NCO's, and ordered, for the first time in the army's history, that the entire infantry be trained in marksmanship, for which purpose every man was to fire twenty rounds. The third rank, which now constituted the light troops of each line battalion, was to be drilled in skirmishing "from time to time," when troops were deployed in open order; "firing should never be by command of senior officers, but be left to the judgment of junior officers, NCO's, and privates." Yorck's committee was to work out detailed instructions

---

[62] For the details of Zieten's career, see Priesdorff, No. 1315; for Roche-Aymon's Prussian service, Priesdorff, No. 1174. With his usual charm and understanding of the Prussian genre, Fontane has described Roche-Aymon's years at the court of Prince Henry in his *Wanderungen durch die Mark Brandenburg*, I, *Die Grafschaft Ruppin*, "Graf und Gräfin La Roche-Aymon."

[63] The work was published in Weimar from 1802 to 1804, and contains a valuable bibliography of about 520 titles on military affairs drawn from Prince Henry's library. Some passages of the text reappear in slightly altered form in the later book, *Des Troupes légères*.

[64] *Preussisches Archiv*, pp. 451–453. In view of this instruction and of the others issued during the following years, it is difficult to understand Shanahan's statement, p. 232, that "no tactical instructions for officers appeared before 1812."

for these subjects, which its agenda grouped under four headings: (1) How could target firing best be taught? (2) How could the third rank be trained most effectively in skirmishing? (3) What were the best methods for teaching field duty? (4) How could field exercises best prepare troops for battle—in particular, for the combined action of infantry, cavalry, and artillery?

The committee decided to draft a set of general instructions, which would guide training until more detailed regulations could be issued on each subject, to be followed in turn by definitive manuals. Through June and July, Yorck, Gneisenau, and Roche-Aymon met on two afternoons a week; their views were transmitted for comment to Bülow and Zieten, who were stationed outside Königsberg, with Gneisenau then working up the final version.[65] The provisional instructions were completed by the first week of July.[66] Evidently they are the regulations that were issued the following month on the training of soldiers who were on extended leave in the regimental cantons, and who for lack of money could not be recalled to the colors.[67] They stated that training was not to be carried out in the "accustomed manner"; instead, the men were to be taught simple close order drill—with the stress on speed and flexibility rather than on precision—the manual of arms, simple volleys, and firing at a target. In order not to disgrace them in the eyes of their relatives and to avoid rendering the military profession distasteful to the population, the soldiers were

[65] Undated letter of Gneisenau to Major v. Pirch, *Preussisches Archiv*, p. 455.

[66] Letter of Gneisenau to Roche-Aymon of 8 July 1808, *Des Troupes légères*, p. 17 of the Preface.

[67] I have not found direct proof that Yorck's committee produced these regulations, but the connection appears certain. A Cabinet Order of 25 July 1808 and orders to the infantry regiments of the same day announced that training officers and NCO's were to be sent to the regimental cantons. *Preussisches Archiv*, pp. 524–527. On 12 August their regulations were issued, "Instruktion für die in die Regimentskantons zum Exerzieren der Beurlaubten zu sendenden Offiziere," *ibid.*, pp. 544–546. This instruction is the only one issued on infantry training between the establishment of Yorck's committee and the spring of 1809. A preliminary draft of the instruction in Gneisenau's hand, which existed in the Prussian State Archives, presumably was the summation he wrote as the committee's secretary and editor.

to be treated gently: "No officer may permit himself to punish his subordinates with the stick, and he must also see to it that no non-commissioned officer takes this liberty with a private soldier. Not even cursing is permissible. . . ."

A few days after Gneisenau had edited the instructions, Roche-Aymon submitted a long manuscript in his native French on the training of light troops, which the committee felt might usefully supplement its brief directions. On 21 July Gneisenau wrote the author: "Your memorandum . . . deserves to be in the hands of every officer. I therefore intend to have it translated by a capable person; we ask your permission for this. If other business didn't take up all my time I should like to translate it myself, *con amore*." [68] The manuscript was printed that autumn as a semi-official publication, and distributed among the army. [69] It was widely used; three further editions appeared in the next six years.

Yorck's committee dissolved itself towards the beginning of August. Their subsequent activities suggest that, except for Bülow, each member was charged to work out more detailed training instructions in a particular field: Yorck took responsibility for the *Jäger;* Gneisenau for the third rank of the line infantry; Zieten and Roche-Aymon jointly drafted orders for the cavalry and the light battalions.

Roche-Aymon's manual of 1808 begins with a dissection of the interacting tactical and strategic factors that had produced the "unbelievable events" of the past fifteen years:

At the start of the Revolutionary wars, the French government decided to introduce new tactics . . . which would give hidden talents scope for development. Instead of the line it chose the column, since this provided appropriate means to direct an enflamed people; regular fire was exchanged for the *tirailleur* system, and thus the basic elements of the French victories were formed. Since skirmishing isolated the soldier in combat, left him to his own judgment, and strongly aroused the ambition of each individual, it necessarily gave the French an advantage over troops drilled to fight only in close formations. . . . The present French emperor improved on this new

[68] *Des Troupes légères*, pp. 17–18 of the Preface.

[69] *Über den Dienst der leichten Truppen*, ed. Count v. la Roche-Aymon, translated by Baersch, Königsberg, 1808. As he had with *Des Troupes légères*, Jähns, III, 2719, mistakes this manual too as a work of Roche-Aymon's father.

system of war. The idea, already sensed by the famous Marshal de Saxe, that the art of war lay solely in the legs, was expanded and realized by Napoleon in his audacious marches; his army achieves a speed of movement so far unequaled by others, and since it is solely designed for fighting it knows neither baggage trains nor supply depots, and its operations are not dependent on the calculations of the quartermaster. But without the organization of French armies into divisions, legions, and corps, the success of these daring marches would nevertheless often be most doubtful. Apart from other factors, this arrangement is so advantageous because through it the efficient combination of infantry and artillery, the two fundamental branches of the service, effectively supports the rather inferior French cavalry. Now the corps and divisional commanders no longer recognize the existence of terrain dangerous to them; they only know more or less favorable ground on which they are able to fight at any time.[70]

As historical analysis this was inaccurate; but the author meant to produce immediate results. If the Revolution had not consciously created its new tactics, the Prussians would now have to do so; the French had not abolished baggage trains and supply depots, but the Prussians must renounce their overreliance on them. Throughout his text, Roche-Aymon tried to impress on the average Prussian officer the view that the preconceptions of linear drill were no longer suited to modern war. He not only explained the methods of organizing patrols and how reports should be written, but discussed the use of maneuver and attack columns, the exploitation of terrain, preferred ways of committing troops to battle in forests, hills, and on level ground, and the coordination of infantry, cavalry, and artillery. A final chapter dealt with training, by which was meant not "those petty frivolities that turn the individual into a puppet and tightrope-walker," but practical exercises that met the demands of field duty.[71] Until more elaborate official instructions began to appear in the spring and summer of 1809, Roche-Aymon's work served as a stopgap that provided officers with practical instructions and helped create among them a more perceptive attitude towards the modern doctrine that was being evolved.

Opposition to tactical reform had not subsided in the interval.

[70] *Über den Dienst der leichten Truppen*, pp. 3–6.
[71] *Ibid.*, pp. 125–138.

As the shock of defeat wore off, the readiness to accept innovation declined, a development that can be traced with particular clarity in the actions of the King. In 1807 he had distinguished with some success between essentials and the insignificant; but his sense of urgency did not last, and in the conflicts between reform and its enemies of the following years he reverted to accustomed ways more often than not, or tended to evade or postpone decisions on the major issues.[72] The *Richtlinien* of 1807 had contained a remark that showed how difficult it was for Frederick William to free himself from the tutelage of linear tactics. Discussing the role of light troops, he wrote, "It is understood that as heretofore light infantry in the field is more often used by itself." [73] This idea went directly counter to the new doctrine, which demanded—if not complete amalgamation of line and light tactics—at least their close and permanent cooperation. During the last war the line battalions had been handicapped and suffered heavily because too often they had fought without the support of their few sharpshooters, who were on patrol or on other detached service. The lesson had been thoroughly appreciated by the reformers. Scharnhorst wrote, "When a company is detached from a battalion, or even separated for only a moment, it takes its rifle section along. No battalion, no company, no section moves without its riflemen." [74] Frederick William's statement, on the contrary, reverted to the separation of tasks favored by the preceding century, and became programmatic, not indeed for the Reorganization Commission but for its enemies—the champions of the old Prussian line. The conservatives' stand was greatly helped by the Cabinet Order of 21 December 1808 with which the King reacted to Scharnhorst's success in eliminating Borstell from the commission. The decree subjected the commission to "irritated criticism" and, more seriously, established the sequence

---

[72] In his review of *Das Preussische Heer vom Tilsiter Frieden bis zur Befreiung*, R. Stadelmann describes the King's behavior in 1808 with unexcelled precision: "He appears to withdraw increasingly to matters of detail, and unmistakably ends up in a kind of Hohenzollern military romp." *Historische Zeitschrift*, CLX (1939), 366.

[73] Paragraph 9, *Preussisches Archiv*, p. 10.

[74] The statement occurs in his essay *Order of Battle*, which is reprinted in Appendix 1 of this work.

that the commission was to follow from then on in its consideration of various topics.[75] The first matters to be dealt with were
uniforms and equipment. In twenty-third place came the formation of a militia, one of the most important projects of the reformers, but a scheme the King wished to delay as long as possible.
Among the miscellaneous topics grouped after the last numbered
item—24: Establishment of a Gendarmerie or Military Police—
was the writing of new regulations. Until these or temporary
substitutes had been drafted, the individual commanders could
continue to drill their men largely according to their own views.

A revealing example of the lack of comprehension with which
even talented soldiers encountered the tactical proposals of the
reformers is afforded by a memorandum that Major Johann Friedrich von Lossau—after 1815 a senior commander and well-
known military historian—addressed to the commission on 21
March 1808.[76] Lossau argued that the old Prussian infantry drill
did not need to be changed, and that linear tactics as a whole were
not outdated. The tactics of light troops, he admitted, should be
improved; but care must be taken that this would not weaken the
line, since "one can't be a line-infantryman and a light-infantry-
man at the same time."

Friedrich August von der Marwitz voiced this fear of contami-
nation by new revolutionary forces more sharply when he wrote:
"The effect of the old Prussian fire has been completely lost, and
we sacrifice an enormous number of men in villages and wood-
land where the French often lure us since they are much more pro-
ficient there than we are, because any Frenchman knows better
how to ensure his personal advantage than the German. . . ." [77]
As was so frequently the case with Marwitz, his sharp intelligence recognized an aspect of the truth, which he then interpreted with extreme nationalistic and caste bias. The native manner of warfare for the loyal Prussian was over open ground, in the
fighting community of his comrades, straightforwardly facing

---

[75] Lehmann, *Scharnhorst*, II, 20. The Cabinet Order is printed in
Preussisches Archiv, pp. 231–235.

[76] *Ibid.*, pp. 332–354; see especially pp. 347–349. Lossau's service data
are given in Priesdorff, No. 1282.

[77] Marwitz, p. 519. It was consistent with this attitude that for the light
service Marwitz advocated temporary free corps rather than fusilier battalions and other light units on the regular list.

the enemy; while the self-seeking, scheming Frenchman sought to ambush, deceive, strike from cover. It was absurd; but Marwitz correctly saw that a fundamental difference existed between the soldier moving and fighting mechanically and the skirmisher.

In his lectures at the School for Officers, Clausewitz attempted to define the true nature of this difference.

The individual hussar and *Jäger* [he said] possesses an enterprising spirit, a confidence in himself and his luck, which someone who has always served in the line can hardly imagine. . . . On the other hand, the hussar and *Jäger* is more respectful of danger in ordinary battle than troops fighting in close order. This is an absolutely necessary quality of light troops . . . in whom the most extreme daring must alternate according to circumstances with intelligent caution. The free play of intelligence, which operates in the little war, this clever union of boldness with caution (I should like to say, this fortunate combination of daring and fear), this is the quality that renders the little war so extraordinarily interesting.[78]

While the debate on infantry tactics continued, innovation was aided by additional changes in army organization. In Frederick William's eyes only those units that had fought until the end of the war deserved a place in the new army. The rest—among them, Prussia's oldest regiments—were struck off the rolls, their remaining personnel was discharged or transferred to new formations. Since *Jäger* companies had been included in Blücher's capitulation, the regiment was dissolved despite the excellent performance of most of its members. Yorck strenuously argued against the decision, which he believed unjust, though he did not go to the length of Blücher, who appeared before the King wearing the now illegal red uniform of his disbanded hussars. Under Yorck's direction, the formation of two new *Jäger* battalions was begun in November 1808; in recognition of the regiment's good service one battalion was incorporated into the Guards. During the same month it was decided to select the best men from those of Goetzen's light infantry units that were still under arms in Silesia and form them into a battalion of sharpshooters.[79] The

[78] C. v. Clausewitz, *Meine Vorlesungen über den kleinen Krieg; Über den Charakter des kleinen Krieges.*

[79] Documents on the founding, organizing, and equipping of the new battalions are printed in Rentzell, pp. 50–52, 391–396; and *Preussisches Archiv*, pp. 530, 678–684, 776–779, 784–786. A few documents of later

Jäger continued to carry rifles, the new *Schützen-Bataillon* was issued muskets, and in other details of dress and equipment resembled the line infantry.[80] To ensure that the men were trained properly and that the drill of the widely scattered companies remained uniform, Yorck, on Scharnhorst's suggestion, was appointed Inspector of the *Jäger* and *Schützen*, a duty he carried out simultaneously with his brigade command.[81] The result of these changes was the breakdown of the isolated position that the *Jäger* had once assumed in the army; now the three battalions of elite light infantry, garrisoned throughout the country, helped acquaint the line with the conditions and methods of the light service.[82]

The process of familiarization was further advanced when the formerly self-contained fusilier battalions were made part of the infantry regiments. Officers and soldiers of the line, drilling side by side with their light battalion, were now regularly exposed to skirmish tactics. It was, however, only natural that the pressure and authority of the line came at times to threaten the tactical characteristics of the light infantry. Until November 1807 the regimental commander had been master in a realm whose first law was the greatest attainable measure of uniformity in drill and appearance. The incorporation of the light battalion brought an alien body to the regimental organization. Friction between the line- and light commanders grew so high that in the last days of 1808 rules had to be issued to define and regulate their relations. Over-all tactical and administrative control was left to the regimental commander, but the chief of the light battalion received

---

date concerning the *Jäger* and *Schützen* are contained in file A 32 of the Scharnhorst Papers. On 17 July 1811, for instance, Scharnhorst is asked to pass on Yorck's suggestion that foresters entering the *Jäger* companies bring their own rifles, the government paying one-third of the weapon's value, which however remains the property of the individual. On 23 July 1811, Clausewitz in Scharnhorst's name agreed to the proposal.

[80] *Das Preussische Heer im Jahre 1812*, pp. 128–129; P. Pietsch, *Die Formations- und Uniformierungs-Geschichte des Preussischen Heeres, 1808–1914*, Hamburg, 1963–1966, I, 159–178.

[81] The Cabinet Order of 14 April 1809 appointing Yorck is printed in Rentzell, p. 54.

[82] Sautermeister's discussion of these reforms (p. 50) is completely misleading, since he confuses the new *Jäger* and *Schützen* battalions with the third rank of the line infantry.

special rights beyond those of other battalion commanders—in particular greater disciplinary independence, and almost autonomous powers in matters of training and drill.[83] It was a necessary and remarkably courageous break with tradition. The distinct position of the fusilier battalion commander was restated in Zieten's "Instruction for Light Troops Attached to Line Infantry" of 10 May 1810.[84] The instruction contains a passage that suggests the prejudice with which the light troops still had to contend: "If a skirmisher makes a mistake in close order drill, he ought not to be disgraced or scolded with expressions that betray contempt of the light service. The commanding officers must strictly see to it that such things do not happen. . . ."

Difficulties were also caused by the many new officers who had been transferred from line units and still knew little about their new duties. The later general von Schmidt, who at this time commanded a light infantry company, writes in his memoirs that most of the newcomers imagined that "the whole art of skirmishing consisted in madly running about," and that they experienced the greatest frustrations in teaching their subordinates to fight as individuals, "particularly without the use of the stick!" [85]

The light battalions needed to be protected against the line mentality; at the same time their own training and that of the infantry in general required much further improvement. Hampered though it was by Frederick William's order to delay the writing of comprehensive manuals, the modernization of tactics proceeded in 1809 by a series of advances in doctrine and organization. Five instructions were issued to the infantry between March and July. The first, written by Gneisenau, prescribed the duties and drill of the third rank and of the light battalions.[86] The tasks of the skirmisher were to protect the closed line and column, to fight in broken terrain, mask troop movements, fill gaps in the

[83] "Instruktion über die Verhältnisse der Regimentskommandeure und der Kommandeure der leichten Bataillone," of 26 December 1808, printed in *Preussisches Archiv*, pp. 860–863.

[84] *Reorganisation*, II, 246–247. The following quotation is from p. 247. The special authority of the fusilier battalion commanders was terminated in 1812 when the army was regrouped to provide an auxiliary corps for the French invasion of Russia.

[85] Schmidt, II, 106–107.

[86] *Instruction über den Gebrauch des dritten Gliedes*. Signed by the King on 27 March 1809, and published as a pamphlet in Königsberg.

front, and produce a more accurate fire than could be obtained from the closed line. Thus, Gneisenau explained, "the third rank is intended for far more important purposes than were the former *Schützen*, who were primarily meant to act as a defense against *tirailleurs* and snipers." The instruction provided simple evolutions and uncomplicated commands; its entire content was realistic, though the actions of the individual skirmisher were still described in schematic detail. Men in the skirmish line should move rapidly and not in cadence; two men should always work closely together; they fire alternately; when loading the soldier steps behind his companion, then moves forward to fire; under certain conditions he is permitted to seek cover, and even to lie down. In the realm of open order, Gneisenau obviously felt, nothing could yet be taken as self-understood. Noteworthy is the little space given to the skirmishers' offensive potential, and the absence of detailed rules for the coordination of open and closed formations.

On 24 April marksmanship instructions were issued to the infantry.[87] At the same time Yorck and Major Ernst von Witzleben, commander of the Guards *Jäger* battalion and Vice-Inspector of the *Jäger* and *Schützen*, released a training guide for riflemen, which contained instructions on how to fire at standing and moving targets from different positions.[88]

In July Gneisenau's brief manual on the third rank was supplemented by rules for the entire infantry, written in line with Scharnhorst's views by Major Johann Wilhelm Krauseneck.[89] The author was another non-Prussian bourgeois who had become an expert in the light service. He began his career in 1791 in Ansbach-Bayreuth, but soon transferred to the Prussian army as *Ingenieur-Geograph*, a specialist position whose holders wore uniform but possessed no military rank. Although he distinguished himself in the Revolutionary wars, his background

---

[87] Excerpted in *Auszug aus den Verordnungen über die Verfassung der Königl. Preuss. Armee, welche seit dem Tilsiter Frieden ergangen sind,* ed. G. v. Scharnhorst, Berlin, 1810, pp. 179–181.

[88] Excerpted in Gumtau, I, 243–244, and Rentzell, p. 55.

[89] *Instruction zum Exerciren der Infanterie.* Signed by the King on 16 July 1809, and published as a pamphlet in Königsberg. On Krauseneck, who ended his career as chief of the General Staff, see Priesdorff, No. 1329, and the good biography published soon after his death by K. F. v. Felgermann, *General W. J. v. Krauseneck*, Berlin, 1851.

proved a handicap and it was not until 1797 that he was given a lieutenant's patent in the fusiliers. During the winter campaign of 1807 Krauseneck attracted Scharnhorst's notice and became a member of his staff. After Tilsit he assisted in reorganizing the artillery, but he preferred infantry service, and in June 1809 was appointed commander of the newly established Guards Fusiliers. The introduction to his "Instruction on Infantry Drill" of 16 July stated that the text was to be considered as no more than a "temporary norm for simplifying the soldier's elementary training, for the removal of all unnecessary formalities from battalion evolutions, which should only serve the requirements of actual combat, and for the expulsion from the realm of training of all complicated positions, steps, and formations. . . . All customary but no longer useful evolutions which the instruction does not mention, are to be regarded as abolished."

The manual was divided into three parts: drill with and without the musket; formations in close order; service of the light troops. The third section summarized Gneisenau's orders for the third rank and the light battalions, with repeated warnings that in their training and employment everything formal and mechanical should be discarded in favor of naturalness and the free play of the individual's intelligence. The section on close order for the first time in an official Prussian publication gave detailed instructions on how to form attack columns. In fact the formation described was a new and easily assembled battalion square; but except that the ranks faced in four directions rather than in one, the square and the attack column were identical.

Finally, on 17 July, the fifth tactical instruction appeared—the "Instruction Concerning the Formation of the Brigades in Battle, for the Attack, etc." [90] This brief document of fourteen paragraphs and four sketches, which expressed the reformers' views on the employment of large units, was distributed only to senior officers and their staffs. The first of its two sections described the new standard line of battle. The brigade deployed into four fragmented layers: fusiliers, and behind them infantry in line, as the first line of battle, backed up by the second line of battle consist-

---

[90] "Instruction in Betreff der Stellungen der Brigaden zum Gefecht, zum Angriff, usw." It is not known to me whether the instruction was printed. A manuscript copy is contained in the Blücher files in the Bundesarchiv-Militärarchiv in Koblenz, Restakten, H 01–1/47, fol. 40–45.

ing of infantry in columns and of artillery, with cavalry and the horse artillery to the rear. The second section outlined the development from this arrangement into the advance and the attack. The fusiliers, partly opened up in skirmish lines, led the way; behind them came the infantry in attack columns. For the final assault the fusiliers withdrew to the flanks and rear and the regular infantry advanced behind its own skirmishers. Skirmish lines and columns were to be the standard means of attack, but the instruction permitted the brigade commanders to depart from this pattern whenever necessary. The weakness of the instruction was the generally passive role it assigned to the cavalry and the inadequate coordination of artillery and infantry; its great merit lay in its treatment of infantry tactics and in the freedom it granted the individual commanders. In place of the shallow and inflexible linear front the troops were now to deploy in depth, in a series of mobile, mutually supporting skirmish swarms, squares, columns, and lines.

Taken together, the instructions of 1809 and their immediate predecessors outlined a new tactical system for the army. Not all points were adequately covered; it was evident that the instructions needed to be combined and elaborated into a single authoritative text. Nor could manuals by themselves shift the army from the Frederician pattern to the modern doctrine that they were developing. The reconstituted General Staff and the military schools helped diffuse the new ideas through the service; but more was needed to turn them into reality on the barrack square and drill field. Once again the light service showed the way. Yorck's supervision of the *Jäger* and *Schützen* was already leading to pronounced improvement in these troops. In the winter of 1809 Scharnhorst proposed that the system of training inspectorates be extended to all light troops—foot and horse—in the army. He suggested that the light units of each brigade combine once a year for extensive maneuvers under the direction of their brigadier, an officer of field rank, subordinate to the commanding Brigadier General. After the light troops had achieved some proficiency in working together, the other troops of the brigade would join them and continue the field exercises on a larger scale. In his memoirs, Boyen writes that the main purpose was to change the army's deep-rooted custom of maneuvering only in long lines over horizontal plains.[91] Again on Scharnhorst's suggestion, Boyen continues, and "to put the whole affair under unified leadership, General Yorck was appointed Inspector-General of all light troops in the army." The Cabinet Order of 17 February 1810, designating Yorck to this position, also ordered him to issue written instructions to all commanders of light units so that they "observed the necessary uniformity in their field-training." [92] Maneuvers that in peacetime prepared officers and rank and file for the realities of war now became a possibility.[93]

[91] *Erinnerungen*, II, 110. The following quotation is from the same page.

[92] *Reorganisation*, II, 204; Voss, p. 25.

[93] That before 1806 Prussian troops did not conduct maneuvers is a frequently encountered misconception. Nor is Shanahan correct when he writes, p. 21, that "it was impossible for the several arms to train with one another. . . . the men were unaccustomed to any drills or exercise that involved more than one regiment." The contemporary literature contains numerous accounts of large-scale exercises that brought together infantry, cavalry, and artillery; see, for example, "Die Preussische Revüe aus den Briefen eines Zuschauers," *Neues Militärisches Magazin*, II, No. 6 (1802), especially pp. 14–22. The decisive difference between maneuvers held before and after 1806 is that in the earlier period maneuvers were designed to train officers, while the common soldier was ignored. See Frederick's explicit statement in the *Military Testament* of 1768; Taysen, *Friedrich der Grosse: Militärische Schriften*, p. 206.

CHAPTER V
The *Reglement* of 1812

FOR some months during the war of 1809 it seemed as though Prussia might regain a measure of independence through the efforts of others. The Austrian defeat turned her back on her own resources. She remained unable, as she had been since Jena, to shape the political forces that dominated the Continent and determined her existence; but these forces were changing. As befitted a client state of the Empire her foreign policies continued to be timid and temporizing; but her civil and military institutions were developing a new vitality, while the French, as Scharnhorst was the first to see, no longer were the power they had been before Trafalgar, the war in Spain, and the crystallization of Napoleon's antagonism towards Russia. In the impending conflict between East and West, Prussia was certain to be involved, if only as a theater of operations, yet the danger carried with it possible advantages. The government negotiated with both sides. Frederick William's sympathy lay with Russia, as did that of most of his advisors; but the French garrisons in the country, the unfavorable geographic circumstances that placed Polish, Saxon, and Westphalian troops within a few miles of every important town and highway, the King's belief in Napoleon's invincibility and his lack of faith in himself and his people made war with France seem unlikely from the first. In June 1810 Napoleon succeeded in having Scharnhorst dismissed as *de facto* Minister of War; and although Scharnhorst continued to head the General Staff and the engineers, the group that worked for a Russian alliance had been dealt a hard blow. Hardenberg's accession as Chancellor also promised a more pliable attitude in Berlin. The Emperor followed up these gains by insisting that recent measures of military preparedness, especially the improvement of Prussian fortifications, be interrupted or revoked. By the early months of 1811 the build-up of French forces in central and northern Germany was reaching serious proportions; but it was not yet known against whom the troops would march. If Prussia was the objective, her army, scattered in small garrisons throughout the state, was in danger of being neutralized and captured before it could mobilize. To meet this threat it was planned to send senior officers to the provinces, with emergency powers that would permit them to act, if need be, on their own. In May 1811, Yorck was on Scharnhorst's suggestion appointed Governor in West Prussia, a post that was expanded in November to the Governor-Generalship of East and West Prussia and Lithuania —an area that bordered on Russia and the Duchy of Warsaw, and would prove equally important whether the future enemies were Russian or French.[1] His instructions were far-reaching—in his own words, they "invested him in special circumstances with a part of the royal power."[2]

Yorck's greatest concern was to achieve a high degree of readiness for his troops, whom he placed as much on a war footing as he dared under the eyes of French observers and agents. He pressed the King and Hardenberg for means to strengthen his command, and for permission to mobilize completely. To supplement his forces in case of war, he and Theodor von Schön, the head of the civil administration in Prussia, planned to arm the population.[3] Organized insurrection, the politicized populace rising against the foreign oppressor, had always been the ultimate weapon in the reformers' politico-military doctrine. As models they took the revolts against social and political change that had erupted throughout Europe during the past two decades. From Russia Stein wrote to Gneisenau: "How a people that revolts energetically and fights courageously should feel and how it should be constituted we are taught by the Vendée, the Tyrol,

---

[1] On 13 May Yorck wrote to Scharnhorst that his new mission might be beyond his abilities. Scharnhorst in his reply ten days later praised and reassured him. Droysen, I, 259–262. The letters are remarkable in their frankness, and confirm the impression given by other correspondence of 1810 and 1811, of a newly intimate relationship between the two men, in which Scharnhorst meets Yorck's stormy demonstrativeness with an unfailingly calm and understanding sympathy.

[2] Droysen, I, 262.

[3] *Ibid.*, pp. 308–309. See also Schön's letters to Droysen of 22 March 1848, 16 March 1850, and 7 July 1850; Droysen, *Briefwechsel*, I, pp. 391–394, 618–619, 654–657.

Spain, Austria." [4] From the military point of view, the Spanish example was the most instructive, and former Prussian officers such as Grolman, Lützow, and Scharnhorst's son who now served in the King's German Legion or in the Spanish army, kept their old comrades informed of the methods and problems of guerrilla warfare. [5]

The whole concept of insurrection met, however, with little favor in Frederick William's eyes—not only for dynastic reasons, judging from his comments on Gneisenau's "Plan for the Preparation of a National Uprising," but from a real horror of the anarchy that would be unleashed. [6] And the King was far from alone in his aversion to a kind of warfare whose chances of success stood in no measurable relation to the threats it presented to the social order. In 1808 Yorck, too, had opposed ideas of insurrection; but at that time the army was in dissolution and little had yet been done to make the people willing in a crisis to take up arms. In the changed circumstances of 1811 he was one of the few senior commanders to support this most revolutionary of military techniques. In Gneisenau's memorandum he was named as one of the men suited to prepare the insurrection. Boyen, another proponent of the scheme, was later to write that the King and Hardenberg feared the idea of a national uprising, and that "in the army too, with the exception of Blücher, Yorck, and Gneisenau, who had now returned from England, the great majority was against a guerrilla war, insofar as now and then something was heard about it. The great majority of officers could not harmonize their tactical training with such a method of warfare." [7] As late as January 1812, Yorck wrote the King:

[4] Letter of 17 August 1811, printed in *Freiherr vom Stein. Briefwechsel, Denkschriften und Aufzeichnungen*, ed. E. Botzenhart, Berlin, 1931–1937, III, 450–452.

[5] See, for instance, Grolman's letter to Gneisenau of 8 June 1810, and subsequent reports, printed in E. v. Conrady, *Leben und Wirken des Generals Carl von Grolman*, Berlin, 1894–1896, I, 232ff.

[6] Gneisenau's essay is printed by Pertz-Delbrück, II, 112–142. In the chapter "Volkserhebung und Kabinettspolitik" in the first volume of his work, *Staatskunst und Kriegshandwerk*, Munich, 1954, Gerhard Ritter has closely analyzed the historical trends behind the reformers' plans for insurrection. See particularly, pp. 100–106.

[7] *Erinnerungen*, II, 104.

If war really should break out . . . it will be a war for our existence. It will decide life or death, and the choice of means must cease
to cause concern if only they can achieve our purpose. Mobilizing the
people *en masse* will, however, hamper the army's operations unless
this mass is properly organized and the insurrection is unleashed only
in those areas where it will not come into direct contact with the
army's movements. . . . Major v. Krauseneck would be particularly well suited to lead such an insurrection.[8]

The mobilization of the people was aimed at the French, but
Prussian policy was about to shift firmly to the opposite side. The
period of diplomatic maneuvering, which in its last days Scharnhorst in a letter to Yorck described as a "stormy, shaky condition . . . a dark and darkening future, a labyrinthian confusion," ended on 24 February 1812 with the Treaty of Paris, by
which Frederick William pledged his support to France in the
coming war.[9] The alliance with Russia, which had been advocated by most if not all reform-minded officers, was discarded.
They had failed in guiding the state; their achievement was
limited to the construction of its new military instrument. But in
this circumscribed task they succeeded remarkably well. In every
field except conscription the schemes for modernization that were
launched in 1807 had been carried forward without meeting
crippling defeat. In the development of tactical doctrine, especially, the past three years had witnessed a decisive turning towards the new. The major steps in this process of accepting
revolutionary methods were the instructions that Yorck issued in
1810 and 1811, the lectures on tactics, given at the War School
for Officers by Tiedemann and Clausewitz, and finally the *Reglement* of 1812.

The first of Yorck's two instructions were submitted to the
King on 17 March 1810, one month after Yorck's appointment as
Inspector-General of the light brigades.[10] The "Instruction for the

[8] Undated report to the King, written towards the end of January
1812, printed in Droysen, I, 520–527. The quotation is from p. 525.

[9] Letter of 26 February 1812, *ibid.*, p. 323.

[10] "Instruktion des General von York für die leichten Truppen zu den
Übungen im Jahre 1810." The text is printed with minor errors and
omissions by Gumtau in the appendix to the third volume of his *Jäger und
Schützen*, pp. 79–100. Frederick William thanked Yorck in a Cabinet
Order of 29 March, and on the same day approved the instruction with the

Light Troops for the Maneuvers of the Year 1810" begins by explaining that written directions cannot cover all details, the elaboration of which is left to the light brigade commanders.[11] The introduction continues with lines that differentiate the basic approaches towards war of the *ancien régime* and the Napoleonic Era:

> Nor can this instruction offer a compilation of entirely new opinions, since as already stated its only purpose is to summarize known truths and experiences into a consistent training guide. Still less is it possible to provide precise formulae for all eventualities in an art such as that of war, in which results depend so greatly on chance, the elements, and—to be particularly noted—on free will, i.e., on the

---

single exception that fusilier battalions should not, as Yorck had recommended, form in two ranks like the *Jäger*, but in common with the heavy infantry in three. *Reorganisation*, ii, 248; Priesdorff, No. 1120. Presumably Yorck wanted gradually to introduce the two-rank formation as the standard for all infantry, light and heavy. Yorck sent a copy of the instruction to Scharnhorst, asking for his opinion, "to which I shall gladly subordinate my own. I shall accept criticisms with gratitude, and will certainly make it my duty to apply them." *Reorganisation*, ii, 248. Scharnhorst's reply of 29 March 1810 was full of praise: "The instruction is so outstanding, so intelligently integrated, so closely bound up with the principles of war, and these are stated in such accurate and just terms, that I have read this excellent essay with as much profit as pleasure." *Ibid.*, ii, 249. Scharnhorst himself at about this time was drawing up maneuver directives for the army as a whole, less detailed than Yorck's instruction, but informed with the same spirit. "Allgemeine Regeln zur Befolgung in den Übungen," printed in Klippel, iii, 523–544. A passage on p. 541 states: "Good marksmanship is always the most important thing for the infantry—it always decides the action. Before the war we taught the men to load quickly, but not well, to fire quickly, but without aiming. This was very ill-considered; we must therefore work with all our might to root out this error." Scharnhorst was clearly spurring on the officers in charge of training, and perhaps said more than he actually believed; nevertheless his words are a further indication that such historians as v. d. Goltz and Jany underestimated the possibilities of aimed fire at the beginning of the nineteenth century, presumably from a tendency to defend the rightness of Frederician tactics as long as infantry weapons had not been improved. In April 1810 Scharnhorst went so far as to write that "For a thinking and informed man, making rifles more common in the army is one of the most important tasks in the entire military profession." Lehmann, *Scharnhorst*, ii, 230.

[11] Gumtau, iii, Appendix, p. 79. The following quotation is from pp. 79–80.

intelligence, courage, or cowardice of the individual parts of the machine. Only general rules can be sketched here. Their appropriate application to prevailing circumstances distinguishes the thinking officer from the one who considers his task mechanically, or seeks the perfect picture of war in the fitting together of learned evolutions.

The first section of the text defines the operational role of light troops.[12] They form "the shield of an army, which is either preparing to strike the enemy with full force while covered by them, or uses them with the intention of blunting the enemy's offensive strength before it can be fully applied." To fulfill these aims, the light forces must be accorded a great measure of flexibility and independence—a factor that "must be firmly kept in mind when establishing rules for light troops." The section continues by enumerating the various tasks of the light foot and horse:

1. Outpost duty, with its subsections of advance- and rear-guards, and of patrols.

2. Direct and indirect cooperation with the tactical actions of the army, both to cover the army's operations and to facilitate their execution. And

3. the war of detachments, to carry out certain special tasks as part of an over-all strategic plan.

The following paragraphs discuss weapons, maintenance, and marksmanship, and open with the definition: "The light infantryman's weapon is primarily the musket, his tactics must therefore be fire tactics, the basic principle of which is to hit the enemy with the bullet." This introduces a statement which perhaps more than any other exemplifies the individuality of Yorck's tactical thought: "If this be done by combining the greatest possible security of the individual with the greatest possible damage dealt to the enemy, then the greatest possible demands of the service are satisfied." Such an axiom—balancing effectiveness with safety, the latter becoming part of the former—spoke a language different from Frederick's rational-heroic aphorisms, or, indeed, Napoleon's smug psychologizing.

The first section ends by recommending field training with live ammunition. The officers are asked to study Scharnhorst's *Handbuch für Offiziere*, which contains a "complete course of instruction" in the theory of firearms.

---

[12] *Ibid.*, III, Appendix, pp. 80–83.

The second part, which forms the main body of the instruction, begins by stressing the significance of skirmishing for the light infantry and recalls Gneisenau's instruction of 27 March 1809, which had already defined the basic elements of skirmishing.[13] Yorck then continues:

Tiraillement is an opened-up battle formation, in which man does not cling to man. On the whole it must be led in one direction, but it affords the individual the advantage of moving freely in any terrain, of firing accurately aimed shots, and of benefiting according to circumstances from all possibilities that the ground offers for personal cover and for hurting the enemy in safety. Skirmish lines permit large areas to be occupied at once, allow outflanking the front of a closely ranged enemy if his superiority is not too disproportionate. The thinness of the skirmish line and the free movement of the individuals composing it not only permit the enemy to be hit with greater accuracy, but also infinitely reduce the danger arising from unaimed volleys (not excluding those of his artillery). Even in former times this manner of fighting was the mark of all irregular forces; but it was left to the modern age to combine these troops and their methods for mutual interaction with the army proper.

The following paragraphs spell out the duties of the light infantry in greater detail:

The light infantryman . . . must occupy the approaches to the army's position—in other words, form the first line of fire; he must often occupy sizable terrain with few men; maintain the connection between the columns that are to decide the main issue; he must hide the movement of these columns and cover their approach; mislead the enemy about our intentions; and finally must choose woods, defiles, and so-called broken terrain for the main stage of his activities.

Obviously serried ranks can rarely move in such terrain. For these duties it is absolutely necessary to adapt to the terrain, and not—as the line does—select the terrain according to its suitability to one's tactics. Thus skirmishing, modified according to circumstances, is the true manner of fighting for the light infantry.

Next Yorck enumerates what the private soldier must learn about skirmishing, and how these skills can best be taught. First, he should understand the proper use of terrain and how to operate as a member of a unit without losing his individuality. Training should start with small groups practising defensive tactics on

[13] *Ibid.*, III, Appendix, pp. 83–92.

level ground. It should become a basic rule that two men always support each other, although "in reality situations often occur in which this cannot be followed slavishly." Nor should the principle of alternate firing be insisted on too pedantically, since the practical object of dissuading men from volleying is simply to teach them not to waste their fire—"the *tirailleur* should hit, and not make noise." After these fundamentals have been mastered, the men proceed to the refinements of skirmishing: the use of buildings in defense, unobserved movement, the choice of cover in forests, hills, and fields—in which connection Yorck mentions Scharnhorst's experience with the French *tirailleurs* before Menin. The next stage is the application of this knowledge to the attack, again initially on level ground, later in broken terrain. Here Yorck confirms others' comments that many officers still imagined skirmishing to consist of "madly running about":

I must also censure an error that has become widespread in the army: the exaggerated running in skirmish lines. It cannot be repeated often enough that the basic principle of fighting in open formations lies in *accurate shooting;* a breathless man simply cannot fulfill this requirement. Certainly the concept of utmost mobility is also attached to light troops, but it must always be subordinated and adapted to the fire-fight.

The final pages of the second section extend these instructions from individuals and small groups to the operations of companies and battalions. In places the text is openly cast in the form of a dispute with old tactical concepts: "One must forget the old notion of wanting to defend everything at once. Force must be met with counterforce, but counterforce is frittered away by detachments." Symmetrical orders of battle are condemned in favor of concentrating "the impulse of the attack (i.e. the superiority of fire) on one point. . . . The whole secret of tactics, regardless of how one looks at it, lies in intelligent disposition of the impulse (just now I can't think of a more suitable term, but hope that I will be understood by any experienced soldier)." Yorck repeats the warning that field exercises and actual combat have nothing to do with parades, and criticizes the unrealistic drill that may still be seen: "Evolutions and maneuvers must always be clear and definite, and never degenerate into trifling." The section concludes with a call for greater understanding of what could be achieved with the new soldier and modern tactics: "So-called impractical terrain, or enemy positions that cannot be attacked, do not exist for the light infantry. . . . If an attempt does not succeed in one place it may perhaps work in another, and what can't be achieved by day should be tried at night, the cover of which has been exploited far too infrequently in recent wars." [14]

The next three sections discuss the duties of the hussars, of outposts, advance- and rear-guards, and of detachments.[15] The text demands that these tasks be carried out with speed and aggressiveness; reconnaissance should take place on a broad front; the hussars must not be tied to the plains, and in contrast to prevailing doctrine should be able to deploy as much as two-thirds of each squadron into skirmish swarms. For all these forces, removed from the center of authority, success lies in the greatest possible exploitation of initiative; at the same time they must always act in conformity with an over-all plan to the extent of sacrificing their individual advantages, and in cases of need even of sacrificing themselves.

The final section—"Principles to be employed in the maneuvers of the light brigades when these are fully assembled"—applies the preceding instructions to the operations of the largest tactical units.[16] Yorck begins characteristically by defining the essential factor involved, and then warning against blindly complying with it: "Mobility lies in the nature of the light troops' manner of fighting and should be apparent everywhere, but it

[14] The impossibility of maintaining tactical control, and the increased opportunity afforded for desertion, had generally ruled out movements after dusk for eighteenth-century commanders. Even during the Napoleonic Era such operations were sufficiently rare as to excite comment. When in 1814 at Athies Yorck put his suggestion into practice and with two corps attacked the French at night, Marmont in his report to Napoleon termed the act an "unfortunate and quite unusual event in war." In his memoirs the French marshal gives this description of his retreat before Yorck's fusiliers: "I shall never forget the music that accompanied us on our march. The signal horns of the light infantry sounded, the enemy halted, and for several minutes fire was directed at us, then silence fell until the music sounded again and prepared us for new fire." A. de Marmont, *Mémoires du Duc de Raguse*, Paris, 1857, VI, 213–214. Marmont admitted heavy losses in equipment but few in men; the Prussians claimed the capture of 2,000 prisoners and 45 guns.

[15] Gumtau, III, Appendix, pp. 92–98.

[16] *Ibid.*, III, Appendix, pp. 99–100.

must never be used at the wrong time, otherwise the means are confused with the end." He again condemns the custom of detaching too many small groups: they are too easily impressed by an aggressive enemy, confusion is inevitable, and defeat of the whole force the result.

During the last maneuvers we still fell too frequently into this old error, proof that we hadn't yet clarified our ideas on the nature of battle, and hadn't been able to free ourselves from the dark, insubstantial idea that we should always adjust our movements to those of the enemy. In this manner we voluntarily cede intellectual superiority to the enemy from the very beginning, and physical superiority can then be achieved only through enormous efforts.

Yorck then delineates his theory of battle, in which the now generally acknowledged principles of surprise and concentration of effort are coupled with a tactical flexibility of his own, which is based on the virtual disappearance of the distinction between light troops and line infantry:

The first stage of maneuvering should be a demonstration; during the initial approach of our firing line, the enemy simply must not know what he is to expect. An extended line of *tirailleurs*, guarded by troops of horse, keeps the enemy occupied, while our attack columns, covered by the irregularities of the ground, march to the flanks and from there impose the main pressure on the battle.

Breaking through the center is a dangerous maneuver; nevertheless it often succeeds in war, if one can rely on the bravery of the troops and on the competence of their leaders, and has some strong flank positions, which the enemy cannot disregard in a possible counterattack. Pursuit of a disorganized enemy . . . should be pushed as far as possible.

Sometimes artillery can be made into the driving force of the engagement; this is possible particularly when the enemy's intentions have been discovered early on. . . .

The instruction concludes: "Finally it is self-understood that the fusilier battalions on maneuvers should never forget that in case of need they are also intended to fight in line; in order to achieve real military bearing and develop the quick responses that are so necessary to them, the *Jäger* and *Schützen* battalions must also master the basic elements of line duty."

Yorck's instruction for the first time in the new army took the soldier from individual training through small-unit tactics to the actions of large commands. The doctrine he presented to the service was consistent throughout; all its parts were shaped by the aim of destroying the opponent's means to resist. Any formalism had entirely disappeared. But the summer maneuvers of that year showed that neither Yorck's intentions nor his methods were yet sufficiently understood in the army. A report he sent the King on 1 August made clear that he was not satisfied with the progress achieved in the months since he had issued his directive.[17] "Almost everywhere," he wrote, "I found that the school-forms of training evolutions had been taken as valid means for the purposes of war: people have surrendered to an illusion of artificiality and have strayed from the true path. . . ." Some of the specific errors that he mentioned were too much drilling on level ground, insufficient attention being paid to marksmanship, failure to understand the flexible nature of skirmish lines and how to draw advantages from the terrain, and ignorance of the proper organization and use of reconnaissance. He concluded: "All things whose incorrect or negligent execution has already caused the defeat of armies, were practiced little or not at all and treated only as matters of secondary importance."[18]

A fortnight later, in a circular of 16 August addressed to the brigadiers of the light troops, Yorck repeated his urging that all drill should be realistic, that units should often train at night, and that "particular attention should be given to the use of the musket, the proper placement, reinforcement, and diminution of the firing-line, the proper distribution and employment of reserves, the alternation of men from reserve to firing line, and finally to the systematic training of the *tirailleurs* in creeping and crawling."[19]

[17] Excerpts are printed by Voss, pp. 49–51. Since May Yorck had been on an inspection tour of the light troops in the army. A Cabinet Order of 12 April 1810, drafted in Clausewitz's hand, ordered Yorck to make certain that officers of light units had "entered into the spirit of the instructions you drafted." *Nachlass Vaupel*, Nr. 48, Heft 17. According to Droysen, I, 238, it was on this trip in July that he made his peace with Scharnhorst. The complimentary references to Scharnhorst in the instruction of 19 March, and the exchange of letters that followed, suggest that Yorck's animosity had disappeared by March at the latest.

[18] Voss, p. 50.

[19] The texts of this and a subsequent circular are printed in Droysen, I, 509–513.

Yorck's instruction of 17 March had called on the commanders of the light brigades to work out supplementary regulations on the drill and maneuvers of their troops. None of these seem to have survived in the original.[20] But the text of one such order with some changes Roche-Aymon later published in his book on light troops, and concrete information on the training Prussian light infantry underwent in the summer of 1810 is thus available.[21] In February Roche-Aymon had been placed at the head of the West Prussian light brigade; on 6 April he submitted to Yorck a manuscript of more than 100 pages regulating the training of his new command, which Yorck approved "in large part."[22] Written, the author states, according to the principle that "the useful should always be preferred to the pretty . . . the simplest and least complicated is the best," the instructions laid down rules for the drill of individuals and units, for field entrenchments, and for the defense of buildings.[23] The men are to go on the range every week, and fire first at fixed, later at moving targets; volleys are to be used in battle only during emergencies.[24] Marching need not be as constrained and exact as that of troops of the line; the steps may be longer, the cadence quicker, and running should be practiced—but with intelligence. Companies should go out on route marches once or twice a week.[25] The evolutions that companies and battalions are to practice particularly are changes of front, forming columns from the line, and vice versa, and forming skirmish lines. "All these movements do not demand perfectly symmetrical order; it is sufficient that the men march in silence,

---

[20] Both Dr. E. Murawski, former head of the Military Archives of the West German Bundesarchiv, and Dr. Arentz, of the Militärgeschichtliche Forschungsamt in Freiburg, assume the brigade instructions to have been among the Prussian army documents that were destroyed during World War II or are in Russian hands.

[21] "Instruction provisoire préparée pour la brigade d'infanterie légère de la Prusse occidentale," *Des Troupes légères*, pp. 110–224. On the background to the writing of the instruction, see *ibid.*, p. 18 of the Preface, and p. 75.

[22] Two days earlier, provisional cavalry instructions drafted by Roche-Aymon and Borstell were published in Königsberg. Roche-Aymon clearly justified Yorck's official evaluation of him as "an educated and exceedingly active staff officer." Priesdorff, No. 1174.

[23] *Des Troupes légères*, p. 115.

[24] *Ibid.*, pp. 116–120.

[25] *Ibid.*, pp. 120–125.

that the ranks don't get mixed up, and that they don't overtake their officers." [26] Great attention should be paid to skirmishing, in which both individuals and groups must be thoroughly trained.[27] The field formations that Roche-Aymon next enumerates are nearly all based on the cooperation of skirmish line and column; the line has almost disappeared as a formation for attack. The section on field fortifications prescribes in detail how men should dig themselves in, how various localities—bridges, woods, roads —can be made secure, and how in general to exploit the terrain for defense.[28] The fourth and last section is a guide to street fighting.[29]

Roche-Aymon's *Instruction provisoire* was a practical, undogmatic manual that ranged from basic drill to field exercises. The only important aspect with which Yorck could not have agreed was Roche-Aymon's argument that a difference existed between light and line infantry, which could be blurred only at the expense of both.[30] Very likely this was the author's genuine opinion; he may also have intended it as a hint to those line officers who as regimental commanders were the direct superiors of the fusiliers, and who might have felt tempted to regularize drill and movement of their light battalions.[31]

The maneuvers of 1810 were the first realistic field exercises on a large scale in the army's history. The troops were instructed to practice patrolling, set ambushes, attempt night attacks, and in other ways freely employ their ingenuity.[32] In view of their back-

[26] *Ibid.*, pp. 125–131.

[27] *Ibid.*, pp. 136–148 and *passim*.

[28] *Ibid.*, pp. 173–200.

[29] *Ibid.*, pp. 200–224.

[30] *Ibid.*, pp. 111–112.

[31] An exchange of letters between Yorck and Scharnhorst the following year still concerns this problem. On 11 February 1811 Yorck complained that regimental commanders would not respect the special position of the fusilier battalions, and interfered with their training. Scharnhorst answered on the 22nd that he agreed with Yorck and that this would have to cease; *Nachlass Scharnhorst*, A. Nr. 29. Already on 1 August 1810 Yorck had vainly requested greater administrative independence for the fusilier battalions; Voss, pp. 50–51.

[32] "Instruktion für die Herbstübungen der Armee im Jahr 1810" of 18 August 1810; *Nachlass Vaupel*, Nr. 49, Heft 18. A Cabinet Order to Yorck of 17 November 1810 again stressed the need for maneuvers to prepare the troops realistically for war; *ibid.*

ground of barrack-square and close order drill, it is not surprising that many officers felt at a loss when ordered to lead their men over uneven ground against enemy parties whose moves were not outlined in detailed programs.[33] After the conclusion of the exercises a Cabinet Order severely criticized their performance, mentioning "significant flaws" that had occurred in the employment of the third rank, particularly the detaching of skirmishers from their supporting formations and the failure to adjust actions to the terrain and the behavior of the opponent.[34] For the maneuvers of the following year, therefore, Yorck issued a further set of instructions "to clear up a certain lack of assurance in plans as well as in execution" that had shown itself during the previous exercises. The "Instruction for the Field Exercises of the Light Troops for the Year 1811" of 16 May 1811 is a more advanced discussion of tactics and operations than its predecessor.[35] Yorck first criticizes the various erroneous ideas of extended order that many senior and junior officers still possessed:

Often it has even been assumed that the tactics of light infantry were nothing more than firing either standing still or advancing in a schematically formed open line; on the contrary, the tactics of light infantry consist in the ability of *appropriately combining in any given situation, according to circumstances and terrain, movement in close formation with a superior well-aimed fire, which can only be achieved in open order* [Yorck's italics].

This sentence defines the infantry tactics that were to dominate European battlefields until the advent of the machine gun. The problem during the first decade of the nineteenth century had been to drive home the point that not just one or two specially trained sections but the entire light infantry unit should be able to skirmish. By 1811 this was accepted; but the need for a continual

---

[33] Many, though not all, exercises before 1806 only presupposed an opponent, so that even an enemy party maneuvering according to a precisely laid-out program was something of a novelty. See Clausewitz, *Nachrichten*, p. 429, and Jany's discussion in *Preussische Armee*, III, 505–509.

[34] Undated Cabinet Order to the *Allgemeine Kriegsdepartement*, written between September and December 1810. *Nachlass Vaupel*, Nr. 50, Heft 19, 64–65.

[35] The text of the instruction is printed in Gumtau, III, Appendix, pp. 101–120. The following quotation is from p. 102.

union of close and open tactics was not yet understood, and the fusilier battalions were in danger of remaining specialists for the secondary tasks of battle. Now Yorck took the further step of insisting on the importance to them of close order: the light infantry must not only be able to fight in skirmish lines but also in the new attack columns of the line infantry. Henceforth, in the realm of light troops the tactical difference between line and light infantry was in principle abolished; it remained only a question of degree and of emphasis.

The instruction continues with examples that spell out the implications of Yorck's definition: "The defense of villages by means of the appropriate use of houses, fences, etc., which give personal cover and permit hitting the enemy from safety, the bayonet attack in closed columns when the enemy has somewhere broken through the skirmish line—these form just as much part of light infantry tactics as does the regular firing of scattered riflemen in woods or on the plains. . . ."[36]

Yorck then warns again that nothing he writes should be slavishly followed:

I repeat once more that there are no unfailing recipes in the art of war; that any number of accidents, unusual determination of the enemy, and a not always equal determination on our side can ruin the best-laid plan. I repeat that there are however general principles, abstracted from experience, which can be safely used as the basis of one's dispositions: *but that the execution of this principle* [sic] *must be coupled with determination and prudence*, and that evolutions designed for the level drill-field play a minimal role in broken terrain [Yorck's italics].[37]

The instruction continues with analyses of operations and exercises, which stress cross-fire, flexibility, the use of counterattacks rather than rigid positions in defense, crawling—"a useful movement that can do infinite good in a large number of cases"— marching and fighting at night, and coordination between the main force and its detachments, patrols, and outposts.[38] The discussion is illustrated by historical examples drawn from the Seven Years' War, the American War of Independence, the cam-

[36] *Ibid.*, III, Appendix, p. 102.
[37] *Ibid.*, III, Appendix, p. 104.
[38] *Ibid.*, III, Appendix, pp. 105–113.

paign of 1800, the War of 1809, and the current fighting in Spain and Portugal. Once again the study of a work by Scharnhorst is recommended—this time the *Taschenbuch* for its discussion of patrolling.[39] The text concludes with a section on horn signals.[40]

To show how the individual soldier could be freed from the impediments of formalism and tradition was the underlying purpose of Yorck's instructions. The training they prescribed was realistic; their own texts were not to be followed word for word, but interpreted in the light of experience and common sense. Tactical differences between fusiliers and the line were minimized; attack- and maneuver-columns became a major factor in operations; force in general was to be concentrated rather than stretched across vast fronts or frittered away in small packets. Battles were won by deceiving the opponent, exploiting the unforeseen, keeping reserves in hand; they were neither chivalrous contests nor pertained to the realm of mathematical certainties. Yorck's instructions shared the quality of many of the reformers' writings in being at once regulations and advocates of a new military attitude. By turning away from the search for absolute

[39] *Ibid.*, III, Appendix, p. 114. Cf. *Militairisches Taschenbuch*, 3rd ed., pp. 3–234.

[40] Gumtau, III, Appendix, pp. 116–120. Horn signals had been introduced in the Prussian army by the *Jäger*, from whom they were adopted by the fusiliers, and afterwards by the line regiments for use by their sharpshooters; Kling, I, 152, and III, 32–33. The fusilier *Reglement* of 1788, pp. 159–160, lists eight calls. This number was soon found to be insufficient and additional calls were devised, until the army came to be infected by a mania for signals, and practicality was buried beneath elegant musical profusion. A Cabinet Order of 18 May 1801 vainly attempted to control the fad; *Preussische Armee*, III, 493. The number of signals, Yorck wrote in his instruction, "has been arbitrarily increased, and their use aimlessly multiplied. . . . In order to achieve uniformity of signals for the entire army, I have submitted proposals to His Majesty the King, and His Majesty has thereupon commanded that the appended calls and their meanings are to be universally observed." Gumtau, III, Appendix, pp. 118–119. Yorck prescribed twenty calls for twenty-two commands, which were later incorporated into the *Reglement* of 1812, and remained on the books until 1889. A few are still used by the West German army today. The whole is another example of the tendency to bracket every eventuality with detailed and complicated rules, which the reformers had to fight in all spheres of the service.

laws that had occupied the previous generation of Prussian theorists and tacticians, they opened war to the free play of intelligence of all of its participants.[41]

· 2 ·

In helping the army progress towards a new way of fighting, the official and semi-official instructions of Yorck, Krauseneck, and others were joined by a body of analytic studies, among which Scharnhorst's essays on infantry tactics, written in 1810 and 1811, were the most valuable. Less tied to the requirements of the moment, seeking to understand both present conditions and the historical developments that created them, Scharnhorst's pieces provided the innovations and proposals for reform with a desirable theoretical depth. The position their author occupied added to their significance; ideas and even actual phrases eventually found their way from the privately circulated manuscripts into the *Reglement* of 1812.[42] A third force in the modernization process consisted of the war schools. Scharnhorst's control over service education enabled him to appoint as instructors men who shared in his tactical views, a power that was nowhere more meaningful than at the *Kriegsschule für die Offiziere*, which Scharnhorst envisaged as the army's supreme educational institution.[43] The Academy was established in Berlin on 2 May 1810; the first term began on 15 October of the same year. Scharnhorst imputed such importance to the task of forming the intellectual elite of the army that despite his numerous other duties he himself lectured to the senior students. The courses on strategy and tactics were read by two of his closest protégés: Tiedemann and Clausewitz.

[41] Yorck's instructions retained their practicality long after the Wars of Liberation. As late as 1851 a Prussian officer, S. v. Förster, published a book with the title *Das Tiraillement im coupirten Terrain nach der Instruction des General von York*.

[42] See pp. 181, 184 below, and the essays and the introductions to them printed in Appendix 1.

[43] For the academy's early history, see L. v. Scharfenort, *Die Königlich-Preussische Kriegsakademie, 1810–1910*, Berlin, 1910, pp. 6–24, and appendices. An excellent analysis of its teaching program during the first decades is contained in E. Kessel's *Moltke*, Stuttgart, 1957, pp. 33–47.

Karl von Tiedemann had been a pupil of Scharnhorst's at the old Academy for Officers in Berlin.[44] After the war, in which he fought as an infantry subaltern, Tiedemann was employed as a member of Scharnhorst's personal staff on a number of confidential missions, and in July 1811 succeeded Clausewitz as Scharnhorst's adjutant.[45] During 1810 and 1811 he lectured on tactics at the War Academy. When in consequence of the Franco-Prussian treaty of 24 February 1812 Boyen quit his post as director of the personnel section at the Ministry of War, Scharnhorst suggested that Tiedemann take his place.[46] Tiedemann however refused, and resigned from the army. A few weeks later, together with Clausewitz and some two dozen other comrades who were unwilling to fight for Napoleon, he entered Russian service.[47] This mass demonstration was an event without parallel in the army's history; to the general public it disclosed for the first time that in some minds patriotism had become a true rival to monarchic sentiment and the principle of military subordination. Except in the cases of men such as Gneisenau or Boyen whose retention the alliance had rendered politically infeasible, Frederick William took the resignations as a personal affront; those officers who went over to the Russians had their properties sequestrated and remained out of favor even after the change of front in the spring of 1813. When Clausewitz asked to be readmitted into the army, he was answered with these lines from the

[44] Tiedemann's biography has not been written. Material on his life can be found in "Tagebuch und Briefwechsel des Oberstlieutenants v. Tiedemann aus dem Jahre 1812," ed. M. Lehmann, *Jahrbücher für die Deutsche Armee und Marine*, XXIV, 1877, 117–148; and there is a brief entry in the *Allgemeine Deutsche Biographie*, XXXIV, 1894, 280–281.

[45] See *Scharnhorsts Briefe*, I, 346–348, 372, 416, n. 2. Officially Clausewitz had been transferred to the General Staff on 19 July 1810, but he continued to work in Scharnhorst's office for another year. *Bundesarchiv-Militärarchiv*, Restakten, Heft 01 1/27, 7, Nr. 270; 01 1/29, 4, Nr. 12.

[46] *Scharnhorsts Briefe*, I, 425; Boyen, *Erinnerungen*, II, 186.

[47] The legend of hundreds of Prussian officers quitting the service in protest was exploded long ago by M. Lehmann in his study "Knesebeck, der russische Operationsplan und die dreihundert preussischen Offiziere von 1812," in *Knesebeck und Schön*, Leipzig, 1875. P. Stulz's recent attempt to convict Lehmann of falsely minimizing the number does not deserve the name of scholarship, but unfortunately is typical of much East German historical writing today. *Fremdherrschaft und Befreiungskampf*, Berlin, 1960, pp. 104–105.

King: "In consequence of your letter of the 11th, I have ordered your process quashed. But you can be readmitted to the service of the fatherland only when you have won the right for special consideration by particularly distinguishing yourself in the coming campaign." [48] In a farewell letter to Tiedemann, Scharnhorst had written: "However events will go now, I cannot condemn your decision because everyone must first see that he remains true to himself." [49]

In Russia Tiedemann was assigned as staff officer to General Pahlen, who held Riga and the northern approaches to St. Petersburg against the Franco-Prussian X Corps of the *Grande Armée* under Macdonald and Yorck. [50] During the early months of the campaign he played an important part in leading the flexible and venturesome defense. At the same time, through letters and outpost interviews, he tried to persuade Prussian units of Yorck's command to change sides and join the Russo-German Legion. [51] On 22 August, during an attack on the Prussian lines, Tiedemann was fatally wounded. [52] A contemporary writes that when news of his death reached Berlin, it was greeted with joy in some circles of society, "to whom the word of command . . . made up their political conscience." [53] Boyen was later to describe him as "an outstanding man in every respect . . . one of the most high-minded and best-educated officers in the Prussian army." [54]

In 1820 the lecture notes of this exceptional officer were dupli-

[48] Letter of 19 March 1813, printed in Priesdorff, No. 1429.

[49] *Scharnhorsts Briefe*, I, 428.

[50] The Scharnhorst papers of this period deposited in the Freiburg archives contain detailed sketches of the fortifications of Riga in Scharnhorst's hand.

[51] B. v. Quistorp, *Die Kaiserlich Russisch-Deutsche Legion*, Berlin, 1860, pp. 9–10. See also Boyen, *Erinnerungen*, II, 239. The German General Staff history of the campaign says that "the Russians continually attempted to induce the Prussian troops to desert," but does not mention Tiedemann in this or any other connection. *Die Theilnahme des Preussischen Hülfskorps an dem Feldzuge gegen Russland im Jahre 1812; Kriegsgeschichtliche Einzelschriften*, XXIV, Berlin, 1898, p. 509.

[52] See the Prussian reports on Tiedemann's death in A. v. Seydlitz, *Tagebuch des Königlich Preussischen Armeekorps*, Berlin-Posen, 1823, II, 38, 51.

[53] *Vor hundert Jahren: Erinnerungen der Gräfin Sophie Schwerin*, ed. A. v. Romberg, Berlin, 1909, pp. 317–321.

[54] *Erinnerungen*, II, 186, 239.

cated in manuscript form for circulation within the service.[55] Although alterations of the original cannot be ruled out, they appear unlikely in view of the numerous editorial footnotes and comments which are in any case appended to the text. The notes generally touch on events in the campaigns between 1813 and 1815, and clearly express the renewed conservative ascendancy of the years after the second Peace of Paris.[56] It was the period of the Carlsbad Decrees, the fall of Humboldt and Boyen, the fateful turning away from political reform. Under the circumstances official approbation of an unconventional work would have been unusual, but in fact Tiedemann's lectures are circumspect both in content and in tone.

For standard combat situations, Tiedemann recommends that one-sixth of the battalion immediately deploy as skirmishers and a further sixth act as *tirailleur* reserve and replacement pool—proportions considerably smaller than those the *Reglement* of 1812 was to advocate for the fusiliers, and somewhat smaller than the permissible figure for the line infantry.[57] He suggests intervals of from 100 to 200 paces between skirmish line and *tirailleur* reserve—*Soutien*—in the attack, and from 300 to 400 paces between skirmishers and the main body.[58] The outside limits are rather longer than the distances prescribed in the *Reglement*, but are consistent with Tiedemann's somewhat old-fashioned views on cooperation between open and closed formations, which seem to stem from an uncertainty about the effectiveness of aimed fire in the encounter of large infantry masses. While the *Reglement* was to envisage skirmishers and column as two aspects of the same effort, Tiedemann throughout his lectures discussed their interaction as that of two bodies which, though interconnected, retained a fair measure of tactical independence.[59]

---

[55] *Vorlesungen über die Taktik; Bearbeitet von einem Offizier des General-Staabes*, lithographed, Berlin, 1820.

[56] The footnotes are signed "A." As several include detailed references to actions of units commanded by Prince August of Prussia, who in the years after 1815 was one of the heads of military instruction in Berlin, it is possible that he was the annotator.

[57] *Vorlesungen über die Taktik*, p. 35; *Exerzir-Reglement für die Infanterie der Königlich Preussischen Armee*, Berlin, 1812, pp. 100, 106.

[58] *Vorlesungen über die Taktik*, p. 36.

[59] *Ibid.*, p. 36.

The core of Tiedemann's lectures lies in a very detailed discussion of the column and of the part skirmishers play in its support. Repeatedly he seeks to convince his listeners of the inadequacy of linear formations, which he attempts to demonstrate both by a profusion of historical examples and by a comparative analysis of column and line. "There are," he writes in one place, "different opinions about the usefulness of column in battle. A conclusion can be reached only by considering the advantages and disadvantages of this formation. The three main disadvantages attached to the employment of the column are:

1. The volume of frontal fire is decreased.
2. The formation is particularly vulnerable to artillery fire.
3. It also affords a good target for line volleys and for *tirailleurs*.[60]

Against this he sets the following advantages:

1. The column has greater speed and flexibility.
2. Order is much easier to maintain in the column than in the line.
3. The column is not vulnerable to cavalry.[61]
4. Columns take up much less space than linear formations, so that if desired more troops can be assembled in one area.

From this Tiedemann concludes that columns should be used:

1. At night, when the line cannot move.
2. Wherever there is reasonable cover against artillery fire.
3. Against cavalry on level ground.
4. In areas where there is little room for extended fronts.
5. In attacks.
6. Where one's intention and strength are to remain hidden.

A seventh point is added in a footnote by the later editor: "When troops are employed that are inexperienced or unreliable, as for instance was the case with the Austrian militia in 1809, and the Prussian *Landwehr* at the beginning of 1813." [62]

Skirmishers assist the closed formations by seeking out and

---

[60] *Ibid.*, p. 80.

[61] By this Tiedemann means that a column could very quickly form squares, the best defense against cavalry. The *Reglement* of 1812, pp. 91–92, prescribed only one method for changing from the column to the square; after 1815 elaborations were introduced. See, for instance, v. Bieberstein, *Die Taktik*, Magdeburg, 1816, pp. 39–41, and figures 11, 13, 16a, and 16b of the plates.

[62] *Vorlesungen über die Taktik*, p. 81.

exploring the enemy's positions, by occupying him along the whole front, and by preparing the assault through aimed fire. "For all these tasks they must get as near as they can to the enemy, and be positioned as advantageously as possible, since on the whole massed volleys are probably still more effective than the fire of *tirailleurs*." Tiedemann hoped to counter the additional danger to which the larger distance from the main body exposed the *tirailleurs* by stiffening the skirmish line whenever possible with troops of light horse and even with mobile artillery.[63]

When discussing the part skirmishers played in full-scale engagements, Tiedemann emphasized their defensive rather than offensive tasks. Only in the assault on fortified positions, he argues, could *tirailleurs* do without the backing of line formations. He regarded them primarily as means to protect the columns, about whose security on the battlefield he shows great concern throughout the lectures, a concern that is reflected in the distance he likes to put between skirmish line and main body.[64]

Once, while they were colleagues at the *Allgemeine Kriegsschule*, Clausewitz commented that Tiedemann's lectures "worked out and illuminated very well the disadvantages of the old tactical methods." [65] This indeed appears to have been their principal value: a closely argued refutation of the main aspects of Prussian linear tactics, which must have been most impressive to the young General Staff candidates. His treatment of the new, on the other hand, was marked by a certain timidity. He followed Scharnhorst and Roche-Aymon in maintaining as much as possible the separate identities of the skirmisher and the line infantryman; but Scharnhorst stressed their close and constant cooperation, particularly in the attack, as well as the importance of aimed fire to a far greater extent than did his disciple.[66]

[63] *Ibid.*, p. 83.

[64] It is interesting, though not too much should be made of it, that the Russian attack on Dahlenkirchen of 22 August 1812, which Tiedemann planned and in which he was killed, was marked by such large intervals between *tirailleurs* and columns that for long periods during the action, according to the report in Seydlitz's *Tagebuch*, II, 32–41, the two functioned almost independently.

[65] In a series of notes and observations on the theory of war, written in 1811; *Clausewitz Schriften*. Communicated by Professor Hahlweg.

[66] Cf. the introduction and Scharnhorst's essays in Appendix 1, especially Paragraphs 1 and 2 of the essay *Order of Battle*.

In this as in nearly every aspect of tactics Clausewitz's lectures on the little war were much less orthodox.[67] Like Tiedemann he wished to demolish the traditional ideas that his listeners might hold on the subject of infantry fighting. "I shall try," he promised in his opening talk, "to remove preconceived opinions and to root out prejudice."[68] But his methods were considerably more dynamic. Early on he made it a point to distinguish between the psychology of the line soldier and the individual fighter, and then went on to argue that in modern war this difference should largely disappear. As might be expected, he did not demand in so many words that the line soldier become more enterprising and self-reliant, but conveyed his meaning by repeatedly demonstrating that the tactics of the little war and modern infantry tactics in general had a great deal in common. Essentially the two were alike since the same basic principles governed both; their dissimilarities were not absolute, but matters of emphasis. In future, skirmisher and line infantryman must use each other's tactics, and this meant that each had to take on many of the qualities of the other. The light soldier must renounce some of his old hit-and-run methods; the line soldier must add a good measure of caution and deception to his exact drill.

Clausewitz's concept of amalgamated tactics springs from his belief that in theory and in practice all forms of war are interconnected, that war is not the realm of small, mutually exclusive groups of specialists—such as, for instance, gunners still tended to be in Germany—but a universal activity in which each aspect influences and is influenced by all others. In his introductory lecture he suggested this formulation: "We employ a classification according to which war is to be divided into large-scale operations and the little war . . . but the borders between the little war and large-scale actions (if I am permitted to use this

[67] See the references to Clausewitz's lectures above, pp. 21 and 147. For reasons that are not known, Clausewitz's manuscript was never duplicated for service use, even though interest in the little war did not wane in Prussia after the War of Liberation. Valentini's old-fashioned treatise, first published in 1799, was reissued several times; Decker's *Der kleine Krieg* achieved three editions between 1822 and 1828, and the following year Duhesme's standard work was translated into German—yet Clausewitz's lectures are incomparably more original and forward-looking than any of these.

[68] *Meine Vorlesungen über den kleinen Krieg*, Introduction.

latter expression, which by the way is neither very learned nor very abstract) blend into each other." [69]

His method of developing this theory is shown in a characteristic section in his second lecture, which deals with the tactical fundamentals of the little war. Clausewitz starts out by declaring that "the use of weapons in battle and in the little war does not differ. Sniping and skirmishing are the same in the little war as in large-scale actions." [70] The text then continues:

Paragraph 1: Infantry is more in the position to decide the issue by fire than by shock, and therefore fights more in open than in close order. [71]

Paragraph 2: In skirmishing, the infantry never completely deploys into open order, but a suitable number of men always remain in close formations. Almost all texts, among them the Austrian *Reglement*, already give this rule for the skirmish formations of line infantry in regular actions, so it isn't a peculiarity of the little war. [72]

Paragraph 3: If circumstances permit, one should combine the fireline mentioned in Paragraphs 1 and 2 with the intention of massive shock. In that case troops should be divided into two parts: the first makes up the skirmish line with its supporting units; the other forms the means for the attack in close order.

Paragraph 4: Where absolute defense is required [i.e., when little ground can be yielded] one should never form simple skirmish lines, but should always retain the major part of one's force for the counterattack in close order.

Paragraph 5: Wherever one wants to penetrate in an attack, one must have troops in close formation in readiness. Although close formations appear generally more suited for the attack, decided advantages are attached to the skirmish line in the attack, even in regular battle. [73]

[69] *Ibid.*, Introduction. Clausewitz contrasts the terms *kleinen Krieg* and *grossen Krieg*. The latter term is awkward even in German and is perhaps best translated as "large-scale operations."

[70] *Meine Vorlesungen über den kleinen Krieg; Über die Taktik des kleinen Krieges oder Verhalten im Gefecht.*

[71] On the margin next to this sentence Clausewitz wrote the word "relative."

[72] On the margin next to the first sentence of this paragraph Clausewitz added the words: "Thus soldiers of the skirmish line who have used up their ammunition can be replaced."

[73] On the margin next to the first sentence of this paragraph Clausewitz added the words: "Here the close formation is the suitable one, and yet under no circumstances can we do without the skirmish line."

The difference in emphasis between Tiedemann's and Clausewitz's views on the role of skirmishers is apparent. To the former they are important auxiliaries, to the latter an integral part of any infantry unit. Lecturing on the little war, Clausewitz was in any case bound to devote greater attention to open formations; he did this however by enlarging on their usefulness in regular battle. Psychologically it seems to have been easier to approach tactical integration from the side of the light service than from that of the line. The professional traditions and feelings of the line officer could not but resist a process that compromised the principle of cohesion, of *Tuchfühlung*, as the army expression had it. To accept the column was not so difficult a step as to accept open formations, with their vaunted irregularities and undoubted problems of tactical and disciplinary control. On the other hand, the *Jäger* or fusilier officer may at times have been impelled to proselytize by a feeling that the future lay with his more natural, less regulated method of fighting. Both ideally and professionally he could only gain from an increasing acceptance of open tactics in the army.

A further aspect of Clausewitz's course deserves mention. One lecture dealt with guerrilla warfare, a subject that lay at the farthest edge of what could be thought of as formal tactics. In the lecture Clausewitz discussed the part that small detachments could play in civil wars and insurrections, and gave examples of special operations that rarely found a place in ordinary campaigns but might succeed in irregular war—for instance, the kidnapping of commanders.[74] The text is remarkable for its disregard of the political consequences attendant upon arming the population; Clausewitz considered armed uprisings simply as a "method of fighting—in other words, in its relation to the enemy." The lecture is an early statement of the thoughts he was later to develop in the equally apolitical chapter "On Arming the People" in *On War*.[75] Even presented with such discretion the

[74] *Meine Vorlesungen über den kleinen Krieg: Über die besonderen Zwecke, welche ein Partheigänger oder ein ähnliches Detasch. haben kann*, Paragraph 6.

[75] Book VI, chapter 26. The lecture referred to its topic by the completely antiseptic term *Nationalbewaffnung*, which was changed in the book to *Volksbewaffnung*—a word that is at once more accurate and more emotional.

technique repelled most officers; willingness to employ it could be found only among the reformers and activists, who saw it as the logical continuation of their view that in a crisis no limits should be placed on the military energies of the state.

· 3 ·

In the late fall of 1810 Scharnhorst persuaded the King that there should be no further delay in preparing comprehensive and definitive manuals, publication of which "would be more useful for the training of the army than all previously issued separate orders, which—scattered and without firm connection with one another—lacked force and effectiveness." [76] On 14 January 1811 Frederick William appointed two commissions, both under Scharnhorst's chairmanship, to prepare new manuals for the infantry and cavalry.[77] Work on an artillery manual, also under Scharnhorst's supervision, had already begun. The members of the cavalry commission—Zieten, Tiedemann's later companion in Russia Alexander von der Goltz, and Lieutenant Colonel von Dolff—based their discussions on the provisional instructions that Borstell and Roche-Aymon had written the previous year. Responsible for the infantry regulations were Krauseneck, Clausewitz, and the royal adjutant Oldwig von Natzmer.[78] At times both commissions met together to coordinate the drill of the two arms, a matter of particular concern to Scharnhorst. The share of the light service in preparing the manuals remained disproportionately large; only three of the seven members were representative officers of the line or of the heavy cavalry, one of whom—von der Goltz—left Prussia the following year and became commander of a hussar regiment in the German Legion, organized in Russia to fight against Napoleon.[79]

Besides the numerous preliminary instructions, memoranda, and essays that had circulated in the army since 1806, the in-

---

[76] *Das Preussische Heer im Jahre 1812*, p. 140.

[77] The Cabinet Orders and other documents relating to the commissions are printed in *Reorganisation*, II, 254–256. See also *Das Preussische Heer im Jahre 1812*, pp. 140, 178–179.

[78] Contrary to Shanahan, p. 183, Yorck was not a member of the commission, but his and Blücher's advice was sought.

[79] Priesdorff, No. 1312.

fantry commission examined manuals of other services, in particular those of France and Austria.[80] On 21 January, Scharnhorst addressed to the Prince of Hesse a request for a copy of the Hessian light infantry manual, having "a very high opinion of its practical value." [81] Several days later he asked Yorck to collaborate with the commission, "which would be a proof of your friendship that I could not treasure highly enough." On 11 February Yorck replied, "I consider the need for a new *Reglement* as such an urgent matter that I myself have already drafted the part concerning the light infantry." Scharnhorst answered, "The judgment of experienced, unprejudiced officers is of great value to me. I know Your Excellency to be such a man, and must admit that I know of only a few others in our army. It would therefore give me particular pleasure if Your Excellency were to assist me by a frank and friendly communication of your opinions." [82] The manuscript of Yorck's proposals has not survived, but the printed *Reglement* clearly shows his hand.[83]

The commission's work proceeded fairly rapidly. As each chapter was completed it was submitted to the King, whose criticisms were incorporated in a final draft. By October the infantry manual had been set up in type; but at this late moment one chapter, "On the Common Errors in the Employment of the Third Rank," was struck out by Frederick William, who then went over the entire text once more, so that the manual could not be issued to the troops until the beginning of 1812.[84] It is not

[80] Jany, *Gefechtsausbildung*, p. 107, opposes several identically worded passages of the Prussian *Reglement* and the French *Règlement* of 1791 in the German version adopted by the Westphalian army.

[81] Draft by Clausewitz "In the name of General Scharnhorst," *Nachlass Scharnhorst*, A 28/29.

[82] *Reorganisation*, II, 254; Voss, p. 49.

[83] Already Scherbening and Willisen, who had access to files in the archives of the General Staff and the Ministry of War that are now lost, write that Yorck's influence on the *Reglement* of 1812 "must not be underestimated." *Reorganisation*, II, 255.

[84] Sautermeister, p. 81, incorrectly writes that "the *Reglement*, on the whole, was completed in June 1811." The progress of the commission's work can be followed in the minutes and drafts contained in the *Nachlass Scharnhorst*, A 28/29. On 7 June the third of five main parts was sent to the King, but a note of 10 July states that the section on skirmishers remains to be done, and changes and revisions continued throughout the fall. The printed manual is dated 15 January 1812, the day generally

known why the chapter displeased the King; of one of its paragraphs the General Staff history comments that it suited the *Reglement* in content but not in form.[85] The passage in question censured the old-fashioned practice of separating light and line formations:

> It is a very great mistake when the movements, fire, and attacks of the third rank, of the guns, and of the closed battalions are not in that connection which the nature of the particular action demands. During maneuvers one often notices the striking error that without any further consideration the movements of the battalion determine the movements of the artillery and of the third rank. This creates false ideas, which the younger officer accepts; the older learns only how to execute evolutions and does not train himself in guiding the action. In war this would obviously lead to highly contradictory and detrimental behavior. The Brigade commanders simply must not permit this fault, and must teach their errant subordinates the true development of action, which consists in the interconnection of all parts, i.e., of the skirmishers, of the close formations, and of the artillery.

These lines are in agreement with the thoughts expressed in Scharnhorst's essay on the reciprocal use of close and open formations; but it is idle to speculate on the author since they equally reflect the concepts of tactical integration held by Yorck, Krauseneck, and Clausewitz.[86]

Despite the omission of this chapter, the infantry *Reglement* of 1812 was a progressive and remarkably effective work. Its text was clear, and so concise that the *Reglement* proved to be the shortest of all contemporary manuals: the French *Ordonnance* of 1791, the British *Rules and Regulations*, and the Austrian manual of 1807 were all three times its length; its 131 pages sufficed to treat most of the subjects on which the Prussian *Reglement* of 1788 had expended 546. In place of the search for detailed uni-

---

given for its actual distribution to the army; but a note of 13 February, mentioning the printing of the infantry and cavalry manuals, suggests that the work might have been published later. Discussion on the most effective manner of wheeling the column was pursued into the spring, until in April a revised version of the relevant paragraph was printed on separate sheets for insertion in the infantry manual.

[85] *Das Preussische Heer im Jahre 1812*, pp. 140–141. The following quotation is from p. 141.

[86] The essay is the third of those included in Appendix 1. See, in particular, Paragraph 5.

formity of its predecessors, the *Reglement* of 1812 stated general rules, and left the rest to experience and sound common sense—the *gesunden Menschenverstand* to which it repeatedly appealed.[87]

The first part of the *Reglement* deals with drill, which is to be founded on the "natural, free, and unforced posture of the individual." [88] The purpose of marching is "to gain territory while at the same time sparing the soldier as much as possible." Three march-cadences are prescribed: the traditional "ordinary" cadence of 75 steps a minute, now almost entirely relegated to the barrack-square and the parade-ground; the quick cadence of 108 steps a minute, which became standard for all evolutions, and could if desired be speeded up to the beat of the drum; and finally the trot without cadence, to cover short distances rapidly in an emergency.[89] This increase in the speed with which the foot-soldier moved made it possible to put the new tactics into execution.

The manual of arms was greatly simplified by the provisions of the second part of the *Reglement*.[90] Only two kinds of firing are prescribed: by command—that is, in volleys; and *Bataillen-Feuer* —individual, aimed fire. On the proper signal, the text states, "every man in the first rank raises his weapon, aims as well as possible, fires, reloads without the least hurry, and makes ready again. Now the man behind him aims, fires, and loads in his turn." [91] When in close formation, the men of the third rank never fired; in emergencies—for example, when squares were formed to repel attacks—they could load the muskets of the other two ranks.[92]

---

[87] Among the important analyses of the *Reglement* are [E. L. v. Holleben], *Militairische Betrachtungen*, Berlin, 1838; G. v. Griesheim, *Vorlesungen über die Taktik*, Berlin, 1855; H. v. Freytag-Loringhoven, "Die Exerzier-Reglements für die Infanterie von 1812, 1847, 1888 und 1906," *Militär-Wochenblatt* (1907), Supplement 1, which traces the influence the *Reglement* exerted on later Prussian manuals; and *Das Preussische Heer im Jahre 1812*, pp. 140–164, 244–256.

[88] *Exerzir-Reglement für die Infanterie*, pp. 1–26.

[89] *Ibid.*, pp. 6–7. The three cadences are identical with, or similar to, those prescribed in English and French drill. See *Rules and Regulations of 1812*, pp. 6, 13–15; and the *Règlement* of 1791, pp. 18, 81–83. However the French quick cadence, the *pas accéléré*, was frequently only 100 steps a minute.

[90] *Ibid.*, pp. 27–42.

[91] *Ibid.*, pp. 41–42.

[92] *Ibid.*, pp. 92, 96. This was also French practice. See Colin, *La Tactique et la discipline*, pp. xviii–xix.

The third and longest part of the *Reglement* dealt with company and battalion formations and with their tactical employment.[93] The company was formed in three ranks, "the nimblest soldiers and the best marksmen" made up the third rank, the other two ranks were arranged by height.[94] Each company was divided into two sections; in the basic battalion formation the eight sections were drawn up in a segmented line of three ranks.[95] The line was not only a drill and parade formation, but could be employed in battle, principally to give fire, but also to gain ground, to withdraw, and even for bayonet attacks.[96] Changes of direction could be executed by wheeling, a concession to eighteenth-century practice, but primarily by the sections forming into columns, which, once the new front was reached, could again be opened up into lines.[97] Closely linked to the *Zugkolonne*—or maneuver column—was the attack column, which became the "battalion's main fighting method."[98] Actually it was a double column, with a front of two sections, i.e. of about forty men, taking up approximately 33 yards.[99] From a battalion in line, the column was generally formed on the two center sections, which was the quickest method, and the one preferred by the French.[100] From the maneuver column it could be formed by doubling the sections, an evolution that the *Ordonnance* of 1791 did not contain. Ac-

[93] *Reglement*, pp. 43–94.

[94] *Ibid.*, 43.

[95] *Ibid.*, pp. 43–44, 46–47.

[96] *Ibid.*, pp. 56–62. Boyen, who was Bülow's Chief of Staff in 1813, writes that at Grossbeeren Bülow attempted to advance his infantry in thin lines under fire, but the resulting confusion made it clear that this use should be deleted from the *Reglement; Erinnerungen*, III, 123.

[97] *Reglement*, pp. 61, 64–70.

[98] *Ibid.*, pp. 70–71; *Das Preussische Heer im Jahre 1812*, p. 151.

[99] Figures and distances for the column are not given in the manual, and have been estimated on the basis of a war-strength battalion of 660 lance-corporals and privates, some of whom are deployed as skirmishers. The frontage is figured at about one pace per man; this may seem narrow, but agrees with Colin's estimate of distances in French drill; *La Tactique et la discipline*, p. xxviii. The French *Règlement* of 1791 gives as little as 50 centimeters to each man in the battalion line; see the plate facing p. 7 of the appendix in the 1816 edition. The Prussian manual also states that in close order drill the arms of adjoining men just touch (p. 33). When squares are formed, each man occupies one pace (30 inches), ". . . which he necessarily requires if he carries a full pack and is to have sufficient room for firing" (Plate 1).

[100] See the *Règlement* of 1791, pp. 236–239, and Plate 26.

cording to the *Reglement*, the double column was to be employed "for the attack, for retreats when threatened by cavalry, etc. Within itself it combines independence, strength, and mobility." [101] The third part of the manual concludes with simple rules for forming squares and for reassembling men scattered in combat.[102]

The fourth part regulates the action of the third rank and the fusiliers.[103] The similarity in wording of certain passages makes it apparent that Scharnhorst's essay *Order of Battle* served as a model for this part of the text.[104] A comparison with Yorck's instructions brings out further likenesses in thought and phrasing, so that Part IV of the *Reglement* may be assumed to have been in the main the joint work of Scharnhorst and Yorck. Its first chapter begins by stating the principle underlying the new tactics:

Infantry must fight on the plains and in broken terrain, against close formations and against skirmishers. Every separate group, battalion, company, etc., therefore has its detachment for combat in close and in open order; for the former the first and second rank, for the latter the third rank.

The detachment for combat in close order must value most highly the composure [*Haltung*] of rank and file, close contact, massed fire, and the bayonet attack; the detachment for skirmishing on the other hand seeks its power in competent aimed fire, use of the terrain, and in the advantages offered by enemy positions and movements. Together with this principal purpose of both detachments, it is nevertheless required that each can take on the task of the other, that if need be the two first ranks of the battalion can fight as skirmishers, and the sections of the third rank can fight in close order.[105]

The last sentence is missing in Scharnhorst's essay, and indeed we know that Scharnhorst never favored the total amalgamation of *tirailleur* and musketeer. The required tactical integration does however reflect Yorck's concept of unified rather than specialized tactics as he expressed it in the final sentence of his instruction of 1810, and again more explicitly in the instruction of 1811. This

---

[101] *Reglement*, pp. 70–71.
[102] *Ibid.*, pp. 91–94.
[103] *Ibid.*, pp. 95–120.
[104] See the introduction to Appendix 1 of this work.
[105] *Reglement*, pp. 95–96.

principle was once more reiterated in the manual, shortly after the passage quoted above: "The sections of the third rank are to be primarily used for combat in open order, although this stipulation by no means removes the need for every infantryman to know how to fight individually." [106]

Skirmish lines were to be employed not only to guard close formations, to mask their movements, and to counter enemy skirmishers, but wherever the ground would create difficulties for the movement of lines or columns, and particularly to prepare and make possible their successful attack: the skirmishers enabled the battalion at the decisive moment to move effectively against "the enemy whom the aimed fire of the marksmen has already shaken." [107] The importance assigned to the skirmish or "fire-line" is again demonstrated in the series of examples with which the chapter closes. In contrast to Tiedemann's lectures, the manual here authorized the immediate deployment as skirmishers of as much as two-thirds of the third rank, while also warning of the danger of fighting at too great a distance from the closed formation. [108]

The second chapter deals with the details of the skirmisher's training and operations. Again it is stated that the best men are to be assigned to the third rank; their training is to aim at creating in the soldier "exceptional ability in the use of his weapon, physical agility, sound judgment, cunning, boldness at the right moment, and self-confidence." [109] The *tirailleur* line knows no methodical kind of musketry; often the two men of a *Rotte* will fire alternately, "but this must never be taught with a pedantic formality"—"common sense and practice will teach the individual better than all the orders that one could prescribe"; features of the ground are to be used for protection and for help in firing accurately and without detection; the skirmish line moves without the least constraint—*völlig zwanglos;* running is permitted in some situations but on the whole it is "disadvantageous, it creates confusion, tires the men needlessly, renders them incapable of loading calmly and firing effectively"—all precepts that echo Yorck's instruction of 1810. [110]

[106] *Ibid.*, pp. 97–98.
[107] *Ibid.*, p. 98.
[108] *Ibid.*, pp. 100–101.
[109] *Ibid.*, p. 103.
[110] *Ibid.*, pp. 105–112.

The chapter ends with a special section on the fusiliers.[111] The flexibility and speed that the manual required of all troops were demanded to an optimum degree of the fusiliers, but their tactics were regulated by an entirely different principle. Throughout the eighteenth century the basic tactical unit of the Prussian infantry had been the battalion; companies were administrative and economic organizations, but unless they were on detached service they possessed no tactical independence. The task of the company commander was to see that his unit maintained its part of the solid line; alignment, cohesion, and orderly volleying were his and his men's prime responsibilities. The introduction in 1809 of the column to all infantry units expanded the range of formations without lessening the complete dependence of the line company's evolutions on the battalion commander. The third rank too formed *battalion*, not company, skirmishers; the individual company commanders could not dispose of these men, whose action was controlled by the battalion commander through a *Tirailleur Capitain*. Now the *Reglement* turned the company into the basic tactical unit for the fusiliers. The relevant passage reads:

> The battalion commander arranges the disposition of the companies and guides their movements in general. The company commanders use the specific advantages that the terrain affords their purpose, they decide which squads or sections are to skirmish, they reinforce or reduce the skirmish line according to the course of the action, choose an advantageous position for the closed sections from which these can easily support the skirmish line, etc. A fusilier company must be trained to develop a skirmish line quickly from any closed formation, and again to reform in line or in column.

Thus the company commander rather than the battalion commander became the man in immediate control of the fire-fight. All formations—skirmish line, line, square, and column—which the heavy infantry executed by battalions, the fusiliers could execute by companies; in combat the fusilier battalion could break into four independently acting bodies, though it was also expected to fight as a standard line formation. This widening of executive control to include company commanders was a further revolutionary development of Prussian infantry tactics, and the last important innovation in the succession of reforms that the Wars

[111] *Ibid.*, pp. 114–115.

of Liberation terminated. Its theoretical and practical antecedents may be sought above all among the *Jäger*, who had always fought in small units, and in Yorck's instruction of 1800, in which he already prescribed the formation of company columns. Yorck again refers to companies as independent tactical units in his "Instruction to the Light Brigades" of 1810. The following year Scharnhorst proposed a measure of tactical freedom for the line company, a suggestion that was however turned down by Frederick William, so that until after the Wars of Liberation the reform remained limited to the light troops.[112]

Part IV of the *Reglement* ended with a chapter on horn-signals, which was taken from the already cited passage on this subject in Yorck's Instruction of 1810. The fifth and final part of the manual "Formation of the Brigade" was closely based on the text of the instruction of 17 July 1809, the earliest and not entirely successful attempt to regulate the combined action of detachments of all services under a single unified tactical command, the brigade.[113] The concept of battle here being evolved was that of a gradual development of sustained force from depth instead of the succession of separate shocks of the Frederician tradition. The standard brigade attack was envisaged as being opened by troops of light horse or more commonly by the brigade's two fusilier battalions, which threw out skirmish lines 100 paces ahead of the closed support detachments. One hundred and fifty paces behind this *Soutien* came the first line of battle, the *1. Treffen*, consisting of three musketeer battalions, generally formed in column, and of two half-batteries of six-pounders. This was the brigade's main force, which exploited the advantages created by the fusiliers and maintained the fire-fight. Drawn up behind them as shock troops and reserve was the *2. Treffen* of the elite grenadiers and the fourth musketeer battalion. Usually the brigade's twelve cavalry squadrons were also kept in reserve and on the flanks, with the missions of defending the infantry against enemy cavalry and of exploiting a possible breakthrough. A battery of horse artillery was to assist the efforts of foot and horse at close quarters, but generally from the flanks so as not to interfere

---

[112] See Scharnhorst's essay "Elementar-Evolutionen eines Bataillons und einer Brigade von 4 Bataillonen," reprinted in *Reorganisation*, II, 258–260.

[113] *Reglement*, pp. 121–131.

with the evolutions of the infantry. If the time was right for a bayonet attack, the fusiliers withdrew to the second line of battle and the musketeer columns preceded by their skirmishers launched the assault.[114]

This gradual build-up of pressure was effected by a constant interaction between the four successive lines of troops making up the brigade: the fusiliers, the two lines of battle, and the cavalry. The thick powder-smoke which quickly obscured the ground made possible the reinforcement, substitution, and withdrawal of units, the shifting of force from point to point, and the replacement of entire lines of battle. Defensive actions and retreats were fought on the same principle of committing units in turn and of wearing down the enemy from a position of depth rather than attempting to break or stop him with one or two all-out efforts. The manual furthermore permitted a very wide range of possible dispositions. Commenting on the standard pattern of the brigade attack, the text states:

> While here His Majesty has given a disposition for an attack in battalion columns, His Majesty nevertheless desires that where circumstances require this disposition be not followed, only the internal organization of the formations remains unalterably according to the instructions of the *Reglement*. Cases in which the disposition of the battalion formations suffers a change are created by the terrain and by other circumstances; if, for instance, the first line of battle has been under fire for some time and the enemy begins to waver, he may be quickly attacked by the two reserve battalions, while the three battalions of the *1. Treffen* form columns and follow the two reserve battalions at battalion intervals.[115]

The weakness of the brigade instructions consisted in the rather vague dispositions given to the artillery, which resulted in an imperfect integration of that arm with the main effort. This was an error of latitude; more serious proved the precise orders that imposed a defensive role on the cavalry and even cautioned against using many mounted troops for reconnaissance.[116] Insufficient combat intelligence and a certain timidity in the employment of large cavalry masses remained a weakness of the

[114] *Ibid.*, pp. 121–128, and Plate II, Figures 1, 2, and 3.
[115] *Ibid.*, pp. 129–130.
[116] *Ibid.*, pp. 129, 131. Cf. *Exerzir-Reglement für die Kavallerie der Königlich Preussischen Armee*, Berlin, 1812, p. 210.

Prussian forces in the campaigns of the following years. But on the whole Part V of the *Reglement*, like the entire work, was a practical, well-thought-out guide to training and operations, whose worth was soon enough proved in action. A mistaken suggestion is sometimes encountered in the literature that the text was issued too late to have had much influence on the training of the army before the final campaigns against Napoleon. Many parts of the *Reglement* had for some years been familiar to the army: they derived from the instructions of 27 March, 16 and 17 July 1809, Yorck's two instructions of 1810 and 1811, and the "Instructions to the Light Brigade Commanders," among others.[117] The separate elements of the reformed tactics were already widely practiced; the *Reglement* pulled them together into a complete and coherent system. It is the condensed expression of all efforts undertaken since Jena to revive and increase the fighting power of the Prussian infantry. That the Prussian troops and their commanders had made an early beginning of learning the new lessons may be seen from the behavior of the auxiliary corps under Yorck in the campaign of 1812, though the line battalions still experienced difficulties in acting with sufficient flexibility, and some of their engagements in open order were mechanical and fumbling. The other half of the army, which was not incorporated into the *Grande Armée*, underwent an entire year's training according to the new manual before war began in the spring of 1813.

The *Reglements* of 1812 for the three services systematized the tactical and operational achievements of the preceding five years, together with certain remnants of earlier usage. Of the three the cavalry manual, while for the first time treating heavy and light horse on an equal basis, was formalistic and defensive-minded. The artillery manual was far superior, though complete integration with the other branches of the army had to await further experience in the field. The best proved to be the *Reglement* for the infantry. It succeeded in codifying the tactical and operational concepts of the few men who step by step over the past years had transformed the army's methods of fighting. That their opinions diverged on some matters of organization and execution did not affect their basic agreement, which derived from

---

[117] Cf. *Das Preussische Heer im Jahre 1812*, pp. 162–163.

both ethical and practical considerations. Whatever their differences on specific social and political questions, they regarded the common soldier and the subaltern as individuals, who possessed dignity and intelligence, and whose physical energy was related to moral factors. Consequently they sought to introduce the force of free will to the battlefield. The flexibility that the *Reglement* of 1812 expected in every infantry unit it demanded with particular insistence from the third rank, and from the fusilier, *Jäger*, and *Schützen* battalions. The actions of the latter three the manual rendered even more elastic by substituting the company for the battalion as the basic combat unit. The light infantry company, which could fight in line, in column, and partly or wholly as skirmishers, thus expressed the concept that Yorck and Clausewitz in particular had developed into the most advanced doctrine of the age: the disappearance of specialist tactics, and their replacement by the complete amalgamation of the methods of the light service with those of the line.[118]

[118] The company column, which Yorck's instruction of 1810 had introduced for the fusiliers, was not authorized for the line infantry by the *Reglement* of 1812, even though the idea gained the support of Scharnhorst. Boyen, too, advocated the company column. See his undated memorandum, written probably between June 1808 and July 1809, excerpted in Meinecke, *Boyen*, I, 187–188. Nor was Yorck's proposal of the two-rank formation accepted. It was not until 1847 that the all-purpose company formed on two ranks became the basic tactical unit for the entire Prussian infantry.

Yorck and the Era of Prussian Reform

I N THE spring of 1812 politics put an end to military reform in Prussia. Except for the concept of universal conscription, which remained in contention and was not to be implemented until the Wars of Liberation, the first part of the reformers' work was done. They and their doctrines now moved onto a larger stage: the years of preparation had ended, the period of testing began.

Under the terms of the Treaty of Paris, Prussia was to provide a contingent of 20,000 men for the invasion of Russia. Three cavalry regiments were detached to Murat's and Grandjean's commands; the remaining force became the 27th Division of the *Grande Armée.* For its commander Napoleon suggested one of the senior Prussian generals, Julius von Grawert. Grawert was duly appointed; but his poor health and doubts about his ability to stand up to French pressure caused the King to create the unusual position of Second Commanding General, which—apparently on Scharnhorst's advice—was filled by Yorck. On 6 June the division was incorporated into X Corps, commanded by Marshal Macdonald, whose orders called for an advance through Lithuania towards Riga, a necessary first step for an attack on St. Petersburg. On 28 June the Prussians crossed the border; some weeks later Grawert fell ill, and on 13 August Yorck assumed the command.[1]

The corps was too weak to penetrate deeply into Russia. For the next four months it waged a campaign of raids and skirmishes in the marshland and sandy plains below Riga, in which the Prussians gained several successes, notably at Bauske, an

---

[1] The most important sources on the campaign of the Prussian corps in 1812 and on the Convention of Tauroggen are the already cited publications by Clausewitz, Droysen, Elze, Seydlitz, and the Military History Section of the German General Staff; *Souvenirs du maréchal Macdonald,* ed. C. Rousset, Paris, 1892; J. d'Ussel, *La Défection de la Prusse,* Paris, 1907; and G. Fabry, *Campagne de 1812: Documents relatifs à l'aile gauche,* Paris, 1912.

engagement that cost the Russians nearly 2,500 prisoners. The active fighting did not prevent the Russians from communicating with Yorck, at first concerning the exchange of prisoners, but soon progressing to suggestions that the Prussians withdraw from the French alliance. Their approaches were met by Yorck with great circumspection, and for the time being led to nothing. By the middle of November the French retreat from Moscow was changing Lithuania from a strategic backwater to an area of major importance, and the Russians, trying to cut Napoleon's lines of communication at Wilna 120 miles to the south, grew more pressing in their appeals. Yorck replied that he could do nothing until he received word from his government. Berlin, however, gave him no guidance. When orders taking account of the changed military and political situation finally reached him on 29 December, they limited themselves to one definite point: if a retreat to East Prussia became necessary, Yorck was again to assume the governorship of the province. By this time Yorck had decided to act on his own.

Napoleon's headquarters had not kept Macdonald informed of the full extent of the French disaster, and it was not until 18 December that X Corps began its retreat towards East Prussia. Macdonald rode with the Westphalian and Polish troops that formed part of his command; some miles behind him came the Prussians. Cossacks harried the extended columns and several clashes with regular troops occurred, until on Christmas day a Russian brigade under Diebitsch moved between the two divisions. Yorck was still the stronger and could have pierced the thin screen, but now he resumed negotiations with the Russians while every day marching a few miles farther west. On the morning of the 30th, following detailed discussions with Diebitsch and Clausewitz, who was serving on the Russian staff, Yorck signed a convention that neutralized the troops under his command for a period of two months.

Yorck's decision completely altered the course of military operations. With Yorck's 14,000 effectives, Macdonald could have stopped the exhausted Russians on the Niemen and Pregel, and given Napoleon the opportunity to assemble his new armies in East Prussia and Silesia with all of Germany for his operational base. Instead the French were compelled to withdraw to central

Germany, and the resultant power vacuum easily induced the Russians to cross their borders and pursue the war in the west. Even more decisive promised to be the political effects. These, however, were not as quick in coming as Yorck had expected. Now or never, he wrote Frederick William immediately after signing the convention, was the time for Prussia to leave her insolent and dangerous ally. The King, on the contrary, felt far from certain that he should turn on Napoleon; he disowned the agreement, ordered Yorck replaced as commander of the Prussian corps, arrested, and brought before a court-martial. The revolutionary step at Tauroggen could reach its goal only if Yorck continued to disregard orders.

On 1 January 1813 Yorck entered Tilsit to rest and refit his men until he heard from Berlin.[2] After more than a week, word of the King's disapproval finally reached him. In the meantime the Russians had proved too slow and too weak to prevent Macdonald from establishing himself in Danzig, where he quickly collected enough reinforcements to become a threat to his pursuers. Already on the 5th Yorck decided to disregard his new neutrality and assist the Russians should their offensive be endangered. On the 8th he entered Königsberg, and there attempted to persuade other Prussian commanders to make common cause with him. "What kinds of opinions are held in Berlin?" he wrote to General Bülow. "Have men sunk so low that they will not dare break the chains of slavery that we have meekly borne for the past five years? Now or never is the time to regain liberty and honor. . . . With bleeding heart I tear the bonds of obedience and wage war on my own."[3] On the 24th he ordered part of his corps to march west on Danzig. He now hoped that by overtly joining the

---

[2] Among the numerous interpretations of the events in East Prussia in the beginning of 1813, the most important seem to me to be Droysen, II, chapters 1 and 2; Lehmann, *Knesebeck und Schön*, pp. 77–347; Ritter, *Stein*, pp. 413–426. An excellent shorter study is H. Rothfels, "Ost- und Westpreussen zur Zeit der Reform und der Erhebung," in *Deutsche Staatenbildung und deutsche Kultur im Preussenlande*, Königsberg, 1931. The military preparations undertaken in East Prussia during this period are discussed in detail in *Das Preussische Heer im Jahre 1813*, published by the Military History Section of the General Staff, Berlin, 1914.

[3] Letter of 13 January 1813, Droysen, II, 41.

Russians and by the military and financial mobilization of East Prussia he would force the entire state into the war against France. The fear and indecision of the King were not his only obstacle. Though proclaimed a rebel, he had to guard Prussian sovereignty against the wishes of some Russian commanders to exploit their military advantage to acquire parts or all of the province. The local estates, which on the whole favored the break with France, feared Russian intentions almost as much as the prospect of acting in defiance of the King by supporting Yorck. Some royal officials refused to obey his orders. At the other extreme, Stein, who had come to Königsberg as the Tsar's representative, was prepared to override any particularist concern for the sake of sweeping Russia and Prussia into a crusade for the liberation of Germany. Yorck, too, looked beyond Prussia's immediate interests. In a letter of 3 January, he had attempted to inspire Frederick William with the words, "Your Royal Majesty's kingdom, though smaller than in the year 1805, is now destined to become the liberator and protector of your people and of all Germans." [4] But he believed that both troops and people could be counted on only if the forms of legality were observed as far as possible: as loyal subjects they were to carry out their king's true wishes, which circumstances prevented him from openly expressing. After intense debates, Yorck, the heads of the civil government, and the leaders of the local notables persuaded Stein to act with discretion and not make use of his Russian powers. A special session of the estates was called, before which Yorck appeared to demand the formation of a *Landwehr* of 20,000 men with 10,000 reserves, chosen and organized according to a scheme that Clausewitz had drafted, and of a volunteer regiment of cavalry, as well as the continuing selective conscription of replacements for the regular forces. With the estate's adoption of Yorck's program on 9 February, East Prussia was committed. It was during these days of excitement and uncertainty that a subaltern in Yorck's corps wrote his family:

Our king sits inactive in Berlin, he pays no attention at all to us here. But I hope General Yorck will act; he is also to assume the planning and organizing of the *Landsturm*. Everyone watches with high expectations. He is now our king, he concludes peace and makes war.

[4] Droysen, I, 503.

There is already little love lost for our king; if he does not declare against France now, anything can be expected.[5]

The decision could no longer be reversed; but it required another five weeks of hesitation and unnecessarily complicated negotiations with the Tsar before Prussia declared war on France.

In his memoirs Boyen wrote that "without Tauroggen and the rising of the East Prussian estates, Scharnhorst very likely would not have succeeded in overcoming the French party [at Court] and the King's indecision." [6] Clausewitz's evaluation is more modest:

It would be unreasonable to believe that had it not been for the decision General York reached at Tauroggen . . . Bonaparte would still occupy the French throne and the French would still rule Europe. Such great results are the effects of an infinite number of causes, or rather forces, most of which would have retained their strength even without General York. But it cannot be denied that the decision of this General had enormous consequences, and in all likelihood very considerably speeded up the final outcome.[7]

Even had they failed to affect state policy, the Convention of Tauroggen and the mobilization of East Prussia would have remained significant, if only because they were among the few actions during the years of reform undertaken in overt disregard of the King's will. No one was more conscious of this aspect than Frederick William. In March 1813 a board of inquiry exonerated Yorck on the pretext that military necessity had forced him to act independently; but during the next few years the King's comments and small injustices made it apparent how difficult he found it to forgive the insult to his authority. Yorck responded with hurt pride and disdain. The honors that he received for his successful generalship in 1813 and 1814 he accepted with a feeling that he once characterized as one of "cold gratitude." He did not, however, persist in his independence, or further attempt to take a hand in the formulation of policy. For a brief period the

<hr>

[5] Letter of E. v. Saucken-Tarputschen to his father, 5 February 1813. The original is apparently lost; a privately printed compilation of Saucken-Tarputschen's diary and correspondence, *Erlebnisse während der Feldzüge von 1812–1814*, which gives the text of the letter on p. 33, is in my possession.

[6] Boyen, *Erinnerungen*, ii, 333.

[7] Clausewitz, *Der Feldzug von 1812 in Russland*, pp. 238–239.

tactical reformer and innovator of military methods and institutions had changed into a political soldier, only to return to the conventional tasks of a senior officer, concerned solely with defeating the external enemies of the state.

· 2 ·

The development of tactics during the second half of the Napoleonic Era was not uniform throughout Europe. By 1812 the army that had given the decisive impulse to Prussian reform was itself losing much of its former flexibility. The decline was mainly due to the effect that the vast French resources in manpower and materiel had on the Emperor's predilections. His interest in infantry tactics, never intense, was outweighed by operational theories, in which the straightforward application of power played a constantly increasing part. Perhaps nowhere did he grant his marshals so much freedom as in the manner in which they deployed their men on the battlefield. When he did issue tactical instructions, he was not always obeyed. As late as October 1813, a few days before the battle of Leipzig, he sought to abolish his infantry's three-rank formation because he regarded "the fire and the bayonets of the third rank as ineffective." [8] His order was ignored, possibly because regimental officers valued the solidity afforded by the deeper formation—especially desirable when they had to make do with half-trained recruits—or simply from an unwillingness to change old habits.[9] The Emperor himself preferred the *ordre mixte* that the *Règlement* of 1791 had codified; but his ideas on infantry and cavalry tactics were not firmly held, and usually he was content if the troops maintained an active fire-fight, and at the decisive moment moved quickly into the assault. Consequently French tactics were extremely diverse; some generals continued to use the supple evolutions that had been developed in the 1790's, others adopted cruder forms.

[8] Colin, *La Tactique et la discipline*, p. xxi.

[9] G. de Chambray, *Oeuvres*, Paris, 1839–1840, v, 381, quotes Gouvion St.-Cyr on the subject: "Napoleon assured me that when peace came, he would form the infantry in two ranks. . . . Napoleon did not wait for peace; already at the battle of Leipzig he had his infantry formed in two ranks, but this idea was rejected everywhere."

The *Règlement* of 1791 remained the army's basic tactical guide. Numerous subsequent instructions took account of fresh experience, and in the years after the Peace of Lunéville it was attempted to bring them together into a new tactical norm, but the campaigns of 1805 and 1806 interrupted the project, which was not taken up again.[10] It has been argued that since the armies of the Empire, unlike eighteenth-century forces, were no longer tactical units, it was only proper that the Emperor delegated responsibility for tactics to his subordinates; but, on the contrary, the very size of the French military organization, which was committed over an entire continent, more than ever made standardization necessary.

The smaller role that open order tactics came to play in the French forces cannot be guessed at from the table of organization. Since 1808 the standard infantry battalion had consisted of four ordinary companies, one company of grenadiers, and one of *voltigeurs*. The proportion of light to line infantry was thus one to five, somewhat weaker than in the new Prussian army. Self-contained units of light troops were no less numerous than they had been during the Revolutionary wars. On the rolls as of 1 January 1812, over 145,000 men were listed as *chasseurs, infanterie légère, tirailleurs*.[11] According to a strength report of the Guards during this same period, out of 42,000 men, 26,160 belonged to formations whose names possessed or once had possessed connotations of the light service.[12] But in most cases this was not a true distinction; the loss of meaning in such designations as *vélite* regiments or *flanqueur* battalions provides one more illustration of the familiar process that turns the irregulars of one generation into the regulars of the next.

A contributory factor in the hardening of tactics was the decrease in quality of the replacements. The incessant campaigns rarely allowed time for their adequate training; learning by expe-

[10] J. Morvan, *Le Soldat imperial*, Paris, 1904, I, 284; Griesheim, p. 64.

[11] Belhomme, IV, 531–533.

[12] Liebert, "Die Rüstungen Napoleons für den Feldzug 1812," *Militär-Wochenblatt* (1888), Supplement 9. In 1814, according to the *Annuaire de l'état militaire de France* of that year, the infantry of the *Vieille Garde* was organized into ten regiments, eight of which bore names derived from the light service.

rience and from the veterans in the ranks could not wholly replace drill, and the result showed in the troops' performance. They were still the best marchers in Europe, but in their evolutions and use of weapons they were becoming inferior. If Napoleon regretted this, the loss in tactical flexibility nevertheless accorded with his inclinations. By 1809 *tirailleur* swarms that could skirmish for long periods, and maneuver effectively by themselves or in coordination with columns or lines, were giving way to a system of massed artillery and monster columns, which minimized the role of individual initiative on the battlefield. Though the Emperor still exploited mobility, writes Liddell Hart, "he unconsciously pinned his faith to mass, and subordinated his art to his weight. . . . [Now] his victories are won less by mobility and suspense than by sheer offensive power, expressed in his new artillery tactics—the massed concentration of guns to blast a selected point." [13] In the six years preceding the Russian compaign, the number of cannon for each thousand men in the army rose from two to nearly five.[14] At times the French still used *tirailleurs* on a very large scale: at the battle of the Thann in 1809 whole regiments deployed completely as skirmishers; at Hanau in 1813 Macdonald advanced with 2,500 men in skirmish lines and 2,500 men in closed formations over a front of 2,000 yards.[15] But more and more the old combination of skirmishers and small columns tended to be reserved for opening the action and for counterattacks against disorganized units, while the main effort was carried out by solid masses with only a few *tirailleurs* in the lead, or even without any skirmishers at all.[16] The strategic concept of concentration of force was degenerating into a self-defeating tactical absurdity.

Throughout the Revolutionary wars and the early campaigns against Napoleon the Austrian infantry continued to fight according to Lacy's manual of 1769, which had been patterned on

---

[13] B. H. Liddell Hart, *The Ghost of Napoleon*, London, 1933, p. 102.

[14] M. Lauerma, *L'Artillerie de campagne française pendant les guerres de la Révolution*, Helsinki, 1956, p. 315.

[15] For Thann, see the combat reports printed in C. Saski, *Campagne de 1809*, Paris, 1899–1902, III, 252–264; for Hanau, *Souvenirs du maréchal Macdonald*, pp. 229–234.

[16] An example of sending columns forward without the protection of a skirmish line is provided by Soult at Pamplona; Chambray, V, 351.

Frederician models. The basic combat formation was the battalion in line of three ranks; the favorite type of firing, volleys by companies, similar to the Prussian rolling *Pelotonfeuer* and equally difficult to maintain in action. Some experiments with more flexible tactics had no lasting results. The disasters of 1805 finally provided an opportunity for general reforms, whose need had been urged by numerous officers, notably Archduke Charles; but although Charles was now appointed Generalissimo of the Armies, he encountered such heavy political and administrative obstruction that his work remained fragmentary.[17] Charles himself was far from modern in his military concepts. He never wholly outgrew the influence of his early mentor, General von Lindenau, who had served as adjutant to Frederick the Great, and had written several books on tactics, one of which has been characterized as "an attempt to out-Saldern Saldern."[18] A service whose most influential reformer was a conservative contending against soundly entrenched reactionaries could never become fully reconciled to the techniques and to the energy and activity demanded by modern war.

The new infantry manual of 1807, of which Charles was the principal author, did not break with the old-Prussian tradition that had rarely proved beneficial to the army. Among its evolutions were some of even greater complexity than those devised by Lacy; the official Austrian history writes with only slight exaggeration that the *Reglement* "incorporated all the refinements and artifices of Frederician drill."[19] It retained the three-rank formation for the infantry, but introduced the battalion column, generally with a front of from 55 to 60 men and a depth of from 15 to 18 ranks. From the line the column formed on the elite right-flank company, an evolution that was slower than the method used by the French and Prussians of forming simultaneously from the two flanks to the center, and rendered the column's use in battle more cumbersome. Although several successes were gained with

[17] Among the analyses of Charles' theories and reforms, the following should be noted: v. Waldstätten's edition of his writings; R. Lorenz, *Erzherzog Carl als Denker*, Stuttgart, 1941; and O. Criste, *Erzherzog Carl von Österreich*, Vienna, 1912.

[18] C. v. d. Goltz, quoted in Jähns, III, 2549.

[19] *Krieg 1809*, published by the *Kriegsgeschichtliche Abteilung des k. und k. Kriegsarchives*, Vienna, 1907–1910, I, 102.

the attack column, the most conspicuous one being the assault on Aspern village, Austrian infantry in 1809 and during the campaigns of 1812 to 1814 usually attacked in line, which was the formation favored by the manual.[20]

The *tirailleurs* needed to clear the path of the attack column came from the third rank, which also provided a battalion reserve, and if required served to lengthen the linear formation.[21] Because of the variety of their duties the men making up the third rank were to be the "brightest, most cunning, and most reliable" in the battalion, soldiers "whose concepts are not limited to maintaining physical contact with the men in front of them." [22] Whenever possible the skirmishers were to act in double teams of two, with intervals of six paces between men; the standard distance between the skirmish line and the closed formation was set at 300 paces—far too great for tactical coordination, but the manual cautioned that these distances should not be timidly observed.[23] However, the main purpose of the skirmishers was to fight defensively and in broken terrain; in true eighteenth-century fashion the manual stated that *tirailleurs* were rarely effective on level ground.[24] Their drill was of an immense complexity, stiffened by harsh punishment: "It was not realized that the soldier, unless he has natural ability for skirmishing, must be carefully trained towards independence." [25]

The troops that did possess a natural ability for fighting in open order, the *Grenzer*, continued to be used for the light service; but their quality had declined since the War of the Austrian Succession and the early campaigns against the French Republic. In training, organization, and equipment they increasingly resembled the regular line infantry, an assimilation that presumably had political motives of sufficient importance to outweigh the obvious military disadvantages. To make up the deficiency in light troops, several *Jäger* battalions were raised, but these units

---

[20] *Exercier-Reglement für die kaiserlich-königliche Infanterie*, Vienna, 1807, Book III, Chapter 3, Paragraph 1. As the manual was issued in at least two different formats, page references can be misleading.

[21] *Ibid.*, Book III, Chapters 1 and 2.

[22] *Ibid.*, Book III, Chapter 1, Preamble, and Chapter 2, Paragraph 2.

[23] *Ibid.*, Book III, Chapter 2, Paragraph 4.

[24] *Ibid.*, Book III, Chapter 2, Paragraph 1.

[25] *Krieg 1809*, I, 113.

did not match their Prussian models in mobility and marksmanship. In contrast to the Prussians, the Austrian *Jäger* formed in three ranks, of which the first two were armed with smoothbore carbines, and only the third with rifles.[26] They trained and fought under the handicap of not having been issued instructions that took account of the particular conditions of their service.

In 1809 the army included nine *Jäger* battalions, a number that had risen to 12 by 1813. The other infantry consisted of 61 line and 17 *Grenz* regiments, to which must be added various *Freicorps* and the *Landwehr*, which Charles and Archduke Johann first raised for the War of 1809. Charles, who in earlier years was opposed to any move that would involve the civilian population in fighting, now accepted the scheme for a militia in order to supplement "the inadequacy of the military resources still remaining to us after fifteen years of fighting and fifteen years of misfortune. . . ."[27] The *Landwehr* proved its worth at Aspern, but neither militia nor the half-hearted attempts at supporting the popular uprising in the Tyrol was sufficient to redress the military imbalance of 1809.

In the later wars of the Napoleonic Era, the Austrians followed the now general Continental pattern of combining column and line, without ever achieving a really successful amalgamation of the two. The troops were hampered by old-fashioned drill, inferior weapons, and pedantic training; many of their officers did not understand the potentials of the new formations. As late as 1813, the Austrian commander-in-chief felt it necessary in his instructions for senior officers to include the advice that "columns or squares can be used to great advantage not only in the defense but also very decidedly in the attack."[28]

In the German states that had not shared the special tradition of light troops found in such principalities as Hesse and Weimar, the armies modernized their tactics at the same time as did the Austrians and Prussians. The Bavarian line infantry, for instance, was not trained to skirmish until 1805; three years later

---

[26] *Ibid.*, i, 75; Rüstow, *Geschichte der Infanterie*, ii, 328.

[27] "Gutachten" of April 1808, quoted in H. Rössler, *Österreichs Kampf um Deutschlands Befreiung*, Hamburg, 1940, i, 319.

[28] Prince Schwarzenberg, "Instruction über taktische Verhaltungen," *Beiträge zur Geschichte des österreichischen Heerwesens*, Vienna, 1872, i, 267.

one-fifth of each company consisted of *Schützen*. In Mecklenburg extended order was introduced in 1808, and in the same year corporal punishment was abolished in all but exceptional cases. By the time of the war of 1809, there was little to chose between the tactics of the French and the tactics of their German allies, who had shifted within a brief period from a general observation of Frederician patterns to adaptations of French doctrine and French organization, though they could match neither the expertise nor the patriotism and Imperial pride that gave impetus to the French manner of fighting.[29]

Very different was the development in Russia. Until late in the Napoleonic wars the Russian infantry fought much as their grandfathers had in the 1750's. Their weapons and training were poor, the general standards of education of subalterns and soldiers too low to encourage commanding officers to renounce their faith in solid mass and the bayonet in favor of greater individual initiative. General Duhesme, who fought against Russian forces in Italy in the 1790's, wrote that although "they possess *Jäger*, we can assert that they have no true light infantry; their soldiers do not have sufficient aptitude for this service. The skirmish lines that they occasionally tried to deploy in their front or flanks did not know how to spread out or to maintain proper direction. The majority of their NCO's are not able to fend for themselves, and there are few who understand how to lead even a small patrol."[30]

Although the Russian light infantry were called *Jäger*, they had nothing in common with their German models. According to a Russian contemporary, the *Jäger* were known for their high morale; otherwise they differed from the line by little more than their green collars. Their training in open tactics was "inadequate

---

[29] See the already cited French and Austrian works on the war of 1809; the tactical studies of the campaign in *Schlachtfelder zwischen Alpen und Main*, ed. v. Reichenau, Munich, 1938, pp. 208–254; and the regimental histories of participating units—for instance, F. Beck, *Geschichte des 1. Grossherzoglich Hessischen Infanterie- (Leibgarde-) Regiments Nr. 115*, Berlin, 1899, pp. 141–164, and F. v. Fabrice, *Das Königlich Bayerische 6. Infanterie-Regiment*, Munich, 1886–1896, ii, 151–263.

[30] P. G. Duhesme, *Die leichte Infanterie*, Berlin, 1829, p. 144. Similar observations were made by Russia's Austrian and Prussian allies in the Austerlitz campaign and during the war of 1807. See E. Mayerhoffer v. Vedropolje, *Die Schlacht bei Austerlitz*, Vienna, 1912, p. 13; Lettow-Vorbeck, iii, 42.

and unpractical." [31] The men were armed with the weak Russian musket or a cheap smoothbore carbine; only 12 privates and one or more NCO's in each company carried rifled weapons. [32] By 1812 the *Jäger* made up more than one-third of the Russian infantry—50 regiments out of over 170—but barring some elite units they fought like regular infantry. The neo-Frederician infantry tactics that had been the norm for the army under Paul remained in force until 1811, but their inadequacy led to widespread disregard of their more complex features, and in 1808 a commission was appointed to work out a new drill for the line and the light troops. As a result the regulations with which the Russian army entered the war in 1812, though still formalistic, paid some attention to open order, aimed fire, and included the attack column; drill was somewhat simplified, and the extremely harsh code of punishment for the rank and file was slightly alleviated. [33] How well the new doctrine was understood and to what extent it was carried out is questionable. Before Riga their Prussian opponents thought that the defenders used skirmishers competently, especially in wooded and otherwise obstructed terrain. [34] Farther

[31] T. v. Bernhardi, *Denkwürdigkeiten aus dem Leben des . . . Carl Friedrich Grafen von Toll*, Leipzig, 1865, I, 197–198. A highly critical discussion of the *Jäger* regiments in the Napoleonic and post-Napoleon period by an expert though unfriendly observer is contained in J. Canski, *Tableau statistique, politique, et moral du système militaire de la Russie*, Paris, 1833, pp. 222–255. Generally in agreement is F. v. Stein, *Geschichte der Entwicklung des Russischen Heeres*, Leipzig, 1895, pp. 171, 245. Stein's book is still the most comprehensive history of the Russian army in the eighteenth and nineteenth centuries by a non-Russian.

[32] The claim by some Soviet historians that all *Jäger* were equipped with rifled weapons must be based on a misunderstanding of terms. I follow A. A. Strokov, *Istoriia voennogo iskusstuai; II, Kapitalicheskoe obshchestvo ot frantszuskoi burzhuaznoi revoliutsii do perioda imperializma*, Moscow, 1965, p. 144, whose figures agree with those given by Stein, p. 239. According to J. S. Curtiss, *The Russian Army under Nicholas I, 1825–1855*, Durham, N.C., 1965, p. 126, the Russian army in the 1830's contained no more than three battalions equipped with rifles.

[33] Strokov, pp. 130, 148–149; L. G. Beskrovnyi, *Otechestvennaia voina 1812 goda*, Moscow, 1962, p. 205.

[34] See the eyewitness reports published by A. v. Schoenaich in "Zur Vorgeschichte der Befreiungskriege: Kriegsberichte von 1812," *Altpreussische Monatsschrift*, IL–L (1912–1913), especially IL, 575–578, and L, 164.

to the south Russian troops were generally outfought, though their tenacity and self-sacrifice dealt the *Grande Armée* irreparable wounds. Despite urgings of their superiors to employ skirmishers backed by closed reserves and attack columns, regimental and battalion commanders preferred to fight their men in the accustomed three-rank linear formation.[35] The tactical backwardness of the Russian troops was matched by the conservative operational views of most of their generals: Wittgenstein's linear order of battle at Grossgörschen on 1 May 1813, lacking almost any depth or reserves, exemplifies the antiquated concepts that continued to dominate the Russian service.

In England the development of a native light infantry had been brought to a halt with the general reduction of the forces after 1783. During the early Revolutionary wars most light troops in the British service were still Hanoverians and other German auxiliaries, and it was not until 1797 that a unit of riflemen was incorporated into the regular army—the 5th battalion of the 60th Infantry regiment.[36] The formation of the Experimental Rifle Corps followed three years later, and in 1803 that of another light infantry regiment. The strength of light units relative to the line remained, however, very much weaker than on the Continent, being at the beginning of the Spanish uprising no more than five battalions among the approximately 65 battalions ready for service in Europe.[37] An order of the Commander-in-Chief on 10 September 1808, declaring that "the proportion of light troops was much too small for the extended scale of the British army," gave the impetus to further expansion, and five additional light regiments were formed by the time of the Waterloo campaign.[38] Each

[35] See the Order of 17 July 1812 by Prince Bagration quoted in Strokov, pp. 149–150.

[36] Hutton, p. 8. On the history of British light infantry during the Napoleonic Era, see volumes IV to X of J. Fortescue, *A History of the British Army*, London, 1906–1920; J. F. C. Fuller, *Sir John Moore's System of Training*, London, 1924; The already-cited work by S.G.P. Ward, *Faithful*, pp. 90–142; and R. Glover, *Peninsular Preparation: The Reform of the British Army, 1795–1809*, Cambridge, Eng., 1963.

[37] This estimate excludes the cadres in the United Kingdom of a further thirty battalions in various stages of preparedness, and the forces stationed outside Europe.

[38] Ward, *Faithful*, p. 95.

line battalion also received a light company.[39] If this still did not constitute a particularly numerous body, the deficiency was made good by the continued employment of foreign auxiliaries, such as the King's German Legion, as well as of *Caçadores* and guerrillas for skirmishing and the purposes of the little war.[40]

Many of the original members of the 5th battalion of the 60th came from central Europe. Their drill owed a good deal to foreign inspiration, as can be seen from *The Exercise of Riflemen and Light Infantry*, drafted by the battalion's first commanding officer, Baron Rottenburg, a German by birth, who had served in the French and Neapolitan armies and fought under Kosciuszko against the Russians.[41] Other German and French texts helped create a more sophisticated concept of the light service in the army—for example, the manual published by the French *émigré* officer Francis Jarry, which, while mainly devoted to the traditional topics of patrols and outposts, contained a few pages on the use of light infantry in battle that stressed their particular advantages over the line.[42] Gradually, however, the foreign school was replaced by a system of drill, evolved by such officers as Craufurd and Moore, that took fuller account of English requirements and attitudes.

Sir John Moore's method of instruction combined careful and realistic training with a mode of discipline that was based on a somewhat higher regard for the private soldier than had hitherto been the custom in the army; he did not abolish corporal punishment but he attempted to bring out a man's better qualities. As

[39] *Rules and Regulations for the Formations, Field-Exercises and Movements of His Majesty's Forces*, London, 1812, p. 66.

[40] The King's German Legion contained troops of the line as well as light troops, the former also receiving training in skirmish tactics. L. Beamish, *Geschichte der Königlich Deutschen Legion*, Hanover, 1832, presents detailed information on the Legion's drill and performance in action. See also L. v. Ompteda, *Ein hannoversch-englischer Offizier vor hundert Jahren*, Leipzig, 1892, pp. 169–173.

[41] Fuller discusses Rottenburg's influence on English tactics in his *Sir John Moore's System of Training*, pp. 77–80.

[42] F. Jarry, *Instruction concernant le service de l'infanterie légère en campagne*, London, 1801, especially p. 197. Two years later an English translation appeared in London under the title *Instruction Concerning the Duties of Light Infantry in the Field*. Jarry became Inspector-General of Instruction at the new Royal Military College; in 1809 and later Scharnhorst was repeatedly invited to succeed him in this position.

one commentator said, he sought to develop intelligence, not to suppress it.[43] The combat formations in which he drilled his men remained linear, but were thinned out to two ranks; in extended order, steadiness and unhurried volleying were stressed more than aimed fire. The linear pattern was not abandoned; instead it was simplified, and Moore tried to improve the quality of the soldier who carried it into effect. Wellington took over Moore's system except for the reform of discipline, which under him reverted to its ancient ferocity. His infantry generally fought in two ranks, though the *Rules and Regulations* of 1812 still stated that this formation "is to be regarded as an occasional exception" for use in broken terrain, "or where an irregular enemy, who deals only in fire, is to be opposed." [44] In the defense, the infantry when feasible formed on reverse slopes, its flanks secured by terrain features, with thick skirmish swarms thrown out, to emerge at the last moment and subject the approaching French columns to a steady fire from flanks and front, succeeded by a short counterattack. Wellington's understanding of terrain was equally sound in offensive operations. Preceded by skirmishers, the infantry advanced in line; but in contrast to the old-Prussian concern for maintaining cohesion, the British battalion commanders were willing to accept large intervals between their units, since these could be covered by skirmishers and the very mobile cavalry and horse artillery. In mountainous or otherwise difficult terrain, attacks by columns of companies were also employed—for example, during the final assaults on the French center at Vittoria in June 1813.[45] Backing up the fighting troops was an efficient staff organization, which concentrated an unusual measure of control in the hands of the Commander-in-Chief.

Here lay the true strength, but also a possible weakness, of the English method. As in the Prussian army of the 1750's and 1760's, everything depended on the central figure. In his admirable study on Wellington's staff in the Peninsular War, S.G.P. Ward writes: "The absence of a commander cannot but lead to some dislocation; but Wellington and his decisions were so essen-

[43] General Sir Frederick Maurice, quoted by Fuller in *Sir John Moore's System of Training*, p. 107.

[44] *Rules and Regulations*, p. 77.

[45] Sir Charles Oman, *A History of the Peninsular War*, Oxford, 1902–1930, VI, 420–421.

tial a part of the command that his absence, had it lasted for no more than a few weeks, and, on occasion, even a few minutes, must almost inevitably have led to failure. It was not the type of command that anyone could wield. . . . All depended on Wellington's presence."[46] From his subordinates the Duke expected not initiative and independent judgment, but the strictest obedience to orders. Unlike the evolving Prussian staff- and command-system, which stated the general objective and left the individual commanders considerable leeway in how to achieve it, Wellington's orders covered a wide range of contingencies, and went into minute tactical and administrative detail.[47]

British officers claimed that the French columns could prevail only against inferior opponents, not over the British line.[48] This article of faith contained an important truth: among the column's advantages was the moral effect of shock, to which well-trained and experienced troops might be immune. It is, however, a mistake to interpret Wellington's victories as a vindication of the line over the column. Wellington's opponents in Spain and later at Waterloo did not exhaust the range of French tactics. In the campaigns between 1808 and 1815, the British forces rarely encountered columnar tactics that exhibited the needed coordination between skirmishers, artillery, and closed formations. The French forces in Spain too often felt compelled to attack uphill, which rendered effective artillery support difficult; against an opponent who had not been weakened by artillery or musket fire the column was likely to fail.[49] The "somewhat ponderous thrust-

---

[46] S.G.P. Ward, *Wellington's Headquarters*, Oxford, 1957, p. 169.

[47] In a well-known incident at Waterloo, Blücher's liaison officer, General Müffling, observed the Duke's system in action. As French troops were recoiling from an unsuccessful attack, Müffling urged two British brigade commanders to fall on them with their cavalry. They agreed that the opportunity was excellent, but refused to take advantage of it since they were not given such freedom. Later Wellington confirmed that had his generals moved without orders, they would have been court-martialed. F. C. v. Müffling, *Aus meinem Leben*, Berlin, 1851, pp. 245–246. It goes without saying, however, that at times Wellington condoned behavior that went counter to his orders—for example, Picton's attack at Vittoria.

[48] Rüstow, *Geschichte der Infanterie*, II, 332.

[49] Graphic examples of the extremely unfavorable conditions under which the French would attack in Spain are afforded by the battles of Vimiero and Bussaco. Oman, I, 254–256; III, 369–383.

ing methods of the French commanders"—as Clausewitz described these tactics—were far removed from the small maneuverable assault columns of the wars of the Republic and the first triumphant years of the Empire.[50] In the same way, Wellington's line differed from classic linear patterns. Its extreme thinness and flexibility permitted deployment in broken terrain; the large numbers of native and foreign skirmishers protected the closed formation in attack and defense. The British army accepted some of the new Continental developments, without discarding the old system completely. Most significantly, it continued to rely on long-serving volunteers from the poorest sections of the population. In a remarkably exact sense, the soldiers' work on barrack-square and battlefield reflected the political and social course of their country in the first decades of the nineteenth century—one of gradual adjustment rather than of revolutionary change.

· 3 ·

The armies of Europe thus reacted in different ways to the stimulus of the French wars. Of them all, the Prussians paid the closest attention to the technique of skirmishing and the amalgamation of skirmishers and column; having once been most deeply committed to the line, they now went farthest to the opposite side. As in every army, the commencement of action was entrusted to light troops and open formations; but the Prussian *tirailleurs* continued to play a major role in the subsequent stages of battle, which typically consisted of lengthy fire-fights interspersed with local attacks by battalion columns that gradually might bring about the opportunity for a decisive advance. In waging this *combat d'usure* the most difficult task was to assure the proper working together of open and closed formations—to effect the shift under fire from column to closed lines or skirmishers, the replenishment of the skirmish line by additional sections of the waiting attack columns, the reassembly of skirmishers into squares to withstand counterattacks. In the campaigns from 1812 to 1815 this coordination was not always achieved. The troops still lacked experience in the new tactics, the more so since not all

[50] C. v. Clausewitz, "Über das Leben und den Charakter von Scharnhorst," *Historisch-politische Zeitschrift*, I (1832), 199. In the particular passage Clausewitz contrasts Scharnhorst's "prudence, sagacity, and cunning" with the schematic tactics of the French.

officers set aside adequate time for extended order drill during training periods. It was rare to find a line officer like the battalion commander who reported his men had made such progress in skirmishing that the unit could at any time be used as a light battalion.[51] More usual was an emphasis on the column, which was the simplest of all formations for recruits to master, and easier than skirmish lines to control in battle. The thousands of conscripts that entered the ranks after the spring campaign of 1813 had no more than nine weeks during which to learn the fundamentals of soldiering, and for simplicity's sake they were trained almost wholly in the main fighting methods of the unit to which they had been assigned. Blücher's biographer writes of these weeks that they were "fully used to drill the troops. But in training there still remained, even in Yorck's corps, the distinction between line and light infantry, between the service of musketeer and fusilier."[52] The quality of training was an additional problem. At the battle of Grossgörschen, the first occasion since 1807 in which Prussian and French troops were opposed, Boyen was unhappy to observe that the French "are not so mechanically drilled and mis-drilled, and thus retain a freer point of view; they grow accustomed to profit from any small advantage that occurs, while the German thinks of nothing else than nervously how to maintain his tactical order."[53]

Tactical coordination was brought to a higher level in the light battalions. Their men were expected to fight in open order, so this most important aspect of their service was not ignored in training, but it was also taken for granted that they could maneuver and attack in column. The excellence of Prussian tactics as they proved themselves in the field lay in this amalgamation. It is an interesting example of the strength with which historical interpretation may be affected by immediate concerns—in this case, to uphold the "Frederician tradition"—that this fact has been largely ignored in German military studies, particularly in the works of the Historical Section of the General Staff that appeared before 1914 and have set the tone for later interpretations. As the

[51] Quoted in H. v. Freytag-Loringhoven, "Wert und Bedeutung des Drills für die Ausbildung unserer Infanterie einst und jetzt," *Militär-Wochenblatt* (1904), Supplement 12, 536.

[52] Unger, II, 57.

[53] *Erinnerungen*, III, 38.

official historians exaggerated the validity of Frederician tactics in the Revolutionary age, so they minimized the importance of light troops and open order tactics in the Wars of Liberation. Instead they suggest that Prussian infantry continued to fight almost entirely in closed ranks. A passage in one of the two introductory volumes of the General Staff history of the Wars of Liberation states the basic theme:

The infantry attack was to consist on principle and as far as possible in a single uninterrupted advance from the approach area to the midst of the enemy. It was to consist in a determined *advance with the bayonet* [author's italics], which was not to be delayed in any way by the individual fire-fight. If individual skirmishing (which was restricted to a few minutes) did not shake the enemy so thoroughly as to render likely the success of the bayonet attack, the first line of battle was to fire volleys.[54]

Such undoubtedly was the ideal of the conservative officer; the reformers never saw infantry combat in this light, their manuals did not describe it in these terms, and it was not the manner in which it typically occurred in the field. The temporary or permanent loss of much of the army's records of the period prohibits a complete refutation of the General Staff interpretation; but the published reports and diaries—including material contained in the volumes of the Historical Section, which contradicts the analytic sections of the same works—suffice to indicate how the army fought in reality.

One need go no farther than the campaign of 1813 to find many instances of the large-scale use of open formations. At Grossgörschen in May the Guards fusiliers attacked entirely in open order, and the three battalions of the adjacent line regiment deployed almost wholly into skirmish lines.[55] At Blankenfelde, on 23 August 1813, a Prussian infantry regiment successfully defended a front of 660 yards "by a violent skirmish action lasting for several hours," in which the third rank fought as *tirailleurs* and the rest of the unit changed from lines into small columns for

[54] A. v. Holleben and R. v. Caemmerer, *Geschichte des Frühjahrsfeldzuges 1813 und seiner Vorgeschichte*, Berlin, 1904–1909, II, 63.

[55] Reports on the extremely effective aimed fire of the advancing fusiliers are printed in Rentzell, p. 66; Conrady, pp. 178–180. Conrady's history of the 6th Infantry regiment, pp. 150–285, contains unusually explicit tactical accounts for the years 1812–1815.

repeated counterattacks.[56] Two weeks later, at the battle of Dennewitz, a Prussian corps, with all its skirmishers deployed ahead of the columns, attacked the French lines with little interruption for two hours.[57] In the battle of Wartenburg, in which Yorck broke the French hold on the Elbe, fifteen infantry battalions—of which as many as five at a time were deployed as skirmishers— for eight hours defended and counterattacked on a front of one-and-a-half miles in the center of the Prussian line, while an enveloping force gradually worked its way around the French right.[58] In the cluster of engagements preceding the decisive encounter at Leipzig, as in the battle itself, the gradual build-up of pressure by skirmishers, lines, and columns was representative of Prussian tactics. At Möckern, on 16 October, a fusilier battalion and two *Jäger* companies, in open formation, attacked Möckern village at the start of the action. The village and the surrounding ground became the center of the fight and changed hands several times; finally, "realizing the uselessness of advancing in closed columns," *Jäger*, fusiliers, grenadiers, and militia, completely intermingled, captured the position permanently.[59] On the same day, to the south at Wachau, a Prussian force first took and then defended the center of the French line, an action that the General Staff account describes as "a *tirailleur* engagement lasting for hours, during which the entire first line of battle of the Brigade Klüx—three battalions of the 7th Silesian *Landwehr-Regiment* —gradually opened up as skirmishers." [60] In the course of the battle the force holding this position grew to thirteen battalions, all fully or partly deployed in skirmish lines. On the morning of 18 October, the Hessian positions south of Leipzig were overrun by strong groups of Prussian *tirailleurs*, supported by troops of hussars.[61] In the early afternoon two Prussian brigades preceded by their fusilier battalions and sharpshooters attacked Probstheida, where Napoleon himself led the defense. A French counter-

[56] R. Friederich, *Geschichte des Herbstfeldzuges 1813*, Berlin, 1903– 1906, I, 400 and map 3.

[57] *Ibid.*, II, 155–156.

[58] *Ibid.*, II, 285–291. The name of the village was incorporated in Yorck's title when he was made a count in 1814.

[59] Friederich, III, 87–89, 95. The part the *Jäger* took in the action is reconstructed in Rentzell, pp. 91–93.

[60] Friederich, III, 336.

[61] Beck, pp. 228–229.

attack regained the village, and only a thick skirmish screen enabled the Prussian columns to withdraw in fair order.[62] The fighting around the walls and in the streets of Leipzig on the following day was naturally enough waged mainly in open formations.

That the General Staff historians inaccurately minimized the part of the light infantry and its methods is also borne out by the army's tables of organization. Out of a total of 46 infantry battalions under arms on 1 January 1813, 15—or nearly one-third— were fusiliers, *Jäger*, and *Schützen*.[63] This proportion of light to line infantry, which marked a genuine, not a ceremonial, difference, was probably unequalled in any other service. But to gain a true picture of Prussian tactical capabilities, the third rank of the line battalions must also be taken into account. It will then be seen that over half of the Prussian infantry consisted of troops that were expected to know how to fight in open formations as a matter of course. This proportion did not materially change in 1814 and 1815. The evidence both of combat reports and the organization of the army goes against the General Staff works. Held in thrall by an "old-Prussian" Frederician tradition largely of their own making, the official military historians have ignored the motives, extent, and implications of the changes that occurred

[62] Friederich, III, 165–166, 179–180.

[63] See Appendices 3 and 4. It may be noted that while the proportion of light infantry battalions rose sevenfold in less than thirty years, that of the light cavalry hardly changed. Of 53 squadrons in the army at the beginning of 1813, 21 were of hussars and uhlans, an increase of about 5 per cent in relation to the heavy cavalry since Frederick's death. The new numerical importance of the light battalions had no pronounced effect on their social profile. Throughout the reform period and the Wars of Liberation, the *Jäger* and *Schützen* continued to include a somewhat greater proportion of bourgeois officers than did the line infantry. In 1809, 55 titled and 12 untitled officers served with the three battalions; in a third regular *Jäger* battalion established in 1813, the bourgeois officers outnumbered their titled comrades 10 to 4, and included the battalion commander. Gumtau, I, Appendices XI, XIV, XVII, XXIII. After the war an internal difference appears among these units. In 1827 only one untitled officer served with the Guards *Jäger*, but 24 are on the lists of the other two *Jäger* battalions. As the army continued to expand during the nineteenth century, it was no longer the branch of service but certain units within it to which social prestige came to be attached.

in the army, and with them passed over an important instance of German reaction to the experience of the French Revolution.

What effect did the increase of light infantry exert on the conduct of war? The immediate changes that the expansion of light troops brought about were of tactical significance, but they carried implications of greater magnitude.

Linear tactics had achieved the maximum of movement and fire compatible with close order. Its system of drill and discipline permitted a great measure of automatic control over the troops' behavior on the battlefield, and thus met the demands of war until it was threatened and superseded by a new principle, more psychological than mechanistic in character, which held that soldiers need not lose their individuality in order to act in unison. From the 1790's on, war is dominated by the concept of separate positions leading to concerted action. Implied is a different view of tactical and strategic control, as well as a different strategic ideal. Eberhard Kessel has well described the change: "If the eighteenth century's theory of war had seen the supreme achievement of the general in the far-reaching exclusion of chance, that of the nineteenth century sought perfection in its utmost exploitation." [64]

The new infantry tactics were infinitely more versatile than the eighteenth-century line, but they involved a loss in mechanical control. At Leuthen Frederick could maneuver a front of twenty battalions as a single body; now in the Napoleonic Era these battalions might act as twenty separate units, many of them divided into closed and open sections. For the general to direct a large number of such fragments, each advancing at its own pace, moving somewhat to the left or the right, deploying to varying degree, meant giving up the measure of certainty that he had possessed when thousands of soldiers marched as one at his command. It is here that the new tactics and the freer discipline that accompanies them reflect the changed operational doctrine and the new spirit of warfare, which they help turn into reality.

At least since the death of Frederick the Great, the three realms of tactics, operations, and what Napoleon called *l'esprit*

---

[64] E. Kessel, "Die Wandlung der Kriegskunst im Zeitalter der französischen Revolution," *Historische Zeitschrift*, CXLVIII (1933), 275.

général de la guerre had not been in agreement in the military institutions of Prussia. In 1806, to give an example, Scharnhorst's intention of pushing the army in six columns through the Thuringian Forest and turning on the enemy wherever he might be found, "to the right or to the left, as circumstances would require," was made illusory by the army's deficiencies in doctrine and training. The Prussian troops, Schlieffen writes, were "in no way prepared for mountain warfare, action in difficult terrain, rapid movements, nor were their generals prepared for the command of large combined forces." [65] In the abstract Scharnhorst's plan was excellent—indeed, it was Napoleonic—but Prussian tactical and operational capabilities were not yet in harmony with the new strategy. Six years later, after the army had been reorganized, these three realms again formed a reasonably consistent whole, and a minimum of energy was wasted in friction between them. To be sure, their relative significance need not remain constant. By the beginning of the spring campaign of 1813 the principles of Napoleonic strategy had become common property to all armies: even if he could not transform his knowledge into action, every commander understood that a combination of mobility, concentration of effort, and retention of strong reserves promised success. With their heavy superiority in numbers and resources, only very grave transgressions against these concepts could have robbed the Allies of eventual victory, while after Leipzig even the most brilliant strategic combinations would not save the Emperor. The fascination of the 1814 campaign lies not in the possibility that its outcome might have been different, but in the conflict of political interests among the Allies and in the lesson on mobility in the defense to which they were subjected by Napoleon. Schwarzenberg and Blücher could commit any number of errors, Napoleon not one, as the consequences of the battle of Laon showed. Once the Allies had launched their concentric advance, strategy could no longer prevent the French collapse—the disparity of force was too great. At such a stage in war a significant weakness in the tactics of the more powerful side may yet negate its other advantages. But in the Wars of Liberation tactical inferiority did not rest with the Allies, or at least not with

---

[65] Schlieffen, II, 166. For the quotation from Scharnhorst's disposition, see *ibid.*, II, 163.

the Prussian army. The danger nevertheless did exist that the Prussians, by not compelling their opponents to stand and fight, would lose the benefits of tactical ascendancy. Scharnhorst, who better than anyone among the reformers understood the mentality and theories of the many maneuver strategists that continued in positions of power, was deeply concerned at this prospect. On his way to Vienna in May 1813, ill from the effect of the wound he had received at Grossgörschen, which was soon to cause his death, he wrote to Knesebeck, now the King's influential *General-adjutant:*

I am again on the move, a terrible inflammation and a 24-hour-long fever during which I raved continuously held me in Zittau. Now I am again on the move, I hope to be still of some use at my place of destination. I beg you to pay attention to one point: always be guided by the opposing positions of the armies, give less value to the strategic dispositions, more to the tactical dispositions. Your eternally affectionate friend. Scharnhorst.[66]

This warning against trying to outmaneuver a genius instead of seeking his armies, forcing the action, and giving the new tactics their head, was wasted on Knesebeck, who until the end of his days believed that victory lay in the occupation of decisive geographic points and in the cutting of lines of communication; but even after Scharnhorst's death, his influence and that of his companions in the work of reform remained sufficient to bring the war to a successful conclusion.

The tactical doctrine developed by Scharnhorst, Yorck, and their collaborators was in agreement with the new dynamics of strategy and with the changed nature of war. If skirmishers and column meant a loss of mechanical control, they also provided the commander with new means to exploit the unforeseen. One reason why stringent tactical control had replaced the more individual combativeness of the *Landsknecht* and the early household troops was the general's wish to neutralize the unintentional and fortuitous, the factor of chance. From Maurice of Nassau's day on, it was believed that this could be achieved only by increasing the rigidity of discipline and the exactness of drill, to the end that the fewest possible obstacles remained between the commander's intention and its realization. Now, after a century-and-a-half in

[66] Letter of 11 May 1813, *Scharnhorsts Briefe*, i, 480–481.

which military absolutism had neared perfection, some of the commander's tactical authority was again delegated to his subordinates, who passed on the increased freedom to the common soldier. It again became feasible to choose a target, to decide whether to stop for loading behind this tree or that bush, to take opportunity of any advantage suddenly presented. And this release of thought and independence on the battlefield brought with it an enormous increase of energy, which not only might cope with the unexpected, but could also more easily bring it about.

The pre-Revolutionary armies were compelled to fear the unforeseen because their means of dealing with it were imperfect. Theory attempted to make up for their limitations in tactics, command structure, administration, and spirit. Men tried to abolish accident by swelling the manuals with rules covering any eventuality, by devising strategies that were based on invariables such as rivers, mountains, the correct tangents of advance and retreat, and by restricting themselves to limited objectives. The attitude born of the French Revolution differed profoundly from this longing for certainty. Clausewitz defined the new approach to war in these words: "War is the realm of accident. In no other human activity must this stranger be given so much freedom, because no other activity is everywhere in such permanent contact with him." [67] This was not an expression of fear; on the contrary, Clausewitz believed that only complete acceptance of the unforeseen as a factor in war rendered military success possible. The same point was made by Yorck when he wrote, "There are no unfailing recipes in the art of war," adding that there existed however such general principles as mobility, firepower, concentration of force, retention of reserves, in whose appropriate application to diverse circumstances could be sought the key to effective fighting. For chance was not to rule without restraint. At St. Helena, speaking of the great captains of the past, Napoleon asked: "Did they become great because they were lucky?"—and answered his own question: "No, but because, being great men, they knew how to master luck. When we investigate the causes of their success, we are astonished to find that they did everything in their power to achieve it." [68]

[67] *On War*, Book I, Chapter III.

[68] Entry for 14 November 1816, M. de Las Cases, *Le Mémorial de Sainte-Hélène*, ed. M. Dunan, Paris, 1951, II, 575.

The acceptance of chance, the relinquishing of closest tactical control on the battlefield, was paralleled by a growing flexibility in operations, and by an increase in the dynamics of war itself. The tamed Bellona had broken free from at least some of the bonds of rationality that had limited her actions throughout the eighteenth century, and contemporaries may be forgiven for having felt that she had shed them all. The early stages of the trend were thus described by Clausewitz:

> The old methods of warfare had collapsed during the Wars of the French Revolution. Because the age and the political conditions had changed, the old forms and methods no longer obtained—this was generally felt, and thrust on us by the French sword. That opinion went further than necessary, that belief in the old was more deeply undermined than was its reality belongs to the usual state of affairs. By their revolutionary measures the French had attacked the old concept of war as though with acid. They had released the frightful power of war from its former diplomatic and financial bonds; now it progressed in its raw form, dragged an enormous mass of force with it, and nothing could be seen but ruins of the old art of war on the one side and fabulous successes on the other; however, a new system of war, i.e., new ways of rationality, new positive forms in the use of force, could not yet be clearly distinguished. War was returned to the people, from whom it had been partially removed by the standing armies; war had thrown off its chains and overcome its imaginary impossibilities—that was all that could be grasped of the development. What structure was to be erected on this broader and firmer basis would only gradually become apparent.[69]

Indeed, the concept of war and the measures needed to turn it into reality had taken long strides towards totality. More of national life was affected, and more was at stake. It is not only the number of combatants that increased after the French Revolution, but also the arsenal of their weapons and methods, and the impetus behind their use. Together with its tactical and operational possibilities, the aims of war had expanded, and the greater threats this posed to the state were more difficult to counter than the unexpected appearance of a fresh enemy division on the battlefield, where reserves, mobility, and independent judgment might overcome the crisis. The weightier imponderables that

[69] "Über das Leben . . . von Scharnhorst," *Historisch-politische Zeitschrift*, pp. 196–197.

compromised the existence of the nation could still, it was argued, be controlled by a commander of genius and by wise statesmanship; but the French Revolution and in its wake the Prussian reformers suggested that in the final resort chance could also be dominated by an instrument which the preceding age did not know how to employ: enthusiasm, popular involvement, *die moralischen Grössen*. It cannot be denied, Clausewitz wrote in Book III of *On War*, that "as matters stand now, far greater scope is given to national spirit [*Volksgeist*]." [70] This he defined as "enthusiasm, fanatic energy, faith, opinion." If these were present and committed, a smashed army, even the conquest of the state, were not irrevocable disasters: the loss of physical power could be made good by giving greater scope to the moral forces, which in the end always prevailed. The moral forces could either create their own forms of effectiveness, or they could be incorporated in the existing system, which meant changing the army's constitution so that popular feeling could find expression in its ranks and be turned to military energy. This was the basis of the Prussian reforms of recruitment, military justice, and admission to officer rank. The new regulations, Clausewitz already announced in 1808, "will in future guide the spirit of a national army, and therefore belong among the most important political appearances of the age." [71]

This political force remained stunted, a useful servant rather than a new master. Regardless how revolutionary some reforms were, no revolution shook state or army; even the loyal outburst of popular enthusiasm in the spring of 1813, which encouraged the government in its resolve to fight Napoleon, is largely the product of patriotic legend-spinners. And yet in his motives and attitudes, as well as in his way of fighting, the new Prussian soldier differed from his predecessor—and this difference mattered. If the feelings of men scarcely affected state policy, they greatly added to state power. Many years after the Wars of Liberation, recalling the eve before a battle, Boyen described the change in these words:

[70] *On War*, Book III, Chapter IV.
[71] "Kriegswissenschaften," *Jenaische Allgemeine Literatur-Zeitung*, 11 October 1808.

Evidently a great change had taken place in our military estate: better treatment of the soldier, greater freedom for the peasantry, the addition of volunteer detachments made up of educated youths, all this had ennobled the warrior's life. Peacetime maneuvers had been kept free from all tricks and were directed only towards service in the field (an achievement of the noble Scharnhorst); the thought of liberating the downtrodden fatherland had become common property, and had elevated the life of the people and the army. The day before the battle the brigade of General von Klüx marched through Borna: if one could imagine 6,000 educated, honorable men walking with determination to a duel of life and death, one would have a picture of this military procession. The artifices of drill with their cul-de-sac of grand parades can only ape such an event, but never achieve it in truth.[72]

In less idealistic language, a British officer after the war made the same point:

It forms part of the discipline in the Prussian army to manage soldiers by exciting their feelings and national spirit in substitution of the old system of making them up into highly drilled machines. . . .

The consideration with which the soldier is treated and the fear of being degraded into the second class certainly have the effect of making him extremely well conducted; and as to his appearance, it is scarcely possible or desirable to exceed it in cleanliness and uniformity.

This system, which is the continuance of the enthusiasm by which the nation rose up in mass during the late war, and which was then very politic, is still worked upon. . . .[73]

The impulses that had created this change weakened after 1815. Soldier and citizen sank, or were pressed, back into that passivity most suitable for a subject, and similar developments can be observed in military doctrine. In the decades of peace that followed on Waterloo much of the *élan* and dedication would in any case have ossified into garrison routine; but the reactionary favorites of Frederick William that now replaced Scharnhorst, Gneisenau, and Boyen strove energetically to bring back as much

[72] *Erinnerungen*, III, 35.

[73] Letter of 4 August 1816 of Sir Henry Hardinge to Sir George Murray; *Murray Papers*, CXXXIV (Add. Mss. 47. 6. 2.), fols. 33–36. I am indebted to Major S.G.P. Ward for making his transcriptions of the Murray Papers available to me.

as was possible of the drill, ceremonial, and barracks-tone that had prevailed until 1806. They were helped by the close attachment that had grown up between the Prussian court and St. Petersburg. "Strangely enough," a Prussian general subsequently wrote, "already during the Wars of Liberation a tendency towards review-tactics began to revive in our army. . . . It was our alliance with Russia that temporarily carried us back to a strong predominance of parade-drill, a tendency towards pettiness, towards military games."[74] Even the *Reglement* of 1812, which had proved itself during three years of war, was now considered too simple, and attempts were made once again to spell out detailed regulations for every eventuality, and to deprive subordinates of their tactical initiative. But too much had occurred and too much had been learned to permit the vindicators of the past more than partial success. The essential gains of the years between 1807 and 1813 were not renounced, and Wilhelm Rüstow's judgment that in the areas of organization and conscription "Prussia remained the state which to the widest extent, even more than the French themselves, took over and retained the principles of the French Revolution," applies with yet greater truth to the army's manner of fighting.[75]

· 4 ·

The man who more than anyone beside Scharnhorst brought about the army's use of revolutionary methods is generally depicted in the literature as an antagonist of reform. This contradiction needs to be explained. To call it into question, however, is not to attempt Yorck's vindication. The honor of historical figures is not our concern, but their ideas and actions are, and Yorck's have rarely received sufficient attention. His interpreters fall into two groups: the students of military theory, institutions, and policy, and the historians of Prussia and of Europe during the Napoleonic Era. The writers that deal with the Prussian army rather than with the state have usually considered Yorck an innovator, though they disagree on the significance of his achievement.[76] Of

[74] Freytag-Loringhoven, "Wert und Bedeutung des Drills . . . ," p. 532.

[75] Rüstow, *Geschichte der Infanterie*, II, 334.

[76] The most important exception to this view is the interpretation that William Shanahan develops in his book, *Prussian Military Reforms*,

the second group, most regard Yorck as adhering to old forms, or even as a violent opponent of change. Their judgments are based on his supposed political views and ignore his work as a soldier. Whether the professional side of a soldier's life may safely be left out of account is questionable, especially if he lived in a society and at a time that placed military conceptions in close relationship to political and social attitudes. But even those non-military statements and actions of Yorck that are drawn on to substantiate his reactionary image require more careful analysis than is usually given them.

How is a man's ideological position determined? The preceding pages have related Yorck's theories and actions to the decisive military trends of his age. A cruder test is possible: Yorck might be compared with his fellow-officers—not the acknowledged reformers, nor with such mediocrities as *Generaladjutant* von Köckritz or the ambassador Friedrich Wilhelm von Zastrow, military courtiers "who looked at war through the spectacles of the old Prussian drill"—but with officers holding positions simi-

---

1786–1814. The relevant lines read: ". . . since the Prussian light infantry had been well-trained before 1806, York was not able to contribute many new ideas. He made no innovations but his recommendations were at least equal to the training measures that had been in use among the best Prussian fusilier battalions. York had a practical turn of mind and his instructions described the light troops as the shield of the army and gave excellent combat advice by stressing the necessity of accurate shooting" (p. 183). The analyses of Yorck and Prussia's military institutions in the preceding chapters show how erroneous this passage is. Shanahan's statement that Yorck's "recommendations were at least equal to the training measures that had been in use among the best Prussian fusilier battalions" leaves unclear whether the years before or after 1806 are meant, but is inappropriate in either case. The reformed light or fusilier battalions were more versatile than their predecessors; but their new tactics, which had first been outlined by Yorck's committee of 1808, continued to develop throughout the years of reform. In the process, Yorck's instruction of 1810 marked the decisive advance. That Yorck was not paying lip-service to modernity is evident throughout his administrative work, his correspondence, and his instructions, with their repeated warnings against executing the new tactics in an unthinking, pedantic manner, as well as in his service in the field. Shanahan's contradictory passage may perhaps be explained by the author's need to bring certain obvious facts into line with his judgment on the preceding page: ". . . the appointment of York as Inspector of Light Troops was evidence of Frederick William's return to military conservatism."

lar to his, the army's senior commanders, the brigade generals and Governors-General.[77] Of the eleven men that with Yorck made up this group in 1811, Blücher, the old *Freicorps* officer Field Marshal Courbière, and Goetzen favored innovation. The attitude of another officer is doubtful. A contemporary characterized Stutterheim, the commander of the East Prussian brigade, as a tenacious fighter who "in the good old days . . . had personally beaten up civilians," and in the literature he is typically referred to as an "arch-conservative officer of the old school." [78] He seems nevertheless to have been a competent man, who made enemies among the activists when in 1809 the King ordered him to reestablish discipline in the Berlin garrison, after the hussar officer Schill had attempted to start an uprising against the French. The remaining seven generals were outright military conservatives. The most flexible in tactical matters was Bülow, of whom Scharnhorst in a letter to Yorck wrote that his attitude and spirit "belong so far as I can judge to our former conditions." [79] In the same letter Scharnhorst described the future field marshal Kleist, who at that time commanded the Lower Silesian brigade, as a "good and sensible man, but an adherent to the old ways of war, of commonplace means, of formalism." Boyen wrote more rudely that Kleist was "personally a very brave man, but so glued to the old forms and so pessimistic about the future that when there was so much as talk about possible innovations in his presence he would become frightened." [80] Similarly, Scharnhorst's old antagonist, Borstell, now Governor-General of Pomerania and the Neumark, despite his personal dash felt most comfortable in the routine of the line.[81] Tauentzien, commander of the Brandenburg brigade, was placed by Clausewitz among those individuals who in 1806 "threw themselves into the yawning abyss of destruction with Frederick the Great's oblique order of battle . . . because of the most extreme intellectual starvation

[77] The characterization of Köckritz and Zastrow is contained in Boyen's *Erinnerungen*, I, 126, 264. See also Hardenberg's evaluation of Köckritz in an essay written probably in 1808, printed in Winter, I, 570–575.

[78] Letter of Privy Councillor G. T. v. Hippel to Colonel L. G. v. Thile of 22 April 1815, quoted in Lehmann, *Scharnhorst*, II, 42; J. Vidal de la Blanche, *La Régéneration de la Prusse*, Paris, 1910, p. 133.

[79] Letter of 29 August 1811, *Scharnhorsts Briefe*, I, 419.

[80] *Erinnerungen*, I, 264.

[81] *Ibid.*, I, 291.

ever brought about by reliance on method." [82] In this group Clausewitz also included the Governor of Silesia and later first commander of the Prussian contingent of the *Grande Armée*, Julius von Grawert. Grawert was a man who had outlived his age. His views on society and the army were the product of the idealistic rationalism that had been so conspicuous among educated officers in the last decades of the *ancien régime*. After Jena he was one of the first to demand that all officers formally justify their behavior during the campaign, and he advocated the admission of more bourgeois to the officer corps, while at the same time proposing the establishment of an elite, all-noble regiment that would serve in the immediate proximity of the monarch.[83] His operational and tactical ideas were as mathematically oriented as Saldern's, so that even a writer loath to criticize any Prussian general declared that he "belonged to those commanders who favored an antiquated, defensive method of waging war." [84] Akin to him in his "very natural preference for the old forms" was Anton Wilhelm von L'Estocq, the Governor of Berlin.[85] The most reactionary of them all was the Governor-General of East Prussia, Field Marshal von Kalkreuth, who had already been a staff officer in Frederick the Great's day, and, as was shown both by his behavior during the war of 1806 and by his violent enmity to Scharnhorst, saw no reason to depart from the old ways. "In the great achievement of skirmishing," Max Lehmann writes, "he saw nothing but organized disorder that had destroyed the magnificent Prussian volleys." [86] Even before the beginning of reform Scharnhorst declared that he did not want to serve under him: "Der General Kalkreuth ist mein Mann nicht." [87]

It is evident that Yorck left his peers far behind in his concern and work for the modernization of the army. The conservatism of

[82] *On War*, Book II, Chapter IV.

[83] Clausewitz, *Nachrichten*, p. 447; Grawert's Memorial concerning the reorganization of the army of 27 September 1807 is printed in *Preussisches Archiv*, pp. 108–119.

[84] Priesdorff, No. 955. See also Boyen, *Erinnerungen*, II, 156–158, and Hiller v. Gaertringen's *Denkwürdigkeiten*, p. 102.

[85] Boyen, *Erinnerungen*, I, 265. See also Scharnhorst's letter to his daughter Julie of 5 March 1807, *Scharnhorsts Briefe*, I, 316–317.

[86] *Scharnhorst*, II, 110.

[87] Letter to his daughter Julie of 28 November 1806, *Scharnhorsts Briefe*, I, 303.

most of the men who occupied the highest positions of command during the years of reform indicates once again the difficulties of the struggle for innovation, and along what lines it was fought. Most writers on the Reform Era, however, give little thought to the military sphere. Instead they base their views of Yorck almost wholly on certain passages in Droysen's biography. Ever since the appearance of the biography in the early 1850's, they have liked to use the terms "old-Prussian" and "Frederician" when they come to describe Yorck, as though such emotive adjectives could do the work of precise categories. Although his book gave them currency, Droysen himself never entirely fell in with these stereotypes. He had written the biography not only because the figure of Yorck and the revival of Prussia interested him as historical subjects, but to achieve a specific ideological task. Later he explained to a colleague, "In communicating with military friends in Berlin, 1845–1846, I often had occasion to hear of the dubious symptoms introduced into the army through the fanciful influence of the Throne; I formed the plan to depict in the typical figure of York the essential substance that the Prussian army possessed and which it should not lose." [88] In the "geistreichen Einflüssen vom Thron" Droysen referred to Frederick William IV's attempts to eradicate what liberal spirit remained among the military, and to turn the army into a weapon that might be used to back up his romantic conception of kingship. Yorck's biography was intended by its author to remind the nation of the energy and courage that came together from many sources and had revitalized the state after Jena. He therefore endeavored to draw a distinction between the idealists—Scharnhorst, Gneisenau, Boyen—the Junker opposition, and a third group of less parochial, far-sighted patriots like Yorck, who, Droysen suggested, derived their strength from the Frederician tradition. But this analysis, whether accurate or not, has proved too subtle for most subsequent writers, who either divide the Prussia of the Reform Era into two contending factions or "parties," or who posit a universal, purposeful patriotism, which reduces to insignificance the antagonisms of the leading figures in army and state. That neither of the two schematic views is appropriate will be readily admitted; but only a very few historians—notably Hintze, Mei-

[88] Letter to Alfred Dove of 16 July 1878, *Briefwechsel*, II, 931.

necke, Stadelmann, and more recently Simon and Ritter—have managed to express their sense of the period's complexities in their writings. Instead Yorck is labeled a "representative of the one great old-Prussian party," which for some writers may carry a positive connotation.[89] More commonly it serves to introduce the conclusion that he was "the principal champion of the beliefs and prejudices of the Junker," or should be counted among "the most spiteful and poisonous opponents of the reform party." [90]

Much of what men thought and did during the years of reform is today beyond analysis. But Yorck's conservatism is one of those larger blanket attributions that still offers scope for closer evaluation. What are the reasons for the view of Yorck as an opponent of the reformers? A survey of the material will lead to four incidents or statements on which this interpretation is founded. Even the indictments of such uncompromising antagonists as Theodor von Schön have not been able to increase their number.[91]

---

[89] The characterization of Yorck as a spokesman of "old Prussia" is by F. Meusel, who considers Yorck and A. v. d. Marwitz to be "intrinsically similar." See his edition of Marwitz's *Memoirs and letters*, I, pp. 32–33 of the Introduction. For another typical academic-patriotic characterization, see F. v. Bezold's lecture at the University of Bonn, *Der Geist von 1813*, Bonn, 1913, p. 12.

[90] The former description is E. Carrias' in his *La Penseé militaire allemande*, Paris, 1948, p. 145; the latter, F. Mehring's in *Zur Preussischen Geschichte: Von Tilsit bis zur Reichsgründung*, Vol. IV, *Gesammelte Schriften und Aufsätze*, Berlin, 1930, p. 101.

[91] Theodor v. Schön, Droysen's single most important source of information on Yorck, first came in closer contact with Yorck when he was appointed *Regierungspräsident* in Gumbinnen in April 1809. In his capacity as civil head of the area he was involved in the schemes for insurrection that were discussed in 1810 and 1811. He contributed to the success of the rising of East Prussia in the spring of 1813 by his talents for mediating between Stein and Yorck and by his own aggressive policies. After the war Schön was appointed *Oberpräsident* in West Prussia, a position that was expanded in 1824 to include East Prussia as well, so that he became the supreme civil authority of the Prussian provinces. As the movement of reaction grew in strength, a loose opposition circle representing both liberal sentiment and a provincial particularism gathered around Schön, and in 1842, after repeated conflicts with the court and the ministry in Berlin, he was dismissed. He lived out his life—he died in 1856 at the age of 84—as a bitter and often outspoken critic of contemporary Prussia.

When Droysen first broached the plan of writing a biography of Yorck,

Without question the most important evidence consists of two letters in which Yorck criticized Stein; the second, written after Stein's dismissal, containing the famous references to mad heads and nests of vipers. The second and third points of indictment are Yorck's supposed participation towards the end of 1808 in an intrigue against Scharnhorst, and his membership in a reactionary club around the same time. Finally, there is his opposition to the reform that deprived the nobility of its special claim to officer positions.[92]

Schön assured him of his help; soon, however, he had second thoughts, both because he doubted Yorck's fitness to be celebrated as an old-Prussian hero, and because he came to disagree with Droysen's historical method. The conflict that grew up between the two men and ended with a complete rupture of their relationship centered partly around Droysen's unwillingness to clarify the mystery of Yorck's family background. Schön was entirely in the right in querying Yorck's noble ancestry; he was less trustworthy in other matters. His opinions of Prussia's leading figures— among them Yorck—had changed radically over the years. During the Reform Era he and the general had collaborated without much friction. Indeed, according to his own letters to Droysen, in the significant debate over the advisability of subversively organizing and arming a *Landwehr* in 1810 and 1811, Yorck had sided with him against Scharnhorst for the most radical course of action. (Letters to Droysen of 22 March 1848, *Briefwechsel*, I, 391–393; 7 July 1850, *ibid.*, I, 655; 15 August 1851, *ibid.*, I, 771. After 1815 his relations with Yorck remained friendly; as Droysen pointed out after Schön's death: ". . . he often urged me to depict the old York more as a villain than a hero. That was one of his confused ideas, which in the course of time had developed more and more crassly, while numerous letters which he exchanged with Yorck until 1825 showed a quite different attitude. . . ." (Letter to Moritz Veit of 6 August 1856; *Briefwechsel*, II, 426.) The reasons behind his change of judgment may be sought in Schön's anger at the reaction's falsifications and misconceptions of the events between 1807 and 1815, his disappointment over his exclusion from power, and his increasing intolerance, as he entered extreme old age, of dishonesty and prevarication of any kind. To a man who in his autobiography recalled with approbation the time at luncheon when Kant told him that he had disproved the necessity of the white lie, the deceptions and ambiguities that abounded in Yorck's background were intolerable. For some decades after his death, particularly in the years after 1871, Schön's credibility was subjected to violent attack; today there is general agreement on the importance of his accounts, though care must be taken to distinguish between his earlier words and deeds and the statements he made towards the end of his life.

[92] See the discussion of Yorck's position on this issue on pp. 130–131.

All this dates from 1808. Two of the points, to be sure, relate to specific events of that year—the privileges of the nobility were abolished by the law of 6 August 1808, and Stein left office in November. It is nevertheless of some interest that during the following years Yorck's name is not linked with the continuing campaign against political and military innovation waged by such men as Kalkreuth and Marwitz. Stein himself did not consider Yorck an enemy in 1812 and 1813, worked well with him in the spring of 1813, and seems not to have castigated him in his correspondence and private papers, though these are filled with violence against personalities at court, in the administration and in the army. Kalkreuth, for example, he describes in one passage as "cunning, jealous, ambitious, maliciously witty, and worn out by military routine and the dominance of a mean and stingy wife." [93] Of Yorck's opposition to Stein's agrarian reforms there can, however, be no doubt. "We all know," he wrote in the first of the two letters printed by Droysen, "that the so-called slavery of the peasants etc. is nothing but philanthropic babbling." [94] This is in keeping with the jargon of the reactionary camarilla; equally to the point may be the allusion to Stein's German rather than Prussian loyalties, "for which we shouldn't reproach him if only he would not compromise the King with them at the present moment." The second letter, which contains the extravagant expression of approval over Stein's fall, is otherwise an unexceptional note, congratulating the recipient, Colonel Adolph Friedrich von Oppen, on his recent promotion, and voicing the hope that "the downtrodden fatherland may again see its former glory." The sentence on Stein is immediately followed by the words: "I hope things will soon improve. Once calmness and good sense return and fate, as one may hope, brings us more favorable times, then I trust that the withered tree, newly revived, shall again bear leaves and fruit." [95]

[93] *Die Autobiographie des Freiherrn vom Stein*, ed. K. v. Raumer, Münster, 1955, p. 36.

[94] It was in this same letter, written towards the end of September 1808, that Yorck discounted the possibilities of insurrection in Prussia.

[95] Oppen, incidentally, was a well-educated and progressive cavalry officer. Himself the son of a bourgeois mother, he advocated an increase in the number of non-noble officers, stood for universal conscription and against corporal punishment. See his Memorial of September 1807 in *Preussisches Archiv*, pp. 91–97. See also Priesdorff, No. 1176.

The story of Yorck's association with a reactionary club seems to be derived from a passage in a letter that General Gustav von Below wrote to Droysen when the historian was collecting material for his biography:

Already during the winter of 1807 to 1808, when I joined the cuirassiers here, a reactionary clique was formed, called the Perponcher Club, which met at a house in the Junkerstrasse. A brother of the ambassador Perponcher, Hünerbein, Kalkreuth (the later gossip-writer), my father's chief of staff Jagow, and also—as Benn declares—York belonged to it, and forged arrows against Scharnhorst's reforms. . . .[96]

This is scarcely conclusive, particularly since there are no further indications that Yorck was closely associated with any of the men named by Below, with the exception of Hünerbein, who served as one of his cavalry leaders and brigade commanders during the campaigns of 1812 and 1813. Indeed the presence of Hünerbein, whose reputation was that of a wit rather than ideologue, lends support to the suspicion that the Perponcher Club was less a political than a social organization.[97] Yorck's criticism of the *Tugendbund*, which Droysen mentions in connection with the club, is equally insignificant; this "well-meaning, but in its aims confused and technically most clumsy organization" was held in very mixed repute, and numbered opponents even among the most radical reformers.[98]

Yorck's attitude towards the question of which classes in society had the right to provide officers was two-sided. He did not resist the admission of bourgeois to officer rank, but opposed the formal abolition of the nobility's special claim to commission— that is, the substitution of schooling and competitive examinations for the institution of officer-cadets. Possibly mindful of his own non-aristocratic descent, as well as of his wife's modest background, Yorck did not argue that the special qualities of military leadership were inbred: they were a matter of education, to be imbued in a boy at an early age, but here the Prussian nobility with its military tradition enjoyed an advantage over

[96] Letter of 5 December 1851, *Briefwechsel*, II, 20.

[97] For Hünerbein's attitude towards the reforms, see Priesdorff, No. 1183.

[98] The judgment is Gerhard Ritter's. See his *Stein*, p. 339.

other groups. Droysen reports that Yorck was highly critical of the nobility, particularly that of the Mark Brandenburg, "which was beyond all help"; nevertheless he held that the children of the nobility should be assured preferential access to commissions. "Until now," he argued, "it had also been considered a duty of the nobility to serve; what would happen if with increasing philanthropy the dislike of the disagreeable military profession grew as well? If the right [to serve] is extended to all, then the nobility's duty is at an end. And doesn't every new universal privilege damage an older privilege of the class that had borne this duty?" [99] Yorck recognized the imperfections of the past, but in this area he feared the effects of a radical legal change. His doubt that the middle class could be relied on to furnish a sufficient number of officers was not entirely unrealistic, considering the widespread opposition of towns, associations, and individuals to the abolition of their traditional exemption from military obligations. Yorck's stand was not very generous, but possibly practical. Once the new regulations were in effect he lived with them better than many of his comrades.

The clash with Scharnhorst towards the end of 1808, termed by Schön "a very dark shadow on Yorck's life," has never been properly investigated. [100] It was closely preceded by an attack on Scharnhorst's reforms by some of the most influential generals in the army. According to a letter of Scharnhorst's to Frederick William of 4 December 1808, Köckritz and Lottum, the two *Generaladjutanten*, had suggested that a number of retired generals be reactivated, and that those officers about to be appointed to the newly created position of brigadier be subordinated to them. [101] Field Marshal Kalkreuth associated himself with this move, which Scharnhorst naturally rejected since its success would have ruined all his attempts to tear down the wall of seniority that had for so long imprisoned the army. [102] Yorck could

[99] The passage is an indirect quotation or summary of an unnamed document, Droysen, I, 209.

[100] Letter to Droysen of 22–23 March 1851, *Briefwechsel*, I, 728.

[101] Letter of 4 December 1808; *Scharnhorst's Briefe*, I, 352–354. The text is also printed in *Preussisches Archiv*, pp. 758–759.

[102] In an unpublished report, Scharnhorst named Kalkreuth and Lottum as the two main opponents of progressive thought. See Ritter, *Stein*, p. 612, n. 23.

scarcely have been involved in this plot, being himself one of the
most junior generals, and at just this time under consideration for
a higher command (to which on Scharnhorst's recommendation
he was appointed on 21 November)—the success of the conservative scheme would have rendered his promotion impossible.[103]
Köckritz and his friends were smarting under their defeat when a
sudden development seemed to present them with an opportunity
to destroy Scharnhorst's power entirely. There are two versions of
the episode. According to Schön and Droysen one or several
English ships had lately appeared off the Baltic coast, chased by a
French raider, and the commandant of the fortress of Pillau had
received an order directly from Königsberg, which the King had
been induced to sign by an unidentified officer, to the effect that if
the British entered the harbor and the French followed, the
French raider should be fired on as soon as it came within range.
When Yorck, who was in over-all command of the coastal defenses, heard of this he hurried to Königsberg, begged Köckritz
to arrange an immediate audience with Frederick William, and
convinced the King that the order if carried out would mean war
with France, and should be revoked.[104] If this is more or less what
happened, Yorck's reaction was presumably caused by fear of the
consequences should the French vessel be shelled, and anger that
the order had bypassed him and gone directly to his subordinate,
the commandant of Pillau. The circumstances under which the
order was issued are obscure; according to Schön a deliberate
provocation of the French was intended. "Yorck knew as well as

[103] The Cabinet Order appointing the six new brigade commanders is
printed in *Preussisches Archiv*, pp. 718–719. Priesdorff, No. 1120, incorrectly gives the date of Yorck's appointment as 21 December. Voss, p. 19,
refers to an otherwise unknown letter in which Scharnhorst wrote Yorck
that he had been advisedly chosen to lead the West Prussian brigade,
since this command, whose area bordered both on Russia and on the
Duchy of Warsaw, presented the greatest political and military problems.

[104] Schön gave three somewhat differing accounts of this incident: one
in his letter to Droysen of 22–23 March 1851; the second in a letter to
Pertz of 6 August 1855 (*Briefwechsel des Ministers . . . Theodor von
Schön mit G. H. Pertz und J. G. Droysen*, ed. F. Rühl, Leipzig, 1896, pp.
50–58), in which he mistakenly assigns the affair to 1809, an error that
is repeated in an essay on Yorck, printed in *Aus den Papieren des
Ministers . . . Theodor von Schön*, Halle a. S., 1875–1891, First Series,
IV, 238–243.

we all did," he wrote to Droysen, "that everything was prepared for our alliance with Austria against France, and that we only longed for a French outrage which we could use as pretext." [105] Firing on the raider would presumably cause French reprisals, which in turn might be used to convince the King that he had no alternative but to fight Napoleon. But at the end of 1808 Prussia was in no position to risk war with France, nor had negotiations with Austria reached the decisive stage that Schön imagined in retrospect. And regardless of the military and political situation, any officer would have been remiss in his duty if he had failed to clarify an order of such importance, which had not even been issued along the regular chain of command. The only aspect of Yorck's behavior that might appear questionable was that he at once sought out the King instead of first speaking to Scharnhorst.

This would also apply to Yorck's actions in the second version of the incident, which is related by Boyen in his memoirs. [106] According to Boyen the English vessel was a man-of-war used to carry despatches between London and Königsberg. Yorck, who did not know of the arrangement, intercepted a letter on the way from Pillau to the ship, suspected that he had uncovered a plot, and informed the King. Whatever the truth, at the time Scharnhorst saw the two events—Köckritz's and Lottum's attempt to reinstate their old friends, and Yorck's interference at Pillau—as part of the same vendetta against him and his program; the fact that Köckritz was involved in both—as *Generaladjutant* he was instrumental in arranging Yorck's audience—and that he and his allies exploited to the fullest Frederick William's subsequent anger over the confusion, lent credence to Scharnhorst's suspicion. [107]

---

[105] Letter of 22–23 March 1851, *Briefwechsel*, I, 728.

[106] Boyen, *Erinnerungen*, I, 345–346.

[107] The already involved episode is further complicated by a divergence of dates in the sources. Scharnhorst's previously cited letter to Frederick William, complaining of intrigues against him, is headed 4 November 1808, which the King corrected to 4 December. The letter includes the sentence: "It was at once hoped that the order to the authorities at Pillau would make it possible to deprive me of Your Majesty's favor, which is more precious to me than anything else on earth." But according to Droysen the presence of the ships was not reported until the middle of December, and Yorck did not hear of the order to fire on the French until 21 December. Droysen based his statement on Schön; may the conflict of

The impression derived from these four episodes, which incorporate our knowledge of Yorck's early attitude towards the reformers, is that he stood in a degree of opposition to the new direction and to some of its leaders during the first years of the Reform Era. On their evidence Yorck cannot be classed with the defeatists, the collaborators with the French, or the virulent and unalterable enemies of any liberalizing and modernizing tendency in the state. But is it possible to consider him with Meinecke as belonging to that "group of men who at least in practice shared some of the most important ideas of the reform, and nevertheless heartily disliked the reformers"? [108] Such an interpretation would indeed seem to take account of the known facts rather more adequately, but Meinecke proceeds to blur his distinction by once again bracketing Yorck with Marwitz. Parts of the old establishment, he writes, had not yet decayed. "Such men as Marwitz, York, and Borstell still represented really vital forces, the old Prussian nobility that had flourished vigorously in the freedom of field and forest and in the discipline of the army. Clearly the reformers underestimated the unbroken, natural potential that lay dormant in this estate." [109]

Yorck however was not a Junker; he can hardly be compared to men such as Marwitz and Borstell, with roots deep in a land that their families had dominated for centuries.[110] What actually lay behind their continuing opposition to Scharnhorst? In a convincing historical and psychological reconstruction, Rudolf Stadelmann has suggested that the clash between Scharnhorst and Borstell in the Reorganization Commission did not so much

---

dates be explained by a slip of Schön's memory, and the day when Yorck heard of the order (or intercepted the letter) in fact be 21 November?

[108] Meinecke, *Boyen*, I, 171.

[109] *Ibid.*, I, 174.

[110] The emotive power of the word "Junker" continues to captivate some historians. In a recent book, *The Fall of Stein*, Cambridge, Mass., 1965, p. 74, R. C. Raack writes of "rough-hewn York von Wartenburg, the archetypical Junker cavalier," the basis for this characterization once again being the famous letter to Oppen. The significance of "cavalier" in reference to Yorck is obscure, but "Junker" evidently is expected to convey the image of a reactionary aristocrat. This is not what the word means, and using it in a wrong sense confuses matters when its use is called for. It is striking how rarely those reformers that were members of East Elbian noble land-owning families—Boyen, for instance, von der Goltz, or Tiedemann—are referred to as "Junkers."

spring from concrete issues—though their differences on these were considerable—as from the fact that Borstell's feudal self-esteem, or, as Stadelmann phrases it, his belief in the "Vasallenrecht des preussischen Dienstadels," necessarily came into conflict with the modern concept of far-reaching authority yielded by an appointed commission.[111] Marwitz too could never agree to replacing an order in which the King was *primus inter pares* among his nobles, and every class and estate had its particular rights and duties, with a system of impermanent, arbitrary administrative measures.[112] Both Borstell and Marwitz and their numerous allies against the civil and military reforms derived much of their strength from their native sphere of an old-established, property-owning aristocracy. Yorck shared in none of their possessions and few of their privileges. He was a man without background, who had to make his way by his own efforts in an environment that at the start was not particularly favorably disposed towards him. Indeed he was one of the *rotutiers* whom Marwitz despised, as he despised everything that failed to fit into his idealized picture of the old order. We are acquainted with Marwitz's opposition to the reform of tactics. He based his defense of the line and of mechanical drill on technical arguments; but these clearly were rationalizations for his recognition that a paternalistic society could not support tactics that gave the individual his head. To Yorck this concern was immaterial. Social preconceptions could not blind him, as they did Marwitz, to the insufficiencies of the old methods. If in 1808 he supported the special claims of the nobility, he never went to the length of Marwitz and disapproved of bourgeois officers as such. In everything pertaining to tactics, and to the equipment, supply, discipline, and education of soldiers, Yorck marked the vanguard of progressive opinion.

The rich and honored tradition that gave so many of the Prussian nobility during these critical years a seemingly impenetrable

---

[111] R. Stadelmann, "Das Duell zwischen Scharnhorst und Borstell im Dezember 1807," *Historische Zeitschrift*, CLXI (1940), 263–276; see especially p. 273.

[112] Cf. the sympathetic yet searching discussion of Marwitz's position and opinions by W. Andreas in his early essay, "Marwitz und der Staat Friedrichs des Grossen," *Historische Zeitschrift*, CXXII (1920), 44–82; in particular pp. 68–76.

self-esteem also made it difficult for them to recognize the needs of a new age. Never would Yorck have been able to defend corporal punishment, as Marwitz did, by relying on his experience in applying the stick to his own peasants.[113] But Yorck opposed beatings not only for reasons of military expediency; he was against corporal punishment on principle. This, at least, is suggested by his actions as chief of the *Jäger* regiment, as army commander in the Wars of Liberation, and again by an incident in the last year of his life.[114] In 1830 he asked the headmaster of a school his grandson was entering never under any circumstances to beat the child: "Even hard scolding, but still more bodily pain, does more harm than good in education since it represses any healthy self-assurance." [115] The headmaster ignored this request, and Yorck withdrew his grandson only a fortnight after his arrival at the school.[116] Yorck's humanistic ideas on education and training—subjects that occupied him throughout his life—appear repeatedly in his correspondence with Major Willisen, the military historian, and with Henrich Steffens.[117] A relationship of great trust and affection such as Marwitz could never entertain towards a bourgeois bound Yorck and the liberal professor, who had been party to Gneisenau's insurrection schemes and later served as a volunteer in the Guards *Jäger*. Indeed, for some years Steffens acted as an informal guardian to Yorck's sole surviving son.[118]

Marwitz and Yorck held such divergent opinions on social as well as on military matters that they cannot be thought of as kindred spirits. Associating the two men is an error produced by a superficial interpretation of Yorck's more flamboyant state-

---

[113] *Ibid.*, p. 60.

[114] Roeder, who served on Yorck's staff in 1813 and 1814, gives numerous examples of Yorck's strong views on the proper treatment of the rank and file—for instance, the episode on p. 87, in which Yorck punished a colonel for having slapped a subordinate.

[115] Letter to Dr. Ulfert of 16 April 1830, *Kleinoels*, pp. 104–105.

[116] Letter to Dr. Ulfert of 2 May 1830, *ibid.*, p. 105.

[117] Letters of York to Willisen and Steffens are printed in *ibid.*, pp. 31–43, 91–92. Cf. the unfortunately too generalized discussion of Yorck's acquaintance with the literary and philosophic trends of his time in Weniger, pp. 173–174.

[118] Cf. Steffen's account of his relationship with Yorck and his son in his memoirs, *Was ich erlebte*, IX, 306–310, 311–312.

ments in 1807 and 1808, insufficient weight given to his activities in reorganizing the army, and inadequate knowledge concerning his family background. Not enough evidence seems to have survived in the archives to make possible a thorough evaluation of his opposition to Stein and Scharnhorst during the year and a half after Tilsit. But Meinecke's suggestion that Yorck's advanced views on reform clashed with his attitudes towards other reformers, a hypothesis that Meinecke himself did not fully explore, indicates another possible area of study that is not ordinarily clarified in official correspondence and the minutes of meetings: Yorck's personality and character. Fortunately numerous accounts of Yorck's traits have been left behind by his contemporaries; they are marked by an altogether unusual unanimity. The accents are placed somewhat differently by different observers, but on the whole all sources agree; only Schön, in old age, saw Yorck as a villainous, unprincipled adventurer, a "Prussian Casanova." [119] The most complete analysis, which includes and relates all the aspects singled out by other authors, is that which Clausewitz wrote on the basis of long and thorough personal knowledge of Yorck.[120] In his *Campaign of 1812 in Russia* Clausewitz described him in these words:

General York was a man of some fifty years, distinguished by bravery and military competence.[121] In his youth he had served in the Dutch colonies, that is, had seen the world and broadened his mental outlook. A violent, passionate will which he hides under seeming coldness, enormous ambition which he hides under constant resignation, and a strong, daring character distinguish this man. General York is an upright person, but he is morose, melancholic, and secretive, and therefore a bad subordinate. Personal attachment is rather foreign to him; what he does, he does for the sake of his reputation and because he is naturally competent. The worst is that under a mask of bluntness and rectitude he is basically very cunning. He

---

[119] See Schön's already mentioned essay on Yorck, written two or three years before his death. *Aus den Papieren*, First Series, ɪv, 238–243.

[120] *Der Feldzug von 1812 in Russland*, pp. 214–215.

[121] In the manuscript this sentence concluded with the subsequently crossed-out phrase: ". . . vorzüglich ausgezeichnet war er durch Willenskraft und Charakterstärke." Clausewitz Papers, *Geschichte des Feldzugs 1812*, p. 111 (b).

boasts when he has little hope, but much more readily seems to consider a cause lost when actually he sees little danger.

He was undoubtedly one of the most distinguished men in our army. Scharnhorst, who considered his extreme usefulness during a period when few had shown themselves useful even more important because it was combined with a great dislike of the French, had always tried to remain on a friendly footing with him, although a suppressed enmity against him always raged in York. From time to time it appeared to be breaking out, but Scharnhorst behaved as though he did not notice it and pushed York into every position where a man of his kind could prove useful.[122]

A brief sketch from the hand of another idealistic reformer, Alexander von der Goltz, reads almost like a précis of Clause-witz's description. Von der Goltz had left Prussia after the French alliance was concluded in the spring of 1812, and with Clausewitz and Tiedemann entered Russian service. During that summer he sent an evaluation of the senior Prussian officers serving in the *Grande Armée* to Stein, with the purpose of giving the Russian high command some idea how receptive individual Prussian leaders would prove if pressed to desert the French cause. "Von Yorck," Goltz wrote, "Lieutenant General, middle-aged, educated, ambitious, dissatisfied, hates France, a univer-sally acknowledged brave and perceptive soldier, more practical than theoretical-minded, easily capable of a daring decision, en-tirely without financial means." [123] Already in June Stein had weighed the possibility of Yorck's changing sides.[124]

The violent temper which Clausewitz marked as one of Yorck's characteristics is frequently mentioned in contemporary memoirs. Its intensity seemed not unrelated to the rank of the individual at whom it was directed. When Yorck unreasonably fell out with a subordinate, he did not hesitate to apologize the following day.[125]

---

[122] The only statement known to the writer which does not concur with Clausewitz's description of Yorck as secretive and cunning is contained in a letter by General v. Natzmer. In June 1850 Yorck's former adjutant wrote to Droysen: "Der General Yorck war nicht der Mann, der anders sprach, als er dachte"; *Briefwechsel*, I, 654.

[123] *Frh. v. Stein: Briefwechsel*, IV, 43. A remarkably similar description is given by Boyen, *Erinnerungen*, II, 196.

[124] In a letter to Gruner of 18/30 June 1812; *Frh. v. Stein: Briefwech-sel*, IV, 30–31.

[125] Among many examples, see, for instance, those reported by K. v. Wedel in his *Lebenserinnerungen*, II, 36–37, 62.

With equals and superiors, he found it difficult to acknowledge himself in error.[126] Gneisenau, with whom he repeatedly clashed during the campaigns of 1813 and 1814, called him an old bear, adding, "He is nevertheless our best general." [127] After 1812 Yorck was frank in his dislike of Frederick William, a feeling that continued unabated beyond his retirement after the Second Peace of Paris until his death in 1830, and that was strengthened by his distaste for the new attitudes in the state, at court, and in the army which emerged during the years of reaction.[128] Behind his numerous quarrels undoubtedly lay the feeling that his command and he personally were not given their due, whether in operational assignments, in the amount or quality of equipment and supplies, or even in the space devoted to his corps in the official reports. The anxious defense against real or imagined slights is a recurrent phenomenon in Yorck's career. Together with this disposition, which at times suggests a lack of self-assurance, went a pronounced desire to demonstrate his independence, particularly to the highest personalities in the state. The rejection of decorations, or the refusal to wear them once accepted, was a convenient method to administer this lesson to the monarch, and

---

[126] "York never shifted responsibility to his subordinates and feared his superiors as little as he feared the enemy—unfortunately he thought it necessary always to fight both." A. v. Janson, *Geschichte des Feldzuges 1814 in Frankreich*, I, 134. Cf. also v. Zwehl, "Der Gegensatz zwischen Yorck und Gneisenau: Eine Psychologische Studie," *Militär-Wochenblatt* (1914), Supplement 10–11.

[127] According to F. v. Stosch, Gneisenau's personal adjutant during 1813 and 1814. See "Die Aufzeichnungen des Generals Ferdinand v. Stosch über Gneisenau," *Militär-Wochenblatt* (1911), Supplement 8, 255.

[128] Yorck's letters and diary entries printed in the collection of family correspondence contain several indications of this feeling. In August 1819, for instance, Yorck refused to appear before the King, who was visiting his county, excusing himself with the "doubtful state of his health." The following month he wrote to his former adjutant Seydlitz, who had voiced the hope that Yorck would attend the royal maneuvers, that he would like to come ". . . if it were at all possible for me to do so. But once I have made my decision I cannot change it. I simply must remain consistent, if only in order not to contradict the statement of the monarch, who some time ago said: The old General Yorck is always consistent, even in his willfulness." Letter of 2 September 1819, *Keinoels*, p. 24.

was resorted to on several occasions. The letter to Köckritz, turning down the post of governor to the Crown Prince, also breathes such an air of independence, which is met with in his letters, reports, and statements for the rest of Yorck's life. But while he claimed to be a stoic and to despise external honors, he wanted the opportunity to reject them. No doubt Clausewitz saw correctly: Yorck was enormously ambitious. This characteristic lends weight to a hint we have from other sources that during 1807 and 1808 Yorck was consumed with envy at being excluded from the Reorganization Commission. In his already cited complaint to the King of 4 December 1808, Scharnhorst wrote that Köckritz and Lottum "are against the changes which Your Majesty has instituted, and through their influence affect very unfavorably all older men who cannot be satisfied with these changes, and all those others who are dissatisfied because Your Majesty has not employed them at court, placed them in the Reorganization Commission, or because they suffer financially from the new arrangements." [129] Yorck was neither one of the senior generals whose career was being cut short by the reforms, nor had he suffered financially from it, and he himself had rejected a post at court. But, so Schön once wrote to Droysen, Yorck "boiled with rage because he had not been included in the labor of building up the new bases of the state." [130] It can be assumed that disappointment at not being immediately called on to occupy a central position in the state figured among the reasons for Yorck's behavior in 1807 and 1808. How significant this emotion was, and what other motives were at play, it is impossible to determine; but Yorck's insulted ambition cannot be left out of account in an estimate of his words and actions at this time. Too often the private expression of his disagreements with Stein have been given the weight of openly stated policy; to some degree at least they were an outsider's expression of envy and anger.

[129] *Scharnhorsts Briefe*, I, 352.

[130] Letter of 22–23 March 1851, *Briefwechsel*, I, 727. It should be noted that the factor of seniority rendered Yorck's appointment to the Reorganization Commission quite out of the question. Scharnhorst's patent of Major General was dated one month after Yorck's, and none of the other members held general rank. If Yorck had been included, either he would have had to be placed at the head of the commission or a Lieutenant General senior to both Yorck and Scharnhorst would have had to be appointed—and in this grade there was no one at once sufficiently active, able, and convinced of the need for change.

It is not true [Delbrück once observed] that words and sentences mean the same whether they are spoken, written, or printed, whether they have been uttered in private or in public. The moment that a word, expressed by a mind conscious of its own impenetrability, is put before the public, it changes its meaning. If one wishes to understand it properly, one must know how to transpose the word from one sphere into another, to translate with systematically practiced skill the word from the language of the diary into the language of historical narrative. . . . Who today still counts it a crime that York jeered at Stein's fall: now the viper's head is crushed. . . . Periods of greatness, of great deeds, also witness great conflicts between those who strive together.[131]

From 1809 on, when Yorck attained great power in army and state, nothing more is heard of his aggressive conservatism. No doubt the lack of evidence need not indicate a true change in his position: pertinent documents may no longer exist, Yorck may have grown more discreet, or—his personal ambitions assuaged for the time being—may no longer have felt the need to oppose. The point cannot be decided with assurance; but what is known suggests that Yorck's antagonism to the reformers in 1807 and 1808 consisted of a certain distaste for legal moves to raise the middle class to the same privileged position in military leadership as the country's nobility, and of a very great measure of resentment and envy. The explanations that historians have sought in ideology are more likely to be found in personal feelings.

· 5 ·

If the depiction of Yorck as a conservative is recognized to be a misinterpretation, the motives for the error also need to be identified. That evidence such as his readiness to take up the revolutionary weapon of insurrection was passed over in silence could scarcely be an accident: on the contrary, for historians to do otherwise would have embarrassed a legend that had grown around Yorck over the years. Nineteenth-century scholars were not always immune to this type of falsehood, nor are their successors today. Sometimes we even consciously succumb to the demands of the legend if it appears to be one that forms "the reflection of a great, though perhaps unjustified, universal feeling." The phrase is Delbrück's; he continues by admitting that

[131] H. Delbrück, "Das 'Tagebuch' Kaiser Friedrichs," *Preussische Jahrbücher*, LXII (October 1888), 409.

when historians face such legends they "will not hesitate to repeat the fables occasionally, and to use them in the awareness that they too are a piece of history—the sediments of strong emotions —and that in the guise of poetry they offer a trace of historical truth." [132]

In the patriotic glow of Wilhelmine historiography a design had been wrought of two elements joining together to achieve the salvation of the state: the reformers, with their spiritual *élan*, their daring and recklessness, and the old Prussian elites, now perhaps lacking the genius of the newcomers, but providing the needed balance with their heroic sense of duty. This contained some aspects of truth, but was simplification in the extreme, and the error was increased by the writers' insistence on clothing one figure with all the attributes belonging to the reign of the great king. The cautious, lackluster Frederick William could hardly fill this part, nor could Blücher, who was too intimately connected with Scharnhorst and Gneisenau; of the other senior commanders only Yorck possessed a sufficiently stricking personality to lend himself to mythologizing. Interpreting Yorck as the representative of Frederician Prussia in all its imagined dark brilliance had the added advantage of rendering harmless his action at Tauroggen. Such independence was acceptable only if it emanated from the most dogmatic royalist of all.

But what did scholars and popular writers imply when they linked Yorck with Prussia's iron age? Since neither Yorck's background, nor the branch of the service with which his most significant achievements were connected, least of all his characteristic independence, qualified him as a convincing representative of the old Prussia, the references were perhaps not to an actual but to an ideal kinship. An intuitive recognition of this abstract resemblance may already have been at work when Ernst Moritz Arndt gave the bond between Yorck and the old monarchy its most poetic expression. His exhortative biography of Stein describes Arndt's first meeting with Yorck, in 1813, in phrases that have been used by historians ever since. Arndt saw "a tall man with full muscular legs that were straight and firm like those of a bronze statue, a broad sinewy trunk, and above it a head with

---

[132] H. Delbrück, "General Wolseley über Napoleon, Wellington, und Gneisenau," *Preussische Jahrbücher*, LXXVIII (November 1894), 312.

sharp, flashing eyes, the forehead grooved like hacked iron, rough like the rough coast of his Pomerelian shore . . . a most genuine model of old-Prussian harshness and courage." [133] Arndt may have wished to suggest only that at Tauroggen and in East Prussia Yorck's moral courage had saved the state, just as Frederick's gigantic self-reliance was believed to have preserved Prussia during the Seven Years' War. But his words may also express a feeling that Yorck did, in fact, stand for something special and new, for which an explanation could be found in the Frederician age.

In the course of Frederick's reign the state had matured into something more than a temporary assemblage of territories, a development that was bringing with it a change in the attitude that men held towards their duties. Officers and bureaucrats were becoming more professional, and more impressed with the ideal which they served. As the organization of which they were a part grew in complexity, new demands were made on their competence and on their loyalties. In their regiments, boards, and offices the abstraction of the state took on firmer shape as a living, separate being, which increasingly interposed itself between the individual and his traditional attachments. Not that the attraction of dynasty, region, and family, of class and economic interests, necessarily declined; allegiance to these could still be usefully combined with work for the state. In particular, while the monarch himself felt and acted as the first servant of the polity, conflicts between allegiance to the state and attachment to the dynasty remained muted. Under weak successors and in response to outside dangers they would erupt, and men might then decide that the state took precedence over all other considerations. To indicate the evolution of this attitude, historians may think themselves justified in depicting Yorck as the representative of the Frederician ethos. In his belief in the primacy of *raison d'état* he was not alone among his contemporaries, some of whom were developing a far wider view of the rights and obligations of the state than he held; but at Tauroggen and during its East Prussian aftermath he demonstrated the force of the new ideal in an unusually compelling manner.

[133] E. M. Arndt, *Meine Wanderungen und Wandelungen mit dem Reichsfreiherrn Heinrich Karl Friedrich vom Stein*, Münster, 1957, pp. 154–155. The work originally appeared in 1858.

· 6 ·

Turning Yorck into a symbol of Frederician Prussia has not been without effect on the interpretation, advanced by other historians, that sees Yorck as the most blatant enemy of reform. But unlike the first legend, this one is void even of poetic truth. Rather it expresses the commonly held misconception that reform is a struggle between two forces: the old and the new. Metaphysically such an image may be justified; in reality the process is always made up not of two but of numerous contending forces, which can be identified and understood only by being sought out on their particular battlefields.

The reform of the Prussian army during the early years of the nineteenth century consisted in the evolution of certain progressive features in army and society, a process that foreign events stimulated and intensified. The reformers put into practice the military ideas of the French Revolution and developed them further, not only to counter the outside threat, but because the seeds of their innovations were already present in Prussian soil. Old and new worked together to nurture and harvest reform; conservative beliefs, self-interest, fear, identification with custom and authority strove to destroy it. In the conflicts over changes in tactics, equipment, discipline, organization, in the debates over the most suitable employment of social and intellectual energies for war, certain issues acquired decisive importance. Though at the time not all men clearly recognized their significance, they separated the genuine proponents and opponents of reform; but the true front was marked less by declarations of principle and programmatic statements, which in any case issued most copiously from such sunshine reformers as Knesebeck, than by the manner in which men actually dealt with specific tasks of change and adjustment. Concern for the education and the dignified treatment of the common soldier, the creation of tactics that realistically exploited the potential of man and weapon in the service of strategies of concentrated power—these issues are better touchstones for the evaluation of the army's reform and of the military reformers than any number of intemperate statements by Yorck.

It has often been pointed out how much the rejuvenation of Prussia owed to foreigners, men who sensed the energy and power immanent in this state, and who as outsiders could see more clearly and act with greater detachment than most natives when it came to modernizing an outdated order. It is equally remarkable that among the soldiers who took a leading part in the reforms and subsequent campaigns many had bourgeois antecedents, and a disproportionately large number had served in light units before Tilsit—or, like the line officers Boyen and Clausewitz, had experimented with light tactics. Often the same individuals are found in both categories. Among senior officers whose fathers or mothers, or both parents, were untitled are Scharnhorst, Gneisenau, Grolman, Krauseneck, Yorck—as well as Yorck's adjutant, Seydlitz, his chief of staff, Zielinski, whose mother was probably Jewish, and his subordinate commander and closest friend, H. W. von Horn. Other men in this group are Diericke, director of the war schools and examination commissions, the three Clausewitz brothers, A. F. von Oppen, Beier, Othegraven, Rode, Aster, Kameke, K. A. and P. F. von Borcke, Steinmetz, Haine, Sell, Creilsheim, Krohn, Schutten, J. C. and F. K. v. Schmidt, Markhoff, Wittich, Keibel, Streit, Hofmann, Rudolphi, Sandrart, Loebell, K. F. von Langen, Zweiffel, Rauch, Sjöholm, the former Saxon and Austrian officers, Thielmann and Roedlich, and the gunners, Neander, Pontanus, J. F. von Oppen, Decker, J. O. von Schmidt, Lehmann, Roell, Braun, Heidenreich, Fiebig, Brockhausen, and Strampff.[134] Of the army commanders and generals of the Wars of Liberation whose service had begun in the infantry, fusiliers and *Jäger* contributed over one-third. A considerable number of regimental commanders and staff officers also emerged from the officer corps of these units.[135]

It was not accidental that so many leading soldiers had connections with the bourgeoisie or served in the light infantry during the formative years of their careers. Hedged in though they were by the formalism of the Prussian line, fusiliers and *Jäger* were

---

[134] All men named held senior command or staff positions during the reform period and the Wars of Liberation, and all reached general rank. The list, drawn from Priesdorff's biographical dictionary, *Soldatisches Führertum*, no doubt is far from complete.

[135] "Rang- und Quartierliste der Königlich Preussischen Armee" of 14 June 1815, printed in *Das Preussische Heer der Befreiungskriege*, III, *Das Preussische Heer in den Jahren 1814 und 1815*, Berlin, 1914, pp. 500–514. The breakdown excludes royal princes and diplomats and courtiers holding military rank.

forcing beds of military thought. After 1789 the methods with which they had timidly experimented came to characterize the tactics of the French republican armies. If the Revolution did not invent the skirmisher, it gave him new value in the field, and, arising out of this, ideological importance. To the *ancien régime* skirmish tactics soon became the tactics of subversion. That one's own light units had possessed little prestige and were officered by men not wanted in the heavy infantry added weight to this feeling. To be sure, skirmish swarms and attack columns were not the only tactical formations with political significance. One of the motives that lay behind their introduction and development in the Prussian army was undoubtedly the fact that linear tactics not only were inadequate but had become identified with the past. Scharnhorst baldly employed the word "line" as a synonym for military reaction. For the revolutionary spirits among the reformers, doing away with the old system was a task in which practical and emotional considerations coincided. On the other hand, the pre-Jacobin existence of light troops in Prussia facilitated the skirmisher's acceptance by realists whatever their ideological conviction, and eventually made it easier for Prussia to fight France without herself having recourse to anarchic weapons—a military factor of some importance in the country's political history.

Just as the adoption of revolutionary methods of warfare did not lead to revolution, so the increasing number of officers with bourgeois antecedents in the army did not coalesce into a force for political liberalization. Even in an age dominated by the aristocracy, progress and the bourgeoisie need not be identical. In the Prussian army the dilution of the nobility in the long run was less a process of democratization than one of upward social mobility.

The educational ideal of the reformers—a community of free, intellectually and morally responsible individuals—in the achievement of which the army was to play a major part, remained unrealized. The reformed army taught men how freedom and individual initiative might be transformed into military effectiveness; through the *Landwehr* and universal conscription it fostered nationalism; but as the school of the nation it failed. After Waterloo Prussia experienced something that other societies—both old and new—are still learning: armed forces cannot be relied on as tools for general reform. In the army the success of the Prussian reformers had been remarkable; but in the political and intellectual climate of the country they could not bring to fruition what seemed to them to be the essential consequences of their military work. Their superlative achievement in one realm, their failure in the other, has affected the affairs of the Germans and of their neighbors to this day.

APPENDICES

APPENDIX 1
Three Essays on Light Troops and Infantry Tactics by Scharnhorst

THE THREE ESSAYS form part of the Scharnhorst Papers, which are deposited in the *Militärgeschichtliche Forschungsamt* in Freiburg im Breisgau.[1] The first and slightest is bound with other documents in a folder (*Nachlass Scharnhorst* B.No. 170) bearing the old inscription: "Drafts and sketches for Scharnhorst's articles, which are partly used in his published work. After 1807." This date cannot apply to our piece, since the century referred to in its opening lines is the eighteenth. It was written after the winter of 1793–1794, the time of the retreat from Hagenau, mentioned in the fifth paragraph, but not much later, judging from the heavily embellished Gothic script, which noticeably differs from Scharnhorst's subsequent somewhat slanted and smoother hand. The text was obviously intended as a contribution to a military journal, and ends with the note "To be continued"; but if Scharnhorst wrote a second part I have been unable to find it.

The essay "On the Need to Have Light Troops" does not compare in originality and intensity of analysis with the two later works; its historical comments are not always accurate, and it betrays a certain awkwardness of phrasing and arrangement that is characteristic of much of Scharnhorst's earlier writing. Nevertheless, the few pages contain significant ideas, among them the need for adapting oneself to the enemy's methods—a matter of life and death for the armies of the *ancien régime*, though by no means generally accepted as such—the principle of the division of tasks, and the importance of independent judgment among the subalterns of light troops.

The first of the other two essays (both catalogued under *Nachlass Scharnhorst* B.No. 101) bears the date 1811 on the title page. Scharnhorst seems to have wished to join it to the following

---

[1] Brief excerpts of the essays are printed in R. Höhn's *Scharnhorsts Vermächtnis*. Collating the originals with transcripts I placed at his disposal, W. Hahlweg has published the German text of the first essay and passages from the second in *Preussische Reformzeit und Revolutionärer Krieg*, *Wehrwissenschaftliche Rundschau*, Supplement 18 (1962), pp. 58–62.

paper, since he later headed the two "First Essay" and "Second Essay." Both are written by a secretary, with some sections closely corrected and revised in Scharnhorst's hand, but the inconsistent paragraphing in the second paper suggests that the manuscript was not quite ready for the printer. That publication was intended is evident from the opening paragraph of the essay "On Infantry Tactics," but what form publication was to take can only be guessed at. The task of private authorship that occupied Scharnhorst during his last years was the completion of the third volume of his *Handbuch der Artillerie*, in which these essays would have been out of place. Perhaps he planned to bring the section on tactics in his *Handbuch für Offiziere* up to date; but the essays are not included in the revised edition issued by Hoyer after Scharnhorst's death. The content of the essay "Order of Battle" makes it, in any case, appear likely that the two papers were combined to form a service directive or a lecture at the new War College, and were to be reproduced only for confidential circulation.

The essay "Order of Battle" clearly served as a model for the section on skirmishers in the *Infantry Regulations* of 1812. The opening paragraph and the first half of the second paragraph of Section IV, Chapter 1, of the *Reglement* are practically identical with the first four sentences in Scharnhorst's essay. The fundamental principle that he states in Paragraph 5: "Infantry combat consists of the mutually supporting action of skirmishers and close formations" is repeated with only a slight change in word order on page 96 of the *Reglement*. There are other similarities; differences are found primarily in the pages on the use of skirmishers in attacking and defending fortified positions. This subject, which was always one of particular interest to Scharnhorst, his essay discusses in some detail, while the *Reglement* devotes only one paragraph to it.

The two papers analyze the historical evolution of infantry tactics and formulate their main contemporary aspects. It is worth noting that Scharnhorst, with thirty years of active service behind him, finds it impossible to state concretely how and where the column has triumphed over the line; he only says that the column has been employed in this and that battle, and apparently to good effect. But there is no reserve in his advocacy of skirmishers. To him, they are the most economical means of achieving results, and in support of his view he argues that though *élan* is a useful quality for *tirailleurs*, the flexibility of the skirmish line makes it in fact a cautious method of fighting—the real reckless-ness lies in the shock tactics of line and column. He does not, however, go back on his earlier advocacy of the division of tasks. *Tirailleur* and musketeer cooperate, but do not lose their separate identities, and Scharnhorst will not take the time even to suggest that an amalgamation of the two might be desirable in future. Here, as throughout the three essays, and indeed in all his techni-cal and tactical writings and actual reforms, Scharnhorst shows himself not so much an innovator or prophet as a careful explorer of prevailing methods, which he expands and reshapes to what he considers are the limits of practicability.

On the Need to Have Light Troops, and Their Uses

Even in the remotest past, armies looked to light troops for their security and support. Because of their light equipment and horses, as well as for their manner of fighting, the Numidians may be considered the first light troops in history. All nations have copied their example, but until the campaigns in the fourth decade of this century only Austria did so with pronounced success; this country very effectively employed Hungarians in her wars. Immediately after the battle of Mollwitz, where the great king experienced and recognized his lack of such units, he made it his first task to strengthen his army with light troops. Already in the 2nd Silesian War he was able to oppose the Austrians with a relatively equal force. His instructive example was followed by the French, the Hanoverians, and the Saxons, all of whom established units of this branch of the service, which until then had been unknown to them. Nevertheless, the proportion of these troops to line formations remained extremely small, until the present war against the French Republic came to remind us of the principle that one should always endeavor to regulate one's dispositions according to the enemy's methods.

Probably never before has a greater number of light troops appeared on the battlefield than among the ranks of the present French army, nor has military history ever been given more irrefutable examples of the essential value of such troops than during this war.

If the campaigns are studied, one may be tempted to hold that at least on the French side this is entirely a war of light troops: the Republic certainly owes most of her victories to her light infantry.

Incidentally, easy as it is for the French nation to organize good light infantry, the main characteristics of which are temperament, enthusiasm, and hatred of coercion, it is equally difficult for her to achieve this goal with her cavalry. None of her provinces can provide horses that equal the Polish and Hungarian breeds in ability to keep going on little feed; nor does the criticism seem unjustified that the French have no great liking for the care and upkeep of horses.

However alert an army may be, and even though it be composed of picked units, it can never prevent raids and harassment if the enemy employs a mass of light troops! The army will melt away from exhaustion and the need for too numerous detachments; this sad experience, which for example was responsible for the unfortunate retreat of the Imperial army from Hagenau, will be proved again and again.

Without a sufficient number of light troops, a commanding general can never acquire speedy news of enemy movements, not even if he sends out masses of spies. Ignorance as much as fear precludes a correct evaluation of intelligence by men who engage in this dangerous occupation. Yes, I dare assert that a great proportion of the pay expended on these people is wasted, and it takes a trained officer, whom experience has made cautious, not to be led into the worst labyrinth by their exaggerated reports. Intelligence gained from patrols is in any case always more precise, since professional soldiers can judge matters more correctly, and their honor is involved. Added to this, if one considers how much energy is taken up by convoys, advance- and rear-guards, outposts, and the covering of forage parties, one will not deny the essential value of these troops. Even on the day of battle or general action they can be used to advantage: by constant skirmishing they weaken and slow up the enemy, by false attacks they mask the main effort, and they harass the enemy by raiding his rear and his flanks.

The argument that today heavy cavalry and line infantry are used for these duties is easily countered by the lesson which we have learned only too often and which recalls a basic tactical principle that we have never transgressed without disadvantage: if we wish to obtain the expected usefulness and profit from heavy troops, we must employ them only in battle.

Some years ago, in a mounted service which because of its high standards and exemplary training cannot be assigned last place in the military world, an active and outstanding general conceived the idea of entirely doing away with the term "heavy cavalry." This ban by itself, without any concrete changes, was to alter the functions and duties of the service. But as so often is the case, it was shown that the name had no bearing on the thing itself. Not a label, but correct use— based on experience—of the various parts making up an entity, determines its truth and permits insight into its nature.

It is also worth some consideration that light troops offer the greatest opportunity for the training of good and useful officers: daily actions accustom them to danger, and by being left to rely more on their own judgment they are taught how to tear themselves from the machine-like process of their profession [*sich aus dem maschinemässigen Gange ihres Metiers rausreissen*]. All previous teaching is as useless as it is unapplicable, and therefore the officers' boldness, judgment, and independence grow almost daily. Turn back to history and my statement will be supported by the honorable examples of a Laudon, a Trenck, Zieten, Seydlitz, Kleist, and Lafayette. The military talents of all these men were developed in the light service.

To be continued.

On Infantry Tactics, 1811

Introduction to Infantry Tactics

Paragraph 1

Since the French Revolution infantry tactics have undergone a change. A survey of combat formations used in the past, and their evaluation by the most famous military personalities, will enable the reader to understand how this development came about.

I. FORMATIONS ACCORDING TO DEPTH OR NUMBER OF RANKS

Paragraph 2

The famous military peoples of antiquity, the Greeks, Romans, etc., formed their dismounted troops in from 6 to 16 ranks. Little by little these were reduced; nevertheless at the battle of Fleurus, in 1690, the French infantry under the famous Luxembourg was still drawn up in six ranks. Not until the Seven Years' War, in 1757, did the formation in three ranks become universal. Shortly before, four ranks were also used; and even at the beginning of the war some armies—among them the Austrian and French corps—still used their infantry in four ranks. In a formation of three ranks, the length of the musket employed enabled all ranks to fire standing up; but usually the front rank knelt to make firing easier for the two rear ranks, while for better defense against cavalry it could push the musket-butts against the ground and level bayonets at chest-height of the oncoming horses [?]. The formation of three ranks being considered the one that permitted all men to fire, it was held the most suitable for modern tactics, in which the effectiveness of infantry supposedly depends on firepower alone. In the French Revolutionary war, in 1794, the awkwardness of the first rank's kneeling when all three ranks fired, and the growing tendency to extend fronts to outflank the enemy, led occasionally to infantry formations of two ranks.

Paragraph 3

While the infantry was gradually evolving from deep to shallow formations, military writers argued about the advantages and disadvantages of both. The famous commentator Chevalier Folard first defended the *ordre profond* in 1727; after him, the greatest general of his age, the Comte de Saxe. In our day, several French officers defended this arrangement, particularly Mesnil-Durand and Maizeroy. Against them, aside from public opinion generally, argued the well-known writers Guibert, Mauvillon, du Puget, Coudray, and others. The advocates of the *ordre profond* were told everywhere that the effect of heavy artillery made this formation impossible. Now one of the best gunners of the time, the Count von Schaumburg-Bücke-burg, joined the debate.[2] In 1773 he wrote a work on the tactics of deep formations, in which he defended them with the greatest ingenu-ity and suggested dispositions that nearly did away with the opposing arguments. Admittedly, the recent wars provided no cases where deep formations conquered, since the troops had all fought in thin lines. However, a solid square of English and Hanoverians had bro-ken the French lines at Fontenoi in 1745, and beaten off all counterat-tacks. In the end, though, it was said, artillery fire disarranged the square.

Paragraph 4

It was not until the wars of the French Revolution that the column once more began to be used for attacks. How and where deep forma-tions prevailed over thin ones cannot be documented; only this much is known through personal experience—that on many occasions, in-cluding the recent campaigns between 1805 and 1809, the French army used columns in battle. The *Instruction concernant les manoeuvres de l'infanterie, Strasbourg, an VIII* contains regulations for the formation of, and evolutions with, battalion columns, etc. The end of the battle of Talavera, 1810, found two full squares on the left wing; at Alexandria they attacked with closed columns; at Preussisch-Eylau, 1807, attacks in column were launched on the right of the town; at Jena columns were used to support the attack.

During the last war the Austrian armies often fought in battalion masses. At Aspern they withstood the attacks of the French cavalry in this formation, and at Wagram it did very good service, particularly towards evening, although the Emperor Napoleon disposed of an enormous amount of artillery.

In the Austrian regulations of 1806 the battalion masses were already completely accepted. In Prussia, in 1808, the King gave the infantry tactical instructions in which he laid down both deep and thin formations for the order of battle: as early as 1804 one could see attacks in column during the Prussian maneuvers.

[2] Count Wilhelm zu Schaumburg-Lippe-Bückeburg was head of the academy in the fortress Wilhelmstein, where Scharnhorst received his first military training. The work referred to in the following sentence is the two-volume *Mémoire pour servir à l'art défensif*, which was printed in 1775–1777. Scharnhorst published sections of the *Mémoire* in a German translation shortly before the French Revolution.

Appendices

II. Order of Battle

Paragraph 5

The conquerors of the world—the Romans—composed their order of battle of lightly armed men (one-third of the total) for skirmishing, and of heavily armed men for combat in close order. The Lacedaemonians and Macedonians, as well as all peoples of the Middle Ages that can claim any lasting military reputation, followed this general scheme. Then tactics developed in different ways, and by the beginning of the Seven Years' War the proper combination of heavy and light troops—or, better, of skirmishers and troops of the line—had been almost completely forgotten. But soon the lack of men able to operate in hilly or wooded terrain was appreciated, and free battalions, free corps, etc., were raised. Duke Ferdinand had nearly 14,000 light troops, which several French accounts of the war have commented on with chagrin. However, at that time such troops were regarded as a species that could be used only to protect the army, to mask its wings and—in broken ground—its front, not as an integral part of every order of battle. Still, this defect was not really felt in major battles, since most of them were fought on plains or around fortified positions, and since none of the armies possessed regular units for dispersed fighting. People therefore retained the forms that accident had brought about.

Paragraph 6

In the North American War between 1775 and 1783, when the Americans fought for their freedom, and in which—having no drill— they sought action in broken terrain where all depends on the natural sense and perseverance of the individual fighter, the English recognized that they lacked the skill for dispersed fighting, particularly in broken terrain. Each battalion was, therefore, given a light (flank) company; the French, who during this war fought on the American side, added a *Jäger* company to each of their battalions.[3] Soon afterwards the Prussian army began to select a number of riflemen from each company, men who were not to fight in close order, but as skirmishers, or rather who were to oppose individual enemy snipers or small mounted raiding groups trying to disrupt the battalions' serried ranks.

Paragraph 7

During the French Revolutionary wars when the untrained French troops could fight trained troops only in broken terrain, the need to

[3] Scharnhorst's historical summary is far from accurate.

train for action in broken terrain was felt even more strongly than it had been in America. Those forces that still lacked riflemen—for instance, the Hanoverians—now acquired them; everywhere more light infantry was raised. In the winter of 1793–1794 the Austrians organized the third ranks of their battalions into units for dispersed fighting; but subsequent campaigns showed that instead they were used whenever a detachment or separate mission was called for.

Paragraph 8

In the meantime the French armies, compelled by the situation in which they found themselves and aided by their national genius, had developed a practical system of tactics that permitted them to fight over open or broken ground, in open or close order, but this *without their being aware of their system*. In the battle of Hondschoote, the actions of Dunkirk, Wervick, Tourcoing, the battles of Mouscron and Wassigny; the attacks on the Weissenburg Line—everywhere in the autumn of 1793 they won through their open order and their *tirailleurs*. In the spring of 1794 the battles of Courtrai, of Mouveaux and Fleurus, were won in the same manner. Decisive actions fought in close order were rare, though not excluded—they occurred only when it was impossible to gain the objective through skirmishers. The French *tirailleurs* attacked guns, and not infrequently silenced them. The fortress Crèvecoeur, covering the control locks of the inundation system around s'Hertogenbosch, was invested by *tirailleurs* who dug themselves in. No gun of the fortress could be loaded and aimed without some of the gunners being killed or wounded. Recently Peschiera was besieged in almost the same way.

Before the assault on Menin in April 1794, 4,000 *tirailleurs* approached the fortress and, firing from the ground, wounded or killed nearly all gunners who attempted to serve their pieces.[4]

A lively regard for honor, for competition and distinctions, the ability to learn quickly and to adapt easily to different conditions and circumstances, make the French soldiers better skirmishers than those of any other nation. Because of this superiority the French were

---

[4] As an Hanoverian artillery captain, Scharnhorst served in Menin during the French siege. The breakout of the garrison, the success of which was largely due to his efforts, established his military reputation which, until then, had been entirely that of a theoretician. See his report "Die Vertheidigung der Stadt Menin und die Selbstbefreiung der Garnison unter dem Major General von Hammerstein," *Scharnhorst: Militärische Schriften*, pp. 1–58. In later years Scharnhorst's pupils—for instance, Clausewitz and Tiedemann—liked to use Menin as an example or illustration in their writings.

victorious whenever they fought in open order and avoided action in close formations. Often victory would not come until three or more days of fighting had passed, but then the more surely, since *they never involved themselves in pitched battles* where chance has such wide scope.

Paragraph 9

The German tacticians still cannot rid themselves of the evolutions of Frederick the Great's autumn maneuvers. Those maneuvers made us forget war: everyone, even the English and French tacticians (not those natural soldiers who led armies in 1793 and 1794, and later), regarded them as the basis of higher tactics.[5] Several able men— Tempelhoff and others—continued to respect these tactics-turned-into-formalities when they commanded in the field.[6] That the mechanics of evolutions alone decided victory was generally believed. Since people occupied themselves very largely with the mathematical principles of fundamental tactics, these became in turn the basis of operations.

Tempelhoff wrote an essay in which—starting from an arbitrary number of bread and supply wagons—he catalogued all movements that in his opinion an army could undertake. He took supply as the centripetal and operations as the centrifugal force; they balanced at a radius of fifteen miles. This pretty equation made people forget a thousand contradictory experiences. The disease was so catching that the soundest heads were affected.

[5] At the beginning of the nineteenth century, the term "higher tactics" was still frequently used to signify major operations, and even strategy as such. Cf. Clausewitz, *Strategie aus dem Jahr 1804* . . . , ed. E. Kessel, Hamburg, 1937, pp. 62, 78–81.

[6] Georg Friedrich von Tempelhoff, author of the well-known *Geschichte des siebenjährigen Krieges*, and a typical military savant of the waning eighteenth century, was director of the Artillery Academy in Berlin between 1791 and 1806.

Order of Battle and Reciprocal Use of Battalions in Close Formation and Riflemen in Open Formation or Tirailleurs

Paragraph 1: Riflemen

Infantry must fight on the plains and in broken terrain, against close formations and against skirmishers. Every separate group, battalion, or company therefore has its detachment for combat in close and in open order.

The detachment for combat in close order puts its trust in the precision of rank and file, in close contact, in massed fire and the bayonet. The detachment for skirmishing seeks its value in competent aimed fire, use of the terrain, and the advantages offered by enemy positions and evolutions.

Paragraph 2

The detachment for skirmishing generally consists of a company of light infantry in each battalion, which in action is deployed either at the rear or in front of the battalion. It may also be the third rank of each company in a line battalion.

This is the arrangement used in the Prussian infantry. In each company, each battalion, one-third of the men, who once made up the third rank, are now designated for combat in open order. The group has its own non-commissioned officers and officers, and is specially trained for this kind of fighting. A battalion of four companies has four sections in two ranks for combat in open order: each section is led by an officer, all four are commanded by a captain. They are called rifle-sections, or sections of the third rank.

Whenever the battalion is formed out of sight of the enemy, the four rifle-sections take up positions fifty paces behind the battalion. When a company is detached from the battalion, or even separated for only a moment, it takes its rifle-section along. No battalion, no company, no section moves without its riflemen.

[Paragraphs 3 and 4 are commentaries on plans and diagrams, which I have been unable to find in the Freiburg archives. They seem already to have been missing in the 1880's, when the Scharnhorst Papers were given their present arrangement.]

Paragraph 5

Infantry combat consists of the mutually supporting action of skirmishers and close formations. In broken country, fighting tends more towards open order and skirmishing: on level ground, more towards close order and the column.

Great mistakes are made in the integration of these two methods, and in leading the skirmishers; this causes me to discuss the employment of light units in more circumstantial detail than our purpose would ordinarily demand.

Henceforth a suitably trained and armed skirmish line, supported by cannon, will advance before our attacking battalions, start the firefight, and keep it going as long as possible. When the men have used up their cartridges, when their rifles misfire, when their artillery vainly calls for reserve ammunition, then our battalions, which so far have not suffered and are therefore in good order, attack in close formation and decide the issue.

When the enemy maneuvers in broken terrain, the riflemen form an advanced line before the battalion, and are supported by cannon, if necessary.

When we are forced to retreat, or when we pursue a retreating enemy, the skirmishers, reinforced by their cannon, must keep the enemy units occupied [?] so that our battalions can maneuver without hindrance. If enemy horse threaten, the reinforced skirmish line should try, if possible, to keep them at a distance, so that they cannot exploit the evolutions or possible errors of our battalions. Wherever a large part of the army is under orders not to attempt decisive actions (the usual conditions of war), when only demonstrations are allowed [here follows a short illegible insertion], a well-posted line of skirmishers and detachments, adequately supported by cannon, should be the only force engaged. In this way the line battalions are not needlessly scattered or weakened; not tied down anywhere, they will remain a force available for any other mission. And should the enemy attempt to drive in the skirmishers, the closed-up reserve force jumps at his throat [*so falle man ihm . . . auf den Hals*]: even the shortest forward movement gives strength.

When fieldworks are defended, the riflemen should be posted behind the parapets, and they and the gunners alone sustain the action as long as the enemy keeps more than 150 paces distance. When he does reach the edge of the trench, he is received by the full volleys of the line units, which have remained closed up safely at the foot of the wall, and have not—as too often happens—squandered their ammunition during the earlier phase of the engagement.

In defending a number of separate fieldworks, the riflemen from the rear battalions and the regimental artillery occupy the intervals between the works, which are manned by the [first] battalion, so that they form one line with the garrison and the guns on the parapets. The firepower of this line may resist the enemy as effectively as though the entire regiment were drawn up against him. The other battalions, forming a second order of battle, will always be ready to attack the enemy wherever he breaks through, and to drive him back. This manner of using riflemen in a delaying defense more or less negates the advantages of the offensive.

If fieldworks are attacked, they should be invested by riflemen at a distance of some 100 to 200 paces. The men disperse in hollows, ditches, furrows, behind trees, hedges, etc., and, backed up by cannon, start a fire-fight and continue it until the garrison has exhausted its ammunition, when it can be overpowered without great sacrifices.

In the defense of a fortress, riflemen using plaster bullets are deployed at 100 or even 200 paces from the glacis in foxholes or small U-shaped trenches, the earth of which is piled up in the enemy's direction.[7] The riflemen should first prevent close enemy reconnaissance; if a regular investment starts, they maintain a steady fire from their holes or ditches—or later from the walls if the enemy has come very near—at the gun embrasures of his fieldworks. In this way many gunners will be killed; they will be forced to rush the laying and firing of their guns, and often these can even be silenced.

If a fortress is besieged, the parapet between the batteries of the second parallel should be built up with sandbags as soon as the parallel has come within rifle-range of the fortifications. During the day sharpshooters are posted behind them who maintain a steady fire at the enemy's gun-ports. Not only does this kill gunners, who are always at a premium during sieges, but within the attacked polygon rifle-bullets will ricochet in all directions, disrupt communications, and in every way considerably increase the difficulties of the defense. Here we should imitate the French attacks in 1794 on Menin, Crève-coeur, Nieuport, etc., where the fire of a few hundred *tirailleurs*, who were constantly relieved, exhausted the garrisons to the limit of their endurance, and forced them to use up their ammunition if they wished to keep the enemy from reaching the edge of the main works.

---

[7] Scharnhorst does not mention this use of riflemen in the chapters on the defense of positions in his early field manual, *Militärisches Taschenbuch zum Gebrauch im Felde.* For the meaning and significance of plaster bullets, see Chapter II, note 99, of the present volume and Appendix 5.

APPENDIX 2
Statistics on the Social Composition of the Officer Corps in the Prussian Army Between 1789 and 1817

THE FIGURES below were taken from the printed Prussian army lists for 1789, 1796, 1800, 1806, and 1817. No lists were published between the last two dates, but the Historical Section of the German General Staff has reprinted a manuscript army list of January 1813, which provided the figures for that year in the table dealing with senior officers.[1] Since the list does not indicate predicates of nobility for captains and subalterns, it could not be used in Table 1.

Ranglisten are not sources capable of establishing fine gradations; the bare fact whether or not an officer carried a title is all they divulge. Moreover they are contradictory, sometimes inaccurate, and out of date the moment they appear: the volume for 1806 prints one colonel's name three times—once with the *von*, and twice without; in 1795, the typesetters ennobled a considerable number of officers, who appeared again without titles the following year. Nevertheless, if used in conjunction with other reference works, such as Priesdorff's dictionary of Prusso-German generals, the *Ranglisten* afford a reasonably accurate dissection of the most important social distinction operating in the army during the period of the French Revolution and Napoleon.

While the other years covered in this summary have been largely ignored in the literature, the social composition of the officer corps in 1806 has received much attention. However, a complete statistical analysis does not exist. The official General Staff study ignores the subject.[2] Most writers even today base themselves directly or indirectly on a paper Kunhardt von Schmidt published at the turn of the century.[3] It is full of useful information, but as Jany already pointed out, Schmidt's interpretations are sometimes unreliable.[4] Indeed, for Schmidt to achieve his figure of 661 non-noble officers serving in 1806—about 9 per

[1] *Das Preussische Heer im Jahre 1812*, pp. 574–636.

[2] [Jany], *1806—Das Preussische Offizierkorps.*

[3] "Statistische Nachrichten über das Preussische Offizierkorps von 1806 und seine Opfer für die Befreiung Deutschlands," *Militär-Wochenblatt*, Supplement 10 (1901).

[4] Jany, *Preussische Armee*, III, 420.

cent of the total strength—he had to include more than 400 men who were officers in form only: ancient NCO's whom it was cheaper to commission and keep employed in arsenals or on duty with invalid companies or fortress garrisons than to retire. As Table 2 indicates, his total of 38 untitled officers of field grade contains only 15 who served in the fighting branches. Nor was Schmidt's paper meant to be a complete study; selected aspects were chosen to defend the honor and reputation of the old Prussian officer corps, and his figures, in themselves not always accurate, become more misleading when taken out of context.

The tables below trace the proportion of aristocrats and commoners in various branches and units of the army over a period of twenty-eight years. Throughout, as might be expected, the presence of untitled officers is considerably greater in light units and the artillery than in the line infantry and heavy cavalry.

It is particularly interesting to see that the years after 1806 show no increase of bourgeois field-grade officers in the favored branches of the service. Even by 1817 only one untitled major can be found in the cuirassiers and dragoons. Ten years later this single representative, too, has vanished. A great increase of bourgeois subalterns is, however, registered from 1813 on; though here again a decline becomes apparent over the subsequent period. Many of the *roturiers* were, in Prince Frederick Charles' phrase, "sons of strange mothers," who had attained commissioned rank during the War of Liberation without possessing all the qualities expected of a Prussian lieutenant.[5] In the years of peace that followed they were gradually eased out. By 1827, to give one example, the number of untitled officers in the four *Jäger* and *Schützen* battalions had sunk from 53 to 35.[6] The officer corps reflected the failure of the reformers to make the army truly representative of the middle classes, though it did not recover its prewar complexion. A minor footnote: the corps included one professing Jew—Meno Burg—who angered Freder-

---

[5] The expression occurs twice in his essay, written in 1860, "On the origin and development of the mentality of the Prussian officer, its appearance and effect." Published as an appendix in K. Demeter, *Das Deutsche Offizierkorps in Gesellschaft und Staat, 1650–1945*, Frankfurt a. M., 1964.

[6] *Army List* for 1827.

ick William III by refusing to be baptized, but nevertheless reached the rank of major in the artillery.[7]

TABLE 1

NOBLES AND COMMONERS IN THE OFFICER CORPS OF SOME UNITS,
1789–1817

		Titled	*Untitled*
1789 [a]	*Jäger*	8	5
	Fusiliers (20 battalions not yet at full strength)	107	8
	Line Infantry [b]	85	0
1796	*Jäger*	45	9
	2nd Magdeburg Fusilier Brigade [c]	45	16
	Line Infantry	223	0
1800	*Jäger*	43	8
	Magdeburg Fusilier Brigade	45	13
	Line Infantry	239	2
1806	*Jäger*	43	8
	Westphalian Fusilier Brigade	44	13
	Line Infantry	254	0
1817	Guards *Jäger* and *Schützen* battalions	29	11
	Jäger (2 battalions)	24	30
	Schützen (2 battalions)	30	23
	Line Infantry [d]	193	162

[a] The list for 1789 includes captains but not subalterns.

[b] For every year but 1817, the entry "Line Infantry" includes the four or five (1789) regiments organized in the same administrative area—*Inspection* —as the *Jäger*.

[c] Despite their different designations, the fusilier brigades listed under 1796, 1800, and 1806 contain the same three battalions.

[d] Four regiments from the same garrisons as the four *Jäger* and *Schützen* battalions.

[7] See his memoirs, *Geschichte meines Dienstlebens*, ed. L. Geiger, Leipzig, 1916.

TABLE 2

NOBLES AND COMMONERS AMONG GENERALS AND FIELD-GRADE OFFI-
CERS IN DIFFERENT BRANCHES OF THE SERVICE, 1789–1817

		Titled	*Untitled*
1789	Infantry [a]	377	2 (?)
	Jäger and Fusiliers	43	2
	Heavy Cavalry	180	0
	Hussars	55	3
	Field Artillery	11	11
1796	Infantry	406	0
	Jäger and Fusiliers	51	3
	Heavy Cavalry	199	1
	Hussars	56	5
	Field Artillery	12	15
1800	Infantry	403	3
	Jäger and Fusiliers	50	2
	Heavy Cavalry	189	2
	Hussars	61	2
	Field Artillery	11	18
1806	Infantry	427	3
	Jäger and Fusiliers	58	2
	Heavy Cavalry	222	0
	Hussars	62	2
	Field Artillery	20 [b]	8
1813	Infantry	148	3
	Jäger and *Schützen*	7	0
	Heavy Cavalry	48	0
	Hussars and Uhlans	24	4
	Field Artillery	15	5
1817	Guards and Line Infantry [c]	177	2
	Jäger and *Schützen*	6	1
	Heavy Cavalry	40	1
	Hussars and Uhlans	43	4
	Field Artillery	14	21

[a] Including Guards, line units, adjutants, etc.
[b] Five officers were ennobled between 1800 and 1806.
[c] Excluding officers on temporary service.

APPENDIX 3

Number and Strengths of Light Infantry Units in the Prussian Army Between 1786 and 1812 [1]

1786

3 *Freiregimenter*. Each regiment contains 2 battalions of 4 companies. Each battalion to consist of 816 officers and men, but full strength has not been reached.

1 *Jäger* Regiment. 2 battalions of 5 companies each. Each battalion consists of 681 officers and men.

Note: An average musketeer battalion of 4 companies consists of 705 officers and men. The grenadier battalions vary from 700 to over 900 officers and men.

1800

24 Fusilier Battalions of 4 companies each. Each battalion consists of 688 officers and men.

1 Jäger Regiment. 3 battalions of 4 companies each. Each battalion consists of 541 officers and men.

Note: From 1798 to 1806 the average musketeer battalion consists of 826 officers and men, the average grenadier battalion of 801.

1806

24 Fusilier Battalions of 4 companies each. Each battalion consists of 688 officers and men.

1 *Jäger* Regiment. 3 battalions of 4 companies each. Each battalion consists of 669 officers and men.

1812

12 Fusilier Battalions of 4 companies each. Each battalion consists of 628 officers and men.

2 *Jäger* Battalions of 4 companies each. Each battalion consists of 429 officers and men.

1 *Schützen* Battalion of 4 companies. The battalion consists of 429 officers and men.

Note: The musketeer and fusilier battalions are equal in strength; the grenadiers have four additional pipers.

[1] The figures are based on the *Reglements* for the infantry and light infantry of 1788, the *Stammliste aller Regimenter* of 1798, and the works on the *Jäger* and *Schützen* by Gumtau and Rentzell.

APPENDIX 4

Proportion of Light Foot to Line Infantry, and of Light Horse to Heavy Cavalry, in the Prussian Army Between 1786 and 1812

THE FOLLOWING FIGURES are taken from the *Stammliste aller Regimenter* of 1798, the table of organization of the Prussian auxiliary corps of 1812 published in Seydlitz's *Tagebuch*, the printed *Army Lists* of 1786, 1800, 1806, and the manuscript list published in *Das Preussische Heer im Jahre 1812*. In Table 1 the army's basic tactical units are employed in the comparison: battalions for the infantry, squadrons for the cavalry. The figures include only units of the field army and leave out of account reserve cadres and garrison companies.

As Appendix 3 shows, over the years the average number of officers and other ranks in a line or light unit varied considerably. The percentages in Table 2 are adjusted to take account of the more significant differences in strength. A number of over-strength grenadier battalions, containing 6 instead of the usual 4 companies, have also been taken into account.

TABLE 1

NUMBER OF LINE AND LIGHT UNITS IN THE ARMY

	Line Battalions	Light Battalions	Heavy Cavalry Squadrons	Light Cavalry Squadrons
1786	141	8	133	100
1800	144 a	27	134	114
1806	149 a	27	145	110
1812	39 b	15	32	21

a Each battalion includes from 40 to 50 sharpshooters.
b The third rank of each battalion is trained to fight as light infantry.

TABLE 2

APPROXIMATE PERCENTAGES OF LINE AND LIGHT TROOPS IN THE ARMY

	Line Infantry	Light Infantry	Heavy Cavalry	Light Cavalry
1786	95	5	65	35
1800	86	14	58	42
1806	87	13	60	40
1812	69	31	60	40

APPENDIX 5
Range, Speed of Fire, Accuracy, and Penetration of Muskets and Rifles

THE MUSKET of the Napoleonic Era could be fired far more rapidly than a rifle using plaster bullets. *Pflasterkugeln* were lead bullets wrapped in a "plaster" or patch of greased wool, cotton, or leather to ensure the greatest possible contact with the rifling. They had to be forced down the barrel with ramrod and mallet, a time-consuming business. Using ordinary cartridges with the rifle increased the rate of fire, but reduced its accuracy. The penetrating power of the rifle, firing plaster bullets, was greater by one-third than that of the musket.

In an analysis of tests carried out under his supervision, Scharnhorst found that hits registered on small targets by rifles compared 2 to 1 with those registered by muskets at 160 yards, and 4 to 1 at 240 yards.[1] On large targets the proportions were 4 to 3 at 160 yards, and 2 to 1 at 300 yards. The relatively better performance of the musket on large targets seems to be explained by the fact that on large targets the musket's broad cone of fire was not such a handicap. The times needed for loading, aiming, and firing were 5 to 2 as between rifle and musket at 160 yards, and 5 to 1 at 240 yards. Thus, Scharnhorst concluded, "Rifle and musket have about the same effect in the same period of time; but the musket needs three to four times as much ammunition as the rifle. Furthermore, under enemy fire a *Jäger* is more liable to aim than an ordinary infantryman because he is convinced that without aiming he never hits at all, and he has been trained and is accustomed to aim from youth on."

Two important points emerge from these figures. In any system of tactics that did not rely mainly on massed, unaimed fire, the rifleman was at least as effective as the musketeer. He was at a disadvantage only when heavy small-arms fire was called for to repel a charge at close quarters. However, his economy in the consumption of ammunition—a factor that could be vital—may be thought to have been balanced by the additional time he

---

[1] For this and the following, see Scharnhorst, *Über die Wirkung des Feuergewehrs*, Berlin, 1813, p. 96.

271

needed to pour his own bullets and to care for his rifle.[2] Wider use of rifles was also inhibited by the lengthy manufacturing process required and the higher cost. A rifle might be fifteen times as expensive as a good musket.

Further, Table 1 shows that a simple change in construction would have raised the accuracy of the Frederician musket by one-third to one-half. And indeed constructing an angled butt that would permit holding the weapon on target was perfectly feasible and practical; as Scharnhorst wrote, "It doesn't create the slightest difficulty to fix a new butt on an old shaft."[3] This should help to dismiss the argument put forward by Jany and other writers that technological deficiencies forbade the more general employment of skirmishing in the old Prussian army. On the contrary, the necessary equipment existed, but the leadership of the army was unwilling to make use of it.

[2] Duhesme, pp. 203–205, considered the maintenance of heavy rifles such a problem that in their place he suggested the use of carbines, which were both lighter and of simpler construction.

[3] "Promemoria" of [?] August 1807, *Preussisches Archiv*, p. 42.

Appendices

TABLE 1

HITS REGISTERED OUT OF 200 ROUNDS FIRED AT A LARGE TARGET [a]

	80 yds.	*160 yds.*	*240 yds.*	*320 yds.*
"Old Prussian" musket, 1782	92	64	64	42
"Old Prussian" musket with angled butt	150	100	68	42
Nothardt musket, 1805	145	97	56	67
"New Prussian" musket, 1809 [b]	153	113	70	42
French musket, 1777–1802	151	99	53	55
English musket	94	116	75	55

[a] Based mainly on G. v. Scharnhorst, *Über die Wirkung des Feuergewehrs*, Berlin, 1813, pp. 79–84. See also Eckardt and Morawietz, pp. 43–57. Scharnhorst gives all distances in paces. Prussia used the so-called Rhenish measurements (1 Rhenish foot = 1.029 English foot; 2 feet 4 inches by Rhenish measurement = 1 pace), so that 100 paces = 80 yards.

[b] The average rate of fire was similar for all weapons: from 2 to 2½ rounds a minute. The "New Prussian" musket had the greatest penetrating power; the French and English muskets were about 9 per cent weaker.

TABLE 2

HITS REGISTERED OUT OF 100 ROUNDS FIRED
AT A SMALL TARGET [a]

	120 yds.	*160 yds.*	*240 yds.*
Prussian rifle using plaster bullets	68	49	31
Prussian rifle using cartridges	51	26	
Prussian musket, 1809		21	4

[a] Scharnhorst, *Über die Wirkung des Feuergewehrs*, pp. 89–96; Eckardt and Morawietz, pp. 80–85.

BIBLIOGRAPHY

1. A Note on Sources

THE Second World War destroyed or scattered many documents that would have been of great value for this study. The bombing of the *Heeresarchiv* in Potsdam early in 1945 constituted a particularly heavy loss. Fortunately the official papers of certain figures, among them Scharnhorst, had been removed in time and are now available at the *Militärgeschichtliche Forschungsamt* in Freiburg im Breisgau. Other remnants of the Potsdam archives have found a new home in the military section of the *Bundesarchiv* in Koblenz. The *Bundesarchiv* also holds the now doubly valuable transcripts that Rudolf Vaupel prepared for the second volume of his publication of documents on the Reform Era, which war and his death prevented him from completing. These collections proved useful, as did certain Clausewitz manuscripts deposited at the University of Münster, and material in the *Rijksarchief* in the Hague on Yorck's life between 1781 and 1786 and on the Regiment Meuron with which he served at the Cape of Good Hope.

Of Yorck's own papers hardly anything has survived. According to a contemporary, he himself lost or destroyed most of his correspondence.[1] The rest in the family archives in Silesia could not be preserved in 1945, and may now be in Polish or Russian hands. The sole document of the Field Marshal still owned by the present head of the family, Count Paul York von Wartenburg, is the original of the Convention of Tauroggen, which the Prussian government always regarded to be of a personal rather than of an official character. Count York was kind enough to lend me a privately printed volume of family correspondence that includes letters of his great ancestor. Very occasionally a letter or document signed by Yorck appears on the autograph market, usually from the last years of his life, although there have been one or two that were written during his active service. The main sources for Yorck's tactical reforms remain his three instructions of 1800, 1810, and 1811, printed in 1834 by Gumtau in *Die Jäger und Schützen des Preussischen Heeres*. Comparing the text of the two instructions from the Reform Era with their originals, now at

---

[1] W. Dorow, *Erlebtes aus den Jahren 1790–1827*, Leipzig, 1845, IV, 70.

Freiburg, reveals minor inaccuracies, but on the whole Gumtau's work is reliable.

Despite its errors and omissions, the most comprehensive collection of documents on the military reforms in Prussia after 1807 is still *Die Reorganisation der Preussischen Armee nach dem Tilsiter Frieden*, edited in the 1850's by Scherbening and Willisen for the *Militär-Wochenblatt*, and later published separately in two volumes. It was to be superseded by *Das Preussische Heer vom Tilsiter Frieden bis zur Befreiung 1807–1814*, under the editorship of Rudolf Vaupel; but only the volume on 1807 and 1808 appeared. Fortunately Eugen von Frauenholz was able to complete his edition of selected documents on German military history, with the publication in 1941 of *Das Heerwesen des XIX. Jahrhunderts*. Both Vaupel's and Frauenholz' works are models of textual accuracy and critical objectivity. The same cannot be said of the third great collection of sources on German military history published during the 1930's, the biographical dictionary of Prusso-German generals, *Soldatisches Führertum*, compiled by Kurt von Priesdorff. The value of Priesdorff's series lies in the very large number of unpublished documents and letters incorporated in the articles. But their selection is frequently inept, and the editor's interpretations express a view that is at once uncritical and perverted by a fervent acceptance of National Socialist ideology.

I have drawn heavily on the official, unofficial, and semi-official military literature of the eighteenth and early nineteenth centuries. The vastness of the printed output in this field is suggested by Max Jähns' masterful discussion of works written between 1740 and 1800 in the final volume of his *Geschichte der Kriegswissenschaften vornehmlich in Deutschland*. The standard authors are available today, either in the original or in later scholarly editions. Many of the more obscure writers, however, are difficult to find even in our best specialized collections, such as the library of the War Archives in Vienna. Some publications—official as well as unofficial ones—deserve the comment Max Lehmann once made on early Prussian *Reglements:* "They have become so rare that they should almost be considered as unprinted archival material." [2]

[2] M. Lehmann, "Werbung, Wehrpflicht und Beurlaubung im Heere Friedrich Wilhelms I," *Historische Aufsätze und Reden*, Leipzig, 1911, p. 136.

Bibliography

Scarcity is not the only problem about the *Reglements*. Like most historical sources they are ambiguous material. Too often, army regulations may represent theory rather than practice. By themselves they cannot tell us how men really fought; certainly from the 1790's on, if not earlier, the tactics British and French troops used in the field are only partially reflected in the manuals. And yet the battles of the period cannot be understood without them. "When we come down to it," Jähns wrote, "the *Reglements* are the most solid and most authoritative deposits of our knowledge of military affairs—if not of its high regions, then of its broad and essential bases." [3] Certain national or cultural differences need also to be taken into account. Not every service disregarded its written instructions as readily as did the British; from the time of Frederick on, eyewitness accounts of battles show a strong correlation between teaching and execution in the Prussian army. The Prussian instructions issued during the Reform Era went, of course, far beyond the codification of officially acknowledged experience; they were attempts at military reeducation, efforts to show officer and soldier how the modern battle should be fought.

A further important characteristic of the manuals is their concern with subjects other than drill or operations. Often they contain information on matters of organization and administration—on pay, equipment, discipline, recruiting. They played a more central role than their modern successors, which form only small items in the mass of constantly changing directives. The significance of the old manuals was reflected in the secrecy that surrounded them. Until 1806 the Prussian *Reglement*, for example, was issued only to officers of the rank of captain and above. Subalterns were not supposed to possess it; the full text was read to them twice a year, and handwritten or even printed extracts of such fundamentals as company drill circulated among them. An officer transferring to a new assignment was obliged to hand over his copy of the manual to his successor. When the army was mobilized, the volumes were collected, wrapped, and sealed, and sent for safekeeping to four previously designated fortresses. [4]

---

[3] M. Jähns, *Geschichte der Kriegswissenschaften*, III, 1927.

[4] E.g., the section "Wie das Reglement wohl verwahrt und keinem Fremden geliehen werden soll," *Reglement für die Königl. Preuss. leichte Infanterie*, 1788, pp. 533–534.

The official documents can be placed in perspective and given their proper value only by consulting the service correspondence, and the eyewitness accounts, diaries, the theoretical and practical discussions that the soldiers of the period produced so copiously. Some of this material was ignored and much of the rest was cavalierly misinterpreted when, after the founding of the Second Empire, the Historical Section of the German General Staff set itself the task of writing the history of Prussia's wars in the eighteenth and early nineteenth centuries. As a collection of sources on all aspects of the Prussian military establishment these studies are indispensable. But their analyses imposed on the conditions of an earlier age the strategic and organizational concepts that the army had learned, often with difficulty and recalcitrance, from Moltke during the Wars of Unification. The profoundly unhistorical spirit that too often informed their work is exemplified by a volume of Frederick's military writings prepared by the Chief of the Historical Section, General Adalbert von Taysen, in which were carefully indicated those parts that the editor considered still valid in the age of the railroad, the telegraph, and the Krupp gun. Max von Szcepanski's judgment on the three volumes dealing with the Prussian army of 1812 and of the Wars of Liberation, holds true for many other publications of the *Kriegsgeschichtliche Abteilung*. They consist, he wrote, "of meritorious detailed labor, a valuable collection of sources, with a commentary that does not go beyond the customary, the officially desired interpretation." [5] A former member of the Section, General Jany, did not shed what Delbrück once called his *Generalstabs-Auffassung* when after the First World War he came to write his unofficial four-volume *Geschichte der Preussischen Armee*.[6] Here, too, a great deal of important information is embedded in a text that rejects historical objectivity as something unpatriotic.

Among writers taking a more critical and creative view of their subject, a pioneer of modern military history, Wilhelm Rüstow, deserves special attention. Rüstow, originally a Prussian lieutenant of democratic leanings, fought under Garibaldi and ended his military career as a senior officer in the Swiss army. Despite its many factual errors, his *Geschichte der Infanterie* remains valua-

[5] *Historische Zeitschrift*, CXXIII (1921), 499.
[6] Delbrück, *Geschichte der Kriegskunst*, IV, 314, n. 1.

ble for the author's intellectual independence and his insights into the political and social nature of war. Hans Delbrück enlarged on Rüstow's fragmented achievement in his grandiose *Geschichte der Kriegskunst im Rahmen der Politischen Geschichte*, which systematically laid bare the connections and reciprocal effects of tactics, strategy, and social and political institutions. In his tradition, but very much in their own manner, such German historians as Rudolf Stadelmann and Gerhard Ritter have explored the impact political and intellectual attitudes had on military affairs of the Napoleonic Era. Somewhat narrower in approach but even more successful are the writings of the French general-staff officer, Jean Colin, who was killed during the First World War. Four of his books, *L'Infanterie au XVIII° sièle: la tactique*, *La Tactique et la discipline dans les armeés de la Révolution*, *L'Education militaire de Napoléon*, and *Campagne de 1793 en Alsace et dans le Palatinat*, constitute a uniquely lucid synthesis that combines detailed military knowledge with an understanding of the intellectual and psychological forces of eighteenth-century France.

In the last thirty years three studies on Prussian military history have appeared that require mention here. The first, Richard Sautermeister's *Die taktische Reform der preussischen Armee nach 1806*, a Tübingen dissertation, discusses tactical change in all branches of the army on the basis of the material in print in the early 1930's. The author hews rigidly to his title: the background to 1806 is treated in 14 pages; aspects separate from tactics but bearing directly on them, such as education and discipline, are ignored; military affairs beyond Prussia's borders are dealt with in a very few sentences, and these contain fundamental errors. It is incorrect, for example, to write that skirmishers were not integrated in French line-infantry units during the Revolution and Empire (p. 34), the more so when this becomes the basis for an assertion of Prussian superiority in organization. The questionable isolation of his subject might have been offset by a comprehensive analysis of tactical change, but this Sautermeister does not give us. His account regards the history of Prussian tactics as one of steady progress up to Frederick's death, followed by a decline lasting until 1806, after which Frederick William III and the reformers carry tactics to new heights. This thesis parallels the tendencies and suggestions of the official studies and of

Friedrich Thimme's article, "König Friedrich Wilhelm III . . . ," in the *Forschungen zur Brandenburgischen und Preussischen Geschichte*, XVIII (1905), but expresses them very much more emphatically. His view of Frederick as a pioneer of modern infantry tactics derives from inadequate knowledge and a confusion of technical terms. Sautermeister's reading of Frederick William's participation in the work of military reform is equally questionable. He suggests that after the collapse at Jena and Auerstedt, the King not only authorized or supported changes, but initiated them and became the "driving force" behind them (pp. 97–98). This interpretation is based mainly on the King's two memoranda of November 1806, which formed "den Anstoss zu den folgenreichsten Verbesserungen in der Taktik, und bildeten die Grundlage für die nun einsetzende Reform der preussischen Armee" (p. 24). Some complimentary references to the monarch in Scharnhorst's correspondence are also cited, though Sautermeister admits that these may have been diplomatic rather than sincere, and finally there is the observation that the King after all bore ultimate responsibility for all that was done. Leaving aside the bizarre aspect of Frederick William's urging on such men as Scharnhorst, Gneisenau, and Yorck, it must be noted that the two memoranda did not propose any tactical change that had not been recommended unsuccessfully long before 1806, and often by the same men who were now charged with carrying these reforms into effect. In certain useful measures the King had always shown interest—in the reduction of the baggage train, for example. Other innovations concerned him less; no question of reform ever evoked in him the same sustained, energetic response as the problems of renaming and reuniforming those regiments that had disgraced themselves in the autumn campaign of 1806. Otto Hintze's evaluation, though still too positive in my view, penetrates to the essence of the problem: "Scharnhorst frequently stated that many of the military reforms were due to the personal instigation of the King; but their realization was nevertheless brought about only through the unceasing moral pressure of the reform party. Frederick William III tended to proffer his suggestions in the shape of hesitant considerations, and from there it was far to a firm decision." [7]

Superior to Sautermeister's very poor work is William Shana-

[7] O. Hintze, *Die Hohenzollern und ihr Werk*, pp. 452–453.

han's *Prussian Military Reforms: 1786–1813*, a study whose main contribution consists in an analysis of the Krümper system and its effect on the performance of the army in the Wars of Liberation. Shanahan raises some useful questions, but his treatment is superficial and often careless, and the result is disappointing.

Finally mention should be made of Reinhard Höhn's *Revolution—Heer—Kriegsbild*, a study in the history of military ideas at the turn of the eighteenth century. An Allied air-raid destroyed most of the copies just after the book had been printed, which led the author to bring out a much shortened version after the war under the new title *Scharnhorsts Vermächtnis*. Both the original and the digest are difficult books. They incorporate much archival research and an exceptional knowledge of German military literature of the eighteenth century; the interpretations are often thought-provoking, though Höhn's most important thesis—Scharnhorst as the mediator between eighteenth- and nineteenth-century warfare—is adopted from Lehmann and Meinecke. This thesis he effectively illustrates, but it is embedded in a strange view of European history: a writer who considers a greater Germany the only equitable solution for the problems of Europe then and now will find the French Revolution and the Napoleonic Era rough grist for his mill.

A further weakness of Höhn's work lies in his treatment of sources. As he points out in *Scharnhorsts Vermächtnis*, many of the documents cited no longer exist, making the work a "source-book." [8] But a comparison of his quotations with documents that were not destroyed and with books of the period shows that Höhn's texts are often unreliable. Usually this is due to his method of interpreting a writer or a theory by pegging the analysis on a great number of excerpts. To fit these into his sentences he is frequently compelled to quote inaccurately. Words, word order, and punctuation are changed; words are deleted, underlined, substituted without informing the reader. Generally the changes are unimportant, sometimes they matter. But more than his ideology or his technique of transcribing, Höhn's historical method is at fault. He addresses himself to the most difficult of all historical problems, the relation of ideas to reality, the transformation of thought and opinion to action. To this task he brings utter

[8] R. Höhn, *Scharnhorsts Vermächtnis*, Bonn, 1952, p. 6.

literalness, untempered by a sense of proportion. The vague pre-
monition of a military theorist he turns into consciousness, an
incidental comment in a philosophic treatment becomes a political
program, intellectual trends he interprets as though they were a
series of administrative changes. I owe a debt to Reinhard
Höhn's work, but largely as a challenge to do better myself.

2. List of Manuscripts, Books, and Articles Cited

1. Manuscripts

Nachlass Scharnhorst, deposited at the Militärgeschichtliche Forschungsamt, Freiburg i. B.

A 28. Instruktion für die leichten Truppen.

A 29. Die Anfertigung eines neuen Reglements für die Infanterie und Kavallerie betreffend.

A 32. Organisation des Jäger-Corps.

B 101. Über die Taktik der Infanterie.

B 170. Entwürfe und Concepte zu Aufsätzen Scharnhorst's, die in seinen Veröffentlichungen nur teilweise verwertet sind. Nach 1807.

Nachlass Vaupel, deposited at the Bundesarchiv-Militärarchiv, Koblenz.

Nr. 46, Heft 15.

Nr. 48, Heft 17.

Nr. 49, Heft 18.

Nr. 50, Heft 19.

Nr. 51, Heft 20.

Nr. 51, Verschiedene nichkollationierte Schriften, 1809–10.

Restakten aus dem Preussischen Heeresarchiv. VI a, Restakten des Grossen Generalstabs (Kap. XLVIII), deposited at the Bundesarchiv-Militärarchiv, Koblenz.

Clausewitz Schriften, deposited at the University of Münster. Meine Vorlesungen über den kleinen Krieg, 1811.

Geschichte des Feldzugs von 1812, after 1817.

Hogendorp Archief, Algemeen Rijksarchief, The Hague.

Inv. No. 11.

Inv. No. 82.

Algemeen Rijksarchief, The Hague.

Kol. Arch. 286.

Kol. Arch. 4280.

Gage MSS., William L. Clements Library, Ann Arbor, Mich.

Amherst Papers, Vol. V.

American Series.

2. Privately Printed Material

Kleinoels: 1816–1871. Letters by Yorck and his descendants, edited by Louise von Katte, and privately printed for the family. In the possession of Count Paul York von Wartenburg.

SAUCKEN-TARPUTSCHEN, E. v. *Erlebnisse während der Feldzüge von 1812–1814.* A compilation of the author's diary and correspondence, privately duplicated for the family. In the possession of the present writer.

[TIEDEMANN, K. v.]. *Vorlesungen über die Taktik: Bearbeitet von einem Offiizier des General-Staabes,* lithographed, Berlin, 1820. In the possession of the present writer.

3. *Regulations and Instructions*

Note: Works cited from documentary collections are not listed.

A. PRUSSIA

Oeuvres Militaires de Frédéric II, Roi de Prusse, Vols. XXVIII–XXX of *Oeuvres de Frédéric le Grand.* 31 vols. Berlin, 1846–1857.

FREDERICK II. "Reglement für die Husaren-Regimenter," 1 December 1743, in E. Count z. Lippe-Weissenfels, *Husatenbuch,* pp. 131–154.

Die Instruktion Friedrichs des Grossen für seine Generale von 1747. Ed. R. Fester. Berlin, 1936.

[SALDERN, F. C. v.]. *Taktische Grundsätze and Anweisung zu militärischen Evolutionen.* Frankfurt, 1781.

Reglement für die Kgl. Preuss. Infanterie. Berlin, 1788.

Reglement für die Königl. Preuss. leichte Infanterie. Berlin, 1788.

Instruction für sämtliche Infanterie-Regimenter und Fusilier-Bataillone. Exercieren der Schützen betreffend. Berlin, 1789.

[HOHENLOHE, Prince F. L.]. *Reglement für die Niederschlesische Inspection.* Breslau, 1803.

ROCHE-AYMON, C. de la. *Über den Dienst der leichten Truppen,* transl. Baersch. Königsberg, 1808.

[GNEISENAU, N. v.]. *Instruction über den Gebrauch des dritten Gliedes.* Königsberg, 1809.

[KRAUSENECK, J. W.]. *Instruction zum Exerciren der Infanterie.* Königsberg, 1809.

Instruction in Betreff der Stellungen der Brigaden zum Gefecht, zum Angriff, usw. Königsberg, 1809. Bundesarchiv-Militärarchiv, Koblenz.

ROCHE-AYMON, C. de la. "L'Instruction provisoire préparée pour la brigade d'infanterie légère de la Prusse orientale, le 6 avril 1810," *Des Troupes légères.* Paris, 1817. Pp. 110–224.

YORCK, H. D. L. v. "Instruction für sämtliche leichte Brigaden zu den Übungen im Jahre 1810," in C. F. Gumtau, *Die Jäger und Schützen des Preussischen Heeres.* Berlin, 1834–1838. III, appendix. Pp. 79–100.

Instruktion für die Herbstübungen der Armee im Jahr 1810, 18 August 1810. *Nachlass Vaupel*, Nr. 49, Heft 18.

YORCK, H. D. L. v. "Instruction zu den Felddienstübungen der leichten Truppen für das Jahr 1811," in C. F. Gumtau, *Die Jäger und Schützen des Preussischen Heeres*. Berlin, 1834–1838, III, appendix. Pp. 101–120.

Exerzir-Reglement für die Infanterie der Königlich Preussischen Armee. Berlin, 1812.

Exerzir-Reglement für die Kavallerie der Königlich Preussischen Armee. Berlin, 1812.

B. OTHER STATES

Règlement concernant l'exercice et les manoeuvres de l'infanterie du premier août 1791. New edition. Paris, 1821.

Règlement provisoire sur le service de l'infanterie en campagne du 5 avril 1792. Strasbourg-Paris, 1792.

JARRY, F. *Instruction concernant le service de l'infanterie légère en campagne*. London, 1801.

Hessen-Casselisches Militär-Reglement für die Infanterie, Artillerie, und leichten Truppen. Cassel, 1802.

PORBECK, H. P. v. "Versuch einer Instruction zu Abrichtung der Scharfschützen der Chur-Badischen Armee," *Neue Bellona*, X (1806), 125–177.

Exercier-Reglement für die kaiserlich-königliche Infanterie. Vienna, 1807.

SCHWARZENBERG, Prince K. "Instruction über taktische Verhaltungen," *Beiträge zur Geschichte des österreichischen Heerwesens*. Vol. I. Vienna, 1872.

Rules and Regulations for the Formations, Field-Exercise, and Movements of His Majesty's Forces. London, 1812.

4. Army Lists

Kurzgefasste Stamm- und Rangliste der Königlich Preussischen Armee für das Jahr 1789. Berlin, 1789.

Rangliste der Königlich Preussischen Armee für das Jahr 1796. Berlin, 1796.

Stammliste aller Regimenter und Corps der Königlich-Preussischen Armee. Berlin, 1798.

Rangliste der Königlich Preussischen Armee für das Jahr 1800. Berlin, 1800.

Rangliste der Königlich Preussischen Armee für das Jahr 1806. Berlin, 1806.

"Rang- und Quartierliste der Königlich Preussischen Armee vom 14.

Juni 1815," *Das Preussische Heer in den Jahren 1814 und 1815*. Berlin, 1914 (1920), pp. 499–621.

Rang- und Quartierliste der Königlich Preussischen Armee für das Jahr 1817. Berlin, 1817.

Rang- und Quartierliste der Königlich Preussischen Armee für das Jahr 1827. Berlin, 1827.

* * *

Etat militaire de France. Paris, 1788.

Annuaire de l'état militaire de France pour l'année MDCCCXIV. Paris, 1814.

5. Published Documents

Auszug aus den Verordnungen über die Verfassung der Königl. Preuss. Armee, welche seit dem Tilsiter Frieden ergangen sind. ed. G. v. Scharnhorst. Berlin, 1810.

FRAUENHOLZ, E. v. *Das Heerwesen in der Zeit des Absolutismus*. Vol. IV of *Entwicklungsgeschichte des Deutschen Heerwesens*. Munich, 1940.

———. *Das Heerwesen des XIX. Jahrhunderts*. Vol. V of *Entwicklungsgeschichte des Deutschen Heerwesens*. Munich, 1941.

Die Reorganisation der Preussischen Armee nach dem Tilsiter Frieden. ed. R. K. v. Scherbening and K. W. [?] v. Willisen. 2 vols. Berlin, 1862–1866.

Die Reorganisation des Preussischen Staates unter Stein und Hardenberg. Part I, *Allgemeine Verwaltungs- und Behördenreform*. Ed. G. Winter. Publikationen aus den Preussischen Staatsarchiven, Vol. XCIII. Leipzig, 1931.

Die Reorganisation des Preussischen Staates unter Stein und Hardenberg. Part II, *Das Preussische Heer vom Tilsiter Frieden bis zur Befreiung: 1807–1814*. Ed. R. Vaupel. Publikationen aus den Preussischen Staatsarchiven, Vol. XCIV. Leipzig, 1938.

SCHOENAICH, A. v. "Zur Vorgeschichte der Befreiungskriege: Kriegsberichte von 1812," *Altpreussische Monatsschrift* (Königsberg/P), IL–L (1912–1913).

6. Letters and Memoirs

ARNDT, E. M. *Meine Wanderungen und Wandelungen mit dem Reichsfreiherrn Heinrich Karl Friedrich vom Stein*. Munich, 1957.

BOYEN, H. v. *Erinnerungen aus dem Leben des General-Feldmarschalls Hermann von Boyen*. ed. F. Nippold. 3 vols. Leipzig, 1889–1890.

Bibliography

BURG, M. *Geschichte meines Dienstlebens.* ed. L. Geiger. Leipzig, 1916.

CLAUSEWITZ, C. v. *Karl und Marie von Clausewitz: Ein Lebensbild in Briefen und Tagebuchblättern.* ed. K. Linnebach. Berlin, 1917.

DOROW, W. *Erlebtes aus den Jahren 1790–1827.* 4 vols. Leipzig, 1843–1845.

DROYSEN, J. G. *Briefwechsel.* ed. R. Hübner. 2 vols. Berlin-Leipzig, 1929.

FREDERICK II. *Politische Korrespondenz.* 47 vols. Berlin, 1879–1939.

HILLER V. GAERTRINGEN, A. Frhr. *Denkwürdigkeiten des Generals August Frhrn. Hiller v. Gaertringen.* ed. W. v. Unger. Berlin, 1912.

HOGENDORP, D. v. *Mémoires du général Dirk van Hogendorp,* ed. D. C. A. v. Hogendorp. The Hague, 1887.

[HORDT, J. L. v.]. *Mémoires d'un gentilhomme suédois écrits par lui même dans sa retraite, l'année 1784.* Berlin, 1788.

Kléber en Vendée (1793–1794). ed. H. Baguenier Desormeaux. Paris, 1907.

LAS CASES, M. S. de. *Le Mémorial de Sainte-Hélène.* ed. M. Dunan. 2 vols. Paris, 1951.

MACDONALD, E. *Souvenirs du maréchal Macdonald.* ed. C. Rousset. Paris, 1892.

MARMONT, A. de. *Mémoires du Duc de Raguse.* 9 vols. Paris, 1857.

MARWITZ, F. v. d. *Friedrich August Ludwig von der Marwitz: Ein märkischer Edelmann im Zeitalter der Befreiungskriege.* ed. F. Meusel. 2 vols. Berlin, 1908–1913.

MÜFFLING, F. C. v. *Aus meinem Leben.* Berlin, 1851.

NATZMER, O. v. *Unter den Hohenzollern: Denkwürdigkeiten aus dem Leben des Generals Oldwig v. Natzmer.* ed. G. v. Natzmer, 4 vols. Gotha, 1887–1889.

ROEDER, C. v. *Für Euch, meine Kinder! Erinnerungen aus dem Leben des Königlichen General-Lieutenants Carl von Roeder,* printed as manuscript. Berlin, 1861.

SCHARNHORST, G. v. *Scharnhorsts Briefe.* ed. K. Linnebach. Vol. I. Munich-Leipzig, 1914.

SCHMIDT, F. v. Erinnerungen aus dem Leben des Generalleutnants *Friedrich Karl von Schmidt.* Vol. II, *Urkundliche Beiträge und Forschungen zur Geschichte des Preussischen Heeres.* XII–XIII. Berlin, 1909.

SCHÖN, T. v. *Aus den Papieren des Ministers und Burggrafen von Marienburg Theodor von Schön.* 8 vols. Halle a. S., 1875–1891.

———. *Briefwechsel des Ministers und Burggrafen von Marienburg*

Theodor von Schön mit G. H. Pertz und J. G. Droysen. ed. F. Rühl. Leipzig, 1896.

SCHWERIN, S. v. *Vor hundert Jahren: Erinnerungen der Gräfin Sophie Schwerin.* ed. A. v. Romberg. Berlin, 1909.

STEFFENS, H. *Was ich erlebte.* 10 vols. Breslau, 1840–1844.

STEIN, K. Frhr. v. *Die Autobiographie des Freiherrn vom Stein.* ed. K. v. Raumer. Münster-Cologne, 1955.

―――. *Freiherr vom Stein. Briefwechsel, Denkschriften und Aufzeichnungen.* ed. E. Botzenhart. 7 vols. Berlin, 1931–1937.

STOSCH, F. v. "Die Aufzeichnungen des Generals Ferdinand v. Stosch über Gneisenau," *Militär-Wochenblatt* (1911), Supplement 8.

TIEDEMANN, K. v. "Tagebuch und Briefwechsel des Oberstlieutenants v. Tiedemann aus dem Jahre 1812," ed. M. Lehmann, *Jahrbücher für die Deutsche Armee und Marine,* XXIV (1877).

WACHHOLTZ, F. v. *Aus dem Tagebuche des Generals Fr. L. von Wachholtz.* ed. C. v. Vechelde. Braunschweig, 1843.

WEDEL, K. v. *Lebenserinnerungen des Generalleutnants Karl von Wedel.* ed. C. Troeger. 2 vols. Berlin, 1911–1913.

7. *Contemporary Works*

ABBT, T. *Vom Thode für das Vaterland.* Frankfurt a. O., 1761.

ANONYMOUS [GROEBEN, G. D. v. d. ?]. "Versuch von der Kriegeszucht," *Krieges-Bibliothek,* I (1755).

ANONYMOUS [GROEBEN, G. D. v. d. ?]. "Bemerkungen über das kleine Schiessgewehr," *Krieges-Bibliothek,* VIII (1770).

ANONYMOUS. *Traité sur la constitution des troupes légères et sur l'emploi à la guerre.* Paris, 1782.

ANONYMOUS. "Von der Ausrüstung der Soldaten," *Militärische Monatsschrift,* I (January 1785).

ANONYMOUS. "Noch etwas über die Ausrüstung der Soldaten," *Militärische Monatsschrift,* I (June 1785).

ANONYMOUS. "Über die Aufklärung des Militairs," *Militärische Monatsschrift,* I (June 1785).

ANONYMOUS. "Über die Ausrüstung und den Auzug des Soldaten, besonders des Infanteristen," *Militärische Monatsschrift,* II (October 1786).

ANONYMOUS. "Die Preussische Revüe aus den Briefen eines Zuschauers," *Neues Militairisches Magazin,* II, No. 6 (1802).

ANONYMOUS. "Gedanken eines Deutschen Officires über die jetzige Verfassung des Soldatenstandes . . . Zum Nutzen Künftiger Feldzüge entworfen," *Neues Militairisches Magazin,* II, No. 6 (1802), and No. 7 (1803).

ANONYMOUS. ("A Royal Prussian Officer"). "Taktische Bemerkungen (vorzüglich in Rücksicht des Werkes: *Geist des neuen Kriegssystems*)," 2nd installment, *Neues Militairisches Magazin*, II, No. 4 (1802).

ANONYMOUS. ("A Prussian ex-Officer). *Grundlinien zur Reorganisation der Armee eines sich wieder konsolidirenden Staates.* Berlin, 1807.

ANONYMOUS. "Notizen über den richtigen Familien-namen und die Abstammung des verstorbenen Feldmarschalls Grafen York von Wartenburg," *Preussische Provinzialblätter*, XX (1838).

ANONYMOUS. "Über die Anwendung der Taktik des Grafen von Bückeburg auf den Dienst der leichten Infanterie," *Neues Militairisches Magazin*, I, No. 4 (1799).

ANONYMOUS. "Über das Feuergewehr der Infanterie," *Neues Militairisches Magazin*, I, No. 8 (1800).

ANONYMOUS. ("An Officer of Hesse-Darmstadt"). "Über die Wirksamkeit des kleinen Gewehrfeuers," *Neues Militairisches Magazin*, II, No. 1 (1801).

[BERENHORST, G. H. v.]. *Aphorismen.* Leipzig, 1805.

———. *Betrachtungen über die Kriegskunst.* 3 vols. Leipzig, 1798–1799.

Berliner Abendblätter (1810–1811), republished in facsimile under the title *Heinrich von Kleist's Berliner Abendblätter.* ed. G. Minde-Pouet. Leipzig, 1925.

BIEBERSTEIN, V. *Die Taktik.* Magdeburg, 1816.

[BLANKENBURG, F. v.] *Schilderung des Preussischen Kriegsheeres unter Friedrich II.: Aus dem Mirabeau-Mauvillonschen Werke von der Preussischen Monarchie besonders abgedruckt.* Leipzig, 1795.

BOREUX, J. J. "Wie lässt sich wohl die Wirkung des Feuergewehres beträchtlich erhöhen, so dass nur wenig Truppen ihr zu widerstehen im Stande sein werden?" *Neues Militairisches Magazin*, I, No. 3 (1799).

BRENKENHOFF, L. v. *Paradoxa, mehrentheils militairischen Inhalts*, n.p., 1780.

BÜLOW, H. D. v. *Lehrsätze des neuern Krieges.* Berlin, 1805.

———. *Neue Taktik der Neuern wie sie seyn sollte.* 2 vols. Leipzig, 1805.

Militärische und vermischte Schriften von Heinrich Dietrich von Bülow. eds. E. Bülow und W. Rüstow. Leipzig, 1853.

CANSKI, J. *Tableau statistique, politique, et moral du système militaire de la Russie.* Paris, 1833.

CHAMBRAY, G. de. *Oeuvres.* 5 vols. Paris, 1839–1840.

CHARLES, ARCHDUKE. *Ausgewählte militärische Schriften.* ed. v. Waldstätten. Berlin, 1882.

CLAUSEWITZ, C. v. *Der Feldzug von 1812 in Russland*. Vol. VII of *Hinterlassene Werke*. 10 vols. Berlin, 1832–1837.

———. "Kriegswissenschaften," *Jenaische Allgemeine Literatur-Zeitung*, 11 October 1808.

———. *Nachrichten über Preussen in seiner grossen Katastrophe*. Vol. X of *Kriegsgeschichtliche Einzelschriften*. Berlin, 1888.

Strategie aus dem Jahr 1804 mit Zusätzen von 1808 und 1809. ed. E. Kessel. Hamburg, 1937.

———. *Vom Kriege*. ed. W. Hahlweg. Bonn, 1952.

CROIX, de la. "Abhandlung vom kleinen Kriege," *Krieges-Bibliothek*, I (1755). Shortened translation by D. G. v. d. Groeben of de la Croix, *Traité de la petite guerre* (Paris, 1752).

DECKEN, F. v. d. *Betrachtungen über das Verhältniss des Kriegsstandes zu dem Zwecke der Staaten*. Hanover, 1800.

DECKER, C. v. *Der kleine Krieg*. Berlin, 1844.

Denkwürdigkeiten der Militärischen Gesellschaft in Berlin. 5 vols. Berlin, 1802–1805.

DUHESME, P. G. Count. *Essai historique sur l'infanterie légère*. 3rd. ed. Paris, 1864.

———. *Die leichte Infanterie*. Berlin, 1829.

EWALD, J. v. *Abhandlung vom Dienst der leichten Truppen*. Flensburg, 1790.

FREDERICK II. *Militärische Schriften Friedrichs des Grossen*. ed. A. v. Taysen. Dresden, 1893.

———. *Oeuvres de Frédéric le grand*. ed. J. D. E. Preuss. 31 vols. Berlin, 1846–1857.

GOETHE, J. W. v. *Campagne in Frankreich 1792*. Vol. X of *Werke: Hamburger Ausgabe*. Hamburg, 1959.

GRANDMAISON, de. *La petite guerre*. [Paris], 1756.

GUMTAU, C. F. *Die Jäger und Schützen des Preussischen Heeres*. 3 vols. Berlin, 1834–1838.

[HOLLEBEN, E. L. v.]. *Militairische Betrachtungen*. Berlin, 1838.

JARRY, F. *Instruction concernant le service de l'infanterie légère en campagne*. London, 1801.

[KNESEBECK, K. F. v. d.]. *Betrachtung über den jetzigen Krieg, und die Ursachen seiner falschen Beurtheilung*. Berlin, 1794.

LE COUTURIER. "Essai sur les manoeuvres des voltigeurs," *Spectateur Militaire*, IV (1828).

LIGNE, Prince C. de. *Fantaisies militaires*. Paris, 1914.

LLOYD, H. H. *Philosophie de la guerre*. London, 1784.

M. v. "Über die Beschaffenheit der französischen Armee," *Neues Militairisches Magazin*, I, No. 4 (1799).

MASSENBACH, C. v. *Übersicht des merkwürdigen Feldzuges am Rhein im Jahr 1796*. n.p., 1797.

Bibliography

MICHAELIS, J. F. *Lesebuch für preussische Soldatenschulen.* Berlin, 1798.

OCHS, A. L. v. "Ein kleiner Beitrag zur Berichtigung der Taktik für leichte Truppen," *Mars*, III, No. 2 (1805).

PORBECK, H. P. v. "Über die Ursachen der vielen Siege und des Kriegsglücks der Franzosen," *Neue Bellona*, II (1802).

———. "Gedanken über einige, die Taktik, der mit der Infanterie verbunden Scharfschützen betreffenden Fragen," *Neue Bellona*, V (1803).

———. "Versuch einer Instruction zur Abrichtung der Scharfschützen," *Neue Bellona*, X (1806).

REICHE, W. v. *Der kleine Partheigänger und Krieger.* Leipzig, 1804.

ROCHE-AYMON, C. de la. *Des Troupes légères.* Paris, 1817.

———. *Über den Dienst der leichten Truppen.* Königsberg, 1808.

———. *Introduction à l'étude de l'art de la guerre.* 4 vols. Weimar, 1802–1804.

[SALDERN, F. L. v.]. *Taktische Grundsätze und Anweisung zu militärischen Evolutionen.* Frankfurt, 1781.

SAXE, M. de. *Les Rêveries ou mémoires sur l'art de la guerre.* The Hague, 1756.

SCHARNHORST, G. v. *Handbuch der Artillerie.* 3 vols. Hanover, 1804–1814.

———. *Handbuch für Offiziere in den anwendbaren Theilen der Krieges-Wissenschaften.* 3 vols. Hanover, 1787–1790.

———. *Militärische Schriften.* ed. C. v. d. Goltz. Dresden, 1891.

———. *Militairisches Taschenbuch, zum Gebrauch im Felde.* 3rd edn. Hanover, 1794.

———. *Über die Wirkung des Feuergewehrs.* Berlin, 1813.

———. Review of J. v. Ewald's *Abhandlung vom Dienst der leichten Truppen*, in *Jenaer Allgemeine Literatur-Zeitung* (1790), No. 352.

SCHOLTEN, J. A. v. *Was Muss ein Offizier wissen, wenn er die Pflichten seines Standes erfüllen will.* Treuenbrietzen, 1782.

SEYDLITZ, A. v. *Memorandum.* "Aus den Akten der Militär-reorganisationskommission von 1808." ed. F. Meinecke. Vol. V of *Forschungen zur Brandenburgischen und Preussischen Geschichte.* 1892.

———. *Tagebuch des Königlich Preussischen Armeekorps unter Befehl des General-Lieutenants von York.* 2 vols. Berlin-Posen, 1823.

TEMPELHOFF, G. F. v. *Geschichte des Siebenjährigen Krieges in Deutschland.* 6 vols. Berlin, 1783–1801.

VALENTINI, G. v. *Der kleine Krieg und die Gefechtslehre,* in *Die Lehre vom Krieg.* 6th edn. Berlin, 1833.

WISSEL, G. v. *Der Jäger im Felde.* Göttingen, 1778.

8. Biographies

BERGHAUS, H. *York: Seine Geburtsstätte und seine Heimath.* Anclam, 1863.

BERNHARDI, T. v. *Denkwürdigkeiten aus dem Leben des . . . Carl Friedrich Grafen von Toll.* 4 vols. Leipzig, 1865–1866.

BOYEN, H. v. *Erinnerungen aus dem Leben des Königl. Preuss. Generallieutenants Freiherrn von Günther.* Berlin, 1834.

BREMEN, W. v. *Yorck von Wartenburg.* Bielefeld-Leipzig [1913].

CHUQUET, A. *Hoche.* Paris, n.d.

CLAUSEWITZ, C. v. "Über das Leben und den Charakter von Scharnhorst," *Historisch-politische Zeitschrift,* I (1832).

CONRADY, E. v. *Leben und Wirken des Generals Carl von Grolman.* 3 vols. Berlin, 1894–1896.

CRISTE, O. *Erzherzog Carl von Österreich.* Vienna, 1912.

DROYSEN, J. G. *Das Leben des Feldmarschalls Grafen York von Wartenburg.* 3 vols. Berlin, 1851–1852.

ENSE, V. v. *Leben des Generals Grafen Bülow von Dennewitz.* Berlin, 1853.

[FELGERMANN, K. F. v.]. *General W. J. v. Krauseneck.* Berlin, 1851.

[FRANSECKY, E. F. v.]. "Gneisenau," *Militair-Wochenblatt,* XLI (1856), Supplement for January–April.

HAHLWEG, W. *Clausewitz.* Göttingen, 1957.

KESSEL, E. *Moltke.* Stuttgart, 1957.

KLIPPEL, G. H. *Das Leben des Generals von Scharnhorst.* 3 vols. Leipzig, 1869–1871.

KOTASEK, E. *Feldmarschall Graf Lacy.* Horn, 1956.

LEHMANN, M. *Scharnhorst.* 2 vols. Leipzig, 1886–1887.

LORENZ, R. *Erzherzog Carl als Denker.* Stuttgart, 1941.

MEINECKE, F. *Das Leben des Generalfeldmarschalls Hermann von Boyen.* 2 vols. Stuttgart, 1896–1899.

OMPTEDA, L. v. *Ein hannoversch-englischer Offizier vor hundert Jahren: Christian Friedrich Wilhelm Freiherr von Ompteda.* Leipzig, 1892.

PERTZ, G. H., and DELBRÜCK, H. *Das Leben des Feldmarschalls Grafen Neithardt von Gneisenau.* 5 vols. Berlin, 1864–1880.

PRIESDORFF, K. v. *Gneisenau.* 4th edn. Hamburg, 1943.

———. *Saldern.* Hamburg, 1943.

REINHARD, M. *Le grand Carnot,* 2 vols. Paris, 1950–1952.

Bibliography

RITTER, G. *Stein: Eine politische Biographie*. Stuttgart, 1958.

SEELEY, J. R. *Life and Times of Stein*. 3 vols. Cambridge, Eng., 1878.

STADELMANN, R. *Scharnhorst: Schicksal und Geistige Welt*. Wiesbaden, 1952.

UNGER, W. v. *Blücher*. 2 vols. Berlin, 1907–1908.

———. *Gneisenau*. Berlin, 1914.

VOSS, W. v. *Yorck*. Berlin, 1906.

WIESE und KAISERSWALDAU, H. v. *Friedrich Wilhelm Graf v. Goetzen: Schlesiens Held in der Franzosenzeit, 1806 bis 1807*. Berlin, 1902.

9. Other Secondary Works

ANONYMOUS. "The Swiss Regiment de Meuron," *Ceylon Literary Register*, I (1931), Nos. 3, 4, 5, 7.

ANDREAS, W. "Marwitz und der Staat Friedrichs des Grossen," *Historische Zeitschrift*, CXXII (1920).

BANNIZA v., BAZAN, H., and MÜLLER, R. *Deutsche Geschichte in Ahnentafeln*. Vol. XI. Berlin, 1942.

BEAMISH, L. *Geschichte der Königlich Deutschen Legion*. 2 vols. Hanover, 1832.

BECK, F. *Geschichte des I. Grossherzoglich Hessischen Infanterie- (Leibgarde-) Regiments Nr. 115*. Berlin, 1899.

Beiträge zur Geschichte des Österreichischen Heerwesens, Vol. I, *Der Zeitraum von 1757–1814*. Vienna, 1872.

BELHOMME. *Histoire de l'infanterie en France*. 4 vols. Paris, 1902.

BERNATH, M. "Die Errichtung der Siebenbürgischen Militärgrenze . . . ," *Südost-Forschungen*, XIX (1960).

BESELER, H. "Blüchers Zug nach Lübeck 1806," *Militär-Wochenblatt* (1892), Supplement 2.

BESKROVNYI, L. G. *Otechestvennaia voina 1812 goda*. Moscow, 1962.

BEZOLD, F. v. *Der Geist von 1813*. Bonn, 1913.

BRESSONNET, P. *Etudes tactiques sur la campagne de 1806*. Paris, 1909.

BÜSCH, O. *Militärsystem und Sozialleben im Alten Preussen, 1713–1807*. Berlin, 1962.

BYVANCK, W. G. *Vaderlandsche Figuren op den Overgang der Achttiende Eeuw*. The Hague, 1927.

CAEMMERER, R. v. Review of C. Jany, *Der Preussische Kavalleriedienst vor 1806*, in *Forschungen zur Brandenburgischen und Preussischen Geschichte*, XVII (1904).

CALLWELL, C. *Small Wars*. 3rd edn. London, 1909.

CARRIAS, E. *La Pensée militaire allemande*. Paris, 1948.

CHALMIN, P. "La Guerre, révolutionnaire, sous la Législative et la Convention," *Revue Historique de l'Armée*, IV (1958), No. 3.

COLIN, J. *Campagne de 1793 en Alsace et dans le Palatinat*. Paris, 1902.

L'Education militaire de Napoléon. Paris, 1900.

———. *L'Infanterie au XVIIIe siècle: la tactique*. Paris, 1907.

———. *La Tactique et la discipline dans les armées de la Révolution*. Paris, 1902.

CONRADY, E. v. *Geschichte des Königlich Preussischen Sechsten Infanterie-Regiments*. Berlin, 1857.

COURBIÈRE, R. de l'HOMME de. *Geschichte der Brandenburgisch-Preussischen Heeres-Verfassung*. Berlin, 1852.

CRAIG, G. A. *The Politics of the Prussian Army, 1640–1945*. Oxford, 1955.

CRESSWELL, M. A., ed. *Thoughts on the Kentucky Rifle in Its Golden Age*. York, Penn., 1960.

CURTISS, J. S. *The Russian Army under Nicholas I, 1825–1855*. Durham, N.C., 1965.

DELBRÜCK, H. "Das 'Tagebuch' Kaiser Friedrichs," *Preussische Jahrbücher*, LXII (1888).

———. "General Wolseley über Napoleon, Wellington, und Gneisenau," *Preussische Jahrbüchen*, LXXVIII (1894).

———. *Geschichte der Kriegskunst im Rahmen der politischen Geschichte*. Vol. IV. New edn. Berlin, 1962.

DEMETER, K. *Das Deutsche Offizierkorps in Gesellschaft und Staat, 1650–1945*. Frankfurt am Main, 1964.

DETTE, E. *Friedrich der Grosse und sein Heer*. Göttingen, 1914.

DIERSBURG, C. R. v. *Geschichte des 1. Grossherzoglich Hessischen Infanterie Regts Nr. 115*. Berlin, 1899.

DITFURTH, M. v. *Die Hessen in den Feldzügen in der Champagne, am Maine und Rheine*. Marburg, 1881.

ECKARDT, W., and MORAWIETZ, O. *Die Handwaffen des brandenburgisch-preussisch-deutschen Heeres, 1640–1945*. Hamburg, 1957.

ELZE, W. *Der Streit um Tauroggen*. Breslau, 1926.

ERNSTBERGER, A. *Die deutschen Freikorps 1809 in Böhmen*. Amsterdam-Berlin-Vienna, 1942.

FABRICE, F. v. *Das königlich Bayerische 6. Infanterie-Regiment*. 2 vols. Munich, 1886–1896.

FABRY, G. *Campagne de 1812: Documents relatifs à l'aile gauche*. Paris, 1912.

[FABRY], "G. L." "Soldats de la Révolution et de l'Empire," *Revue d'Histoire*, XXXVII (1910).

FÖRSTER, S. v. *Das Tiraillement im coupirten Terrain nach der Instruction des General von York.* Berlin, 1851.

FONTANE, T. *Wanderungen durch die Mark Brandenburg: Die Grafschaft Ruppin.* Berlin, 1862.

FORTESCUE, J. *A History of the British Army.* 13 vols. London, 1899–1930.

FOUCART, P. J. *Campagne de Prusse (1806) Jéna.* Paris, 1887.

———. *Campagne de Prusse (1806) Prenzlow-Lübeck.* Paris, 1890.

FREYTAG-LORINGHOVEN, H. v. "Die Exerzier-Reglements für die Infanterie von 1812, 1847, 1888 und 1906," *Militär-Wochenblatt* (1907), Supplement 1.

———. *Krieg und Politik in der Neuzeit.* Berlin, 1911.

———. "Wert und Bedeutung des Drills für die Ausbildung unserer Infanterie einst und jetzt," *Militär-Wochenblatt* (1904), Supplement 12.

FRIEDERICH, R. *Geschichte des Herbstfeldzuges 1813.* 3 vols. Berlin, 1903–1906, in *Geschichte der Befreiungskriege 1813–1815.* 9 vols. Berlin, 1903–1909.

FULLER, J. F. C. *British Light Infantry in the Eighteenth Century.* London, 1925.

———. *Sir John Moore's System of Training.* London, 1924.

"Zur Geschichte der Einnahme von Berlin im Oktober 1757," *Urkundliche Beiträge und Forschungen zur Geschichte des Preussischen Heeres,* I, No. 4 (Berlin, 1902).

GIERATHS, G. *Die Kampfhandlungen der Brandenburgisch-Preussischen Armee, 1626–1807.* Berlin, 1964.

GLOVER, R. *Peninsular Preparation.* Cambridge, Eng., 1963.

GOLTZ, C. v. d. *Von Rossbach bis Jena.* Berlin, 1906.

GRIESHEIM, G. v. *Vorlesungen über die Taktik.* Berlin, 1855.

HAARMANN A., and HOLST D. "The Hesse-Hanau Free Corps of Light Infantry, 1781–1783," *Military Collector and Historian,* XV, No. 2 (Summer 1963).

HAHLWEG, W. *Preussische Reformzeit und Revolutionärer Krieg. Wehrwissenschaftliche Rundschau,* Supplement 18 (September 1962).

HARTUNG, F. Review of P. Schmitthenner's *Politik und Kriegsführung,* in *Historische Zeitschrift,* CLVIII (1938).

HERZFELD, H. *Die moderne Welt, 1789–1945.* 2 vols. Braunschweig, 1957.

HINTZE, O. *Geist und Epochen der Preussischen Geschichte.* Vol. III of *Gesammelte Abhandlungen.* ed. F. Hartung. Leipzig, 1943.

———. *Die Hohenzollern und ihr Werk.* Berlin, 1915.

———. "Die Hohenzollern und der Adel," *Historische Zeitschrift,* CXLI (1914).

Höhn, R. *Der Soldat und das Vaterland während und nach dem Siebenjährigen Krieg.* Weimar, 1940.

———. *Revolution—Heer—Kriegsbild.* Darmstadt, 1944.

———. *Scharnhorsts Vermächtnis.* Bonn, 1952.

Holleben, A. v., and Caemmerer, R. v. *Geschichte des Frühjahrsfeldzuges 1813.* 2 vols. Berlin, 1904–1909, in *Geschichte der Befreiungskriege.* 9 vols. Berlin, 1903–1909.

Höpfner, E. v. *Der Krieg von 1806 und 1807.* 2nd edn. 4 vols. Berlin, 1855.

Hutton, E. *A Brief History of the King's Royal Rifle Corps.* Winchester, 1917.

Jähns, M. *Geschichte der Kriegswissenschaften vornehmlich in Deutschland.* 3 vols. Munich-Leipzig, 1889–1891.

Janson, A. v. *König Friedrich Wilhelm III. in der Schlacht.* Berlin, 1907.

Janson, A. v. *Geschichte des Feldzuges 1814 in Frankreich.* Berlin, 1903–1905.

Jany, C. *Die Gefechtsausbildung der Preussischen Infanterie von 1806.* Vol. v of *Urkundliche Beiträge und Forschungen.* Berlin, 1903.

———. *Geschichte der Königlich Preussischen Armee.* 4 vols. Berlin, 1928–1933.

———. *1806: Das Preussische Offizierkorps und die Untersuchung der Kriegsereignisse.* Berlin, 1906.

Jedlicka, L. "Das Milizwesen in Österreich," *Wehrwissenschaftliche Rundschau,* ix (July 1959).

Jonquiere, C. de la. *La Bataille de Jemappes.* Paris, 1902.

Kessel, E. "Die Wandlung der Kriegskunst im Zeitalter der französischen Revolution," *Historische Zeitschrift,* cxlviii (1933).

Kling, C. *Geschichte der Bekleidung, Bewaffnung, und Ausrüstung des Königlich Preuss. Heeres.* 3 vols. Weimar, 1902–1912.

Krieg 1809, published by the *Kriegsgeschichtliche Abteilung des k. und k. Kriegsarchives.* 6 vols. Vienna, 1907–1910.

Krieg gegen die Französische Revolution: 1792–1797, published by the *Kriegsgeschichtliche Abteilung des k. und k. Kriegsarchives.* 2 vols. Vienna, 1905.

Lauerma, M. *L'Artillerie de campagne française pendant les guerres de la Révolution.* Helsinki, 1956.

Lehmann, G. *Die Ritter des Ordens pour le mérite.* 2 vols. Berlin, 1913.

Lehmann, M. *Knesebeck und Schön.* Leipzig, 1875.

———. "Werbung, Wehrpflicht und Beurlaubung im Heere Friedrich Wilhelms I," *Historische Zeitschrift,* xxxi, New Series

(1891), reprinted in *Historische Aufsätze und Reden*. Leipzig, 1911.

———. "Yorcks Entlassung aus dem preussischen Dienst," *Historische Zeitschrift*, LXV (1890).

———. "Yorcks Wiedereintritt in den preussischen Dienst," *Historische Zeitschrift*, LXIV (1890).

LETTOW-VORBECK, O. v. *Der Krieg von 1806 und 1807*. 4 vols. Berlin, 1891–1896.

LIDDELL HART, B. H. *The Ghost of Napoleon*. London, 1933.

LIEBERT. "Die Rüstungen Napoleons für den Feldzug 1812," *Militär-Wochenblatt* (1888), Supplement 9.

———. "Über Verfolgung," *Militär-Wochenblatt* (1883), Supplement 8.

LIPPE-WEISSENFELS, Count E. zu. *Husarenbuch*. Berlin, 1863.

LYNCKER, A. v. *Die Altpreussische Armee, 1714–1806, und ihre Militärkirchenbücher*. Berlin, 1937.

MAHON, P. *Études sur les armées du directoire*. Vol. I. Paris, 1905.

MARGERAND, J. *Armement et équipement de l'infanterie française du XVIᵉ au XXᵉ siècle*. Paris, 1945.

MAYERHOFFER v. VEDROPOLJE, E. *Die Schlacht bei Austerlitz*. Vienna, 1912.

MEHRING, F. *Zur Preussischen Geschichte: Von Tilsit bis zur Reichsgründung*. Vol. IV of *Gesammelte Schriften und Aufsätze*. Berlin, 1930.

———. *Historische Aufsätze zur Preussisch-Deutschen Geschichte*. Berlin, 1946.

MEINECKE, F. *Das Zeitalter der Deutschen Erhebung*. Göttingen, 1957.

Mittheilungen aus dem Archiv des Königlichen Kriegsministeriums. Vol. III. Berlin, 1895.

MOMMSEN, W. *Geschichte des Abendlandes von der französischer Revolution bis zur Gegenwart, 1789–1945*. Munich, 1951.

MONTBÉ, A. v. *Die Chursächsischen Truppen im Feldzuge 1806–1807*. 2 vols. Dresden, 1860.

MORVAN, J. *Le Soldat impérial*. 2 vols. Paris, 1904.

Offiziere im Bild von Dokumenten aus drei Jahrhunderten. Vol VI of *Beiträge zur Militär- und Kriegsgeschichte*, published by the *Militärgeschichtliche Forschungsamt*. Stuttgart, 1964.

OMAN, Sir Charles. *A History of the Peninsular War*. 8 vols. Oxford, 1902–1930.

Der Österreichische Erbfolgekrieg, 1740–1748, published by the *Kriegsgeschichtliche Abteilung des k. und k. Kriegsarchives*. 9 vols. Vienna, 1896–1914.

OSTEN-SACKEN und von RHEIN, O. v. d. *Preussens Heer von seinen Anfängen bis zur Gegenwart*. 3 vols. Berlin, 1911–1914.

PALMER, R. R. "Frederick the Great, Guibert, Bülow: From Dynastic to National War," in *Makers of Modern Strategy*. ed. E. M. Earle. Princeton, 1961.

PARET, P. "Clausewitz and the Nineteenth Century," in *The Theory and Practice of War*. ed. M. Howard. London, 1965.

———. "Colonial Experience and European Military Reform at the End of the Eighteenth Century," *Bulletin of the Institute of Historical Research*, XXXVII (May 1964).

———. "Jena," *Great Military Battles*. ed. C. Falls. London-New York, 1964.

PECKHAM, H. H. *The War for Independence: A Military History*. Chicago, 1959.

PHIPPS, R. *The Armies of the First French Republic*. 5 vols. London, 1926–1939.

PIETSCH, P. *Die Formations- und Uniformierungs-Geschichte des Preussischen Heeres, 1808–1914*. 2 vols. Hamburg, 1963–1966.

Pirmasens und Kaiserslautern. Vol. XVI of *Kriegsgeschichtiche Einzelschriften*, published by the *Abtheilung für Kriegsgeschichte* of the General Staff. Berlin, 1893.

POTEN, B. v. *Handwörterbuch der gesamten Militärwissenschaften*. 4 vols. Bielefeld-Leipzig, 1877–1880.

POTEN, B. v. "Das Preussische Heer vor hundert Jahren," *Militär-Wochenblatt* (1900), Supplement 1.

Das Preussische Heer der Befreiungskriege, published by the *Kriegsgeschichtliche Abteilung II* of the General Staff. 3 vols. Berlin, 1912–1914 (1920).

PRIESDORFF, K. v. *Soldatisches Führertum*. 10 vols. Hamburg, 1936–1945.

QUIMBY, R. *The Background of Napoleonic Warfare*. New York, 1957.

QUISTORP, B. v. *Die Kaiserlich Russisch-Deutsche Legion*. Berlin, 1860.

RAACK, R. C. *The Fall of Stein*. Cambridge, Mass., 1965.

REICHENAU, v., ed. *Schlachtfelder zwischen Alpen und Main*. Munich, 1938.

RENTZELL, D. *Geschichte des Garde-Jäger-Bataillons*. 2nd edn. Berlin, 1894.

RITTER, G. *Staatskunst und Kriegshandwerk*. Vol. I. Munich, 1954.

RÖSSLER, H. *Österreichs Kampf um Deutschlands Befreiung*. 2 vols. Hamburg, 1940.

ROSINSKI, H. *The German Army*. London, 1939.

ROTHENBERG, G. E. *The Austrian Military Border in Croatia, 1522–1747*. Urbana, Ill., 1960.

ROTHFELS, H. "Ost und Westpreussen zur Zeit der Reform und der Erhebung," *Deutsche Staatenbildung und deutsche Kultur im Preussenlande*. Königsberg, 1931.

Rückzug und Verfolgung. Vol. I of *Beiträge zur Militär- und Kriegsgeschichte*, ed. H. Meier-Welcker, published by the *Militärgeschichtliche Forschungsamt*. Stuttgart, 1960.

RÜSTOW, W. *Geschichte der Infanterie*. 2 vols. Nordhausen, 1964.

———. *Die Lehre vom kleinen Kriege*. Zürich, 1864.

SASKI, C. *Campagne de 1809*. 3 vols. Paris, 1899–1902.

SAUTERMEISTER, R. *Die taktische Reform der preussischen Armee nach 1806*. Tübingen, 1935.

SCHARFENORT, L. v. *Die Königlich-Preussische Kriegsakademie, 1810–1910*. Berlin, 1910.

SCHLIEFFEN, A. v. *Gesammelte Schriften*. 2 vols. Berlin, 1913.

SCHMIDT, K. v. "Statistische Nachrichten über das Preussische Offizierkorps von 1806 und seine Opfer für die Befreiung Deutschlands," *Militär-Wochenblatt*, Supplement 10, (1901).

SCHMITTHENNER, P. *Das Deutsche Soldatentum*. Cologne, 1938.

———. *Politik und Kriegsführung in der neueren Geschichte*. Hamburg, 1937.

SCHNACKENBURG, E. "Die Freikorps Friedrich des Grossen," *Militär-Wochenblatt* (1883), Supplement 6.

SHANAHAN, W. *Prussian Military Reforms: 1786–1813*. New York, 1945.

Der Siebenjährige Krieg, published by the *Kriegsgeschichtliche Abteilung* II of the German General Staff. 13 vols. Berlin, 1901–1913.

SIMON, W. *The Failure of the Prussian Reform Movement, 1807–1819*. Ithaca, N.Y., 1955.

STADELMANN, R. "Das Duell zwischen Scharnhorst und Borstell im Dezember 1807," *Historische Zeitschrift*, CLXI (1940).

———. Review of *Die Reorganisation des Preussischen Staates unter Stein und Hardenberg*. Part II, *Das Preussische Heer vom Tilsiter Frieden bis zur Befreiung: 1807–1814*. Vol. I. *Historische Zeitschrift*, CLX (1939).

STEIN, F. v. *Geschichte der Entwicklung des Russischen Heeres*. Leipzig, 1895.

STROKOV, A. A. *Istoriia voennogo iskusstuai*. Vol. II, *Kapitalisticheskoe obshchestvo ot frantszuskoi burzhuaznoi revoliutsii do perioda imperializma*. Moscow, 1965.

STULZ, P. *Fremdherrschaft und Befreiungskampf*. Berlin, 1960.

SZCEPANSKI, M. v. Review of *Das Preussische Heer der Befreiungskriege*, in *Historische Zeitschrift*, CXXIII (1921).

Die taktische Schulung der Preussischen Armee durch König Friedrich den Grossen während der Friedenszeit 1745 bis 1756. Vols. XXVIII–XXX of *Kriegsgeschichtliche Einzelschriften*, published by the *Abtheilung für Kriegsgeschichte* II of the German General Staff. Berlin, 1900.

TAYLOR, A. J. P. *The Course of German History*. New York, 1962.

Die Theilnahme des Preussischen Hülfskorps an dem Feldzuge gegen Russland im Jahre 1812. Vol. XXIV of *Kriegsgeschichtliche Einzelschriften*, published by the *Abtheilung für Kriegsgeschichte* II of the German General Staff. Berlin, 1898.

THIMME, F. "König Friedrich Wilhelm II, sein Antheil an der Konvention von Tauroggen und an der Reform von 1807–1812," *Forschungen zur Brandenburgischen und Preussischen Geschichte*, XVIII (1905).

TRANSFELDT, W., and BRAND, K. H. v. *Wort und Brauchtum des Soldaten*. Hamburg, 1959.

TSCHIRCH, O. *Geschichte der öffentlichen Meinung in Preussen*. 2 vols. Weimar, 1933–1934.

USSEL, J. d'. *La Défection de la Prusse*. Paris, 1907.

VANICEK, F. *Specialgeschichte der Militärgrenze*. 4 vols. Vienna, 1875.

VIDAL DE LA BLANCHE, J. *La Régénération de la Prusse*. Paris, 1910.

WARD, C. L. *The War of the Revolution*. ed. J. R. Alden. 2 vols. New York, 1952.

WARD, S. G. P. *Faithful: The Story of the Durham Light Infantry*. London, 1963.

———. *Wellington's Headquarters*. Oxford, 1957.

WENIGER, E. *Goethe und die Generale der Freiheitskriege*. Stuttgart, 1959.

ZWEHL, v. "Der Gegensatz zwischen Yorck und Gneisenau. Eine Psychologische Studie," *Militär-Wochenblatt* (1914), Supplement (1914).

INDEX

Names of scholars who are mentioned in the text, or to whom attention is called in the notes, are italicized.

Index

Index

Index

Index